The Mohican World
1680 - 1750

A full-length portrait of Etowaukaum, chief of the River Indians, was painted in London in 1710 by John Verelst and engraved by John Simon. The painting captures some typical cultural exchanges: Etowaukaum is wearing a linen shirt and a trade blanket rather than the furs common a century earlier, yet he retains facial tattoos and his clan, shown by the turtle at his feet.

The Mohican World
1680 - 1750

Shirley W. Dunn

PURPLE MOUNTAIN PRESS
Fleischmanns, New York

The Mohican World, 1680-1750

First Edition 2000

Published by
Purple Mountain Press, Ltd.
1060 Main Street, P.O. Box 309
Fleischmanns, New York 12430-0309
845-254-4062, 845-254-4476 (fax)
purple@catskill.net
http://www.catskill.net/purple

Cover painting, "The Mohican Grandfather,"
copyright © 1997 by L. F. Tantillo.
Used by permission.

Library of Congress Cataloging-in-Publication Data

Dunn, Shirley W. (Shirley Wiltse), (date)
   The Mohican world, 1680-1750 / Shirley W. Dunn.-- 1st ed.
      p. cm.
   Includes bibliographical references and index.
   ISBN 1-930098-12-X (pbk. : alk. paper)
   1. Mohegan Indians--History. I. Title.

E99.M83 D858 2000
974.6'004973--dc21
                                                    00-062777

Manufactured in the United States of America on acid-free paper.
1 2 3 4 5

Table of Contents

Preface

THIS VOLUME is intended as a companion volume to *The Mohicans and their Land, 1609-1730*, my previous book about the Mohicans. It keeps the same format. As before, a substantial listing of Mohican deeds and Mohican names are provided as appendices. The two books form a set which surveys the history of the Mohicans for over a century and a half.

Events of the late seventeenth century and of the first half of the eighteenth century stimulated changes in the Mohican world. The previous successful balance of Hudson Valley Algonquians with the environment at the time of the arrival of European traders, before Indian populations dropped and the fur trade brought conflict with the Mohawks, can be demonstrated from early travelers' accounts. Considerable village relocation characterized the first adjustment to European visits, and next, after two decades, Mohican land began to be dispensed for European farms. By the 1650s, there is evidence of Mohican settlement along the Housatonic River. This volume takes special notice of Mohican communities developing inland from the Hudson River.

Both in the Hudson and the Housatonic watersheds, late seventeenth century English and Indian wars also affected Mohican life. The resulting dislocations destroyed the fabric of society. Although the relative calm after Queen Anne's War in the early eighteenth century permitted the Mohicans to regroup, colonial expansion inevitably pressed upon Mohican population centers. Mohican history in the eighteenth century is the story of the response to that colonial pressure. As acknowledged owners of the land, the Mohicans wielded influence disproportionate to their numbers. It was remarkable that such a small minority exercised so much direct and indirect control over colonial development. This influence has been unrecognized and therefore little studied.

The second book illuminates further the differing concepts of land ownership and community control held by Mohicans and colonial landowners. In the Hudson Valley, Indian ancestors of eighteenth century Mohicans had signed deeds which, in colonial eyes, conveyed permanent ownership of the land to European immigrants. If the land was unoccupied, however, new generations of Indians felt the land had been abandoned and returned to their use. The Mohicans reasoned that proper family lines, each headed by a sachem, should be paid when colonial farmers finally wished to divide up and settle the land. Moreover, some early land transactions between Indians and Europeans were forgotten; the Indians using the land were unaware it had ever been sold.

In the eighteenth century, sale of land contributed to the livelihood of Native Americans when traditional ways of life were circumscribed. The Indians at Stockbridge acknowledged their need to derive income from their lands. When they complained to Sir William Johnson in 1762 about tracts that were being occupied by colonial settlers without purchase of an Indian title, they explained: "If this way of dealing is allowed to be continued, we must all be ruined, having little else besides our Lands at present to depend on. . . ."

Foremost in Indian lives was the need for guns and European goods on which Indians had become dependant for daily living and for defense. Cultural survival was underwritten by the exchange of Indian land for goods, yet at the same time some land retention was essential. Possession of alluvial flats with adjacent high ground ensured locations for Indian villages and spaces for the rotation of fields. Woodlands were essential for supplies and firewood. Control of vast hunting grounds defined the ability to bring home game and the Indians' ability to trade.

Various temporary solutions were found to the seemingly unresolvable conflict between retaining land and the need to sell it. Moreover, other pressures affected Mohican decisions to sign away land. Friends of the Indians desired land, while Colonial governments allocated land and expected Indian cooperation in providing deeds. Ruthless speculators devised ways to coerce land away from Indian owners or took advantage of their good will and illiteracy. The Mohicans were intelligent and rational. They were, as Henry Hudson noted, a good people. They struggled against a sophisticated society which used the tools of literacy - deeds, diaries, books, letters, petitions, laws and intricate government regulations, to name but a few - often against their interests.

This book and its predecessor trace a number of different Indian experiences with land sales. Some land transactions were mutually satisfactory. These were acknowledged by Mohican chiefs as deliber ate and just. Some sales caused controversy. Although the recorded deeds make absorbing reading, without interpretation the respectful legal terminology may put too good a face on the sale of Indian land. Many sales came after-the-fact, when settlers were already establishing farms. Deeds, therefore, must be supplemented by documents which suggest the volatile political and demographic forces of the times.

I have done my best to keep Mohican interests central to this book. As a result of Indian reverses, a fair number of colonial settlers felt concern for the dwindling native population; although these colonials wanted to help the Indians, most could see improving native survival only through the lens of the Protestant religion and in terms of English or German culture. The result was the establishment of Christian missions, which, although far from successful, were stepping stones to change.

Voluminous archives such as those of the Moravian missionaries, accounts of the Stockbridge mission, and sources dating to the formation of planned colonial towns in the Housatonic Valley have proved invaluable in Mohican research. In some cases, these resources have given voice to Mohicans. For example, the literate Moravians kept daily records of their experiences in Indian villages. They also wrote revealing letters and appeals for their converts. In addition, documents from colonial landowners such as Robert Livingston and Richard Sackett have provided data about relationships between colonial landlords and Mohican leaders. In the eighteenth century the Mohicans drew closer to Indian Commissioner Sir William Johnson and appear often in his papers. War records provide insights into Indian (and English) cultural advances and regressions. The many land transactions called Indian deeds are a staple source of information for Mohican locations, names and relationships. The Mohicans gave an impressive number of deeds within their large territory, and many more remain to be collected

Despite all the sources, absence of the Mohican language, in particular, is a formidable obstacle to understanding Indian social relationships and history, while mythology largely has been lost. Please bear with the variations of Mohican names. Despite my attempts to standardize names for the reader's convenience, occasionally it is necessary to vary a name according to general use or the document being used. It has been inspiring to me through research to uncover details about the lives of individuals and families in the seventeenth and eighteenth centuries. Numerous interesting and historic figures have emerged. These include Etowaukaum, Abraham of Shekomeko and Manhaet, his mother, Metoxon, Catharickseet, Towetemack, a woman of Greene County, and Konkapot, Umpachanee, Solomon, and Hendrick Aupaumut of Stockbridge, among many others.

Documents reveal the complexity of Indian society. For example, an Esopus Indian casually notes exactly where the ancient boundary line fell between the Mohicans and the Esopus Indians, friendly neighbors but entirely separate groups. His information is confirmed in an Esopus document from a century earlier. Moreover, this sachem explained that if any Indian hunter shot a deer or bear beyond his nation's limits, it was necessary to divide the game with representatives of the neighboring nation. Such subtle customs are rarely recorded.

There is no sure way of predicting where absorbing information will be found. The documentary research for this book has ranged far, taking me to previously unknown sources in new places. Mohican research provides a constantly expanding horizon. Besides the Dutch and English sources of the Hudson Valley, New England and Pennsylvania archives have produced an almost overwhelming flood of material to be sifted. Increasingly, archeology also is revealing patterns of Algonquian Indian life.

Although I have acknowledged some of the considerable Mohican contributions to colonial events, there is more to be learned and written on this subject. The obsessive concentration of Indian studies in the east on the Iroquois is a thing of the past. The increased interest in Algonquian studies portends valuable volumes on Mohican life and on neighboring nations in the future.

I have tried to emphasize connections between the different locations where Mohicans resided. The steady, comfortable interchange of individuals among Mohican sites in the eighteenth century illustrates an enduring feeling of national unity as well as complex family relationships in all corners of Mohican territory. Until recently, this national unity was scarcely understood or acknowledged. Catskills, Mohicans and Westenhooks were thought to be separate nations, when, research shows, they were one.

The Mohicans retained this strong tribal identity in the eighteenth century despite the cutural adaptations made necessary by events. The unity of Mohican social and institutional fabric speaks for itself in this volume.

Acknowledgments

MANY PEOPLE have contributed information or given other assistance in the preparation of this book. My husband, Gerald Dunn, has accompanied me on many research trips, has edited text, and has helped in other ways. Our son, Geoffrey Dunn, has provided essential computer assistance.

The New York State Library Research Resident Award of 1997-1998 made Library resources easier for me to use. In addition, I have consistently received gracious assistance from Jim Corsaro and other staff in the Manuscripts and Special Collections room. At the New York State Archives, James Folts supplied indexes and research guides and took an interest in my research. The East Greenbush Community Library has procured obscure sources through inter-library loan. Polly Pierce, librarian in charge of Mohican records at the Stockbridge Library, was very helpful in opening the Library's collection for my use.

While this book was in process, the Native American Institute (NAI) was formed. Created by Richard Powell and headquartered at Columbia-Greene Community College, NAI has helped expand Mohican research. Membership in this organization enlarged my circle of contacts; the resulting NAI Research Committee has been extremely supportive. I would like to thank NAI members Steve Comer, Lion Miles, John Michael Smith, and Richard Walling for providing research and sources. In addition, committee members Stanley Joseph, John Michael Smith, and Lion Miles have read and commented on parts of the manuscript.

Ruth Piwonka also read and offered valuable comments on part of the manuscript and has provided sources. George Hamell, Ethnology Collections Manager of the New York State Museum, helped me examine artifacts and obtain a photograph of a unique artifact. My thanks to Lila Parrish for hospitality and to James Parrish, who gave time to a tour of sites in the Great Barrington area. He has supplied additional information and provided photos of artifacts, as well. Others who have contributed research tips or copies of documents include Ned Pratt, Warren Broderick, Harold Zoch, Robert Grumet, Debbie Winchell, Jen Crowley, and Linda Crowley.

Melinda Camardella contributed research and photographs from the Shekomeko area. William Morrill has suggested research sources and provided his valuable map of the Livingston Manor spur. Site Director Bruce Narramore and Bob Engel at Clermont State Historic Site were most accommodating in providing access to Livingston documents.

Arlee Davids of the Mohican Wisconsin Library and Museum, Dorothy Davids and members of the Mohican Nation Historical Committee at Bowler, Wisconsin, and Sherri White, Mohican Repatriation Representative, have provided information and pictures of artifacts. Genealogist Mildred Adriance has accompanied me on research trips and provided leads on books available. My appreciation goes also to Harold Nestler, of New Jersey, a bookdealer and author who has taken an interest in my search for sources. I have had welcome translation help from the New Netherland Project, through Charles Gehring and Janny Venema.

Special thanks go to L. F. Tantillo for permission to reproduce his 1997 painting, *The Mohican Grandfather*. My appreciation is extended also to David Wolfe, whose collection includes two powder horns owned by prominent eighteenth-century Mohicans. In addition to providing photographs of the pieces, he commissioned the drawings which show the surfaces of the powder horns.

Purple Mountain Press publishers, Loni and Wray Rominger, have been supportive of the book as well as flexible about deadlines. Several people have written or called me as a consequence of their interest in my first book, *The Mohicans and Their Land 1609-1730*. The expressions of good will from so many interested people is both encouraging and challenging.

Shirley W. Dunn
March, 2000

I.
Managing the Environment

"They live in summer mostly on fish. The men repair to the river and catch a great quantity in a short time, as it is full and furnishes various sorts. The arrows they use are pointed with little bones, iron or copper, with which they, being good shooters, shoot deer, fawns, hares and foxes and all such. The country is full of game. . .as appears by skins which were brought on board. Oxen and horses there are none."[1]

THE ENVIRONMENT in which the native population lived at the time the Dutch arrived in the early 1600s was rich but challenging. The fertility of the soil and the sweetness of the air were marvels to the Dutch. The changeable Hudson River was far different from the controlled stream of the present, being sometimes sluggish, shallow and choked with sand bars, and at other times dangerously high and out of control. Similar fluctuations occurred in other streams on which Mohicans lived. Rivers were festooned with dead trees and vegetation extending into the water; many small streams cut through the banks. After floods, sand bars and riverbanks were altered.

When the first Europeans arrived in the upper Hudson Valley, they encountered scattered flourishing native communities, whose members were husbanding the resources of family and tribal territories. They had devised routines to raise crops and store food which, as a rule, prevented hunger. To achieve this success, Native Americans in the Hudson Valley utilized their environment. Indians gradually degraded any area where they lived by collecting wood for fuel; by harvesting bark, reeds and saplings for houses; by taking plant materials for nets, canoes, weapons, and food containers; by using weeds, stones and earth for dyes and medicines; by killing and processing a selection of wildlife; by gathering edibles; by clearing land; by raising and storing crops; by occupying living spaces; by making cooking and storage containers; and by the other activities of living. They occasionally moved to pristine locations, allowing their previous settings to return to a natural, but altered, state. Moreover, they did not leave their territorial forested areas intact. Archeologist Roger Moeller has proposed that destruction of the forest by the Indians was a primary factor in their survival.[2]

It is important to take a brief look at ways of life early in the contact period in order to understand the changes which took place within the next two centuries, changes with which this book is concerned. Whatever the setting, activities of daily life were not casual. Providing food, shelter, clothing, and weapons for a large and varied population of many age levels and abilities required leadership and shared knowledge. The essential acts of living—gardening, hunting and fishing, gathering wild foods, processing and storing food, making clothing and weapons, building shelters, and burning the land—were communal, not individual, acts. The processes were carefully orchestrated by village elders to ensure adequate production and supply of food and necessities for group living. The management process also involved imposing restrictions on individuals which ensured the continued existence of resources for future use. Recognizing these management activities underscores the complexity of the seemingly simple Indian life.

There are adequate descriptions of Indian life in very early European sources but little is written that is specifically tied to a single tribe or nation. The newcomers from overseas found it hard to separate the Indian groups and rarely took note of differences among them, although differences must have existed. Consequently, information used for the following description of the life of Hudson Valley Indians has been drawn from nearby regions, as well as from the Hudson Valley. Each location is identified.

Evidence of controlled burning which occurred over 3000 years ago has been unearthed in the Housatonic Valley of Massachusetts.[3] This ancient method of vegetation control had the effect of favoring those trees, shrubs, and flowering plants which could survive fire; burning completely altered the physical environment, leaving sections of the forest blackened for months. Fields recovered in a season, but with altered vegetation. Burning was an important Indian tool for clearing and improving land for cornfields, as well as for opening the understory of the forest to encourage the growth of grasses and berries which attracted game. Deliberate attempts to keep certain areas open may have verged on cultivation.

The Hudson Valley Indians regularly set fire to selected woods and fields. Burning initiated by the Indians had several benefits for their way of life. Vander Donck wrote that the Indians "have a yearly custom of burning the woods, plains and meadows in the fall of the year, when the leaves have fallen and when the grass and vegetable substances are dry. Those places which are then passed over are fired in the spring in April. This practice is named. . .bush-burning." The purposes were, he said: "First, to render hunting easier, as the bush and vegetable growth renders the walking difficult for the hunter, and the crackling of the dry substances betrays him and frightens away the game. Secondly, to thin out and clear the woods of all dead substances and grass, which grow better the following spring. Thirdly, to circumscribe and enclose the game within the lines of the fire, when it is more easily taken, and also, because the game is more easily tracked over the burned parts of the woods."[4] An occasional burn in a woodland prevented more serious outbreaks in the future. In addition, some fires occurred naturally.

Coping with a river required special skills. Soils near the river and on islands were made rich by the frequent floods which deposited silt and debris on them. Inland, alluvial flats along streams were subject to standing water. Raising maize, beans, and squash meant planning for alternate flooding and subsequent drought. Access to essential materials was important. A Hudson Valley Dutch writer of the 1640s noted that the country had hills of fuller's earth, and "several sorts of fine clay, such as white, yellow, red and black, which is fat and tough, suitable for pots, dishes, plates, tobacco-pipes and the like wares."[5] New York Mohican villages near later Coeymans, Schodack Landing and, especially, Castleton were located near the clay banks of the area which provided material for pottery. Certain areas, such as the hills near Coxsackie, contained valuable flint suitable for projectile points.

Raising Maize Was Essential

The indigenous population appeared prosperous to the Dutch. Henry Hudson in September 1609, described the success a Mohican community he visited had in stockpiling food. He found, stored in a large longhouse, a great quantity of maize (corn) and shell beans, and, he said, "there lay near the house, for the purpose of drying, enough to load three ships, besides what was growing in the fields."[6] Maize was the cornerstone of Mohican diets. In addition, the Mohicans in 1609 had on hand tobacco and squash, and wild grapes to offer to the ship's crew at a time, late summer, of abundance in provisions.

A map of c.1630, now at the Library of Congress, showed a Mohican plantation on the east shore at the present City of Rensselaer. When Kiliaen Van Rensselaer received a map in 1632 showing his new purchases near later Albany, he was elated to find along the west shore of the Hudson River below Fort Orange a swath of cleared land of 200 morgens (400 acres) "which had been seeded before by the savages."[7] Van Rensselaer's map showed additional cleared land on islands in the river and in extensive fields along the shore north of Fort Orange.

In pre-contact times, hills and swamps were not needed for farming in Mohican territories, a sign that the native population had not reached a level which forced them to use less than desirable locations. Mohican historian Hendrick Aupaumut later wrote that the Indians of old cultivated only fertile locations along rivers, creeks, and ponds for raising corn, beans, and squash. This was the Mohican pattern even as late as 1734, when it was reported by a New England minister that Mohicans "make little or no use of any but interval [intervale] land."[8] Seventeenth century Mohican locations along the Hudson and Housatonic rivers, on the Catskill Creek, on the Kinderhook and Roelof Jansen Kills, and near Saratoga Lake, as well as on the ponds of western Connecticut and Massachusetts, bear out this preference.

Indian farming routines caught the attention of European observers. The lives of Hudson Valley and Long Island Indians were briefly summarized by Englishman Daniel Denton in a small book of 1670. After discussing how the native population had been greatly reduced by Indian wars and by disease, he wrote, "They live principally by Hunting, Fowling, and Fishing: their Wives being the Husbandmen to till the Land, and plant their Corn." Denton explained that Indians built movable tents, which, he added, "they remove two or three times a year," having, however, their principal quarters where they plant their corn.[9] According to this definition, Henry Hudson, in September 1609, had visited a village site which contained the principal quarters of a Mohican community. The temporary lean-tos or small wigwams mentioned by Denton were for hunting and fishing locations. In the 1640s, Adriaen Van der Donck wrote, "Their castles and large towns they seldom leave altogether. From other situations they remove frequently."[10]

At the close of the winter and in early spring, when the hunting season was ended and the stock of dried provisions from summer and fall was nearly exhausted, *sapaen* (thin mush made with dried, pounded corn, to which dried beans or preserved meat might be added) could be the standard food available. Providing adequate winter storage was a serious consideration for the women. Dried meat and fish and stored vegetable products mold and decay easily under damp conditions and can be attacked by mice and insects. Samuel de Champlain noted that the Indians along the St. Lawrence River "continue [planting] until they have enough for three or four years' provision, for fear lest some bad year, barren and unfruitful, should come upon them."[11]

Adriaen Van der Donck, after becoming acquainted with the Indians of the Hudson Valley in the 1640s, wrote that some garden products had been known to natives from the earliest times. The Indians themselves said that their corn and beans were received from the southern Indians, who had received their seed from a people who resided still farther south; Hudson Valley Indians told Van der Donck that they ate "roots and the bark of trees instead of bread, before the introduction of Indian corn or maize." Champlain was told that Indians to the south of the St. Lawrence River were "bark eaters," but it is estimated that corn has been raised for over one thousand years in the northeast, gradually becoming more important.[12] If, indeed, the Delawares came from west of the Mississippi River, and if, according to tradition, the Mohicans were a segment of the Delawares who subsequently moved to the Hudson Valley, it is likely they brought maize with them. Maize horticulture encouraged the establishment of villages; a sedentary village life enhanced security and population survival. Not surprisingly, preservation of the village and its productive fields became a goal of land management when colonists and Indians began to share land.

A description of Hudson Valley Indian gardening was given in the 1640s by Van der Donck: "Before the arrival of the Netherlanders, the Indians raised beans of various kinds and colours. . .they furnish an excellent food, of which the Indians are especially fond. They have a peculiar method of planting them. . .when the Turkish wheat (Indian corn) or, as it is called, maize, is half a foot above the ground, they plant the beans around it, and let them grow together. The coarse stalk serves as a bean prop, and the beans run upon it. They increase together and thrive extremely well, and thus two crops are gathered at the same time."[13] There were other benefits: in the proper soils, beans supplied nitrogen, a major nutrient needed by corn, as well as calcium to augment Indian diets. In times of drought, mulching was important in gardening. Weeds pulled from Indian gardens were carefully laid in the rows to conserve moisture.

Maize was described as an adaptable crop, readily grown in almost every kind of soil; nevertheless it required frequent hoeing by the women to discourage weeds and, because it had to be protected from animals and birds, young people were assigned to guard the crop. Skill in husbandry was needed to produce consistent corn crops: New England Indian women "knew how to cull out the finest seed, to choose the fittest season for planting, to measure the distance for the planting holes, to worm the corn, prune it and dress [mulch] it as needed."[14] Ample stocks for winter required a community in residence for the summer months.

Squash was raised in the same fields. The large leaves of squash planted between the rows shaded the roots of beans and corn. Hudson Valley natives gave much importance to squash. They did not always wait for the squashes to ripen, but gathered them as needed and immediately placed them on the fire. Squash provided food in the season before corn was ripe. Samuel de Champlain wrote that the Indians "also eat many summer squashes, which they boil and roast under the ashes."[15] Calabashes or gourds also were grown; they had very little pulp, and were raised chiefly for the hard and durable shells. Dried gourds were used to hold seeds, spices, and personal items, and for bird houses. The calabash was the common water-pail of the natives; some were very large. While Indians did not routinely smoke it, tobacco for ceremonies was also grown. It was dried for religious ceremonies and for smoking in stone pipes passed during conferences, and was used by chiefs and medicine men for ritual purposes.

Dried or parched corn, the staple food, required laborious preparation. Examples of methods come from Samuel de Champlain, who wrote the following about food preparation by Indians on the St. Lawrence in 1616: "Their principal food and ordinary provision is Indian corn and Brazilian beans, which they prepare in various ways. They pound it [corn] in wooden mortars and reduce it to meal, from which they extract the meal dust by means of certain winnowing fans made from the bark of trees; and then from this meal they make bread, with beans. These beans they have first boiled into soup, like the Indian corn, so as to be easier to beat, and they put the whole together. Sometimes they add blueberries, or dried raspberries, sometimes pieces of deer's fat. Then, having steeped the whole in lukewarm water, they make bread [from it] in the form of cakes, which they bake under the ashes. And when they are baked, they wash them, and wrap them in leaves of Indian corn, which they fasten to them, and put them into boiling water." Bread with beans, wrapped in corn leaves, was for special occasions, Champlain said. Usually Indians made a simpler kind of corn mush by putting two or three handfuls of pounded Indian corn in an earthen pot full of water, and boiling it, stirring it frequently so it would not burn or stick to the pot. "Then they put into this pot a little fish, fresh or dry, according to the season, to give flavor to this *migan*, which is the name that they give it." The smell of this dish made with aged fish was strong and unpleasant to Champlain.[16] Ripe corn also was roasted, he noted.

Women and girls worked together in the fields. Senior women decided how much of the best grains to set aside for seed for the following year. Farming was a carefully programmed activity, and, in addition to the practical aspects of crop raising, gardening was attended by appropriate celestial timing, religious ceremonies and essential sacred offerings which were thought to be necessary to ensure spiritual help. These ceremonies were ways the Indians could influence the spirits which they believed existed in the rocks, trees, and animals around them.

The Indians cleared land for fields by girdling or burning the trees. Planting began among the

A stone smoking pipe hatchet with an effigy face was found by Ken Mynter in 1965 at a Mohican village site in Castleton, New York. He donated this and other artifacts to the Arvid E. Miller Memorial Library-Museum in Bowler, Wisconsin.

Courtesy of the Museum and the Stockbridge-Munsee Band of Mohican Indians.

standing dead tree trunks; as the trunks fell, they were burned in heaps
by the women. The charcoal and ash were scattered on the soil.
Champlain reported, "They clear it [the land] with great difficulty,
as they have no proper tools for the purpose. They strip the trees of
all their branches, which [trees] they burn at their base, in order to
kill them. They clean up the ground between the trees, then plant
their corn at distances of a pace, putting about ten grains in each
place."[17]

When a cultivated plot became exhausted, another site was selected, and the abandoned land grew up to brush and then forest again.
The process of regrowth might take only twenty years on rich sites
before young trees filled the clearings, according to the Indians. Some
land, however, lay in the flood plain, which might be repeatedly
scoured by ice during high water, so that few trees grew. This land
would regain fertility from the debris left by floods, but planting on
it risked the loss of the crop during the course of the growing season.
It has been noted that clearing also could lead to erosion as part of
"fundamental biotic change."[18] By abandoning exhausted fields and
hard-packed village sites over thousands of years, the indigenous
population had altered the nature of the flora and fauna of the area.

There were many ecological implications from Indian farming.
Edge, the meeting place between forest and fields produced by native
fields, or by natural or deliberately set fires, was one of the most
prolific locations for both plants and animals. Shadbush, wild cherry,
elderberry, sumac and other small berry-producing trees, and sassa-
fras, with medicinal roots, favored the edges of woods. Abandoned
fields and edge areas provided browse or prey for deer, elk, bear, grey
foxes, squirrels, and chipmunks; open fields of weeds and flowers
aided many insects as the vital new growth on abandoned plots
proceeded through various stages from shrubs to trees and the soil
gradually developed new layers of compost from leaves and debris.

Depending primarily on soil conditions, the time between relo-
cating to new corn fields might be long or short. In 1613, Samuel de
Champlain described how this cycle of land use required that villages
be relocated in the St. Lawrence Valley: "They sometimes move their
village at intervals of 10, 20, or 30 years, and transport it 1, 2, or 3
leagues [a league was about three miles], for their soil becomes worn
out in producing corn without being fertilized; and so they go to clear
another place, and also to have wood [for fires] more accessible. . . ."[19]

Slash-and-burn horticulture, not highly regarded today, never-theless was successful for the Mohicans and other eastern Indians as long as there was plenty of alternate land to which crops could be rotated. According to early Dutch accounts, those conditions were being met in the Hudson Valley at the time of first contact. However, one archeologist has proposed that competition for arable land was the cause of some Indian tensions as a result of an ever-increasing North American native population, especially along the Mohawk River.[20] This seems not to have been a problem along the Hudson, where the Mohicans controlled such a large territory; the value of defending and retaining an extensive territory is obvious. Unfortu-nately, once European settlement began, extensive land losses from war with the Mohawk Indians and from land sale to the colonists, as well as the limitations imposed by colonial farming, restricted peri-odic relocation.

The Science of Gathering

In addition to agriculture, a carefully managed cycle of gathering occurred in the fields, swamps, and woods. The process of harvesting useful wild products was closely tied to the abandonment of fields and to the burning of woods and fields. Erosion, sunlight and altered soil composition gave entry to opportunist seeds, including those of many valuable plants used for dyes, bait, insect control, other house-hold processes, and for medicinal or ritual purposes, as well as for food. As anyone who has vacant Massachusetts, Connecticut, Ver-mont or New York fields knows, grasses, blackberries, raspberries, strawberries, milkweed, Joe-Pye weed (named for a Mohican Indian), goldenrod, amaranth, pokeweed, sumac, and many other sun-loving plants soon appear in them. On sandy, acid soil, blueberries, huckle-berries, sarsaparilla, plantain, lamb's-quarters and hazelnuts can flour-ish.

Indians harvested chestnut, basswood, elm and oak bark, and various fibers, such as Indian hemp (spreading dogbane) and milk-weed, in the woods and swamps. Oak and elm bark were used to cover houses, and various basts were twisted into ropes for nets. Selected reeds, grasses and rushes were used for mats and baskets. For example, on a surveying trip with the Mohican sachem Catharickseet, land-owner Robert Livingston was shown a small lake within his land's boundaries where the Indians got the rushes from which they still, in the eighteenth century, made mats.

Rev. Charles Wolley, a visiting Englishman who wrote about New York City and the Hudson Valley in the 1670s, mentioned that the Indians "make thread of Nettles pill'd when ful ripe, pure white and fine, and likewise another sort of brownish thread of a small weed almost like a Willow, which grows in the Wood about three feet high, which is called Indian hemp, of which they likewise make ropes. . .of this they make their Bags, Purses or Sacks which they call *Notas*. . . Their work is weaving with their fingers; they twist all their thread upon their Thighs; with the palm of their hands, they interweave their Porcupine quills into their baggs; their needles they make of fishes or small beast bones, and before the Christians came amongst them, they had Needles of Wood, for which Nut-wood was esteemed best, called *Um-be-re-mak-qua*; their Axes and Knives they made of white Flint-stones. . .They make their Candles of the same wood. . .which they call *Woss-ra-neck*. . . ."[21] Sinews also were used where string or thread was needed.

One example of a weed that springs up on abandoned areas is chenopodium, also known as lamb's-quarters or goosefoot, a ubiquitous tall plant having several varieties. Some types produce a nutritious grain from which flour can be made. The leaves can be cooked like spinach. Chenopodium varieties have been found on Hudson Valley and New England archeological sites, as well as in midwest sites, in South America (where it was used by the Incas) and in ancient sites in Europe. One early historic account states that the Indians used a plant similar to *orache* to make a powdered purple dye for their bodies. Orache is a name for one type of chenopodium. The account follows: "There, however, are various plants from which the Indians prepare several fine, lovely and bright colours. . .A certain plant springs up and grows in the country, resembling the *Orache* or golden herb, having many shoots from the same stalk, but it grows much larger than the Orache. This plant produces clusters of red and brown berries, which the Indians bruise, and press out the juice, and pour the same on flat pieces of bark, about six feet long and three broad, prepared for the purpose; these are placed in the sun to dry out the moisture. If it does not dry out fast enough, or if they intend to remove, which they frequently do in summer, then they heat smooth stones, and place the same into the juice of the berries on the bark."[22] The dry substance was then scraped off the bark and put into small bags. When used by Indians to produce a purple color, it was tempered with water.

Many other dyes also were produced from local materials. In 1723, Cadwallader Colden noted that "I have seen fine Reds and Yellows & good black (the Country people say they have seen all colors) died [dyed] by the Indians with some roots & weeds, which grow plentifully in the country."[23] A list of the herbs which the country near New York City afforded, given by Denton in 1670, included, "Purslain, white Orage [orache], Egrimony, Violets, Penniroyal, Alicimpane, besides Saxaparilla very common. . . ."[24]

Seventeenth-century accounts mention a variety of locally available wild food plants: several kinds of plums (shadbush and other berry-producing plants were included here), small cherries, small apples (crabapples), hazelnuts, black currants, gooseberries, and blue India figs. Strawberries grew in abundance, turning the fields and woods red. Strawberries, reported Van der Donck, ripened the middle of May and continued until July. There were blueberries, huckleberries, cranberries, raspberries, and black caps, artichokes, ground-acorns, ground-beans, wild onions, and leeks. The ground nut, or "Indian potato," is identified as *Apios Americana*, a tuber-bearing perennial legume of wet locations, difficult to find today. It produces a "smooth, sweet, slightly turnip-like flavor."[25]

There is also a dwarf ginseng called ground-nut. Charred butternut and hickory shells, and several kinds of seeds, including raspberries, chenopodium, smartweed, hickory nuts, grasses, buckwheat or sedge, purslane, and viburnum or hackweed were found during an archeological dig at a Mohican site on an island near Albany.[26] These finds do not necessarily represent Indian use, as some could have been carried to the site accidentally. Chenopodium once had extensive use in New England.[27]

There were many Indian medicinal uses for plants. Van der Donck noted the several kinds of roots and fruits used by the Indians. The Indians were able "with roots, bulbs, leaves, etc. [to] cure dangerous wounds and old sores," he explained.[28] A plant today called Joe-Pye weed could be used to cure fevers, while monarda species (bee-balm) also were used medicinally. Snake-wort was a remedy for the bite of the rattlesnake; the Indians reportedly held this plant in such high esteem that many of them carried some of it, well-dried, with them. Denton commented "nay, did we know the vertue of all those Plants and Herbs growing there (which time may discover) many are of opinion, and the Natives do affirm, that there is no disease common to the Country, but may be cured without Materials from other Nations."[29]

The life cycle of useful plants was understood by the skilled women of a village. Productive locations were well-known, and harvesting was planned for optimum times. Many foodstuffs, both wild and cultivated, were available only for short periods in any one year; accurate knowledge of every plant's life cycle was imperative. For example, ripe nuts would be stolen by squirrels and other animals if not gathered quickly. Berries had to be gathered before they spoiled or were eaten by birds. This complex unwritten lore of the fields and woods was continually being taught to the young by mature Indians.

Van der Donck wrote "chestnuts would be plentier if it were not for the Indians, who destroy the trees by stripping off the bark for covering for their houses."[30] The result was vine-covered dead stumps standing in the woods, trees from which the bark had been stripped by the Indians. Some practices seem wasteful. Van der Donck also noted the Indians cut down the chestnut trees and cut off the branches in season to gather the nuts. At the time, chestnuts, a fast-growing wood, made up a large percentage of forest trees, possibly as much as every fourth or fifth tree in certain areas, and the supply might have seemed unlimited. Not every use of resources, however, was necessarily wise; community activities were governed by convenience and tradition.

The Indians also cut trees to make canoes, which were frequently made from the boles of the tulip poplar. The tulip poplar was also called white-wood and canoe-wood. Wood from the forest was burned for cooking and also for heat in freezing weather, when people slept close to their fires. Native indoor winter temperatures probably were lower than in today's homes, but some heat was necessary. Firewood was stored in or near wigwams. Hudson Valley natives apparently did not often cut down living trees for firewood, but gathered deadwood for that purpose. The deadwood would burn readily because it was dry and seasoned. This practice helped preserve live trees and removed deadwood from the forest. Availability of firewood often was a factor in village site selection.

Hunting and Fishing

Hunting and fishing were major resource uses which affected the ecological balance of the environment as well as the comfort level of the Mohicans and their neighbors. When the Dutch arrived, game was plentiful and furs and skins were commonly used instead of cloth in the Hudson Valley. Henry Hudson's crew was offered otter and beaver furs by Mohicans near Catskill. The Indians were practiced hunters. William Wood in New England later noted that beaver and otters were too cunning for the English; only the Indians had the skill to catch them.[31] Large game was hunted by large or small groups, and occasionally a whole village organized to drive white-tailed deer or elk into corrals by making loud noises or rounding them up with walls of fire. Elk were found in the northeast until late in the seventeenth century. The two species did not frequent the same haunts, according to the Indians. As late as 1714, Indians near Claverack Creek in present Columbia County used as a landmark a path, deeply etched into a streambank, where the elk used to cross.[32]

Champlain wrote about a semi-permanent, large deer trap made of logs that took twenty-five Indians ten days to build. Deer were driven into the enclosure by men beating sticks. William Wood wrote in New England that the Indians sometimes used hedges, "a mile or two miles long, being a mile wide at one end and made narrower and narrower by degrees, leaving only a gap of six feet long over against [opposite] which, in the daytime, they lie lurking to shoot the deer which come through that narrow gut. . .In the night, at the gut of this hedge they set deer traps, which are springs made of young trees and smooth-wrought cords, so strong as it will toss a horse if he be caught in it."[33] That snares were a Mohican hunting technique is confirmed in a deed of 1665, which specifically relinquishes the right of the Mohican sellers or any future Indian claimers to set deer traps on a tract of land in present Albany County.[34] Spears and the bow and arrow also were used to obtain meat and fish.

Deer bones, fresh-water mussel shells, fish bones and scales, and sturgeon scutes (plates), found at one archeological site from the late 1500s on Papscanee Island, south of later Albany, in Mohican territory, indicate the variety of the native diet. Denton wrote of the Indians, "The meat they live most upon is Fish, Fowl, and Venison; they eat likewise Polecats, Skunks, Racoon, Possum, Turtles and the like."[35] A special meal for an honored guest might include, according to Van der Donck, beavers' tails, bass heads with parched corn meal, and very fat meat stewed with chestnuts.

The Dutch author, Adriaen Van der Donck, wrote in the 1640s that deer were incredibly numerous in the country. "The Indians through the year and every year (mostly in the fall) kill many thousands and the wolves, after the fawns are cast, also destroy many, still the land abounds with them everywhere, and their numbers appear to remain undiminished." Mohican deeds contain frequent mention of Indian men who could not be present for the signing because they were away hunting. Turkeys, ducks, swans, geese, and even pelicans, as well as multitudes of passenger pigeons, filled the skies in season, as Van der Donck wrote, and flew "to and fro, across the country in the spring and fall seasons." He also declared, "In spring and fall the waters by their movements appear to be alive with water fowl, very noisy; swans so plenty that bays and shores appear as dressed in white drapery."[36]

Passenger pigeons arrived in clouds in the spring. It was recounted that the Indians, when they found the breeding places of the pigeons (where the birds assembled by the thousands), frequently removed to those places with their wives and children, to the number of two or three hundred in a company. There they lived for a month or more on the young pigeons, which they took by pushing them from their nests with poles and sticks. The Indians also caught the birds in nets. The passenger pigeons haunted beech forests, where they dined on beechnuts when they became ripe. The removal of some birds may have been valuable to the passenger pigeon flocks, which came in such numbers as to destroy the forests where they roosted. The balance between the Indians and the passenger pigeon was ancient; a gradual increase in the native population of the Hudson valley might have altered the relationship if Dutch settlement had not intervened. The extinction of the bird was not caused by Indian hunting but by extensive hunting and environmental change in the late nineteenth century. Another Atlantic seaboard game bird taken by the Indians which later became extinct in the twentieth century was the heath hen, the eastern race of the prairie chicken.[37]

Also eaten were swans, ducks and geese, quail or Bob White, which had a wide range at the time, and partridge (ruffed grouse) and many songbirds. The wild turkey was a popular game bird, as well as a clan symbol. "The turkeys sleep in trees and frequently in large flocks together. They also usually sleep in the same place every night.

. . The Indians take many in snares, when the weather changes in winter. Then they lay bulbous roots, which the turkeys are fond of, in the small rills and streams of water, which the birds take up, when they are ensnared and held until the artful Indian takes the turkey as his prize."[38] In addition, turkeys were shot from their roosting trees with arrows.

Among the animals noted in the Hudson Valley were beaver, otters, bear, squirrels, deer, elk, and wolves. One early Dutch account noted there were many bears, of a shining pitch-black color. The heavy fur of the black bear was prized for Indian coverings, and the claws were used for adornment. When the Indians hunted active bears in summer or fall, they dressed in bearskins to disguise themselves and their scent, but, the Indians recounted, most bears were taken during their sleeping season, when they were easily killed. Bear meat and bear fat were staples of Mohican life as late as the eighteenth century.

A fat dog or bear might be kept on hand in a cage for feasts or special meals, such as those honoring visitors like Henry Hudson, who was offered a meal of dog meat by the Mohicans. The dogs mentioned by Champlain "of which they have store to hunt with"[39] were common also in the Hudson Valley, although early accounts say little about Indian dogs being used for hunting. However, there were dogs around the villages. One observer, Reverend Wolley of New York, reported Indian dogs were only wolves taken when young. Probably the reason for this erroneous statement was that Indian dogs had a wolf-like appearance. David Zeisberger, who had lived among the Delaware and Iroquois Indians for many years, wrote in 1780, "Dogs they likewise possessed in former days, of a kind still to be found in considerable numbers among them. These may be readily distinguished from European dogs. . .The ears of Indian dogs rise rigidly from the head and the animals have something of a wolfish nature, for they show their teeth immediately when roused."[40]

Wolves, described as "not so large and ravenous as the Netherlands wolves are," were numerous. According to recent DNA studies, the local wolves were red wolves, common in the east.[41] To protect colonist's farm stock, wolves were hunted for a bounty by both Indian and colonial men after the arrival of European settlers.

Fish, a mainstay of the Mohican diet, were plentiful. When shad, herring, the huge striped bass, and other migrants came in from the sea, the Indians along the Hudson and Housatonic rivers were ready to catch as many as they could eat and preserve. Shellfish were collected as well. New York Bay abounded with very large oysters. Large oysters grew not only in vast beds along the coast, but well up into the Hudson River from Staten Island to the present Tappan Zee Bridge.[42] Accounts noted that sometimes towards the spring of the year, Indians went in large numbers to the seashores and bays, to take oysters, clams, and all kinds of shellfish. Dried, the meat could be preserved a long time. Shell heaps were a common sign of Indian occupation.

For fishing the Indians devised numerous methods. In the Housatonic River, for example, are the remains of V-shaped stone weirs which directed fish into a catch area. Baskets made of rushes were also set in streams as weirs. Fishing nets were tied using hand-twisted twine. Fish were speared also at night from canoes by the light of burning pine knots. Sturgeon in the Hudson were speared. At times fish were plentiful enough, both on the Hudson and in smaller streams, to be scooped up in baskets. These varied methods, common to the eastern seaboard, were noted by artist John White in the Carolinas in 1585; Samuel de Champlain drew Indian weirs in the early 1600s on his maps of New England. In the St. Lawrence Valley, according to Champlain, Indians fished even in winter, using several holes to insert a single large net under the ice.[43]

William Wood, too, wrote of the fishing skill of the Indians of New England: "In this trade they be very expert, being experienced in the knowledge of all baits, fitting sundry baits for several fishes and diverse seasons; being not ignorant likewise of the removal of fishes, knowing when to fish rivers and when at rocks, when at bays, and when at seas. Since the English came, they be furnished with English hooks and lines; before they made them [lines] of their own hemp more curiously wrought of stronger materials than ours, hooked with bone hooks."[44]

Game caught by Indian hunters was shared with relatives in the village according to protocol, providing for the support of family and community members. The old people in a village relied on the young men for primary supplies of meat, fat, hides, and furs. The obligation to provide for village and family members became a very heavy responsibility for the young warriors. Although stored crops and dried meats helped bridge interruptions in food supplies, when the hunting cycle was disrupted by wars which drew young men away, the dependant village population quickly suffered. When young men died in war, the food supply of the old people, women, and children became precarious.

Because they were of such importance to the yearly cycle, hunting and fishing were carefully regulated by custom and leadership. The subtleties of this control are hard to pinpoint, as they were not written down for future study. Leaders of a village or family were instrumental in determining favorable times to hunt, fish and plant. Religious ceremonies were conducted to assure that animals would allow themselves to be caught. As part of their early and arduous apprenticeship in the arts of hunting and war, male children became adept at killing small animals and birds for their households, so there were few chipmunks, squirrels or woodchucks around a village. Wolley wrote that a boy of seven could shoot a bird flying. Good hunters were honored by community approval, prestige, and choice marriages.

While hunting activities seem unrestricted, in actuality acts by individuals or groups were limited. Taking more game than could be processed or used at one time was proscribed. Hendrick Aupaumut, an eighteenth-century Mohican leader, lamented that it was not until the whites came that the Mohicans were tempted to waste their game.[45] Hunting in excess brought danger of retaliation from animal spirits, who might absent themselves from their accustomed haunts so the village would go hungry.

Housing

Indian dwellings were shown in numerous drawings on seventeenth century maps—from Spanish territory in Florida up the seacoast to Maine, on the St. Lawrence River, and in central New York and the Hudson Valley. The Indian house was a nearly universal map artifact. Since it is shown in varied lengths and heights, the maps imply that there were variations among houses. On maps, however, there were no stylistic distinctions separating linguistic groups, such as the Algonquians and Iroquois.

The popular seventeenth- and eighteenth-century name for an Indian residence, wigwam, also did not distinguish between the two groups, but was used by Europeans on maps and drawings for the homes of both Iroquois and Algonquian. Nor were dwellings of the two groups necessarily different in size. Henry Hudson visited a Mohican residence in 1609 which housed ample supplies of corn and fifty-seven people who were present, as well as probable women and

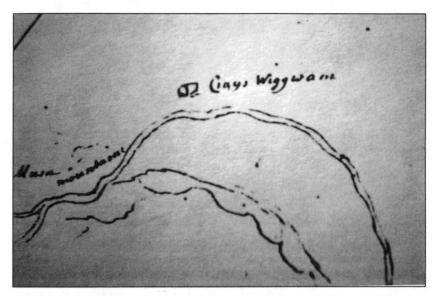

The dwelling of Cray, a Mohican, shown on Richard Sackett's 1704 survey, illustrates the longhouse form of the typical Mohican wigwam. Cray's wigwam was near Amenia, in Dutchess County, New York.

New York State Archives, Indorsed Land Papers, 4: 20

children who were absent. The wigwam of Umpachanee at Sheffield, Massachusetts in 1734 was about fifty or sixty feet in length.[46]

All that remains of Henry Hudson's lost journal of his visit is found in a 1624 printed text published by Johannes de Laet. The 1624 text is improperly translated in *Narratives of New Netherland*, a popular reference book. Correctly translated from the Dutch, Hudson's account should read: "These [fifty-seven people] I saw there in a house well-constructed of oak bark, and rounded as if it had been an arch. . ."[47] In other words, Hudson saw what today would be described as a longhouse. Adriaen Block, one of the first Europeans who visited the Mohicans, arrived only a year or two after Henry Hudson. Drawings on Block's map echo Hudson's 1609 description of a Mohican dwelling.[48]

Varied building lengths and heights are suggested by Adriean Block in drawings of Hudson River longhouses on his 1614 map, and the location of longhouses among the trees is interesting. William Strachey, in Virginia in 1618, stated that Indian houses were commonly placed "under the covert of trees, that the violence of foul weather, snow or rain, cannot assault them nor the sun in summer annoy them." He mentioned that the dwellings were as "warm as stoves, although very smoky."[49]

Chiefs in Virginia, according to a c. 1612 map by John Smith, had larger longhouses than the rest of the villagers. To afford extra size, in larger houses the vertical side wall of a house was framed separately from the rounded roof, and the two parts were lashed together on cross ties and along a purlin in order to keep tension on the arch of the roof saplings. The building of a frame for an Iroquois longhouse was described in 1724 by Lafitau. He explained that the lodges rest on posts flanking each compartment. "The square frame being raised, the Iroquois make the roof framing with long poles bent in an arc which they cover also with bark sheets a fathom [six feet] long and from one foot to fifteen inches wide. These bark sheets overlap like plates." This house contained the extra height framing and vertical sides shown in illustrations engraved from John White's c. 1585 drawings in the Carolinas and copied on John Smith's map. Both methods of framing could be used.[50] The Mohicans had similarly larger longhouses for chiefs. Mohican historian Hendrick Aupaumut wrote that members of a Mohican village would help in building their sachem a long wigwam.

An unpublished map of c. 1630 of Indian dwellings and a Dutch trading post on the side of Delaware Bay, drawn by an eye-witness, shows a more rounded end to Indian longhouses than on those on other illustrations, with doors on the side. Later illustrations make clear that when the ends of a longhouse were closed off to extend storage areas, doors were moved to the sides of the dwelling. Occasional archeological reports have mentioned side doors on longhouse outlines and side doors are clearly shown on some later illustrations.

Interestingly, one Indian structure on the Delaware Bay map is small, and probably was nearly round, rather than rectangular. Samuel de Champlain's maps of coastal New England depict buildings of different shapes and lengths, which include both longhouses and circular structures. These maps show that some houses might be round. Nicholas Denys, a seventeenth century Frenchman who wrote about the Mic Macs of Maine, had a simple explanation for variations in size. He said, "If the family is a large one, they make it [the wigwam] long enough for two fires; otherwise they make it round...."[51] Roger Williams observed of the Narragansetts of Rhode Island, "Two families often live together in a round house, about

A c. 1630 map of Delaware Bay shows a trader's house near an Indian village.
The wigwams have entrances on the sides and one is round.
Algemeen Rijksarchief, the Hague, the Netherlands

sixteen feet across. When a house is to be built, the men generally set up the poles. Then the women cover the outside with mats [bark was used in the Hudson Valley], and line the inside with finer mats./. .Generally their houses are open. A hanging mat serves for a door. When someone comes in, he lifts it up, and then it falls back by itself."[52]

The character of life in a longhouse of the Nyack Indians, located in Brooklyn near Fort Hamilton, was described by Jasper Dankaerts about 1679. Dankaerts was an agent for the Labadist sect; he and a companion, Peter Sluyter, were visiting possible locations for the sect in America. They came to a plantation where an old Nyack woman was threshing dried Turkish beans out of the pods by means of a stick. She told them she was eighty years old; they were amazed at her strength and dexterity. They went to her habitation, a longhouse, where they found a group of Nyack Indians, consisting of seven or eight families, totaling about twenty-two people. The account continued:

Their house was low and long, about sixty feet long and fourteen
or fifteen feet wide. The bottom was earth, the sides and roof were
made of reed and the bark of chestnut trees; the posts or columns,
were limbs of trees stuck in the ground, and all fastened together.
The top, or ridge of the roof was open about half a foot wide, from
one end to the other, in order to let the smoke escape in place of a
chimney. On the sides, or walls, of the house, the roof was so low
that you could hardly stand under it. The entrances, or doors,
which were at both ends, were so small and low that they had to
stoop down and squeeze themselves to get through them. The doors
were made of reed or flat bark. In the whole building there was no
lime, stone, iron, or lead.

They build their fire in the middle of the floor, according to
the number of families which live in it, so that from one end to the
other each of them boils its own pot, and eats when it likes, not
only the families by themselves, but each Indian alone, according
as he is hungry, at all hours, morning, noon and night. By each fire
are the cooking utensils, consisting of a pot, a bowl or calabash
[gourd], and a spoon also made of a calabash. These are all that relate
to cooking.[53]

Dankaerts noted that their other household articles consisted of
a calabash of sweet water for drinking, a small basket for maize and
beans, and a knife. Although the Nyack Indians, by the 1670s, had
guns, powder and lead, they had nearby also an Indian canoe "without
a nail in any part of it." Such canoes were sometimes forty feet long.
The group also had fish hooks and lines, and scoops to paddle with
in place of oars.[54]

"Their household furniture is slight and scanty, consisting of
mats and wooden dishes, hatchets made of hard flint stone by dint of
savage labor, and tubes for smoking tobacco formed likewise of flint
stone ingeniously perforated, so that it is surprising how, in so great
a want of iron implements, they are able to carve the stone," reported
a 1633 book describing New Netherland.[55]

Adriaen Van der Donck in the 1640s gave a detailed account of
the method of construction of a typical native dwelling in New
Netherland. He wrote:

When they build a house, they place long slender hickory saplings
in the ground, having the bark stripped off, in a straight line of two
rows, as far asunder as they intend the breadth of the house to be,
and continuing the rows as far as it is intended the length shall be.

Those sapling poles are bent over toward each other in the form of an arch, and secured together having the appearance of a garden arbour. The sapling poles are then crossed in the form of lathing, which is well fastened to the upright work. The lathings are heaviest near the ground. A space of about a foot wide is left open in the crown of the arch. For covering they use the bark of ash, chestnut, and other trees, which they peel off in pieces of about six feet long and as broad as they can. They cover their houses, laying the smooth side inwards, leaving an open space about a foot wide in the crown, to let out the smoke. They lap the side edges and ends over each other, having regard to the shrinking of the bark, securing the covering with withes to the lathings. A crack or rent they shut up [cover], and in this manner they make their houses proof against wind and rain. They have one door in the centre of the house. . .From sixteen to eighteen families frequently dwell in one house, according to its size. The fire[s] being kept in the middle, the people lie on either side thereof, and each family has its own place [a bench with partitions on each side] for sleeping and storage. . .Such is the construction of an Indian dwelling in every place, unless they are out on fishing and hunting excursions, and then they erect temporary huts or shanties.[56]

Summary

Due to the productivity of the region, the techniques very briefly mentioned above usually provided ample food for the Mohican population as well as reserves for the winter ahead, provided the delicate yearly cycle was followed. It is believed that the Hudson Valley environment was productive enough to encourage steady population increases. This in turn led to more hunting and gathering. Farming was expanded in turn. Ample food lead to further increases of population, a cycle of success. This gradual expansion rippled across Algonquian territories, but was interrupted by the arrival of Europeans. The old stand-off between the Mohicans and the Mohawks was broken as a result. Although they had been enemies long ago, Dutch accounts confirm that fighting began between the Mohawks and the Mohicans only after fur-trading with Europeans had brought the Mohawks into Mohican territory.

The complex circumstances noted above, fine-tuned management of farming, gathering, and hunting, and balance in tribal relations, all of which affected resources management and community survival, soon were jeopardized. Within a few years after the arrival of Europeans, aspects of Indian life were altered and Indian material goods changed. Conversely, many things about Indian life remained the same. Longhouses, for example, still were the common Mohican wigwams in the eighteenth century, and hunting and gardening featuring maize, beans, and squash continued. Ceremonies and rituals continued as of old until the missions began.

Initial acceptance of European tools, clothes and weapons was not dictated by need, but rather by desire, convenience and imitation; it was a social exchange. The need for adaptation in the second century after the arrival of the Dutch and English had deeper roots. In the eighteenth century, cultural change was forced on the native population by wars and by the expansion of the colonial population, with resulting loss of land, as the following chapters demonstrate. The information given here is intended as a yardstick against which to measure this change.

II.
The Mohican Network

"They say they belong to a place called Wayattano, at the
head of Stratford River."[1]

WARS sparked by the European presence were culturally
disruptive influences for all Mohican communities in the
latter half of the seventeenth century. Before recovery
from the Esopus Wars and the 1660s war of the New England Indians
against the Mohawks could occur, King Philip's unsuccessful rebellion swept New England in 1676, bringing terror to neutral Indian
nations as well as to English settlers.

This war was not the end of the series. Within a few years, a deadly
war between the English and the French was fought across New York
and northern New England in the 1690s, to be followed by Queen
Anne's War in New England early in the eighteenth century. The
repeated violence strained native populations. Once the series of wars
ended, after 1720 a flood of white settlement was released into
Mohican areas. The effects of these crises, wars followed by land loss
due to settlement, caused a breakdown in the once finely tuned
management of Mohican resources.

It will be valuable to look briefly at these wars. While the
outbreaks between the Waranawankong Indians at the Esopus and
Peter Stuyvesant's forces in the late 1650s and early 1660s had not
removed the Mohicans from their settlements north of Esopus at
Catskill and at present Leeds, the wars had disrupted hunting patterns
and Indian alliances. As the Esopus Indians were harrassing settlers
and confronting Stuyvesant's troops, their Mohican and Wappinger
neighbors tried to help them while avoiding fighting. Indian media-
tors from Schodack, from Catskill, and from villages on the Kinderhook Creek and the Roelof Jansen Kill made trips into Esopus
territory with messages from the Dutch of Fort Orange. While the
Indian emissaries helped retrieve Dutch prisoners, they also prevented
their Esopus Indian friends from attacking Dutch farmers at Catskill

and Leeds. Such provocation would have drawn Stuyvesant's troops into Mohican territory and the Mohicans into the fray.[2]

The Mohicans, the Wappingers, and the Mohawks were the three noncombatant Indian nations most affected by the Esopus Wars. The Mohawks, too, tried to avoid the fighting. After the hostilities ended, there remained much resentment among the Esopus Indians against the Mohawks as well as against Stuyvesant's regime. The Esopus blamed the Mohawks for the loss of many men in the war; the Mohawks in turn threatened to attack the Esopus, to quiet such accusations.

As the Esopus hostilities wound down, a major Indian war erupted. A coalition of Indian nations from New England and the Hudson Valley united to attack the Mohawks, who had been harrassing the Wekquaesgeeks at the south end of the Hudson River, taking away their beavers and goods. Also subject to tribute were the Pacamtecocks and Sokoki of the upper Connecticut River, the Moheagans of Connecticut, and other New England and St. Lawrence River groups, including the Abenakis.[3] There was great agitation among Algonquian-speaking Indian allies as they considered means to end the Mohawk menace.

A pattern of aggression had made the Mohawks despised bullies against whom their victims were finally rebelling. To most of the Indian victims, all-out war seemed the only effective solution to the Mohawk aggression. Since the Mohawks were valued allies to the European residents of Fort Orange and Beverwyck (soon to be Albany), this made the Fort Orange environs vulnerable to attack from New England Indians aiming to destroy the power of the Mohawks.

Because Mohican circumstances were unique, however, the Mohicans were an exception to this consensus. Their relationship with the Dutch population at Beverwyck and Fort Orange restrained their involvement. Fort Orange and Beverwyck were central to Mohican trading locations and also contained powerful Mohican protectors, such as Jeremias Van Rensselaer. The Mohicans, as a result, tried to ward off attacks which might include the Dutch fort or the adjacent small village of Beverwyck. Since they would not permit an attack on the village and fort, they remained neutral, despite a long-standing antipathy for the Mohawks. The politics of the colonies had a place in Indian actions, as well. The English, unhappy with Dutch efforts to control the Mohawks, encouraged New England Indians to attack

Dutch sites. One result was a random attack on an outlying Dutch farm at the mouth of the Kinderhook Creek in summer 1664 in which a tenant farmer and his family were killed.

In 1663, as the New England Indians gathered in Mohican territory preparing to attack, they were emboldened by possession of guns, now widely available. (Indian warfare, which in the pre-contact era had not resulted in great numbers of casualties, became more lethal with the advent of firearms than it had been in the past.)[4]

Although Mohican territory east of the Hudson would be the staging area for the coming fighting, the Mohicans temporized about joining as long as they could. As a delaying tactic, supposedly to defend themselves, the Mohicans had requested permission of the Mohawks to build a fort on the Kinderhook Creek, in present Columbia County. It was probably near that fort that the New England Indians gathered. By October, 1663, as a result, the Mohicans unavoidably were swept up in the preparations for war. The Mohicans and the Catskill Indians left behind their maize plantations, "yea, had offered to sell divers maize plantations to the Dutch for a piece of cloth." The Dutch of Fort Orange came in canoes to remove unharvested corn from abandoned Mohican fields.[5]

Here was an extreme example of the damage war could do to normally well-organized Indian communities. As a result of the disturbance, the Mohican families near Albany and at Catskill would lose a crucial winter's supply of maize, squash and beans; they would, as well, forego fishing and hunting and seasonal preparations such as setting aside seed corn, drying meat, preparing furs and skins, mending nets, gathering wood, and performing fall religious ceremonies. Since villages in different localities were involved, villagers would find it hard to help each other. During the coming year, they would be forced to rely on fresh meat for food rather than vegetable crops—provided enough warriors returned from the fighting to hunt. In addition, women and children would be removed from their traditional villages to strange locations, where locating supplementary foods such as nuts and berries would be more difficult than at home.

It was likely the population would become further indebted to traders for much-needed articles. If, in the excitement, the Mohicans sold away their land to Europeans in order to get war supplies, as indicated by the 1663 report, they might never be able to return to their traditional community sites. This crisis may explain why the Mohicans relocated their earlier settlements. After the war, they were back in the Schodack area. In the 1730s their chief, Ampamit, had a village on an island opposite Schodack Landing, but he had little land left for cultivation and complained that some Indians had to pay rent for corn land.[6]

In October 1663, a Mohawk informer carried a warning of a possible Algonquian attack to his great *nytap* (friend), Rensselaerswyck tenant Peter Winne, who was farming near present Castleton-on-Hudson, New York. The Indian friend told Winne that all the Indians from east of Fort Orange had assembled and were to come in five days to attack Fort Orange. The large group of Indians, reported to be about five hundred strong, was said by the Mohawk informer to be located three miles east of Claverack, a distance of over nine miles by English measurement. (The "Claverack" referred to was Claverack Landing, a farmers' dock on the Hudson River at the present City of Hudson, not the later inland community.)

Mohicans from Westenhook Appear

Mohicans living inland in a village on the west side of the Housatonic River in an area called Westenhook were involved in the Indian war preparations. The prospect of the war brought one of the earliest documentary references to this segment of the Mohicans. The war group assembled east of Claverack in 1663 was described as consisting of the "Mahicanders, the Catskills, the Wappingers, those of Esopus, besides another tribe of Indians that dwell half way between Fort Orange and Hartford."[7] This latter reference was to the Mohicans of Westenhook on the Housatonic River.

The Housatonic River was regarded as the half-way point between the Albany area and Connecticut to the east. Hubbard, for example, in his narrative of Indian wars of the 1670s, places the "Ausotunnoog river in the middle way betwix Westfield and the Dutch river and Fort Albany."[8] The large Indian village half way between Albany and Hartford on the Housatonic River was familiar to the Dutch. By the early 1650s, this community of Indians had been acknowledged by mapmakers, although the Housatonic River was not yet recognized on maps. As a result of information obtained from Indians or travelers, an unidentified Indian settlement known to be in the Westenhook area was shown on mid-seventeenth century maps above the head of an imaginary stream which, emptying into Long

Island Sound near New Haven, rose in the west in Housatonic
territory.

Errors had arisen very early on maps as a result of confusion
between the minor Quinnipiac River, near New Haven, and the
longer Housatonic River, a few miles to the west. The Quinnipiac
River was discovered as early as 1614; Adriaen Block had called it the
R[ivier] van den Roden Bergh or "River of the Red Hill" on his map
of New England and it was shortly thereafter shown on William Jansz
Blaeu's early *Atlas* of 1617.[9] Early mapmakers had no knowledge of
the course of the Quinnipiac, a small river bearing to the northeast.
They drew it as a waterway extending into the area where the
Housatonic River actually runs. The result was a map misrepresenta-
tion which continued into the eighteenth century. As late as 1753, a
resident wrote of the Housatonic, "This river, tho' it be navigable for
eight or ten miles from the mouth of it and extends itself cross the
Colony of Connecticut and almost cross the Province of the Massachusetts, more than a hundred and twenty miles into land, yet it is
not laid down in any of the maps which I have seen of this country."[10]
When the absence of the Housatonic River on early maps is understood, the Mohican identity of the location shown becomes clear. The
community shown on maps was actually on the west side of the
Housatonic River, not on or even near the Quinnipiac.

The first map to pinpoint the Westenhook Indian site with a dot
was a first-state Jansson-Visscher map of 1651. The Indian location
was embellished as the map was copied. By 1655 another popular map,
copied from the first and attributed to Hugo Allardt, titled "Novi
Belgii," showed a substantial Indian community, in the form of a
house encircled by dots, at the head of *Rodenberghs Rivier*, in the area
in reality served by the Housatonic River. The similar 1656 map
which accompanied Adriaen Van der Donck's *A Description of the
New Netherlands* also showed the Indian site, as did several other maps
in the Allard, Montanus and Jansson-Visscher series.[11] A comparison
of these old maps to a modern map places the Indian settlement in
the western corner of Connecticut, near the Taconic range.

The river was not entirely overlooked. In 1720 a German mapmaker updating old map plates added a "Stratford River," another
name for the Housatonic, to his map. On this map, an Indian location,
labeled Kiyaeck, is shown on a tributary of the Stratford (Housatonic)
River.[12]

Maps of the mid-seventeenth century ignored the Housatonic River. The location of Rodenburgh's River was imaginary. The Mohican Indian village in the circle (top left) was real, however, and was located on the Housatonic River. Map of New Netherland 1651.

Manuscripts and Special Collections, New York State Library

There is little doubt that the Indian settlement shown on the mid-century maps is the same one noted in the 1663 reference to the Indians half way between Fort Orange and Hartford; only a brief time, about a decade, had elapsed between the appearance of the map in 1651 and the 1663 account. The Indians listed in the war group of 1663, the Mahicanders, the Catskills, and the Indians between Fort Orange and Hartford, were not three separate nations but three groups of Mohicans. The three populations were related, and individuals moved freely between locations, as subsequent deeds show and as some of the natives later testified.

The other groups mentioned in the 1663 report, the Esopus and Wappingers, were separate nations. Soon after this event, the Wappingers became acknowledged allies of the Mohicans. The Wappingers lived south of the Mohicans on the east side of the Hudson; in 1643 they were described as "living on the North River about half

ways from Fort Orange" to New Amsterdam.[13] The Esopus villages
once had been across the river from the Wappingers. By 1663, the
Esopus Indians at the Indian war gathering must have been few, since
their nation had been severely damaged during the Esopus Wars by
Stuyvesant's army. The Esopus who were ready to fight the Mohawks
apparently were survivors who had been given refuge during the war
in Wappinger and Mohican territories. They no longer could return
to their confiscated land and, when the Esopus fighting was over,
some settled among the Mohicans and Wappingers.

War Against the Mohawks

The war of the eastern Indians against the Mohawks began in
earnest in 1663. The Mohicans finally joined in 1664, the year the
English took over New York. Despite this major governmental
turnover, there was little opportunity for change around Fort Orange. The constant Indian hostilities halted trade and caused hardships
for the colonists of Rensselaerswyck and Albany. After the intervention of Albany officials, fighting was halted by a truce in 1666. The
Mohawks agreed to "stop bothering the Mohicans." As Connecticut
had encouraged its Indians to attack the Mohawks, the Mohicans
accused Connecticut of keeping the Mohican chiefs from settling with
the Mohawks.[14]

When the war broke out again, a crucial battle was fought at
Kinquariones on the Mohawk River.[15] Finally the war was reluctantly concluded by the participants at an Albany conference in 1672,
after another intercession by Albany leaders, including Jeremias Van
Rensselaer, Director of Rensselaerswyck.[16] There was no clear winner
and the participants remained mutually hostile. Thereafter, although
there were outbreaks of fighting, there was a reduction of aggression
on the trails, and trade was resumed.

The fragile 1672 peace with the Mohawks had been in effect for
two years when Jeremias Van Rensselaer died late in 1674. The
influential Van Rensselaers for over forty years had been major
purchasers of Mohican land and had maintained close and peaceful
associations with the nation's leaders. Jeremias Van Rensselaer, who
became Director of Rensselaerswyck in 1658, had been one of the
most dependable friends of the Mohicans at Albany. As the Mohicans
had come to rely on his protection, with the loss of his restraining
influence, they expected a renewal of attacks by the Mohawks. The

distressed Mohicans mourned Van Rensselaer's death at a conference at Albany in February 1675.

The Mohicans had to cope with another change. The Dutch colony was transferred permanently to the English early in 1675. At the conference, the Mohicans requested that they would not be exiled or destroyed by the English, "something they have never done to the Christians." The English assured the Mohicans they would be protected and were welcome to stay in the Colony. In light of the changing situation, the Mohicans at the 1675 conference declared: "[You] Say that the English and the Dutch and their people are now one and the Dutch are now English. Thus we Mahikanders, the highland Indians, and the 'western corner' Indians are now one also. . . ."[17] In response to the perceived Mohawk threat after the death of Van Rensselaer, the chiefs of the Mohicans in 1675 had arranged a defensive alliance with the neighboring Highland Indians and with the western corner Indians.

The Highland Indians were identified as Wappingers and Wekquaesgeeks by Frances Lovelace in a 1669 letter. He wrote, "I beleeve I can resolve your doubt concerning what is meant by the high Land Indians[;] amongst us The Wappingoes and Wickerskeck etc. have always been reckoned so. . . ."[18] The Wappingers, south of the Mohicans in present Putnam County and lower Dutchess County, lived north of the Wekquaesgeeks or "Wickerskecks" who were in present Westchester County and the Bronx. Wekquaesgeek land had been claimed as far south as the East River by the "Wickerscreeke Indians" in 1649, and land to the north was sold by them in 1671.[19] Frederick Philips, in the present North Tarrytown area, in 1680 obtained permission to purchase from the Indians additional land "on Each side of the Creeke Called by the Indians Pocanteco att Wickerscreeke." However, land in later Putnam County and at Poughkeepsie was sold in 1683 by Highland Indians who were apparently Wappingers.[20]

The western corner Indians mentioned in the 1675 alliance were the Mohicans of the Indian village at Westenhook, on the Housatonic River. Later statements showed they considered themselves to be brothers of the Mohicans on the Hudson and some of them may have come from there. The friendly alliance of Mohicans, Wappingers and Wekquaesgeeks, extending from Mohican territory to present New York City, was different from the century-old codified organization welding the Iroquois into a single nation. The Hudson River group was simply a loose federation of the Mohicans with neighbors to the south. It was noted by a Mohican descendant, John Quinney, that the associated nations had a yearly meeting.[21]

Temporary alliances were commonly arranged among Indian nations when a single nation was not strong enough to survive a perceived threat or accomplish a goal without help. Such assistance from friends was not mandatory. Speakers bearing gifts and wampum belts were sent from the nation in need to possible allies. Using formal but persuasive oratory, the emissaries spoke at charged council meetings. If successful, they enlisted the young men of the neutral nation to fight beside them. Philip Metacom, during King Philip's War, had approached the Catskill Indians in the same manner for help, and the western Indians later similarly requested aid of the Mohicans. Long before, the Mohicans had requested help against the Mohawks from Algonquian nations on the St. Lawrence River. Samuel de Champlain had persuaded these nations to refuse the request of the Mohicans.[22]

Lag in European Settlement

The succession of wars and the uncertainty about colonial jurisdiction slowed English settlement of the region west of the Housatonic River, except along Long Island Sound. This vacuum preserved for the Mohicans in interior parts of present Columbia and Dutchess counties, in the northwest corner of Connecticut, and in the western reaches of Massachusetts a late-seventeenth century haven. These isolated villages became essential to Mohican cultural survival as Mohican land in New York was lost.

Much of the Mohican land lying in the Hudson Valley was gone by 1700. West of the Hudson and along the Mohawk River Mohican land had been appropriated by the Mohawks after a Mohican defeat in 1629; further land loss came when Kiliaen Van Rensselaer, taking advantage of their loss to the Mohawks, was able to buy land for his farms from the Mohicans. In 1630 and 1631 he obtained for his colony extensive tracts of land on the west side of the Hudson River above and below Fort Orange, reaching two days' journey to the west, and also one parcel on the east shore, opposite Fort Orange.

Other land sales followed. After 1630, and particularly in the decades after the ending of the Esopus Wars in 1663, Dutch traders and farmers obtained Mohican land at Claverack, Kinderhook, Saratoga, Half Moon and Schaghticoke, as well as at Catskill, at Coxsackie, on the Roelof Jansen Kill, and elsewhere in present Columbia, Dutchess, Greene and Rensselaer counties in New York.[23]

Mohican isolation at inland sites was by no means complete. Housatonic Mohicans maintained very close connections with relatives in villages in adjoining counties of New York, with the chief sachem in his village at Schodack, as well as with Albany traders, according to Indian deeds and documentary accounts. Stream drainages lead naturally from one area to the other. For example, the upper courses of the Roelof Jansen Kill, which rises in Columbia County and flows into the Hudson River, were close to the headwaters of the Green River, which also rises in present Columbia County, New York, but flows east into the Housatonic River between Great Barrington and Sheffield, Massachusetts. A little farther south, the Webatuck (Ten Mile) River flows from New York's Dutchess County into the Housatonic drainage. Indian trails, such as the one that passed through later Great Barrington, led from New England to the Hudson.

Within a few years after the great war of the Indian nations of New England and the Hudson Valley against the Mohawks ended in 1672, Indian villages were disturbed during the Indian uprisings between 1675 and 1676 known as King Philip's War. Although the Mohicans on the Housatonic and on the Hudson River did not participate in the fighting, they sympathized with Philip Metacom's forces. Once again, as they had in the Esopus Wars, Mohican settlements sheltered Indian refugees. And once again they were on the opposite side from the Mohawks.

In summer 1676, it was reported to Governor Andros that some of Philip's men were about to cross the Hudson River "near Esopus" to seek warriors, in the traditional Indian manner of asking friendly nations for help. The Catskill Mohicans, not far from Esopus, had a substantial village inland near present Leeds on the Catskill Creek and were probably the sought-after accomplices.[24]

Early in August 1676, a party of about 250 New England Indians was pursued by English soldiers to the Housatonic River, crossing at a ford which was probably "in the upper part of Sheffield," now Great Barrington.[25] The fugitives, camped on the western shore of the stream on Mohican land, possibly believed they had entered the safety of New York territory. The group was nevertheless attacked by Connecticut soldiers. About 200 of the Indian fugitives, some wounded and others ill, fled westward into New York, where the

New England troops were not allowed to follow. After this escape, Connecticut troops were refused permission by New York's Governor Andros to sail up the Hudson River in pursuit of the survivors.[26]

The escapees, many of whom were women and children, reached a Dutch-speaking village on the east side of the Hudson River, probably Kinderhook, then crossed the Hudson below Albany and were sheltered among Mohicans at a place called *Paquiage*, most likely the village identified with one of the large flats at present Leeds, New York. The identity of this flat is mentioned in a deed of 1678. The same productive flat, identified as "the maize land named Quaiack" was mentioned in another deed.[27] The location was apparently the one where Philip Metacom had hoped to find recruits for his rebellion. Here in 1996 the presence of a contact period Indian village was confirmed by an archeological dig near the hamlet of Leeds, New York.[28]

Refuge during the War

During King Philip's War, Mohicans residing in the Housatonic area were threatened by Connecticut and Massachusetts soldiers, who had little interest in distinguishing between Indian friends and enemies. Because it was dangerous to go hunting or to travel in New England, New York territory looked like a safe retreat for neutrals for the duration of the war. That Mohican villagers moved from the Housatonic Valley into nearby New York as the war progressed is related in area history books.[29] This tradition is confirmed by documents of the period.

Relations were strained between New York and the New England colonies, who wanted the help of New York's Mohawks against Philip's forces. The New York Council and Governor pursued a course of admitting refugees from the war into New York. The Wickerscreeke (Weckquaesgeek) Indians, for example, were permitted to take refuge on the north end of Manhattan Island. The Wickerscreekes soon paved the way for the Westenhook Mohicans to enter New York.

On April 27, 1676, the Colonial Council in New York reported that "Severall Indyans appeared before the Governor in the Fort; they say they belong to a place called Wayattano, at the head of Stratford River, with them were some Wickerscreeke and some Stamford Indyans. The sagamore [chief] of Wickerscreeke came with them.

They declare themselves to bee good friends and desire to continue so and make a present of about ten deerskins, a beareskin and 4 small beavers, given at three times repeating their desire of friendship; The Governor accepts of it, and promises protection to them within [the boundaries of] this Government [New York] but will not undertake anything without; That hee had heard from the Wickerscreeke Indyans that they are good Indyans and now finds them so, and they may have all friendship and freedom here, so long as they behave themselves well. The Governor presents them with three Duffells Coates, one to the Wickerscreeke sachem, the other two, to the two chiefs from Stratford River."[30] The Indians from the Stratford (Housatonic) River were welcome, but to obtain protection, the Wayattano petitioners would have to move over the border into the colony of New York. Once again, war was having a disruptive effect on the cycles of community management.

King Philip's War was at its height. With the New York government's permission, the Mohicans of Wayattano now took shelter in safe areas of New York Mohican territory, such as at Tachkanick (later spelled Taconic) and along the Kinderhook Creek. The movement of some Mohican residents into New York during King Philip's War probably accounts for the presence in Columbia County of Mohicans identified as Westenhook Indians who sold tracts of land along the Housatonic River.

Wayattano is at Westenhook

The first New York land transactions recognizing the Westenhook locale began when Indians sold some land in present Columbia County on October 1, 1679. The sellers were five men: Wieshaghcaet, his two brothers, Powhyates and Maxinhaet, and their two cousins (or nephews), Waespacheek and Pinonock, "all Westenhoek Indians."[31] The land sold lay on both sides of the Kinderhook Creek, rather than at Westenhook on the Housatonic River. This and other deeds show Mohicans from Westenhook exercising control of land in sections of the all-inclusive Albany County (later Columbia and Rensselaer counties) in New York. In the 1670s their sphere was not limited to the banks of the Housatonic River, sometimes called the Westenhook River (or Creek). Conversely, when land was sold along the Westenhook Creek in 1685, and again in 1703 and 1704, when land for the Westenhook Patent extending west to the Van Renssclaer

patent was sold, the Indians involved were not identified as Westenhook Indians. The reason seems to be that the term "Westenhook"
merely referred to a locality. It was not a tribal name.

The two European purchasers of the Columbia County land were
Dirck Wessels (Ten Broeck) and Gerrit Teunis (Van Vechten), of
Albany. At this date the men rarely used the surnames by which their
families were later known. Both were prominent at Albany, and both
served on the Albany Council. They had many significant dealings
with the Mohicans and other Indian nations. Dirck Wessels functioned as recorder and translator for the Albany Council at Indian
meetings. He was deeply involved in land speculation and for a time
was associated with Robert Livingston. Both Dirck Wessels and
Gerrit Teunis were Indian traders; they had previously obtained other
tracts of land in New York Colony from Mohicans.

It is likely some of the resident Mohicans remained at Housatonic
Valley locations during the war, while others moved back when the
war ended, although they probably chose new sites for their villages.
Mohicans east of New York's borders sold two large tracts of land to
trader Dirck Wessels and a company of investors in 1685. Subsequently, Indians from Westenhook considered joining a Mohican
community at Tachkanick in present Columbia County, on the west
side of the Taconic range. Possibly in response to the 1685 transaction,
in January 1687 Indians from the Indian community identified as
"Wawyachtenok or Wayattano," considered moving into New York
to join their relatives at Tachkanick. Their speaker was Peter d' Wilt
(Peter the native); he was accompanied, and therefore sponsored, by
Indians of Tachkanick, the Roelof Jansen Kill, Kinderhook, and other
River Indians.

To get permission to come over the colony border, they opened
a dialogue with Robert Livingston on the subject. From this dialogue,
it developed that their village of Wawyachtenok/Wayattano lay not
far to the east of Tachkanick, which was a tract west of the Taconic
Mountains purchased by Livingston from the Mohicans. Tachkanick
lay along the headwaters of the Roelof Jansen Kill near present-day
Copake and West Copake, but, as Livingston extended his borders,
it eventually included secluded valleys in the mountains. Tachkanick
was located on a Livingston map of 1714.

Locating Wawyachtenok/Wayattano

Although the New York-Massachusetts border was still vague, the Wayattano/Wawyachtenok group believed they lived in Massachusetts, not in New York. They were asking permission to enter the New York colony. The village at Wawyachtenok was connected to Tachkanick by a path, according to an Indian deed given to Robert Livingston in 1685: "The southerly bounds [of the land called Tachkanick] beginns on the other Side of that creek [Twastawekak] that Runns along the fflat or plain over against [opposite] Minnissichtanock, where Two Trees are markd and Runns along the foot of the high mountains, to the Path that goes to Wawyachtenock, to a hill called by the Indians Mananosick, where Two Trees are marked, on the Southwest Side of the Path. . . ."[32] An accompanying crude map made for Robert Livingston at the time of the purchase shows the path going through the mountains. On this map, however, the path led to Westenhook, suggesting that Wawyachtenok was within Westenhook, or that the two words meant the same thing.[33]

The names of the Wawyachtenok sachems involved in the discussion with Livingston were Wanamanheet, Pinawee, and Pachkanass. Wanamanheet was apparently the same man as Wanemenhet, a Mohican sachem who previously, in 1648 and 1650, had sold a mill creek and a parcel of land at Schodack on the Hudson River. When fellow Schodack Indians testified about his land in the Albany Court in 1664, he was not present. Possibly Wanemenhet, having sold his land, had removed to the Housatonic area. As he was a sachem, a family entourage very likely accompanied him.[34]

Although the Wawyachtenok group received permission to enter New York, after their discussions with Livingston, they decided not to make the move. Their explanation involved other Indians to whom they were related, who lived farther south on the Housatonic River. The dialogue was recounted in a Livingston memorandum of 1687 titled, "What the Wawyachtenokse Indians have said to Robert Livingston, Proprietor of Tachkanik, in the presence of Johannes Wendel and Hendrick Cuyler, Aldermen, in the City of Albany, the 24th of January 1686/7." Their statement was entered in Livingston's Indian Records as follows:

1. First, as an introduction, [the Indians] said that they were brethren with the Indians of Tachkanik, Roeloff Jansens Kill and other River Indians. Give 1 deer skin.

2. Say that if the Indians of Wawyachtenock would come to plant on Tachkanik, the other Indians who live further down will be afraid and could easily be destroyed for they have a very small heart. Give 4 deer skins.

3. Say they are definitely decided to stay on Wawyachtenok as the other Indians who live further down among the English with whom they are related would be afraid. Give 3 deer skins.

4. Would like to be considered as brethren and to be in a covenant since Tachkanik lays near to them. Give 4 deer skins, and 2 wildcats, and 1 fox.

(To give deer skins or furs at a conference was part of Indian protocol. Usually the Indians were offered gifts in exchange. The statement was translated by Capt. Dirck Wessels, Albany recorder, the Albany trader who knew the Westenhook Indians well and who was prominent among the purchasers of their Housatonic land in 1685 and again early in the eighteenth century.)

Robert Livingston responded:

I understood that some of the Indians of Wawyachtenok would like to come and plant on Tachkanik and come under this government. Therefore I have made that known to his Excellency [the Governor] who said that the path is open for all good Indians to come here in this government where they will be welcome and well treated if they behave themselves well. As you are decided to stay on Wawyachtenok, that is all right, but if you would like to come and live at Tachkanik or anywhere else in this government, you will be given a tract. Has been returned: 1 half barrel of beer, 1 small barrel of rum, and 1 roll tobacco."[35]

The related Indians who lived farther down on the Housatonic River, whom the Wawyachtenok Indians felt might be destroyed if left unprotected, were apparently the Mohicans in a village called Weatauk (Wiataak) near later Salisbury, Connecticut, and, in addition, those in villages on the lakes farther south, near later Sharon, Connecticut. It was fortunate the Wawyachtenok group decided not to move into New York. By remaining at Westenhook, they may have avoided an epidemic of smallpox which struck Schaghticoke and other Hudson Valley Indian encampments about 1690.

The Community of Wawyachtenok

The documents quoted above demonstrate that a significant Mohican location known as Wawyachtenok, also called Wayattano, existed east of Tachkanick. According to the Indians' testimony it lay not far from Tachkanick. It probably was the active Mohican community shown on maps of the 1650s and mentioned in 1663. While its precise location is uncertain, several later documentary references to Wawyachtenok/Wayattano help to locate the tract or village. The community seems to have been situated west of the Housatonic River, not far from the border between Connecticut and Massachusetts.

One possible location for Wawyachtenok was a site one mile north of present Great Barrington where an Indian village traditionally known as "the Great Wigwam" or "the Great Castle" once existed near the customary fording place and Indian path on the river. A nineteenth century historian of Great Barrington suggested that "This [Great Wigwam] locality is where the Congregational Church now stands, and to the east and south of that building."[36] This interpretation seems to be based on the finding of burials in the vicinity of the church. Documents quoted below, however, indicate the Indian village and the ford were north of Great Barrington. An early military road went west from the vicinity of the ford, cutting through the mountains to the Tachkanick area in Livingston's patent. The road, used by traders, soldiers and provincial officials, forded the Housatonic River near the Great Wigwam and did not take present Route 23, as has been suggested, but instead followed a well-worn route no longer used over the mountain. [37]

The Great Wigwam location was a point of measurement for the committee which laid out proprietors' lots for the town of Sheffield in 1724. The committee reported "that ye Lower Township shall extend up the Maine River [the Housatonic] from ye Path yt goeth over ye river by ye Great Wigwam, something above ye middle falls, which is something above a half a mile from said path." According to Charles Taylor, the nineteenth-century historian, the Middle Falls were those occupied at the time (1882) by the Berkshire Woolen Company.[38]

The Great Wigwam location also was noted by a visitor going down to attend a service at Mahaiwe with John Sergeant in November 1735. The visitor wrote, "The services were held in a wigwam about a mile from the base of Maus-waw-se-ki [Monument Mountain]. The Indians gathered here from Indian Town [Stockbridge], and from the 'Great Wigwam' - at the ford a mile or two south."[39] This measurement also places the location and ford north of today's village of Great Barrington.

According to the above account of 1687, the Indians said they belonged to a place called Wayattano (which they also called Wawyachtenok) situated at the head of Stratford River. Stratford was another of the several names attached to the Housatonic River. After the founding of the community of Stratford near its mouth, the Housatonic was called the Stratford in its lower reaches. Wayattano or Wawyachtenok was at the head of that segment, not at the head of the whole river, which rises north of present Pittsfield.

Wawyachtenok was located more specifically in two documents dating to 1702. On March 12, 1702, Robert Sanders petitioned, with others, for the "Tract of unappropriated Land in the Hands of the Native Indians Proprietors lying in Dutchess County to the Westward of Westenholks Creeke and to the Eastward of Pogkeepke [Poughkeepsie] in Dutchess County aforesaid called by the Indians by the Name of Wayawnagtanock who are willing to sell the said Tract to your Petitioners." Although the petition implies the tract was in New York's Dutchess County, the events cited above indicate Wawyachtenok was east of the contested Massachusetts border. Since at the time New York claimed land into the Housatonic Valley, Sanders and other speculators turned to the New York government for permission to buy. The March 12 description was made more specific in a second petition of March 30, 1702, for other land nearby. The second petition of Sanders, with Abraham Gouveneur and others, described Wassaic, in Dutchess County, New York, a tract in southeastern Amenia, as "to the southward of Wayanagtanock, to the westward of Westenhoeck Creek."[40] Thus, Wawyachtenok, west of the Housatonic, was north of an imaginary line extending east from Wassaic.

By 1703, according to a deed for Westenhook, an unnamed settlement which the Westenhook Indians intended to retain was within a tract extending on both sides of Westenhook Creek between waterfalls in northwestern Connecticut and a waterfall called Packwack, opposite the "bounds of the Colony of Rensselaerswyck and Claverack." [41] The south line of Claverack was the north boundary of the Livingston Patent, and fell opposite a point south of Great Barrington. The Wawyachtenok settlement clearly was within later Massachusetts boundaries.

The name Wawyachtenok continued to be used in connection with the Westenhook Indians. In 1689, another war affecting the Mohicans loomed. Hostilities between the English colonies and Canada threatened, and an attack by the French on Albany appeared imminent. On September 17 the Albany trader, Robert Sanders, was ordered by the Albany Council to endeavor "to procure the Indians of the Long Reach, Wawyachtenok and Esopus to come up here [to Albany] to lie out as scouts upon the borders of this country." [42] The Indians of the Long Reach were the Wappingers and Wekquaesgeeks, while the Indians of Wawyachtenok were the Mohicans of Westenhook.

The threat of attack on Albany in 1689 was real. The frightened Albanians were calling on all Indian friends to surround their city to protect them. In fact, an attack by the French and some Canadian Indians did materialize the following February of 1690, but was diverted to Schenectady, where many of the Dutch villagers were massacred or captured.

The Mohicans below Albany (*i.e.* at Schodack and Catskill) accepted assignments around the city of Albany to ward off approaching attackers. Incidents in the 1690s, including one in 1696 when Mohicans were rewarded for killing French Indians marching to attack Kinderhook in later Columbia County, show the worth of the Mohican net around the city. [43] Whether Mohicans from Wawyachtenok came over to Albany to join the other Mohicans as scouts lying out around Albany is not certain.

Despite extensive references to the name, no document has been found that specifically connects Wawyachtenok with the Great Wigwam site. That a Mohican village called Wawyachtenok existed within the bounds of Westenhook is well established, however.

The Ottowa Connection

As this 1689 war with the French approached, a large group of loyal Mohicans, who had lived for six years among the Ottowa Indians, finally came home rather than fight against their English friends. A request to the Five Nations, who were warring with the French, to "Open a safe Path for the Northern Indians and Mehikanders who are at Ottowawa to come home. . . ." had been made by Governor Dongan in 1687. The Mohican group had been tempted away from the Hudson River by the need for beaver furs to pay their debts. At the invitation of the Ottowas, they had left their homeland "and hunted with good Success of many Beavers, being 50 Men, [and also] Women & Children 60, In all 110. . . ."[44] The Ottowas had old obligations to the Mohicans and were among their dependable western friends, according to the Mohican historian Hendrick Aupaumut.

By April 1690, when the New York government was in the hands of Jacob Leisler, the Mohicans remaining with the Ottowas were warned by the French to take up the French cause or face retaliation. The Mohicans sent word to Albany that they needed aid to get home. To help them return to the area, four Mohicans were sent from Albany to make the arrangements with the Mohawks for safe passage. The Mohican group among the Ottowas was waiting for this escort "from us with 2 Christians whome wee have ordered with other Mehekanders living on the River to go to them and Convey them through the Macquaes [Mohawks] land hither. . .further they tell us of 60 persons belonging to them of the same nacon [nation] that are designed for Esopus with Bevers. . . ."[45] The beavers apparently were for trade at Esopus and represented some of the fruits of their Ottowa/Niagara stay.

The Mohicans arrived safely on the Hudson River but were struck by a smallpox epidemic which spread through the camps of Albany's Indian allies. In September 1691, at an Albany conference, a proposition was made by the Senecas "to the Mahekanders that came last year from Ottowa." The Senecas condoled with them, "Wee are sorry children that you have lost a great many men the last year as well by the mortallity of the small pox as otherwise. Wee reconcile the loss of that blood." The Mohicans had brought along to safety a Seneca captive, for which the Senecas gave thanks. The term "children" was apparently merely a figure used to express the tenderness felt by the Senecas. In the same address, the Mohicans and Schaghticokes were addressed also as "Brothers and Cousins."[46]

It is interesting that in 1689 New York merchants, concerned the colony of New York would be lost to the French, urged that several forts should be built on the frontiers for protection. These included a large fort proposed to be built on Lake Ontario, "at Oniagra

[Niagara], Wyachtanack, or such other place there...." [47] Very likely the name "Wawyachtenok" from the old site west of the Housatonic River had been carried to the shores of Lake Erie by the Mohicans who were hunting among the Ottowas.

Thus another war intruded on the stability of Mohican villages.

The Ottowas and the Mohicans remained friendly. After the war's end in 1699, Ottowa Indians came to Albany to trade; names of Ottowas were entered in the account book of Everett Wendell, Albany trader.

During the period of the war with Canada, Rev. Benjamin Wadsworth, a Boston minister who later became President of Harvard, in 1694 went with a large group on horseback from Boston to Albany to attend a meeting between commissioners of Massachusetts and Connecticut and the Iroquois. After a stop at Westfield and an overnight stay in the woods, he and his group camped a second night at "Ousetonuck formerly inhabited by Indians." *Housatunnuk* was the name applied in the eighteenth century to the area between Sheffield and Stockbridge where the Mohican villages of Skatehook and Wnahktukook were situated. Wadsworth's party very likely had come along the established trail to the fording place above present Great Barrington. The brief reference by Wadsworth has led some historians to suggest that all Indians had removed from the Housatonic Valley at the time, an idea certainly not supported by the documents of the period. Wadsworth's party may have come upon the Great Wigwam or the Wawyachtenok site near the ford, however, and found it deserted.

The Indians near the ford may have moved to a new village location before 1694. Later references from the mid-eighteenth century placed the village of "wanaghtonack" at Stockbridge, Massachusetts, where it was associated with the sachem Konkapot. The name through usage became "Wnahktukuk." Possibly Indians of this village were descendants of the Wawyachtenok. According to one nineteenth-century Mohican, the name "Wnokhtuqkook" meant "head of the stream," a definition the Indians of Wawyachtenok had given for their location in 1676. [48]

The Westenhook or Housatunnuk area was perceived as a wilderness. Even half a century later, Rev. Samuel Hopkins, writing in 1753, called the area "the vast uncultivated Wilderness between *Connecticut* and *Hudson's* Rivers, as also in all the Northern Borders of this Province." [49] The lack of English knowledge about the Housatonic River was illustrated in Wadsworth's journal. He regarded the journey as a trip through the unknown. He was not even sure where the river ran. He wrote from the Housatonic, "Throu this place runs a very curious river, the same (which some say) runs throu Stradford; and it has, on each side, several parcels of pleasant, fertile, intervale land." On his return a week later, he traveled back toward Boston by a more southern route. From Claverack, his party went about twenty miles inland to "Turconnick" (Tachkanick). South of Tachkanick, after lodging in the woods, the group came to the upper reaches of a tributary of the Housatonic, the Ten Mile River, also called Weebu-tuk River.

Wadsworth explained that Ten Mile River, "called so from its distance from Wyantenuck, runs into Wyantenuck river, by ye side of which we rode, (I believe) 6 or 7 miles, and then passed [crossed] ye same a little after sundown. . .Wyantenuck river is ye same that passeth throu Ousetonnuck; it is Stratford river also."[50] Thus Wadsworth noted yet another local name for the Housatonic River; in one section it was called the Wyantenuck River.

The Ten Mile River empties into the Housatonic a few miles below present Sharon, Connecticut, at Gaylordsville. From that point, the travelers rode south beside the Wyantenuck/Housatonic "six or seven miles" before they crossed the river at a location different from the earlier crossing on the way to Albany. They then proceeded east to Woodbury. Wyantenock is the name of a large tract of country in the vicinity of New Milford. Due to its southerly location, despite the superficial similarity of the name, Wyantenock was demonstrably not the locale of the Mohicans' Wawyacht-enok/Wayattano.

A Network of Mohican Villages

By the late seventeenth century, there were other Mohican villages along the Housatonic River in addition to the major location documented by maps fifty years earlier. Mention was made in 1676 by the Wawyachtenok Mohicans of Indian relatives who lived farther down the river, closer to the English settlers. These Mohican settlements in northwest Connecticut were steadily augmented by Mohicans removing from the Hudson Valley.

Moreover, there also were Mohicans west of Catskill, across the Hudson River. The old Mohican village still existed at Schodack, along the Hudson. Gideon Hawley in 1753 had noted an Indian village near Kinderhook. There was a village of Stockbridge Indians at Nassau, in Rensselaer County, in 1760 and an Indian village on the Spencer Town lands in present Austerlitz when the Indians tried to sell them. In addition, Mohicans resided at Tachkanick, probably on or near Copake Lake. Farther south in the Berkshire hills, a Mohican village called Shekomeko existed by the 1720s. Thus several Mohican communities were known in the Housatonic Valley and nearby in New York. In the first third of the 1700s, a network of associated Mohican villages still lay on either side of the colonial settlers along the Hudson.

Part of this network was described in September 1725, in a letter from Governor Talcott of Connecticut. He wrote:

"There is also a place Called We-a-taug, Nigh the North Wt Corner of this Coloney, lying upon Ow-see-tum-ac [Housatonic] River, a tribe of about 50, and on sd River about ten miles Northerly at a place called Ow-see-tum-ac, another tribe of about 30; these last as yet but seldom trade or Come many of them further into our Coloney than to New Milford."[51]

Included in the network, near present Salisbury, Connecticut, was the community of Weatauk, noted above; the name has several spellings, including *Wyatiak* and *Wiataak*. This community later was swollen to unusual size. An account from the early nineteenth century recollects that as late as 1740 there were about seventy wigwams at Weatauk.[52] This number of houses seems to be far too large; it probably was exaggerated or incorrectly copied. However, it is clear that a large community developed there, including many more than the nucleus of fifty people described in 1725. On Indian Pond northwest of Sharon, Connecticut, several miles to the south, was the Mohican community called Wequadnach (Wukhquatenauk); near to Wequadnach was a smaller, unnamed village on another pond. On a 1707 journey, Robert Livingston found an occupied Indian house on a lake near later Lakeville. The wigwam on the lake was representative of Mohican family locations scattered throughout the area.

Of the two villages associated with Indian Pond, the Rev. Cotton Mather Smith, long-time pastor of the Congregational Church in Sharon, wrote in 1800 to Benjamin Trumbull, who was compiling a history of Connecticut, that before the settlement of Sharon in 1739, "there were between two and three hundred Indians that resided in the northwest part of the town in two villages; the one [Wequadnach] by the side of a large pond, now known by the name of Indian Pond, which consisted of about twenty-five wigwams; the other village was situated in a large meadow at the south end of a large pond, now known by the name of Mudge Pond, containing about ten or fifteen huts or wigwams."[53] Reverand Smith identifies these Indians as probably part of the Stockbridge tribe, and subsequent land deeds and Moravian records confirm they were Mohicans, with close connections at Stockbridge and to the Hudson.

To the north of the Connecticut line the Great Wigwam site was above present Great Barrington, in Massachusetts. This old site, mentioned above, was used as a landmark by a committee appointed by the General Court which was planning to develop land bought from the Mohicans. The committee reported about ten Indian families were living in two communities on the Housatonic River.

Although the Great Wigwam site may have been abandoned earlier, in 1734 a few Mohicans were living there.[54] In addition to this small settlement, John Sergeant reported that four or five Mohican families lived in each of two communities north of the Massachusetts line; each group was headed by a respected sachem. Other Mohicans were scattered nearby.

One sachem, Umpachanee, with his family and four other families, in 1734 resided at Skatekook or Mahaiwe "near the late residence of William W. Warner, deceased, in the extreme north part of Sheffield." Indians came up to Mahaiwe from the Great Wigwam site at the ford, "a mile or two two south,"[55] to hear a presentation by John Sergeant in 1735 about a possible mission and school. Mahaiwe, or Skatekook, the village of Umpachanee, was reported to be one mile from the base of present Monument Mountain. The name should not be confused with Skatikook (Pachgatgoch), an Indian village near Kent, Connecticut.

The second sachem, Konkapot, with four or five families, lived on land known as the Great Meadow, called Wnahktukook by the Indians. Konkapot's village was at the present community of Stockbridge, Massachusetts. A nineteenth-century history of the area reported "The dwelling of Konkapot stood on a knoll, on the east side of the county road, a short distance north of the brook which bears his name."[56] The name of Konkapot has been perpetuated in the area; two Konkapot Rivers and Konkapot Mountain still appear on maps.

Small groups of wigwams or single wigwams were here and there, such as at present New Marlboro and Pittsfield in Massachusetts, according to local history books, and there undoubtedly were additional isolated wigwams and family hamlets, as well as seasonally occupied hunting lodges. In 1714 Robert Livingston was entertained and fed by the residents of one of these wigwams while on a surveying trip.

Mohican Ownership

In summary, in the seventeenth and eighteenth centuries Mohican villages were located in the Housatonic Valley of western Massachusetts and northwestern Connecticut, and in remote areas of New York as well as on the Hudson. Individual Mohican families associated with these villages were scattered along small streams and ponds. A substantial Mohican population lay protected in the vast forested area. These communities were mentioned in both New England and New York records. Protected to some degree from smallpox by their isolation, annecdotal records suggest that early in the eighteenth century, the Mohicans in this network were experiencing a resurgence. This helped to augment the perilously low Mohican population in the Hudson Valley at the end of the seventeenth century.

Housatonic Valley land deeds of the eighteenth century, discussed in the next chapter, affirm the Mohican ownership of land on both sides of the Housatonic River from a point north of Kent, Connecticut, to as far north as a corner of Vermont and east to the Westfield River. In addition, the Mohicans detailed their ancient occupation of the area in protests and documents. For example, in an Indian deed of 1763, Benjamin Kokhkewenaunaut, "Chief Sachem of the Mohhekunnuck River Indian or Housatunnock Tribe. . ." and seventeen of his fellow tribesmen were described as "Indian hunters and Claimers of the land lying in the Western part of the said Province of the Massachusetts Bay from the Great River called Hudsons River on the west part and a River called Westfield River on the East part. . . ." The Westfield River is an angled tributary on the west side of the Connecticut River. While the western branch of the Westfield River begins only a few miles east of the Housatonic River, the main body of the stream lies about twenty-five miles east of Stockbridge. The Mohicans' Massachusetts claims were described as extending from a line twelve miles west of the Hudson River to the Westfield River (or from wherever the dividing line between the two colonies might be established), "being thirty-six miles in breadth, more or less. . . . "[57]

Konkapot, at a conference with a Massachusetts General Court committee, in 1736 said, "All the land east of what I have sold to the committee, as far as the Farmington river, and south to the Connecticut line is all my land."[58]

In a petition of 1762 presented to the Massachusetts Council and House of Representatives, the Mohicans wrote "That your memorialists are the descendants of Indians who were the ancient & original owners & Inhabitants of the Lands lying in the western part of ye province. . . as far as a river called by the English Westfield River. To the east, beyond that, your Memorialists acknowledge belonged to other Nations."[59]

Indian Artifacts

As a further indication of the once viable Mohican population, there is ample evidence of extensive Indian burials and artifacts in the Housatonic Valley. Indian graves were commonly found near the river in the nineteenth century and even earlier. One of the earliest accounts is the following, from a letter written in 1800 by the Rev. Cotton Mather Smith, who had lived at Sharon for over fifty years: "Tradition has handed down what the oldest inhabitants repeat, that on Millerton Road, not far from an old ore bed at the foot of Indian Mountain, was an Indian Village. Here arrow heads used to be found and in the meadow by the lake Indian skulls have been ploughed up."[60] The lake mentioned is Indian Pond, on the New York border northwest of Sharon, Connecticut, and the Indian village was known in the eighteenth century as Wequadnach.

Another report mentions a find of pottery, bones, and shells in a rock shelter on the west side of the road near the foot of Indian Mountain. A detailed reference to Indian burial places near Salisbury, Connecticut was given by Hon. Samuel Church, son of Nathaniel Church, in a historical address presented in 1876. He said, "The Indian burial places, as well as any thing, designate the places of Indian settlements. There was one on the eastern side of the north pond [i.e. Wequadnach]; another on the east side of the road leading through Weatogue [Weatauk] and a little southerly from the old burying ground on my late father's farm and still another. . .on the bank of the Housatonic, on the old White farm. This probably belonged to an earlier race than the Indians found here by our fathers. The annual encroachment of the river by the spring freshets, upon the banks, frequently exposed the bones of buried Indians, which upon exposure, became dust. These exposures have long since ceased. . . ."[61] A reference to the same burial grounds in a tourist guide of 1887 mentions artifacts as well as skeletons. "The old Wetaug burial ground of the Indians is situated on the bank of the [Salmon] river near this place [Salisbury]. The wearing of the river at one time washed out many skeletons that crumbled to dust upon exposure and

Artifacts from separate Indian sites in the Housatonic Valley include a long stone pestle with an effigy head and a pecked-stone mortar. The heavy mortar was located beside a spring at Great Barrington, Massachusetts.

Courtesy of the Great Barrington Historical Commission, Charles J. Taylor Collection; photographs by James Parrish

*Pottery shards are among artifacts, probably Mohican,
found in the Housatonic Valley.*

Courtesy of the Great Barrington Historical Commission,
Charles J. Taylor Collection; photograph by James Parrish

brought to light many Indian relics in the way of weapons, implements, and so on, a large number of which Mr. Little has in his
possession."[62]

An extensive collection of Indian artifacts which belonged to
historian Charles J. Taylor became the property of the Great Barrington Historical Commission. These may include some of Mr.
Little's collection. The artifacts are stored at the Ramsdell Public
Library at Housatonic.

Also well-remembered in the nineteenth century was the old
Council Elm of the Indians on "Wetaug road running along the
earthen base of Ashley Mountain, parallel with the Housatonic
River. . . a quarter mile south of Robert Little's house."[63] Taylor
mentions another relic, a fishing weir in the bed of the stream at Great
Barrington "of Indian construction, composed of large stones, laid
together in the form of the letter *V*, with its point down the stream."[64]
An early mention of an Indian burial place farther north on the
Housatonic is one described as near *Kaphack* in the deed of 1685.
Kaphack has been located as in the north part of Sheffield in a
nineteenth-century history of Berkshire County.[65]

The north part of Sheffield became Great Barrington. The site of
Kaphack was most likely west of the village of Great Barrington, on
the slope of the mountain, just north of the Sheffield line, near a
twentieth century golf course. However, Charles Taylor, in his
History of Great Barrington, published in 1882, recounts the finding
of many Indian skeletons in the course of construction of houses
within the hamlet of Great Barrington. His report included the
discovery of "a large number of bodies" on a sand bluff north of the
Agricultural Fair Grounds.[66] Other burials were found elsewhere in
and near the village in the nineteenth century.

A local history states that "At the southerly slope of Mt. Peter
[at the south end of Great Barrington], arrow points abounded a few
years since, and in the summer of 1878 in opening the stone quarry
on the eastern side of this elevation, a well-preserved mortar for
pounding corn was uncovered, cut partly, perhaps, by the aid of
natural agencies, in the surface of the solid rock, whilst at the same
time, in evidence of the practical use of the mortar, a broken stone
pestle was dug up in the soil at the foot of the rock."[67]

Another traditional Mohican burial place was at present Stockbridge. Indian bones were found there "in preparing ground for the
foundation of a meeting house in 1784." According to an 1887 guide
book, "Their [the Indians'] burial place, before the establishment of
the [Stockbridge] mission, was in the rear of the home of Col. James
F. Dwight, on a bluff overlooking the meadow." This latter burial
place is the one later memorialized with a stone monument at the
west end of Main Street, Stockbridge.[68]

Artifacts have been found in many sites along the Housatonic
River, suggesting that villages from time to time were located close
to most of the rich alluvial flats suitable for raising corn, beans and
squash. While stone artifacts and projectile points may date to pre-
historic societies, surviving Indian graves probably dated to the
seventeenth and eighteenth centuries. Little is known of earlier times.
The archeological record eventually may throw more light on the
pre-historic era. For example, archeological finds at Kampoosa Bog,
near Stockbridge, included hearths, tools, and bits of pottery left by
unknown groups in the area over 2000 years ago.[69]

Summary

Documents of the historic period demonstrate the existence of a network of Mohican communities dating to the seventeenth and eighteenth centuries. The documents also show the close connections between the groups near the Hudson River and across the hills in the Housatonic Valley. These interchanges leave little doubt that they were the same people, part of a physically scattered, but united, nation. The Housatonic Valley assumed increasing importance for the Mohicans as the Hudson Valley filled with European settlers. The history of a few of the Mohican settlements in the Housatonic Valley and in the Taconic Hills of New York will be explored in the chapters to come.

III.
Mohican Land in the Housatonic Valley

". . .here it was yt a heap of Stones in the Indian language was commonly called Wawanaquassick." —Statement of Mohicans on a Livingston boundary inspection in 1712.

THE FIRST COLONIAL SETTLERS among the Mohicans of the Housatonic area came from the Hudson Valley, despite the intervening hills. This was in large part because Dutch New Netherland originally extended east to the Connecticut River, visited and mapped by Dutch explorer Adriaen Block by 1614. In 1634, the Dutch fort called *Good Hope* was erected on the Connecticut River near present Hartford, Connecticut, following a Dutch land purchase from the Agawam Indians. However, traders from Massachusetts quickly established a competing English settlement nearby and a second English community at Springfield. Hartford and the eastern half of Long Island were conceded to the English by Petrus Stuyvesant in the Treaty of Hartford of 1650, as he could not hold the locations.[1]

Under English royal charters, both Connecticut and Massachusetts claimed land extending far to the west across and beyond the Dutch colony of New Netherland. In the effective charter of Connecticut, obtained from Charles II in 1662, the colony's stated boundaries were Narragansett Bay to the east, Massachusetts Bay Company to the north, and Long Island to the south, with no limits to the west until the ocean was reached. Despite the fact that New Netherland became English New York, the extreme western limit given to Connecticut ensured future conflict over the western line. Successive English Kings refused to settle the Connecticut-New York boundary issue.

Massachusetts first claimed land in New York Colony under the patent of New England, granted by James I in 1620, which included North America between forty and forty-eight degrees of latitude "throughout the main land from sea to sea, provided the same or any part be not actually possessed or inhabited by any other Christian prince or state. . . ."[2] Since aboriginal populations were not organized into states and were not Christian, their ownership was passed over. However, under this definition, New Netherland was clearly possessed by another Christian state. By 1615 it contained a small fort with a resident population on Castle Island on the upper Hudson; Dutch traders had frequented the Hudson River since 1610. When a charter was given to the Dutch West India Company in June 1621 to manage the territory, colonization soon began.

The dispute between New York and Connecticut dragged on until 1731, when a line twenty miles east of the Hudson River finally was established. This placed Weatauk, near later Salisbury, and the Mohican community of Wequadnach, at Indian Pond near Sharon, in western Connecticut. They were close to a strip of land given to New York called the Oblong, or the equivalent land. It replaced land ceded by New York to Connecticut along the shore of Long Island Sound.

Under the 1662 charter, the elected General Assembly of the Colony of Connecticut had power to lease, grant, or sell any land not covered by a document of sale previously approved. Indian lands were not exempt, as the Indians were considered merely occupants of their locations. Indian claims to cultivated fields and village sites were considered valid but could be challenged if documents existed showing earlier land sales; this happened at Sharon, Connecticut. Indian claims to unoccupied hunting grounds were acknowledged, but only to the extent that the natives were to be paid when the land was settled.

The Connecticut Assembly, after 1662, anxious to avoid appropriation of Connecticut lands by James II and encroachment by the Colony of New York, was quick to grant private titles to its western lands. In the 1660s, and in the years following, the Assembly granted tracts to Connecticut residents who had performed special military service in Indian wars or who had other preferments. An early country grant of fifty acres was given in 1668 to Robert Ross for land near later Salisbury. Other grants were given in 1672 to John Wheeler for one hundred acres and one for 150 acres to Joseph Hawley in 1687. In 1720, William Gaylord, who had bought the latter two earlier grants, obtained another fifty acres with a partner.[3] These country grants carried a requirement that the Indians were to be paid when the land was occupied by the grantee.

Thus, much of the land of the Mohicans in northwestern Connecticut was disposed of without their knowledge. None of the grants was claimed immediately. The grants, made for political purposes, were merely paper; the area was considered a rocky wilderness in dispute between two colonies and was very unsafe during wartime. However, the seventeenth century grants later became more desirable and set the scene for eighteenth century pressures on the Connecticut Mohican population.

English settlement along Long Island Sound, below Mohican territory, gradually moved west of the Housatonic River. New Haven was established in 1637. In 1646, a New Haven trader set up a post on the Housatonic above present Derby, Connecticut. Stratford was established near the mouth of the Housatonic. A New York boundary south of present Westchester County (below Mohican territory) had been reached with Connecticut as early as 1650, but above it the Housatonic River became the temporary boundary line before 1731 between the competing colonial governments of New York and Connecticut.

Farther north, the boundary between New York and Massachusetts was not fully resolved until the 1790s. New York occasionally claimed land east to the Housatonic, although after 1773 a boundary twenty miles from the Hudson River was generally understood to exist. The boundary dispute delayed organized settlement of the towns planned in western Massachusetts from 1726 until about 1736. After this Massachusetts began to permit development of the towns laid out earlier, without benefit of a formal boundary agreement. Over the decades, various appointed commissions failed to establish the New York-Massachusetts boundary line, leaving bad feelings between the two colonies over land claims and confusing the Indians of the area, as well.[4]

Major New York land grants stretched into the Housatonic Valley in both Massachusetts and Connecticut, on the presumption the land was in New York territory. New York owners of these grants lost their lands when the Connecticut boundary was established. Local Mohican sachems, when they were propositioned by New England residents for new Indian deeds in the eighteenth century along the Housatonic River, no doubt were assured that the land could not remain the property of New York patentees to whom the Indians had previously given deeds.

Indian Land Sales Begin

Westenhook, which came to be a name associated with the Housatonic River, did not originally mean the waterway. Instead, it referred to land west of the Housatonic River and east of present Columbia County in New York. Two significant purchases of Indian land at Westenhook, tracts lying in Massachusetts and northwestern Connecticut, were made early in 1685 by some highly placed New York colony speculators headed by Lucas Santen, Treasurer of the Colony. Others in the group were Albany Indian trader and Council member Dirck Wessels, and Cornelis Van Dyke of Albany. The Westenhook land sale to these men was witnessed and, therefore, sanctioned, by Wattawit, chief sachem of the Mohicans at the time. He lived at Schodack, on the Hudson River. Five Mohican Indians from Westenhook traveled to Albany to sign the deed and to receive payment.[5]

Evidence of the Housatonic Valley connection between these signers and Hudson Valley Mohicans is found in the names on the deeds. The Indians who sold the land on the Housatonic at Westenhook in February 1685 were Nishotawa, Awaanpaak, and Panematt, the son of Ottonowaw, acting for his father. Ottonowaw, called in another deed "the lame Indian," was one of the group identified as "Mahikan Indians" who had sold land near the Hudson River on the Roelof Jansen Kill to Robert Livingston in 1683.[6]

For the February 4, 1685, Indian deed to Lucas Santen and company, Dirck Wessels, trader, was apparently the contact person and translator. The deed conveyed eight flats on a creek called Westenhook. The land extended north from the north line of "land of Machaktehank." This line was south of "the great fall of waters called by the natives Pawachtuek," thought to be south of the Massachusetts-Connecticut line.[7] The tract continued north into Massachusetts on both sides of the Westenhook Creek to a creek called Wata Pichkaak, reportedly today's Konkapot Brook in Sheffield, Massachusetts. The western boundary was given as the "flat land belonging to Panaskanek," and otherwise the limits were "into the woods from both sides of the creek Eastward and westward to the high hills as far as the owners' propriety stretches."[8]

On March 25, 1685, more land—located in Massachusetts north of the February 4, 1685, purchase—was sold by Westenhook Mohicans to the the same coalition of New York Colony men. However, for this parcel, the Westenhook Creek (Housatonic River) was the eastern boundary. This second purchase included two flats on the west side of the river lying north of the flat "called Taashammik formerly belonging to nishotowa, awaanpaak, and ottonowa," which had been conveyed in the previous deed.

The new purchase extended into the hills almost to Tachkanick. It was bounded on the west "keeping the Same bredth into the woods westerly, as farr as the Land belonging to an Indian called Tattem- shatt, being near the Land called Tachkanik." The purchase extended north to an Indian burial ground near a plain or flat called Kaphack.[9] The Westenhook tract's boundary "near the Land called Tachkanik" indicates that the second 1685 purchase stretched from the Westen- hook Creek into the hills west of present Sheffield. Land on the east side of the Westenhook Creek was not included in the second Indian deed.

Tataemshatt, whose land was near Tachkanick, was identified in 1682 as a Catskill sachem, yet he was among Mohicans who sold land on the Roelof Jansen Kill in 1683 to Robert Livingston. He was a participant, with his brothers and several women, in the sale of Tachkanick to Livingston in 1685. His nickname was *Gose*, and a stream bearing his name ran into the Claverack Creek.

It appears that the Mohicans expected to continue to hunt on both Westenhook tracts of land, although this was not mentioned in the deeds. They had been able to continue to hunt and fish after the sale of the Roelof Jansen Kill in 1683. As the Westenhook land was never occupied by the New York owners, the natives were able to use the land there for many years.

The Mohican who sold the second tract of Westenhook land on March 25, 1685, was Panaskenak; he was empowered by his brother, Tatankemitt, who was away hunting. Panaskenak signed with the picture of a turtle, suggesting he was a member of the turtle clan. A fellow Indian named Machaneek was a witness; two days later Machaneek and others sold to Dirck Wessels two flats and adjoining woodland on the west side of the Kinderhook Creek, some twenty- five miles away in Columbia County, New York. As noted above, Dirck Wessels and Cornelis Van Dyke had purchased Mohican land on the Kinderhook on October 1, 1679, and together they had obtained other land from Mohicans opposite Albany in 1678.[10] Cornelis Van Dyke was an active speculator in Indian land. He had been a partner in purchasing Indian tracts in Saratoga and Catskill.

The two Westenhook purchases in which John Spragg, Lucas Santen, Dirck Wessels, and others were involved in 1685 remained in limbo, probably because Lucas Santen fell into disfavor, lost his position as Treasurer of the Colony, and returned to England in disgrace. On February 22, 1687, Lucas Santen gave a deed to William Smith of New York for all Santen's interest in the tract of land "purchased in company with John Spragg and others, from the Indians, and known by the name of Westenhook." Whether Santen had a right to sell seems doubtful, under the circumstances.[11] His sale to William Smith, however, defines the territory known as Westenhook as the tracts purchased in 1685.

While the extensive goods and money paid to the Indians for Westenhook would seem to have been lost by the New York purchasers, that was not the case. There was continued contact between the Indians of Westenhook and the Albany traders. Trader Robert Sanders reported in 1703 that the Wawyachtenok Indians in the Westenhook area were willing to sell their lands.

Spurred to action, the reorganized Westenhook proprietors took action to save Westenhook for themselves by obtaining Indian mortgages for the same land which the Westenhook Indians had sold them in 1685. The new coalition included trader Dirck Wessels and Peter Schuyler, Albany's first Mayor. He was an Indian commissioner much admired by the Indians and also a leader in the militia. None of the 1685 Indian sellers participated in the new land transactions nineteen years later. The intervening nineteen years had seen a smallpox epidemic along the Hudson River and a war between the English and the French in which the Mohicans had participated as scouts around Albany. Probably the original Indian signers had died.

A Unique Indian Transaction

The close relationship between the Mohicans and trader Dirck Wessels unfolded in the official documents which led to the Westenhook Patent, given by New York to the new owners early in the eighteenth century, in March 1705/1706, (i.e. in 1706). The date is frequently, but incorrectly, given as 1705. The documents began with a Westenhook Indian deed of October 1, 1703, signed by two members of the native community on behalf of others who were not present. The bounds of this deed on "the creek called Westenhook" began at an Indian burying place near the flat called Kapack (the flat and the burial ground in the later Great Barrington area were mentioned in the deed of 1685) and ran northerly on both sides of the creek "to a fall or rift in the creek called by the Indians Sassgtonack unto the woods westerly to the bounds of Kinderhook and Patkook [and] eastward into the woods four English miles."[12] Patkook was a specific location at a waterfall at the intersection of Cornelis's Kill (also called Gose's kill) and the Claverack Creek in Columbia County. The locale formed a disputed boundary mark for part of the Van Rensselaer Patent for the lower manor, in present Columbia County.

The boundaries of this new 1703 parcel therefore were similar to the more northern of the two 1685 parcels, with a significant addition. Land extending eastward into the woods four miles on the east side of the Westenhook Creek, withheld previously, now was included.

The Mohican signers were Tapaset and Pittonack (also known as Pinonock), heirs of the deceased Indian named Mataseet. They signed for their other friends and relatives. Witnesses were Mackhataw and Onesat. Pinonock, a sachem, in 1679 had signed a Columbia County deed. These acts indicated his connection to both places. The value of 110 beavers and twelve otters already had been provided by the traders. Thus, this 1703 Westenhook deed gave land to satisfy a debt the Mohicans incurred with the traders. According to later testimony by Wessels and Schuyler, the Indians owed the furs to the traders for trade goods obtained on credit and already consumed.

A map of c. 1726 drawn by Cadwallader Colden, Surveyor General, illustrates the vague boundaries of the patents lying west of Westenhook. According to his map, which noted that the boundaries were uncertain, the Westenhook Patent ran west across parts of present Columbia County to join the Van Rensselaer patent and the Kinderhook Patent. The map stated that Peter Schuyler and the other owners of Westenhook claimed 200,000 acres.[13] Although the Westenhook patentees could claim land as far west as Patkook, the Van Rensselaers also claimed that land. Colden was angry about the large New York grants held by wealthy men with little return to the Colony or the King's interest.

A second Westenhook document of October 2, 1703 was signed by the same two Indians, Tapaset and Pinonock, heirs of Mataseet, in behalf of a man called Akamaagkamin (Attamaghkamin) and his brother, Sokam, and all other Indians with any claim to the land at Westenhook.[14] The October 2 tract was south of the land conveyed one day earlier. It began on the south side at a falls in the Westenhook Creek called Tapgtonak (also spelled Sapgtnack), ran north on both sides of the creek past the falls called Packwack, and into the woods westerly to the bounds of the Colony of Rensselaerswyck and Claverack. Rensselaerswyck proper lay in present Rensselaer County; Claverack was the term used for the Van Rensselaer tract in later Columbia County.[15]

A Unique Arrangement

This latter parcel, containing the Indian village and fields, included specific reservations in the text. The Indians partly conveyed the land to the buyers with the intent that the land would be secured in a patent held by the buyers for the Indians, who had resolved to continue their settlement there. Peter Schuyler, Dirck Wessels, John Johnson Bleeker, and John Abeel agreed to resign the land for the Indians' settlement, until the time the Indians were willing to receive the full payment.[16] Thus, the land would be reserved for the Indian community. It would not be settled by Europeans until the Mohicans were ready to give it up. This open-ended mortgage allowed the Mohicans to satisfy their debts, while remaining in their Westenhook territory on the Housatonic.

However, the traders would obtain and hold a patent for their land. The Mohicans were to be paid twelve and one half beavers and six duffel coats whenever they gave up the location. With this arrangement, there must have been a constant temptation to take the goods and relocate, but for two decades that did not occur. In Albany, at the signing, Capt. John Johnson Bleeker gave the Mohicans additional merchandise worth the sum of six pounds thirteen shillings.

Trader Dirck Wessels of Albany had developed a significant relationship as a supplier of goods to the Mohicans, was familiar with their territory, and was anxious to acquire their land. As a trader, he seems to have been interested primarily in the trade the natives could provide. By restricting European settlement and farm development on this large tract of land, he and his associates could hope for a small but steady supply of furs and for regular Westenhook customers. This action of reserving Indian land was an unusual exception to the general pattern of European expansion. Undoubtedly, the buyers also expected the land to appreciate in value, so they could sell it some time in the future when the Indians were gone.

The agreement was signed by Schuyler, Wessels, Bleeker, and Abeel but not by any Indians. However, a paragraph added to the deed by the sellers stated that at Albany, on October 6, 1703, the Indians received on account from Capt. John Johnson Bleeker, in merchandise, the value of six pounds and thirteen shillings. The acknowledgement of payment was signed by Tapaset with his mark (a turtle) and by Pinonock with his mark (a line atop three legs). The two Mohicans had visited at Albany for at least four days.

In September 1704, these same four buyers obtained a third Mohican deed for the more southerly 1703 parcel of land along the Housatonic River. The land was described as extending from the falls called Sapgtanok northerly on both sides of the creek past the falls called Pachwack and continuing north to Kapagkagh. For this land an additional group of Indians received goods to the value of sixty beaver skins. The sellers were Sankhank, Catharickseet and Walleg-naweek on behalf of all their relations.[17] These three Mohicans represented a group with interests in the land who did not sign on October 1, 1703. Perhaps they had complained about being omitted. This last document was necessary to include all Indian owners before the coalition of traders could apply for their New York patent. Catharickseet was the respected and long-lived sachem who had extensive dealings in the Livingston patent.

Thus, Mataset (now deceased), and Tapaset, Pinonock, Akamaagkamin, his brother Sokam, Sankhank, Catharickseet and Wallegnaweek were among the Westenhook community members early in the eighteenth century; they had rights to the land sold in 1685 at Westenhook by Nishotawa, Awaanpaak, Panematt, Panaskenak, and his brother Tatankenat. Because Panematt had been given the right to sell by his father, Ottonowaw, a Mohican who in 1683 sold land in present Columbia County on the Roelof Jansen Kill to Robert Livingston, the genealogical trail leads back to the Mohicans on the Hudson River.

In consequence of these purchases, the next year, on July 11, 1705, Dirck Wessels, with Peter Schuyler, Bleeker, Abeel, and others, petitioned for a patent for the tracts of land on the Westenhook Creek, which they received the following spring. Dirck Wessels explained in his patent application that they wanted the land for trading with the Indians. The application cited the purchases made from the Westenhook Indians in 1685, 1703 and 1704. The group's petition related "that the petitioners had, several years before [i.e.

1685 and 1703], advanced money and goods to the Indian proprietors of land on a creek called Westenhoek. . ." and stated that the Indians mortgaged the premises to the petitioners. The traders had made further advances of money and goods to the Indians and had purchased the lands from them on the first and second of October 1703. Moreover, "the Indians being unable to pay the sums previously advanced, or to obtain the money and goods which they wanted from any other party, the petitioners had condescended to make these further advancements and take deeds of the lands."[18]

The governor of New York, Edward Viscount Cornbury, granted a patent for these lands to Peter Schuyler, Dirck Wessels, John Abeel, John Janse Bleeker, Ebenezar Willson, Peter Fauconier, Daniel Cox, Thomas Wenham and Henry Smith, known as the Westenhook Patent. The patent covered large tracts of land extending northerly along the Housatonic River from a point below Great Falls in Connecticut to a point north of Stockbridge in Massachusetts. Nineteenth-century historian Charles Taylor explained his interpretation of the bounds: he believed the patent of Westenhook on the south extended to the mountains on both sides of the river and in Sheffield it ran west to Mount Washington. The north boundary (a rift called Packawack) he believed was the falls at Glendale or the limestone gorge just above. Sasigtonack—"water splashing over rocks"—he identified as the falls at the north end of Great Barrington village.[19]

A document of 1754 stated that the north line of the patent of Westenhook was eighteen miles north of the Connecticut line.[20] How this distance was determined is not certain. A point eighteen miles north of the Connecticut line on a modern map, following the curves of Route One, falls at Stockbridge, Massachusetts, but it has been suggested that the northernmost point of Westenhook was north of Stockbridge.

While the Schuyler-Wessels group left the Indians in possession of the land as promised, trade with the Mohicans probably continued. There is no evidence that New York's Westenhook proprietors made any improvements in the Housatonic Valley. Instead, after many years, the proprietors were taken aback, and protested, when New England settlers began to occupy farms on the land, and when townships were proposed in Massachusetts and Connecticut. Robert Livingston's farmers encroached as well; a few were arrested. In April 1724, Philip Livingston wrote to his father, Robert, "Peter Hoogeboom is arrested here for trespass by the Patentees of Westenhook.

He came to me for advice. I do not understand such matters. I suspect it [Hoogeboom's farm] lies in Dutchess County if it be in this province. . . ." According to historian Charles Taylor, the Westenhook Patent covered a large part of the later towns of Sheffield, Great Barrington, Stockbridge, West Stockbridge, Mount Washington, Egremont, and Alford. It also included the town of Salisbury and parts of Canaan in Connecticut.[21]

The New Yorkers were dismayed by the Connecticut boundary with New York adopted in 1731 and by the formal establishment by the Connecticut Assembly of a town (Salisbury) in the northwest corner of the state where the Westenhook proprietors had prior title. Even more outrageously, from their perspective, Massachusetts had begun erecting two towns in 1724 within the bounds of the Westenhook Patent, despite the fact that the boundary between New York and Massachusetts had not been formally fixed. This action by Massachusetts had long-range consequences for the Mohicans of the Housatonic Valley.

The Mohicans were approached by a Massachusetts "settling committee" sent by the General Court to clear the Indian title for the two proposed Massachusett towns. The prominent sachem Konkapot and other area Mohicans gave an Indian deed in 1724 for the land on which the proposed towns were to be laid out. The tracts conveyed were within land previously sold by the Mohicans in 1703 and 1704 to the Westenhook proprietors. The Mohicans were advised that the land no longer belonged to the New York proprietors because it was in Massachusetts.

Four hundred sixty pounds in hand, three barrels of cider and thirty quarts of rum were offered to Konkapot and his counselors. The payment offered by the committee was overwhelming, and the natives had no choice but to get what they could out of the situation. Moreover, the Indians were assured that they could continue to live in the area. A small reservation, a narrow strip dividing the proposed townships, was set aside for them. They probably expected to continue to hunt and fish on all the land, as they had done since 1685 on other tracts sold in Connecticut, Massachusetts and New York.

Evert Wendell, a lawyer and probably the trader who had dealt with many Mohicans at Albany, launched a futile legal effort on behalf of the Westenhook patentees. Acting as attorney for the owners, including some who were heirs of the earlier proprietors, including Jan (John) Janse Bleeker, Philip, son of Peter Schuyler and

others, Wendell in 1726 entered a petition requesting the Governor
of New York to intercede with Massachusetts so the proprietors
could continue in the peaceable possession of Westenhook. He explained that the people of Connecticut and Massachusetts were pre-
tending that Westenhook would fall into their boundaries whenever
the partition line was fixed. However, Wendel's action was unsuccessful and all land east of the proposed new state line was confiscated as
Masssachusetts proceded with settlements without waiting for the
state boundary to be finalized.[22]

Although by giving new deeds for the land, the Mohicans ended
their valuable association with the Albany traders, this relationship
was probably near an end in any event. Massachusett's premptive
actions established by *fiat* the boundary between the two colonies.
What could not be foreseen was that this action by Massachusetts
would soon end Mohican isolation in the Housatonic Valley. Development of towns would limit the group's future options and pros-
perity.

Dirck Wessels, Peter Schuyler, and their associates were not the
only Hudson Valley purchasers of Mohican land in the Housatonic
Valley prior to the setting of the colony boundaries. Farther to the
south, Robert Livingston purchased from the Mohicans of the Roelof
Jansen Kill their New York land which extended into the hills west
of the Housatonic Valley. He obtained, as well, a spur which extended
into Connecticut. Farther south, Richard Sackett purchased from the
Mohicans residing in Connecticut and New York land near Amenia,
New York and additional land in Connecticut extending to within
two miles of the Housatonic River. In addition, a few Dutch farmers
from the Livingston Patent took up residence among the Mohicans
of Weatauk, near present Salisbury, Connecticut. These changes,
discussed in a subsequent chapter, affected the Connecticut Mohican
villages at Salisbury and Sharon and the mission village at Shekomeko.

Robert Livingston and the Mohicans

As early as 1680, Robert Livingston petitioned Edmund Andros,
New York's Governor General, for permission to buy land from
Indians "willing to Dispose of the same" on the Roelof Jansen Kill.[23]
This significant creek reaching far inland is notable for its deep bend.
Located in today's Columbia County, New York, it is a tributary of
the Hudson River. According to mid-seventeenth-century Dutch

*Three Indian villages on the Roelof Jansen Kill were shown on a
Dutch map of 1651. Robert Livingston bought flats along the creek
from the Mohicans in 1683. Map of New Netherland 1651.*

New York State Library, Manuscripts and Special Collections

maps, three Indian villages were located along this creek. A New
Netherland map of 1651 showed an Indian village on the east side of
the creek not far inland from the Hudson River, as well as two
locations near each other on the south side of the deep bend of the
stream.

Beginning in 1683, Livingston purchased parcels of land from the
resident Mohicans, and, using these Indian deeds, obtained New York
patents for his Manor of Livingston. The purchases set in motion a
familiar relationship between Robert Livingston and the Mohicans,
extending across several decades. Robert Livingston supplied the
Mohicans with significant amounts of goods which improved their
material comfort. In exchange, they eventually gave up their village
and hunting locations on the west side of the Taconic range. In 1729
Robert Livingston was succeeded as Lord of the Manor by his son,
Philip, who was succeeded in 1749 by his son, Robert, Jr. Livingston
documents relating to Mohican land, which will be discussed below,
can be summarized as follows:

1683	Livingston bought three flats and woodland along the Roelof Jansen Kill from the Mohicans who lived beside the creek.
1685	Livingston bought land at Tachkanick from the Mohicans.
1686	A special patent, erecting a Manor, included more land than the previous Indian purchases and added a spur of land extending into Connecticut. The document made Livingston Lord of the Manor.
1688	An Indian woman from Catskill was paid for her right to one of the flats bought in 1683.
1688	Livingston bought from the Mohicans the land at Tachkanick which they previously had reserved for themselves.
1697	Livingston bought from two Mohican women a parcel on the south side of the Roelof Jansen Kill a little above the farm where Johannes Dykman lived. The land ran east to the high hills.
1697	A month later, he gave another payment for the same land to the Indian man who had made the arrangements.
1707	Livingston, with one of his sons and three Indian guides, made a tour into Connecticut to inspect the south line of the spur.
1712	Livingston enlisted the aid of Mohican sachem Ampamit and of Catharickseet to locate Indian landmarks on the boundary line between his land and Henry Van Rensselaer's land. The south line also was examined.
1713	May 11, the Mohicans made a deposition concerning Robert Livingston's acquisition of the Manor lands.[24]
1713	May 11, the Indians conveyed *Gochkomeckkok* to Robert Livingston. This parcel was located in their former reserved land.
1714	Catharickseet, a sachem, and other Mohicans assisted Robert Livingston and surveyor John Beatty in surveying the boundary line around the Manor and the spur into Connecticut. The map produced by the surveyor, which showed the boundaries of Livingston Manor mentioned in the Patent, included areas which the Mohicans soon maintained had never been purchased from them.
1718	Mohicans contended land in the northeast corner of the Manor had never been bought. They gave up their claim on the north line of the Livingston Patent in exchange for cancellation of all debts they owed to Livingston and received additional goods from him.
1721	An Indian release of a tract called *Waintas* was given to Livingston.
1722	Indians sold land to Livingston at *Wichquapakhat*, on the Livingston Manor spur into Connecticut.
1724	Mohicans gave a quitclaim for the north line of the Manor.

1725   Tsioas (also known as Shabash or Abraham) and Winnigh Po,
        Mohicans, received a gift from Livingston in recognition of
        the land sold by their mother and another woman in 1697,
        while they were still children. In return, they promised to
        make no land claims against Livingston Manor.

1757   Mohicans at Stockbridge gave a deed to New Englanders for
        land in the Town of Mount Washington in the hills between
        Livingston Manor and Massachusetts, on which the Living-
        stons had settled farmers long before. The Indians claimed
        the Livingstons had never bought the land from them. The
        farmers claimed they were in Massachusetts, where the Liv-
        ingstons had no land rights and, therefore, were not on Liv-
        ingston land.

1768   Mohicans identified boundaries of Livingston Manor, in connec-
        tion with Cadwallader Colden's charges against the Van
        Rensselaer Patent.

After Livingston obtained his first Indian deed in 1683, the
Hudson Valley Mohicans continued to hunt on their former land. A
reservation in that first deed given to Livingston granted the Mohicans "the power of free fishing in the [Roelof Jansen] Kill and to be
able to hunt Deer in the said limits, provided they shall bring the head
to the purchaser."[25] In addition, one woman, Tamaranchquae, reserved the right to plant for four years on a little "Hook of Land
which shall be shown to her and no more."[26]

Because they were allowed to hunt and fish throughout their old
locations, the greatest initial change for the Mohicans was loss of their
village sites and established cornfields on the flats along the Roelof
Jansen Kill, not far from the Hudson River. After the flats and
woodland were sold, Mohican villagers seem to have left their earlier
locations and gathered to the east, in the lake-studded region near the
mountains. This region, called Tachkanick, took in the modern town
of Copake and areas in the hills to the east.

Livingston's original modest July 1683 purchase from the Mohican Indians in New York on the Roelof Jansen Kill resulted in the
first Livingston patent, issued by Governor Thomas Dongan on
November 4, 1684. The patent repeated the boundary description of
the 1683 Indian deed for three flats along the creek and woodland
beyond. The Indian deed did not state acreage but some 2000 acres
were included when the 1684 patent was issued. This was more land
than the three flats beside the creek contained, and must be attributed

to the vague reference to woodland or to an unjustified expansion of the purchase.[27]

There were two similar versions of the 1683 Indian deed, signed six days apart. The first served as a contract of sale; it listed the extensive payment promised, in five days' time, of sewant (wampum), blankets, duffels, strouds, shirts, stockings, guns, powder, lead, caps, kettles, axes, adzes, paint, scissors, looking glasses, fish hooks, awls and nails, tobacco, pipes, bottles and kegs of rum, beer, knives, coats and tin kettles—a windfall in Mohican eyes— and an indicator of the needs and desires of the late seventeenth-century Mohican communities on the Roelof Jansen Kill.[28] Clothing needs included blankets, pieces of wool cloth, and shirts. Moreover, hunting depended upon European guns, lead for bullets which the Indians molded, and gunpowder for hunting. Stone axes, replaced by Dutch tools similar to the ones given here, had not been used for decades; earthen pots, too, were things of the distant past. Bottles and kegs of rum, now much desired commodities, were routinely included in transactions.

The second document, of July 18, 1683, was the legal deed to the property. The deed included the statement that the sellers had been paid. They received money as well as the goods promised. The Mohicans who signed the deed and shared the goods were Ottanowaw, Tataemshatt, Tamaranchquae (a woman), Wawanetsawaw (a woman), Newamee (the daughter of Tamaranchquae), and Auxhys (Ottonowaw's son's daughter). Kosshecko (a Wappinger sachem), Moneetpa (possibly Manueenta, of Catskill), and Kachkehant were Indian witnesses. Five years later, "a certain cripple Indian woman named Siakanochqui of Catskil" was paid a cloth garment and a cotton shift for her share in one of the flats which had been sold.[29] These connections demonstrate that the Roelof Jansen Mohicans had ties to the Catskill Mohicans as well as to those of the Housatonic Valley and those at Schodack.

Livingston's first 1684 New York patent was followed in 1685 by his application to Governor Dongan for permission to purchase "about two or three hundred acres, which in time might prove a Convenient Setlement" at Tachkanick, on the Roelof Jansen Kill "behind [east of] Patcook." Patcook or Patkook, noted above as a point on the west line of the Westenhook Patent, was a locality named for a waterfall on a small creek called Cornelis's Kill, where the small creek joined the Claverack Creek. Patkook, also spelled Pattenhook or Pathook, was noted in Westenhook deeds as a point in the Van Rensselaer patent line.

Livingston justified his 1685 application by complaining that his first tract, comprising the Indian flats on the Roelof Jansen Kill, was "much contrare to Expectation, very Little being fitt to be Improved. . . ." In June 1685 he was granted permission to buy the additional 200 acres he requested, and consequently on August 10, 1685, he obtained a deed from the Mohicans for the "Land called Tachkanik. . .behinde Patkook."[30]

In the second Livingston Indian deed, the tract was described as at Tachkanick, east of Patkook "on a creek that runs into the Hudson River and there called the Roelof Jansen Kill; all the land and low hills." The Tachkanick area, about fifteen miles inland, was south of the headwaters of the Roelof Jansen Kill, where there were substantial flats and small lakes. The hills were in the Taconic range of eastern New York and western Massachusetts. By soon expanding into the mountains, where he leased a farm to John Hallenbeck in 1692 or 1693, and to a few others early in the 1700s, Livingston demonstrated the boundaries of his purchase.

While the Indian deed did include the low hills and all Indian rights "to the eastward of a creek called Twastawekak," the north-south Livingston line drawn in the mountains included "two fifths of the. . .town of Mount Washington" in Massachusetts.[31] At the time, of course, the Massachusetts boundary was not settled. Later, during rent disturbances of the 1750s, as noted above, Mohicans at Stockbridge believed Livingston Manor farms in the mountains were on land never purchased from their ancestors.

A patent for the land at Tachkanick was obtained by Robert Livingston from Governor Dongan on August 27, 1685. The land included not only the two hundred additional acres proposed but "about six hundred Acres as by the Indian deed of sale."[32] Thus was established a persistent pattern of taking more land than was proposed; Livingston was not the first landowner of the era to expand his boundaries, nor the last. The Indian deeds were vague enough to permit this license and Governor Dongan was happy to oblige his friend.

On July 22, 1686, moreover, Governor Dongan issued a special Livingston patent which combined the land in both previous patents with additional land, a spur extending into Connecticut near later Salisbury. The spur is not shown on a sketch map of the Tachkanick

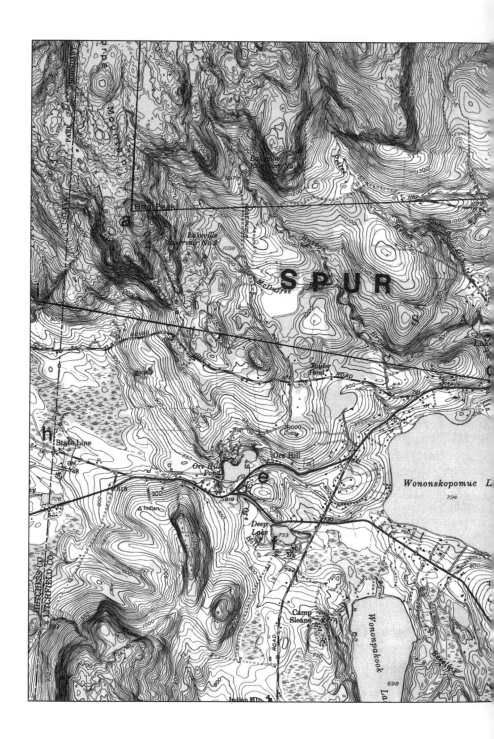

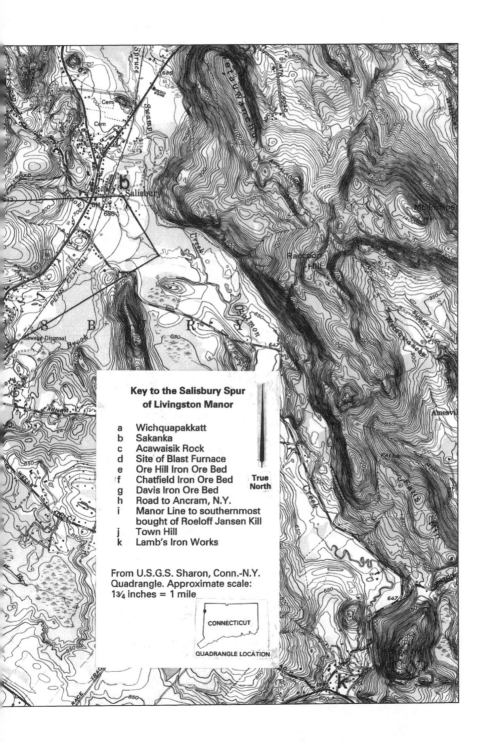

Key to the Salisbury Spur of Livingston Manor

a Wichquapakkatt
b Sakanka
c Acawaisik Rock
d Site of Blast Furnace
e Ore Hill Iron Ore Bed
f Chatfield Iron Ore Bed
g Davis Iron Ore Bed
h Road to Ancram, N.Y.
i Manor Line to southernmost bought of Roeloff Jansen Kill
j Town Hill
k Lamb's Iron Works

True North

From U.S.G.S. Sharon, Conn.-N.Y. Quadrangle. Approximate scale: 1¾ inches = 1 mile

CONNECTICUT

QUADRANGLE LOCATION

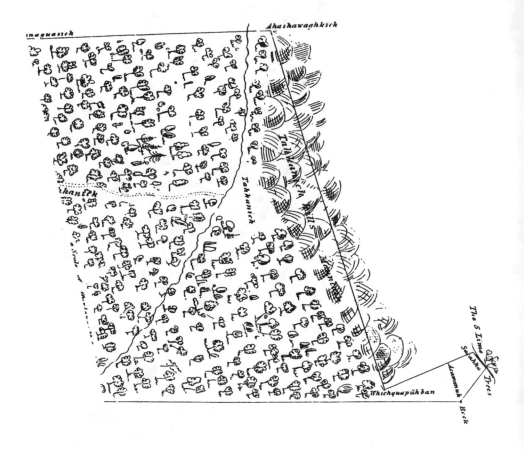

Above: *The map of Livingston Manor drawn in 1714 includes the eastern boundary in the Tachkanick Range and the spur into Connecticut. Robert Livingston traveled the spur with a surveyor, four neighbors and three Indians in 1714. Along the way, they stopped at the wigwam of Metoxon at Salisbury.*

Map from O'Callaghan, *Documentary History* 3: 690

Overleaf: *A modern map by William Morrill recreating the spur of Livingston Manor extending into Connecticut helps identify the landmarks on the map drawn for Robert Livingston in 1714.*

Courtesy of William P. Morrill, Lakeville, Connecticut

purchase which accompanied the 1685 deed. The third patent thus would appear to include another unwarranted taking of land, but, interestingly, in 1714, sachem Catharickseet, formerly of Tachkanick, and other older Mohicans were willing to identify the Connecticut landmarks outlining the spur for a surveyor. They were aware of and possibly had been paid for the Connecticut segment. In 1715, as a result of the Beatty survey, Livingston obtained a confirmatory patent for Livingston Manor, which also contained a detailed description of the spur.[33] In 1722, Livingston listed a payment for a piece of Indian land along or in the spur.

In 1707, Livingston and his son, Philip, aided by three unnamed Indians, made a tour of the south and southeast bounds of the manor and examined the spur. After two days of struggling over hills and sleeping in the open, they came in Connecticut to "two lakes called Wanapakaook where a great Indian house was. . . ."[34] The lakes were immediately south of Lakeville, Connecticut, where one lake still bears the name "Wononpakook."

At Livingston's request, the 1686 patent had elevated his land-holdings into a manor. He became the first Lord of Livingston Manor, with the prerogatives and prestige which accompanied that status. Like the Van Rensselaers to his north, Livingston planned to hold most of his land in perpetuity, while giving leases to farmers who would be tenants on his land.

The goods paid to the Mohicans for Tachkanick in 1685 included 630 guilders, wampum, blankets, strouds, duffels, guns, kettles, casks of rum, beer, gunpowder, lead for bullets, coats, shirts, axes, stockings, hoes, knives, rolls of tobacco, iron pots, awls, serge coats, hats, caps, shoes, edges, knives, planes, bottles, and jugs. Indian land near Albany outside of Rensselaerswyck had become far more valuable, in terms of goods that could be obtained for it by the Mohicans, than in earlier days.[35]

Despite a pent-up desire for land for new farms, there was a strong sense among the colonial settlers in the 1680s that it was necessary to keep the Mohicans happy and not give them any cause to move elsewhere. Troubles with French Canada loomed. The New England Indians at Schaghticoke, north of Albany, with whom the Mohicans had close ties, were being openly courted by the French with offers to remove to Canada. Albany residents and their connections in the countryside were concerned that the local Indians, as well, might defect to the north with their friends. Such a departure would leave

the Albany area without the protection of an Indian buffer in the
event of French raids. Thus, while large bonuses for land reflected
rising land values, they also at this time reflected concerns that if the
Mohicans left, Albany would be exposed.

In 1685, when the natives sold land at Tachkanick, they hoped to
continue to reside in the area. To ensure village space and cornfields,
they reserved a tract for themselves. The pattern of setting aside land
for cornfields and a central village was repeated in the Housatonic
Valley. The reservation of land illuminates the natives' assumption
that, as long as they saved land for their wigwams and cornfields, there
would be opportunity for hunting and fishing either on the land
which had been sold or elsewhere in their remaining unsold territory.

Several Mohicans visited Albany to sign the Tachkanick deed.
The signers were: Tataemshatt, Michiel, Tawaheese, Nishotawa, Mi-
nasees (a woman) Tantapenowa (Netapoe's wife), and Mamattittaw-
awpe. The only person present who had signed the previous deed was
Tataemshatt, who was Michiel's brother. Michiel was also known as
Waquassamo. Another brother, Amesett, was at Canada and did not
sign. Tantapenowa was Tataemshett's mother. Tawaheese (Tawihaes)
was an older brother of Ampamit, the Schodack leader who later
became chief sachem of the Mohicans.

Soon the Mohicans released the special tract, described as within
Robert Livingston's land called Tachkanick, which they had held
back. On February 17, 1688, the Mohicans sold Livingston the land
"which the said owners had reserved for themselfs to Plant upon
when they sold him Tachkanik, with the land called Quisich kook
lyeing upon this side of Roelof Jansens Kill near Tachkanik, haveing
the said Kill on one side and the hill on the other side together with
all our Right and Title northward and Eastward as far as the west and
hithermost end of the Lake called Achkoockpeek [Copake Lake], and
from thence down Southerly on both sides of the Said Roelof
Johnson's [Jansen's] Kill till you come to a flat called (blank)."[36]

In 1686, Quasighkook or Quisichkook was described in a document as a piece of woodland overgrown with small trees and bushes,
lying on the west side of the Roelof Jansen Kill, containing, with the
marshes lying there, about two hundred acres. Livingston may have
bought the land because Philip Schuyler had applied for a license to
buy it from the Indians.[37] With this purchase along his north line,
Livingston's collection of three Indian deeds began to describe more
completely some large parts of the land he claimed. In Mohican eyes,

the northeast corner, including Copake Lake, remained unpurchased, as did a segment on the south line.

Development of the Livingston lands into European farms was slow. Livingston did not build his own house on the Manor until 1699.[38] However, as he planned to establish a large tenant farm on his new purchase at Tachkanick, Livingston began the contruction of a wagon road from Patkook (near present Claverack) to Tachkanick shortly after he obtained the Indian deed of 1685. The road was gradually improved. In 1711, Robert Van Deusen, a Livingston farmer, declared that for about twenty-five years he had worked on Livingston's road from Tachkanick to Patkook.[39]

With the road under way, Livingston offered a few early farm leases on his eastern land. One of his first leases was given in May 1687 to Mattheus Abrahamse Van Deusen, an Albany county farmer from the Claverack area, who settled on intervale land at Tachkanick. (Columbia County had not yet been formed from Albany County.) Thus, very quickly there was a colonial presence within or near the formerly reserved Indian land. Van Deusen's ten-year lease was for eighty acres.[40] Livingston was to supply materials, and the tenant farmer was to erect buildings and develop the farm in exchange for deferred rent.

In 1694, a traveler, Rev. Benjamin Wadsworth, described the condition of the early wagon road and mentioned a Livingston farm at Tachkanick: "'Tis about 20 miles from Clauvrick to Turconnick [Tachkanick]; the way is generally good, being all of it waggon way; there are some bad swamps in this way, several bad bridges, one bad hill; the land seems to be good; tis well cloth'd with a young growth of wood, especially white-oake. About 2 mile from Turconnick, we left a small pond on the left hand: a little farther, we left another on the right hand; about a mile farther, another on the left hand. At Turconnick (which is a very stately farm of Mr. Levinstone's) we baited [ate] and refreshed horse and man. . . ."[41] If it was at the Van Deusen farm where Wadsworth stopped, as seems likely, it appears Mattheus Van Deusen and his family had accomplished many of their goals in seven years and were exemplary tenants.

By 1686, Livingston's patent or charter for his Manor stated point to point boundaries around his Indian purchases which, in Indian eyes, still enveloped more land than his Indian deeds contained. These extended boundaries were set down on the 1714 survey map, mentioned above. The map's legend gave a figure of 160,240 acres of land encompassed in Livingston Manor.[42]

Tenants were few, however. In 1702 the New York Governor, Earl Bellomont, complained to the London Board of Trade that "Mr. Livingston has on his great grant of 16 miles long and 24 broad, but 4 or 5 cottages as I am told. . . ."[43] The Governor's observation about Livingston's dearth of farmers was accurate. The Livingston Manor map of 1714 showed, besides Livingston's Manor House by the river and his mill nearby, only five houses. (However, the surviving version of the map is a copy by E. B. O'Callaghan. The original may have included additional names.) A census of 1714 listed more farmers than appear on the map, but the number was still small. The lag in Livingston farm settlement was of great benefit to the Mohicans who continued to hunt and fish on the land. The long lull in settlement, however, gave the Indians a false sense that they could sell land to obtain needed goods without suffering consequences.

Possibly Robert Livingston's success in amassing land came because he cultivated very good relations with Thomas Dongan, administrator of the New York Colony, as well as with the Indians. Livingston, who traded with the Indians in addition to holding responsible offices as Secretary of Albany and Indian Commissioner, obtained the Indian deeds he needed by offering the Mohican villagers large quantities of desirable goods, as well as by extending credit and by being friendly and accommodating. He also dealt with Mohicans in official capacities, representing the Governor, as when he handled requests of Mohicans to move into New York from Massachusetts in 1686. This incident has been recounted in the preceding chapter.

Livingston's purchases, especially of the Indians' reserved land at Tachkanick, had important long-range implications for the Tachkanick Mohican community. Sale of their lands reserved for planting ensured the villagers at Tachkanick soon would move elsewhere, especially when Livingston established a farm in the area. Documents show that some moved to the east side of the mountains into Massachusetts and Connecticut. The Indians maintained that they had not sold the land lying north and east of Achkoockpeek (Copake) Lake, however. It is likely the Mohicans had a community there; one researcher in the nineteenth century believed there was an Indian village on the north shore of Copake Lake.[44]

The matter of ownership of the northeast corner was resolved in 1718 when Catharickseet and his family desisted their claim on the north line of the Livingston Patent in exchange for cancellation of all debts they owed to Robert Livingston.[45] This transaction indicates that Livingston, probably through a family member or a trader, still provided a trading post as late as 1718.

Despite their land sales to Livingston, the slow pace of farm settlement on Livingston Manor and New York's desire to encourage protective Indian settlements persuaded the Mohicans to stay in the Tachkanick area. As late as 1686 Mohicans still lived at Tachkanick. In 1686, fellow Mohicans on the Massachusetts side of the mountains considered joining their relatives at Tachkanick and were told by the New York Governor and Robert Livingston that they were welcome and that land would be given to them. The Massachusetts Indians chose not to come, but the incident indicated a continued Mohican settlement at Tachkanick.

Two years later members of this group at Tachkanick sold their reserved land there. Indians involved in the 1688 Livingston purchase of reserved land were not named, but possibly present at the transaction was a young man, Catharickseet, from Tachkanick. Catharickseet was described as a Westenhook Indian but moved to other locations. He was a son of a Mohican known as "Goose" or "Gose" who was a witness to a 1697 Indian deed given to Robert Livingston by two Indian women.[46] Goose was the nickname of Tataemshatt.

Catharickseet in 1704 was one of the Mohicans who made a sale of land at Westenhook to Dirck Wessels, Peter Schuyler and others, land that became part of the Westenhook Patent. He figured largely in subsequent relations with Robert Livingston. With a few other Indians, Catharickseet knew where the old boundaries of the Livingston Patent had been drawn, including the north line, which on its west end adjoined the Van Rensselaer line.

Catharickseet, therefore, proved valuable to Robert Livingston when, in 1712, the boundary with Henry Van Rensselaer to the north was questioned by Van Rensselaer. In dispute was the precise location of a heap of stones called by the Indians Wawanaquasick or Mawanaquasick, which marked a point in the south line of the Van Rensselaer property and consequently a point in the north line of Livingston Manor. Van Rensselaer claimed the stones were farther south than Livingston believed they were. The question arose whether, in the Mohican language, only one certain heap of stones had the name Wawanaquasick or whether all heaps of stones were called Wawanaquasick. If the latter, then it might be impossible to decide which heap of stones was intended in the original deed of 1649, giving Van Rensselaer the advantage.

A local Indian well-acquainted with the area that is now Columbia County was David Annahakenic. Testifying in a 1768 case against Van Rensselaer, when Annahakenic was seventy-six years of age, he gave an interesting version of why Indian stone heaps were found. He said that before any white people came there, the sachems, being all of one nation and finding themselves settled at different places, ordered these monuments to be made as a mark of the union of the tribes. Annahakenic said he received his information from Makepanet, a sachem, who received it from his father. Makepanet's father was a chief who was living when the English came to the area. Makepanet charged his son to hand down to others a memory of the meaning of the monument. The statement seems to be a valuable reference to the unity of the Mohicans at Westenhook, the Mohicans at Catskill, and the Mohicans on the Hudson.[47] Various reasons, however, were given by Mohicans for the stone heaps.

Annahakenic, as a young man, had accompanied the two proprietors, Livingston and Van Rensselaer, and other Indians to the stone heap in 1712. He testified that there were five elderly Indians at Wawanaquasick whose names were Tataemshatt, Wampopeham or Michiel, Ampamit, Menonompa, and Catharickseet.[48] The names are familiar from the deeds. Catharickseet was well-known and Ampamit, his son-in-law, later became the chief sachem of the Mohican nation. These men were Mohicans of stature, respected by the landowners and farmers as well as in the Indian community.

A document now at Clermont State Historic Site tells more about the 1712 excursion: "We whose names are underwritten doe certify & declare yt upon ye 8th day of April 1712 [we] were desired by Rt Livingston, owner of ye manor of Livingston to accompany him and ye Sachem with Seven Indians to ye Place called Wawwanaquasick from where ye sd Livingston would Runn his line to wachankasick upon ye River Pursuant to ye Patent of ye manor. & yt henry Renselaer and his Bro'r Kiliaen was desired to by them to go who professed yt as soon as they came upon ye sd place ye Sachims all empowered with . . . & divers of Indians yt live thereabout as also an old Indian called (blank) father in law to Ampamit whom Mr h Renselaer had brought along with him, & ye sd Sachem & also ye Indians as soon as they came to ye top of a high hill where Several heaps of Stones were ye northernmost a big heap & about 60 yard 2 oyr [other] heaps he sat down and said that was called wawanaghqua-sik, and being asked if there was no oyr Place thereabout called wawamaquassik he said no, that here it was yt a heap of Stones in the Indian language was commonly called wawanaquasik but yt no heap of stones wch was near there but had anoyr name, as yt heap of stones."[49] A recollection by Johannes Dykeman indicates the sachem whose name was missing in the above account was Catharickseet.

The line was settled by the two proprietors in 1716. Many years later this dispute was recollected by old farmers who lived in present-day Columbia County, then Albany County, which at the time included the whole upper part of New York Colony. Their testimony names some of the Indians who accompanied the party of Livingston and the Van Rensselaer brothers. A Livingston Manor farmer, Johannes Dykeman, eighty-one years old in June 1770, gave his account of the 1712 attempt to settle the boundary line between the patents of Hendrick Van Rensselaer and Robert Livingston. Dykeman explained that he was present about sixty years before when Kaghter-oukseet (Catharickseet) identified the place on the boundary line where an Indian stone heap lay as Mawanapoguasick and as the boundary between Van Rensselaer's land and Livingston's. He said that Hendrick Rensselaer and Robert Livingston were present when the place was identified. Van Rensselaer said Mawanaquasick was more to the south and the Indian insisted the place he had pointed out was the true Mawanaquasick. A dispute between Mr. Van Rensselaer and the Indian followed.[50]

The east boundary of the Van Rensselaer Patent for the so-called lower manor later was in dispute. Land in present Columbia County had been bought from Mohicans, headed by an influential sachem, Pamitepiet, also known as Keesiewey or Cornelis, in 1649. Additional land was obtained from Keesiewey in 1670. The 1649 boundaries were vague but included lands at the Claverack along the Hudson River and inland called Pothamhasik, Patkook and Stichsooch, ten flats along the Hudson River and on the creek beyond the Claverack, Ten Points Island (now Vastric or Rogers Island) and to the east "so far landward as the sellers own."[51]

Thus the eastern boundary remained in doubt. By the early 1700s, the Van Rensselaers were claiming that they owned twenty-four miles inland. A confirmatory patent of 1717 did not make the boundary any more specific. The Mohicans in 1754 claimed the eastern portion had never been purchased from them. In 1767, a New York supreme

court trial charging the Van Rensselaers had illegally enlarged their
boundaries was brought by Lt. Governor Cadwallader Colden on
behalf of the Crown. Although a jury decided the issue in favor of
the Van Rensselaers, in 1772 Johannes Van Rensselaer surrendered a
large portion of his eastern lands to the King in exchange for a new,
uncontested patent for his remaining Claverack land. This action did
not restore the land to the Mohicans, however.

Indians probably enjoyed being called upon to show where old
boundary lines fell; their voices were considered authoritative on
questions of Indian landmarks. Catharickseet's judgment was of
import in settling the line between the two estates; he recognized his
position and did not hesitate to insist he knew best. In 1714, when
the sachem was living in Connecticut a few miles from present
Salisbury, he helped Livingston and surveyor John Beatty survey the
Livingston Patent line. The survey began at the point on the north
line where the disputed stone heap of 1712 was situated. Catharickseet
was one of three Indians who accompanied the 1714 survey party,
which along the way stayed at the Indian wigwam of Metoxon
(Corlaer) for two days. The farthest points of Livingston's acquisi-
tions were declared to be the outside boundaries of his territory. Also
measured was the spur, a point of land extending into Connecticut.

The scribbled but thorough field diary kept by Livingston of that
outing provides a rare glimpse of a stay in a Mohican establishment.
It shows that as late as 1714, in isolated areas, some things, such as
quonset-shaped wigwams and traditional foodstuffs, had changed
little from earlier years. Indians still were making rush mats for their
wigwams, with rushes cut from an area lake. The difficulties encountered by these hardy men, both colonials and Indians, in bush-wack-
ing the line along the hills and reaching Connecticut were vividly
portrayed.

A substantial part of the diary follows. The group visited the
Connecticut spur, reciting familiar landmarks. Livingston mentioned
Indian locations, in particular placing the area chief, Metoxon, in the
Salisbury area in 1714, as well as giving other insights into Indian life
early in the eighteenth century:

> Journal of our Journey in Running the line of mannor Livingston
> from Manaquasik [Wawanaquasick] where the stone heaps Ly to
> the Southermost bought [curve] or bounds of Roeloft Janse's Kill:
>   Tuesday the 13 of Octobr 1714 the surveyor Mr. John Beaty
> accompanied with 4 Christians and 3 Indians vizt. Jacob Vosburgh,

Martin Vosburgh, Baltus anspagh, John Conraet Pein and myself
Rob't Livingston owner of the Mannor of Livingston & Catricseet
[Catharickseet] Panamat & John We Sett out from the mannor
house about 9 a Clock & went to the Pine Boss [woods] & came to
Claes Brusie's [house] about 12 found a Turkey by the way that
Claes had Shot 2 days before We came to Mananaquassik where the
Stone heaps lys about 3 a Clock, we measur'd from the stone heaps
to the Smal Rivulet that Runs at the End of the s'd hill where the
same ends, & is 164 Rod. the Cours [was] South 21 degrees westerly.
we lay al night at the Brook at the Rok where a Tree grows out of
the Rok that is split.[52]

Weddensday the 14th of octr 1714 we start from the Stone
heaps calld mawanaquassik & Set our Course South 71 degrees East
but after we went a mile began Seing the Top of the hill that wass
cal'd ahaschewaghkick [near Hillsdale][53] on the northward of the
hills of Taghkanik [which] lay now Easterly [therefore] the Course
was alter'd South 78 degrees Easterly or Eastwards goes Southerly
and after that we had gone 2 miles throu Roks and hill we came to
a Flatt or Plain wch we call the horse nut Flatt & a little after 4
miles we came to a large Flatt wch we call the X [Christian] Flatt
& on the East end thereof Lodg'd at the end of a vuynt crouple boss
[swampy woods] wch was a little above 5 miles

Thursday the 15 of octobr we continued the Course East 12
degrees South cam presently to a flat wch we call the Long flatt
where there is a fine mash [marsh] & so cam then ye valey where
is an . . . & so over the creek call'd Roeloft Jansens Kill Scit[uate]
& so to the End of Taghkanik hills called ahaschewaghkick being
about 8 1/2 miles from the stone heaps, where we made a stone
heap and all the 6 Christians cut the cross on the Trees and Cutt a
. . . also it was about 2 a clock when we got there & from there we
[set the] Course South. . . 2 degrees east & came to a Smal Rivulet
att Beshes' Pas about 4 miles where we lodged al the way Barren
and was forcd to go on the west side of the hills because the East
sides are so mountainous it was Impracticable to Hurry

We had Snow to night

Friday ye 16 of octob we went from ye last Creek around
Besses' Pas & came to ye Land of Taghkanik, 1 1/4 mile so that it
is 5 miles from ahashewaghik to Taghkanik, I went to Roelofts
Daghter [daughter] & got a Suply of Provisions & went from
Tahgankik along ye hills ye Course: 6 degrees E. & having went 5
miles from Taghkanik came to ye place yt Crosses from ye west
Ridge of hills to ye hills of Taghkanik cald Papsengaghit, where we
Lodged a cold n.[night] w wind

Saturday 16 [sic] October went from our lodging wh was very cold frost and came to wighquapakkat [Bird Peak] is about 4 miles except 6 Talys & ye Course was. . . , ye course is S. 6 deg East, & ye 6 Talys is S: 72 degr East ye 2 markd trees yt was markd 7 year ago we markd Each wth X & ML being cut out they Stand on each side of ye Riverlet yt ye Path goes over to go to awankapakak, ye end on ye North Side hanging over ye Path & from thence we went to Awankapakok where there is two Smal Lakes and Some aple Trees where Potchay livd but no. . .there now . . .nor land & so proceeded to ye flat calld Nakaowanich or Nakawasik as ye Indian says where ye Indians Lay vizt [to wit] Corlaer [chief Metoxon] and Panawaghowe we went to Sakashqua by ye Creek under ye hill & found ye Tree we marked 7 years ago ye Surveyor could not Reach it before night So we took up our Lodging in ye Indian house.

Sabbathday 17 Octob 1714 we remained at ye Indian house our horses were gone ye way back as yesterday fetched them back and mark Vosburgh & John Pein went to westenhook wh is about 4 miles from here.

Mondagh 18 octob 1714 we went from the Indian house where we had laid agn ete ye beans & fatt of venison & Bear flesh & followed ye Cours to ye South East corner of Sakachqua [Salisbury area] we went to ye n: East End of ye Land cal'd Sakachqua & markd a tree X by ye Creek yt Runns along ye foot of a hill & then along sd kil til anoyr Small Creek comes into it where 5 linden or lime Trees and an Esh [ash] tree are all in a Cluster together we markd 3 with X and then set out and by setting off new came where ye Indian house stands where we lodg'd & so to ye South East End of ye Nakawanich or Nakaowank where ye Course S 40 d: w from ye flat call'd Sakaghqua to ye South side of ye flat called Nakaewsik by a Blak Rok where 2 white oak trees are markd X by a mans gut [cut] & then our Course to ye Southermost Boght of Roelift Jansens Kill n:75 deg'r: west & as soon as we got up ye hill from ye said flatt we saw ye Lake called awankepakook on ye Left which is a Large Lake ye Indians say Sacket & Comp have boght to ye midle of sd Lake we went with said course to Wighquapakket is 2 miles where we Lodg'd where ye foot Path crosses ye white brook ye Land was about 150 yds to ye southward, it was a Cold night & I Sprained my hip with Carying great Log to ye fire.

Tuesday ye 19 Octob 1714 we set out from wighquapakkat & continued ye Course about 3 miles to (blank) & it is in abt 5 m. . . & there ye guide Catharukseet changd ye Course 9 degrees more northerly to n: 66 northerly & they came to a Place cal'd Tapasksit a little Lake where ye Indians get ye Rushes they make their matts of the land came to ye South end of sd little lake, they have gone

today 7 miles & 4 miles ye East course so yt is from ye flatt where
ye Black Rokes call'd nakaowasik in all about 9 3/4 miles & we saw
little or no land valuable nor Swamps except one here hard by & a
fine Plain we saw a mash by ye way wh ye line crossed about two
miles of.[54]

On Wednesday, Livingston and the group made it to the southernmost curve of the Roelof Jansen Kill and stayed the night at Jacob
Vosburgh's. The next day, Thursday, they noted the land occupied
by the Palatines and went to Vincent Roushe's farm, and then, a little
before sundown, Livingston went home temporarily to his own
mansion by the river. However, the following days were filled with
survey work for him as well as the Indians, as Hendrick Van Rensselaer was anxious to run his line "from where Goses Killetie Runs into
ye Patkooks kil and so [west] to wahankassik in Hudsons River over
against [opposite] Catskill, & ye Indian Catarakseet Gooses Son Says
yt Place has anoyr name cald Quaghkakaghik where there is a Path
very deep formerly made by ye Elks, there being a Small Claykuyl
[clay creek] near it, where ye Elks used to come, & from thence yt
Place has this name. . ."[55] Apparently elk had roamed the area until
a short time before this outing. Elk and white-tailed deer did not
frequent the same areas.

In 1743, Catharickseet, although very old, was still in demand.
Robert Livingston had died and his son, Philip, was in charge.
Catharickseet aided surveyor Charles Clinton in determining the
north line of the Little Nine Partners Patent, which was the Livingston patent south line. He went to the familiar points of reckoning:
"Saturday, the 14th. Two Indians, Cabrickset and Tasawight conducted him [the surveyor] to the place Sakaqua, and showed him a
large pitch pine tree 'now dead' marked by a chip out of the east and
west sides, standing in a cleared field of Thomas Bayless [in present
Salisbury village]."[56] The Indians said this tree was marked by Justin
Vosburgh twenty-eight years ago by the direction of Mr. Livingston
who was then present. Cornelius Knickerbocker, who had a farm
near the Mohicans of Weatauk, now Salisbury, and Thomas Lamb,
of Connecticut, were the interpreters for Mr. Clinton and these
Indians on the 1743 trip.[57]

Catharickseet seems to have been consistent in his testimony and
loyal to Livingston interests. In 1743, the boundaries of the Livingston spur were contested by Richard Sackett. Although Catharickseet
accepted payment from Richard Sackett and Isais Ross, proprietors

active in the Little Nine Partners Patent, Philip Livingston could rely
on Catharickseet's knowledge and integrity. He wrote to his son,
Robert, Jr.: "Ye ones [Indians] who brought yr father [read grandfa-
ther] to ye Rock know best where it was and what land was comprehended in ye mannor patent I do not mean yt of 1714 which is only
a Confirmation, the old Indian Catontsect now says still tho im-
ployed by Sackett and Roos that all the land there is called Nak-
awasick."[58]

There had been other Livingston Indian deeds. In 1697, two
Mohican women sold to Robert Livingston a parcel on the Roelof
Jansen Kill "a little above the farm belonging to Robert Livingston
where Joh[annes] Dykman now lives. . . ." The residence of Johannes
Dykman, shown on the map of 1714, was on a wagon path leading
southeast from Livingston's mill and manor house. This deed of July
7, 1697, was signed by Mohican women Mylady (nickname) and
Manhagh, and by Goose (Tataemshatt), Catharickseet's father.[59]
Witness to this transaction was Pennanack (Penanock) a Westenhook
Indian.

A note dated August 14, 1697, signed by Goose, was appended to
this deed. The note stated that Goose was employed by the two
women to dispose of the land to Livingston, and also contained the
statement that the purchase included all the land as far as the high
hills, a notation that could be used years later to justify Livingston
ownership in the Taconic mountains. Earlier deeds had mentioned
low hills, i.e. foothills.

This 1697 deed for land at the river also proved valuable in a later
boundary dispute involving Livingston's land. Peter Schuyler had
purchased land south of Robert Livingston's on the Hudson River,
land which was passed to Martinus Hoffman. Hoffman had leased a
parcel to Cornelis Lowrence, who encroached on Livingston's dock.
A case involving ownership of the dock at the boundary line was due
to come to court. For evidence, in the second quarter of the eighteenth
century, a Livingston descendant was trying to get the testimony of
Cornelis Lowrence. Young Robert wrote to his brother that Cornelis
Lowrence "was to shy and would not speak one word without first
looking to Hoffman he acknowledged he had been with you, [and]
Father, and two Indians, he promist to come to see me but believe
Hoffman won't let him he has been at Hoffmans whole fortnight,
Hoffman promist my son he would bee for me and my son when
Cornl Lowrence hired the place but I am informed he has been at my

landing last tuesday, the 20th instant and that he sayd my landing was the place [i.e. the line]. . .I have an Indian deed of the Squa MyLady and Manhagh dated the 7th day of July 1697 whereto was witness my Br Johannes Livingston and Johannes Beekman now [then] 47 years old I believe it is Johannes Beekman the Smith that was our neighbor at Albany if he be alive I am advised he must be supeoned to prove that Indian deed or his handwriting. . . ."[60]

In 1725, Livingston gave Manhagh's two sons, Abraham and Winnigh Po, duffels, powder, shot and rum at their request. They complained that they had never received any of the payment given to their mother for her sons. In making this gesture, Livingston secured a confirmation of the purchase and their approval of his settling two farmers on the land called Pachowasit. Moreover, they promised never to make any claim on Livingston's land, a promise Abraham kept through all his land recovery efforts, detailed in another chapter.[61]

In 1714, the elder Robert Livingston also was engaged in a boundary dispute with Richard Sackett, acting on behalf of the Little Nine Partners Patent. On both sides Livingston was beset with boundary challenges. He needed to come to a settlement with Van Rensselaer about the north line of Livingston Manor; on the south, Beekman as well as the Little Nine Partners encroached. The Livingstons' welfare often depended upon the Indian deeds or on testimony by surviving Mohicans. Robert Livingston, his sons, and grandson needed and received Mohican help.

Although Robert Livingston's long-time relationship with the Mohicans was marked by Indian claims for land not purchased and by counter-claims by Livingston for payment of debts owed to him by the Indians, there was little suggestion of ill-will. He understood the uses of credit and the Indian need for goods. The opportunistic Livingston, who could not have obtained his large acreage without deeds from the Mohicans, was a flexible, able, and persuasive person. The Indians probably respected not only his status at Albany but his courage, physical stamina, and willingness to associate with them. Livingston seemed to enjoy the trips with Indian guides around his borders under difficult conditions. It is clear that while the relationship between Robert Livingston and the Mohicans was not entirely amicable, he felt completely safe in traveling among them, and he trusted their memories, honesty, and allegiance.

IV.

The Mohicans and the Albany Traders: Aspects of Indian Debt 1680 to 1720

"The 19 martens entered higher up, . . . [Aeijawassen] acknowledges to be indebted for, in excess to what I find him to owe by the book. In case he pays the same, return to him the value of 19 martens, for the sake of doing justice to him and to myself."[1]

THE RELATIONSHIP of the Mohicans with the traders who bought their furs was complex. The Mohicans came to depend on the fur traders for essential guns and cloth, while the traders depended on Indian customers to ensure continued trade. To encourage trade, the dealers offered credit; the result was that most Indians obtained goods they needed in advance and paid later. Mohican Indian debts incurred with traders at the end of the seventeenth century demonstrated the Indian dependence on selected imported products. Typical Mohican purchases showing this dependence in New York and in western Massachusetts are recorded in lists of goods paid for Indian land and in the surviving account book of an Albany trader, who kept a record of his Indian trade late in the seventeenth century and early in the eighteenth century.

Although the original large Mohican population in the Upper Hudson Valley was greatly diminished within two decades after the Dutch arrived, Mohican communities survived near Dutch and, later, English farms and villages. The Mohicans were recognized as owners of large tracts of land within the upper Hudson River and Housatonic River watersheds. Mohicans delivered messages, worked for European farmers, sold corn to Dutch housewives, supplied fur traders, and patronized Dutch taverns. Mohicans helped protect the first Dutch traders and later Beverwyck and the City of Albany which it became, and fought beside New York and Massachusetts colonials in the French and Indian Wars and, later, in the Revolutionary War. Along the Hudson River and in the Housatonic Valley, these two ethnic communities, European and Native American, shared living space through the eighteenth century. The fur trader offered a significant connection between the two.

Mohican social and kin obligations, spiritual practices, and material culture were very ingrained, rivaling those of the Dutch in staying power. That is not to say that the Mohican way of life did not change. The Mohicans had adopted material items from European sources which had meaning to them or made their life easier, within their own traditions. These material additions did not completely alter their existing lifestyle as new goods could be substituted for parallel products formerly of their own making. For example, wool cloth in the form of duffels or strouds was used for Indian blankets and clothing instead of valuable skins and furs, which were sold to the newcomers. Brass kettles, axes, and knives were substituted for former earthen pots and stone tools. Metal projectile tips replaced or augmented stone or bone. After about 1640, natives of the Hudson Valley acquired guns and became adept at using them; they thereafter altered many of their hunting methods.

Within a few decades the Mohicans, as well as other Indian nations who had contact with the Europeans, became dependant on these new products and stopped creating many of their former material goods. Gunpowder and lead needed for their guns came from the Dutch. This dependency drove the Mohicans and all other Indian groups to continue the fur trade. This trade changed, however, as hunters had to go farther afield to find furs.

Besides hunting, lesser sources of trade goods for communities existed. Mohicans counted heavily on the frequent Indian conferences held at Albany, at which the Governor sometimes spoke to the assembled Indian nations. After the conferences, the Governor or Albany's Indian Commissioners distributed gifts of guns and supplies, shirts, hatchets, knives, pipes and tobacco, and kegs of rum to the Indians present, gifts which sachems carefully shared with their relatives and villages. In addition, Albany officials made payments to friendly neighbors such as the Mohicans to keep them pacified when events went awry, such as when a European murdered an Indian, when an alliance seemed to be faltering, or when war with the French threatened. Sir William Johnson, Indian Commissioner, gave out quantities of goods at conferences to support Indian allies, especially during wartime.

Moreover, it was possible for the Mohicans to obtain goods for services to the colonial community. For over a century, Indians collected bounties for killing wolves which harassed European live-stock, helping to drive these animals to extinction in the area. Individual natives were paid for other jobs: they carried documents and messages to Esopus or New Amsterdam, found lost farm horses in the woods, rescued captives, and harvested fields. On occasion, they were paid for services as scouts or fighting units. Indian women sold corn door-to-door or worked in Dutch-American households. Baskets, brooms, and canoes were manufactured for sale. Thus the Indians creatively put together sources to obtain products which had become a necessary part of their lives.

Alcohol figured heavily in some of these earnings, especially in payments to men. The intoxicating alcoholic beverages of the Dutch were entirely new to the northeastern Indian experience when the Dutch arrived. The natives quickly altered their culture to include beer, brandy, wine, rum and, after apple trees were established, hard cider. There was not, however, time to evolve a system of cultural control for this addictive drink. The intoxicating beverages, even when used only for special occasions, had a detrimental effect on the behavior of individuals and groups; moreover, sporadic alcohol abuse led to fights and murders among Indian family members and friends. Even more seriously, the use of alcohol led to an interruption of patterns of care and sustenance within the village setting. This was evident in the impoverished Indian villages adopted in the eighteenth century by Moravian and Congregational missionaries.

A recollection of Indian village life free from war and the unhappy effects of alcohol came from Mary Jemison, a Scots-Irish woman who after captivity had elected to remain with the Senecas. She had lost two much-loved sons in alcoholic fights. She related: "No people can live more happy than the Indians did in times of peace, before the introduction of spirituous liquors amongst them. Their lives were a continual round of pleasures. Their wants were few and easily satisfied; and their cares were only for today. . .If peace ever dwelt with men, it was in former times, in the recesses from war, amongst what are now termed barbarians."[2] War and alcohol, as Jemison observed, were the two great destroyers of peaceful village life.

Responsible Indian leaders repeatedly acted to restrict the flow of alcohol to Indians. At a 1702 conference, a sachem requested Lord Cornbury to keep secure the gallons of rum given the Indians as a present until the conference was over, lest the Indians might start drinking it and become unfit for business.[3] Indians at Stockbridge, newly reformed from drinking, urged their allies to give up alcohol. One string of wampum carried by a messenger brought an answer to Stockbridge Indians from the Shawnees: "Brother, I thank you for your word of advice; you told me drinking was not good. I now leave it off, and you shall not find your brother drunk again."[4]

Moreover, except at conferences, alcohol was not free. Paying for it drained off large resources that should have supplied families and old people with clothing, guns, and tools. Alcohol use contributed to debts owed to traders and led to mortgages, which resulted in the loss of Mohican land. Of special interest in the debt record, therefore, are the outlays for alcohol.

Buying on Credit

When Indians ran low on needed supplies, they could turn to the *handelars* (fur traders) for an advance on goods. The result was that to a substantial extent the Indians adopted the Dutch system of credit. If they had no furs on hand, they obtained the products they wanted first and paid later, as the Dutch routinely did. For merchants, the Indian trade was highly speculative. War, sickness or hunting failure for other reasons could leave the traders with unpaid accounts and no furs to send off to Europe on the sloops sailing down the Hudson.

The Albany merchants with whom both the Dutch and Indians dealt maintained a delicate balance between supplying products in advance of payment and later collecting the agreed upon price. For example, after Sybrant Van Schaik, a trader, died, his wife was advised in 1686, "Also, as about two hundred beavers of book debts are found which the savages or Indians owe, on which at present little can be counted, the aforesaid mother binds herself to pay the aforesaid children the just half of what shall be received therefrom."[5] There is ample evidence, however, that the Mohicans recognized their obligation to pay. After the mid-seventeenth century, most went far afield to obtain furs for the purpose. In 1689, about 110 Mohicans were with the Ottowa Indians near Niagara Falls in search of furs. In 1708, Indians from Schaghticoke had gone to present Vermont to hunt with the explicit intent of catching up on their debts; they were afraid to return home, they said, "for if we come now while we have no beaver, we shall but run more in debt."[6]

Trade goods which Indians needed usually were to be paid for with furs—most commonly beaver, otter, or marten—and with deerskins. Payment, however, was not entirely in animal products. Wampum was welcome. Indian corn, when available, was also welcome. Although the practice was illegal, traders stole corn from Indian fields at Schaghticoke to pay debts while the owners were away. Moreover, mortgaged land went as payment to traders for debts that were not paid off by a specified time.

A picture of life in an Indian village after the fur trade began adorned this map of 1671. In front of their longhouse, Indians package furs for transport to a trader. Map by John Ogilby, titled Nova Belgii Quod nunc Novi Jork vocator Novae Angliae & Partis Virginiae Accuratissima et Novissima Delineatio.

Courtesy of James Hess, Heritage Map Museum, Lititz, Pennsylvania

The loss of land for debt could occur informally. In 1718, for example, the extended Mohican family of sachem Catharickseet claimed woodland and meadows lying on the north side of Livingston Manor, which Robert Livingston had included within the bounds of his manor. Livingston persuaded the Indians to desist from their claim by forgiving all debts owed to him by Catharickseet, his wife, Nanakema, her brother, now dead, and Catharickseet's sister's husband, also now dead. In addition, Livingston presented them with four shirts, eight mugs of rum, one barrel of beer, and twenty pipes.[7] Thus he obtained the land.

Numerous parcels of Mohican lands in New York and in western Massachusetts were lost after being more formally mortgaged for goods and alcohol. For example, the sachem Manueenta (nicknamed Schermerhorn) in 1675 gave a 2 1/2 year mortgage for one half of the land belonging to the Indians at Catskill. The mortgage was the result of a debt worth eighty beaver skins and fifteen otter skins which "diverse Indians" owed to trader Jan Clute.[8] This debt was paid off years later to clear the title, but by a settler to whom the Indians had sold the land, not by Schermerhorn, the Indian.

Traders Encourage Debts

Indian debt served the trader. To profit from the sales of the furs he acquired from them, the trader had to attract Indian customers. Indebted customers achieved that end by returning to the trader with furs on every trip to Albany to pay debts. They then would take new goods on credit, which would bring them back again with more furs. Among the traders, it was understood that certain Indians belonged to certain traders. Sometimes, therefore, a debt owed to one trader might be paid to another, with the understanding that the payment would be passed along to the proper person.

Repeat customers were important because of the intense competition for Indian furs, competition which Dutch and English officials were unsuccessful in regulating, despite numerous ordinances. Some Indians were accosted in the woods, some were beaten and conveyed to a certain trader's house even when they intended to go elsewhere, and some were robbed of their furs. As a result, special houses where the Indians could trade were set up on the outskirts of Albany. These flimsy structures were renewed periodically, as in 1698, when the Albany Common Council noted that "It is thought convenient by ye News of ye Peace that one or two houses be made upon ye hill, for ye Indians, as formerly, and Care shall be taken for to have ye Materialls ready to build in ye Spring by all ye Traders who doe any wise pretend to ye same."[9]

In addition, natives accused some traders of taking advantage of them by offering alcohol before trading began. They then were tempted to drink away the profits from their furs, without acquiring needed goods for hunting or supplies for their villages. In 1722,

Ampamit of Schodack, eloquent sachem of the Mohicans, offered this indictment at a conference: ". . . the matter is this, when our people come from hunting to the town or plantations and acquaint the traders and people that we want powder and shot and clothing, they first give us a large cup of rum, and after we get the taste of it we crave for more, so that in fine all the beaver and peltry we have hunted goes for drink, and we are left destitute either of clothing or ammunition. Therefore, we desire our father [the Governor] to order the tap or crane shut, for as long as the Christians will sell rum, our people will drink it."[10]

At the 1722 conference, Governor Burnett chided the Indians, the women as well as the men, for being often drunk and for squandering their Indian corn for rum. Historically, alcohol has posed serious problems within many societies. Among the Dutch and English, many of whom drank beer daily, individuals frequently became addicted and ruined their lives. Modern research into how brain chemicals are regulated by genes has shown that some gene combinations are particularly susceptible to alcohol addiction; as a result of twentieth century research, alcohol dependence today is recognized as in part a physical problem.[11] This information helps to explain why many Indians, as well as numerous Europeans, found it difficult to stop drinking. The dangerous consequences of group binges were recognized. Women, children, and visitors often retreated to the woods to avoid violence when liquor was brought into a village and carousing began.

Despite repeated ordinances forbidding the sale of alcohol to the Indians, the lucrative practice continued. Not every one in the Indian societies of the seventeenth and eighteenth centuries wanted the tap shut. As many Indians wanted alcohol, the issue divided the Indian population. In 1653, Esopus chiefs, for example, foreseeing fights and trouble, begged Kit Davits, a trader, not to sell brandy to the Indians.[12] Yet, despite the concerns of leaders, Kit Davits found ready customers. Indian participants at conferences were angry if alcoholic drinks were not given to them. In addition, many Indians connived with dealers to get alcohol illegally, and enterprising Indians peddled brandy to their fellows.[13] Women often carried home liquor for their men and some Indian women sold liquor to make a living.

European drinks also might be obtained casually from Dutch farmers, who always had a supply of beer, rum, or cider in the cellar. For example, according to Court Minutes, drunken Indians from

Schodack, having obtained rum from a local farmer in 1656, were locked up at Albany until they were sober. At Esopus, Indians who had been paid in rum for helping a farmer harvest corn became noisy and attracted the attention of soldiers, who led an attack on the Indian revelers. This fray started another round of the wars between the Dutch settlers and the Esopus Indians.[14] In the 1740s, Massachusetts adopted a law which allowed only licensed dealers to sell alcohol to natives. The law was intended to protect the Indians from obtaining alcohol easily from individuals.

Other trade goods as well as alcohol were essential. To obtain desired products without furs or corn in hand, the natives sought traders with a substantial store of trade goods who were willing to extend credit. Records indicate this often meant the trader would wait a year or two, and occasionally even longer, for the return of the hunters. As a result, most upper-Hudson traders were headquartered in Albany or Esopus and had other sources of support to tide them over lulls in this variable, although profitable, trade.

In Pennsylvania, Ohio, and western New York, traders setting up posts far from home base were occasionally murdered by marauding Indians who took their goods. However, in eastern New York and western Massachusetts, traders and other travelers were safe among the peaceful Mohican Indians. Traders could go into the country to meet their Indian customers and to collect debts. In 1710, the Mohican Indian chief known as Corlaer or Metoxon, headquartered in an Indian village in northwestern Connecticut, was listed as a buyer in an Albany trader's book.[15] Possibly the trader had previously visited the Mohican village in Connecticut. Indians as well as traders might travel far to deal with fur traders. Westenhook land transactions and mortgages illustrate the familiar interaction of Housatonic Valley Mohicans with Albany-based fur traders.

Traders as Friends

Although there were complaints, traders were valued links between Indians and colonial society. Not all traders tried to cheat their Indian customers, despite this modern impression. On the contrary, some traders became dependable resources for Indian villages and were vital to Mohican lives. To be near a friendly trader with shelves of duffels (cloth), shirts, gun supplies, and kegs of rum became important for Mohican villagers in the seventeenth and eighteenth centuries. To fill this need, native settlements not close to Beverwyck (later Albany) sometimes invited colonial traders to settle near them. The Mohicans of Columbia County, for example, requested that some of the Dutch join them in the 1640s and even threatened to encourage rival English settlements if they did not do so.[16] The desire for the presence of traders was not limited to the Mohicans. The Dutch village at Esopus was begun on the invitation of the Waranawankong (Esopus) Indians. The fur trade was paramount to the Iroquois. In 1701, a French report concluded that "when the Iroquois would see that goods would be furnished them at a reasonable rate, far from insulting us, they would protect and respect us, having no better friends than those who supply them at a low rate."[17] Thus, post-contact Indian community behavior was shaped by the need for trade goods and, as when the Mohawks weighed the offerings of two competing European powers, even national alliances could be affected.

An outstanding seventeenth century example of a trader who was an Indian friend was Jan Dareth. A prominent Albany merchant and gunsmith, he learned the Mohican language, translated deeds for the Mohicans, and accompanied Mohican leaders on risky diplomatic excursions. He made valuable reports to Albany officials about the results of their missions.[18] Some traders adopted the Indian way of life, lived in or near native villages, and learned to converse in their language. As a result, the traders served as translators when needed and became allies of their customers, who appreciated their support. In 1675, for example, Schermerhorn, a Mohican sachem at present Leeds, New York (west of Catskill in Greene County) donated land to a fur trader, Jan Pieterse Bronck, "for a liberality shown him [Schermerhorn] and for friendship enjoyed."[19] Jan Bronck built a cabin by the creek near Pachquiack, one of the great flats at Leeds, and traded on the outskirts of the Indian village there.

In another situation, a grandson of Arent Van Curler, who had the same name and perhaps could use to advantage Indian memories of his grandfather's reputation, reputedly maintained an Indian trading post in present Washington County in the eighteenth century. According to local legend, his location was protected by the Mohican Indians from attacks by Mohawks or Canadian Indians. A building owned by Van Curler still stands on the site.[20]

About 1730, Mohicans in the Housatonic Valley attracted a Kinderhook trader, Joachim Van Valkenburgh, to live among them.

The group gave Van Valkenburgh a farm and the trader remained with the Indians at Westenhook almost a decade. He was an especially close friend of Konkapot, chief of the Mohicans at Wnahktukook, later Stockbridge. Despite this friendship with a trader, Konkapot was described as sober and he never drank to excess. Accommodations between Indians and traders varied according to the personalities, honesty, and kindness of individuals involved and were affected by Indian wars, disease, hunting success, alcohol, and wars between European powers.

New England Traders Want Mohican Furs

It was not only the Dutch and English on the Hudson River who were interested in profits from Mohican trade. Mohican Indian contacts with European goods and culture came from English neighbors to the east and south as well as from the Colony of New York. By 1640, Mohicans on the Hudson below Fort Orange were accused by Kiliaen Van Rensselaer of by-passing Dutch merchants by sending furs to New England traders. The route from Schodack was apparently by way of one or more Mohican villages at Westenhook, in the Housatonic River valley.[21]

New England's merchants were familiar with Albany, of course. For example, Springfield trader John Pyncheon traveled to Albany at least three times, and described the trip as a "long, troublesome and hazardous journey."[22] New Englanders crossed the Housatonic River at recognized fording places, such as near present Great Barrington, where there was a Mohican village, as they traveled to Albany for conferences or to Canada on diplomatic missions. Other Mohican settlements were on the routes which took travelers to Albany via Kinderhook.

Mohicans could deal with English traders at Hartford, Springfield, Stamford and New Haven, and with the New Haven outpost above present Derby. Mohicans were friends also with surrounding Indian nations, including the Indians of Stamford, Connecticut, who were near the English on the shore of Long Island Sound. Most important, perhaps, was the trading post "which Governor Hopkins of Connecticut, set up in 1641 at Woronoco," near present Westfield, Massachusetts.[23] By the 1650s, this trading post appeared on Dutch maps as Pinser's *handel huys*. On the eastern edge of territory claimed

by the Mohicans, the trading house was within a day's journey of
Mohican villages on the Housatonic River.

"Pinser" was the wealthy and influential John Pyncheon,
headquartered at Springfield, Massachusetts, and the son of William
Pyncheon, Springfield's founder. John Pyncheon later financed the
establishment of Westfield and other communities by purchasing
land from local Indians (not, however, Mohicans). He was "indispen-
sable as the Massachusetts colony's agent to the western [i.e. New
York] Indians."[24] In 1677, the Mohicans were thanked publicly by
merchants John Pyncheon and James Richards for not joining an
attack on settlers in Maine made by some of the New England Indians;
the two merchants hailed the Mohicans as friends now and in the
future.[25] However, by the 1670s the fur trade in Massachusetts had
declined, and the Mohicans there had fewer furs with which to buy
merchandise. Their thoughts were turned to dealers on the Hudson
River who would offer credit or who would give mortgages on
Mohican land. This the New England traders were not as likely to
do, since the Westenhook territory was claimed by New York at the
time.

When furs were scarce, land became a major item of exchange for
products used by Indian communities. Beginning in the seventeenth
century and continuing into the eighteenth, traders supplied goods
to the Mohicans in exchange for mortgages on land. These mortgages
for land were rarely, if ever, paid off by Indians, with the result that
the land was lost to the natives. Mortgages demonstrated a community or family need for the products of the traders. The Indians were
often aware they might not be getting full value for their lands;
however, land sales maintained relationships with valued traders.
Indian sellers believed that accepting gifts worth less than the land
obligated the purchaser to bestow future favors on them. According
to a modern writer, "Europeans held up their part of the bargain by
periodically giving gifts confirming the validity of the original deed
or satisfying the demands of Indians claiming not to have been paid
for their share of the land."[26] Both sides understood these mutual
obligations, although sometimes only lip service was paid by Albany
mortgage holders who resold the land as soon as it was theirs. The
loss of land gives an intimation of the far-reaching effect of Indian
debt.

Of necessity, as the century passed, new trapping grounds were
developed far away. Mohicans joined some Iroquois in raids into

Virginia and Maryland in the 1680s, and, with the Minisinks, in 1681 returned "with furs from as far away as the Spanish frontier [Florida]."[27] When colonial delegates from Virginia and Maryland protested the incursions, which had resulted in murders of some settlers and travelers, the Mohicans and others promised to go farther to the west in search of beaver.

Several western nations owed obligations to the Mohicans for past assistance. "Mahican and other 'Loups' had actually been exploring the Midwest already since about 1669. . . . it appears that, in the 1670s, the Mahican and Esopus. . . gained permission from the Ottawa and Miami to exploit the latter's game resources. By 1680, there were two bands of New England and River Indians living among the Miami. . . . Mahican prestige in the Midwest was acknowledged by the Iroquois, who requested them to arbitrate for peace with the Miami and Ottawa in 1687."[28] Some Ottowas traded at Albany, according to the account book of an Albany fur trader, discussed below.

Fur Traders of the Albany and Housatonic Areas

Despite its uncertainty, trading was considered a very profitable venture. Young men of established Albany families customarily were started out as Indian traders. The fur trade could be a stepping stone to the legal profession, ownership of stores, sloops, or mills, and to politics, land speculation, and government appointments.

Among traders important to the Mohicans in the seventeenth and early eighteenth century were men whose names appear often in the Albany records in other connections. Several of these traders held important posts in the administration of the City of Albany, were appointed as Indian Commissioners (a seeming conflict of interest with trading), and became major landholders. Robert Livingston, Secretary of Albany and secretary to the Indian Commissioners, and a major landowner, for whom the Indian trade was a useful sideline, was an example of a man who combined many posts to his advantage.

Well-known fur traders included Robert Sanders, who spoke and understood the Mohican language well enough to act as an interpreter. He had obtained Mohican land north of Albany at present Lansingburgh in exchange for Indian debts, and he arranged for the City of Albany to pay him instead of the Indians if Albany claimed the Indian land. In 1682, he was described in a letter as meddling and talkative, and as concerning himself with Indians in matters of public import, to the prejudice of the Government.[29] Shortly after, with Myndert Harmense Van Den Bogaerdt, he leased land which included the site of present Poughkeepsie. Despite Sanders' unpopularity, as war with the French loomed in 1689, his familiarity with the natives along the Hudson River proved valuable to the English. In 1693, Major Dirck Wessels, accompanied by Robert Sanders, was sent by Governor Benjamin Fletcher on a mission to the Five Nations, to persuade them not to consider an offer of peace from the Governor of Canada.[30]

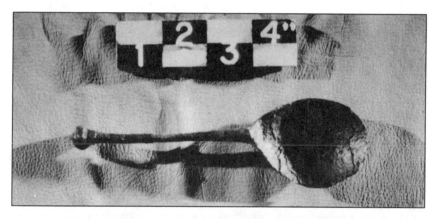

Goods found on Indian village locations between Sheffield and Great Barrington, Massachusetts, suggest connections with the Hudson Valley. They include a Dutch pewter spoon and the head of a trade axe.

The Great Barrington Historical Commission, Charles J. Taylor Collection; photographs by James Parrish

In 1702, Robert Sanders, with others, petitioned for the tract called Wayawnagtanock (Wawyachtenok) west of the Housatonic River which the Indians were reportedly willing to sell. This was apparently the same tract already claimed as a consequence of 1685 Indian deeds by fur trader Dirck Wessels and associates. These men quickly stepped in to secure the land again by giving goods to the Mohicans in exchange for mortgages. Shortly afterwards, Sanders and others as a substitute requested a license to buy from the Mohican Indians land at Wassaic, in present Dutchess County, New York, land which lay to the south and west of Wawyachtenok.[31]

Indian traders who appear in the Albany County records include the early combination of Jan Thomas Whitbeck and Volkert Janse Douw, in-laws who shared a farm on Papscanee Island on the east side of the Hudson and maintained locations in Albany. The two traders had numerous early contacts with the Mohicans, from whom they bought islands lying near their farm, as well as Schodack Island in 1663 and adjacent Schodack mainland in 1664. In 1665 Volkert Janse Douw obtained land east of Kinderhook from the Mohican Indian, Wattawit, "out of friendship and because of an old debt for maize."[32] Other early traders were Abraham Staats, who by 1654 had a trading post among Mohicans at the mouth of the Kinderhook Creek, and Jan Dareth, mentioned above, a friend of sachems Aepjen and Keesiewey.

Additional familiar fur dealers were Gerrit Teunis Van Vechten, who lived south of the present City of Rensselaer, on the east side of the Hudson not far from the Witbeck-Douw farm, as well as at Catskill, and Jan Clute at Catskill. Jan Bronk of Coxsackie traded at Leeds, west of Catskill. Dirck Wessels (Ten Broeck) of Albany, with Peter Schuyler, supplied goods to the Mohicans living at Tachkanick and Westenhook. Both served as Indian Commissioners for the City of Albany.[33] Major Dirck Wessels was deeply involved in Mohican land purchases and was closely associated with Robert Livingston. Records suggest Wessels' late seventeenth century and early eighteenth century influence on the Mohicans was the most pervasive of any of the traders of the period.

There was also Joachim Van Valkenburgh of Kinderhook, who in the 1720s and 1730s lived near Wnahktukook, a Mohican village on the Housatonic River at present Stockbridge. Van Valkenburgh, whose language was the Dutch of the Hudson Valley, could manage a little English and he learned some Mohican, as well.[34] His languages were an indication of the culture of the times. Members of Dutch families still spoke Dutch at home and in Albany, but carried on business in English at New York. Traders learned Indian languages, in order to converse with their Indian customers. The language exchange extended both ways; some Mohicans, because of their connections with Dutch residents and traders from the Hudson River, understood the Dutch language, while Mohicans of the Housatonic Valley learned English.

Van Valkenburgh, who became the trusted friend of the sachem Konkapot, had learned the Mohican language as a youth in Kinderhook. He farmed the "40 acres of meadow and 250 acres of upland adjoining"[35] which he obtained through a gift from Konkapot, who came from the Hudson River area and may have understood a little of Van Valkenburgh's Dutch. They were friends. Van Valkenburgh, as the resident trader, lived in harmony with his Indian friend and the Mohican community at Westenhook, although, along with other goods, he sold alcohol to both Dutch and Indian customers until the arrival of the English mission.

Van Valkenburgh was an example of a trader who served as a bridge between his Indian customers and friends and the European culture which was affecting their lives in many ways. As a Kinderhook resident, he had from his infancy been conversant with the Mohican Indians, particularly those bordering on New England.[36] As interpreter, he accompanied Konkapot to Springfield when Konkapot was to receive a Captain's commission from Massachusetts Governor Belknap. Moreover, he translated English into the Mohican language for John Sergeant, the missionary who came to Stockbridge, and helped him learn the Mohican tongue. The versatile Van Valkenburgh, although he proved useful to all parties at the time the English mission was established at Stockbridge in 1734, was resented by the English who disliked his Dutch background and who also wished to control the Indians at Westenhook without interference.

Goods Needed by Mohicans

Deeds for Indian land which list the European payment to the Mohicans and their fellow nations give some evidence of the adaptations in Indian communities. In the eighteenth century, unfortunately, merely listing a lump sum of money or stating that goods worth a certain sum were paid to the Indians became the usual form on Indian deeds. Many seventeenth century transactions, however, include a list of the items provided. In 1685, for example, goods given by trader Dirck Wessels for land in Columbia County on the Kinderhook Creek included: five fathoms of wampum, two bags of gunpowder, three fathoms of duffels cloth, three shirts, one kettle, two axes and four bars of lead.[37] Alcohol, if it was provided in this case, as seems likely, was given separately, probably to the sachem involved.

Deeds given in 1685 by the Mohicans for two Westenhook parcels of land to Dirck Wessels and his associates listed valuable items of clothing and guns and related items. Products given for the first parcel included: twenty fathoms of black wampum, twenty fathoms of white wampum, four blankets, three fathoms stroudwaters cloth, six fathoms wool duffels cloth, two stroudwater coats, three duffels coats, three children's coats, six shirts, three guns, four kettles, four bags of powder, six axes, six pairs of stockings, two hoes, two half vats of strong beer, four vats of rum, twelve pairs of scissors, twelve combs, two rolls of tobacco, twenty knives, twenty bars of lead, and thirty awls.[38]

For the second tract of 1685, different Mohican individuals received: one fathom of duffels, one blanket, one kettle, one gun, two shirts, two bags of powder, four bars of lead, four knives, one coat, two axes, two pairs of stockings, one half vat of beer, two vats of rum, and forty fathoms of white wampum.[39] The three major categories accepted as payment by Mohicans in most land transactions were cloth and other clothing; guns, along with lead, flints and powder; and alcohol. In addition, there were occasionally paints, knives, axes and kettles, minor luxuries. The numbers of kettles being given had declined greatly from former years, when kettles were considered a priority item.

By the 1680s, larger quantities of goods were being given than the Mohicans had received for land in prior years as land had become more valuable. The lists of goods obtained for land were similar to commodities purchased directly by the Indians from the traders, according to a surviving account book.

The Wendell Account Book

An Indian trader of the late seventeenth and early eighteenth centuries was Evert Wendell, based at Albany, whose remarkable account book of his Indian trade has survived at The New-York Historical Society. From internal evidence, it appears that the keeper of this account book was Evert Wendell, son of Capt. Johannes Wendell, an Albany merchant. Although there was more than one person named Evert Wendell, the particular keeper of the Indian book is identified through references in the book to his father "Hanes" (meaning Johannes), to his brother "Hanes," and to "our Susanna," his sister.

The Wendells were an entrepreneurial family. Family members, women included, engaged in trade. Wendell's grandmother was Elizabeth, a daughter of trader Robert Sanders. She also was a fur trader. Evert Wendell mentions a book of accounts kept by Hester, probably his cousin. Another relative, Jacob Wendell, served as a mercantile link between Albany and Boston in the early decades of the eighteenth century and became one of the original proprietors of Pittsfield, Massachusetts, which was first known as Wendell's Town.[40]

Evert Wendell, the keeper of the account book, was born February 8, 1681, and died in 1750. He married Engeltje Lansing in 1711. In addition to the Indian trade, Wendell sold rum, grain, and general merchandise in Albany, from which trade a second account book survives at The New-York Historical Society. Wendell kept a grist and saw mill, became an attorney, and served as a commissioner of Indian Affairs.[41] Since his father was a merchant, it seems likely Evert Wendell took over some existing fur trade accounts at the beginning of his career. He would have been young, only sixteen or seventeen years old, when his account book began in earnest. As his father died in 1692, undoubtedly he assumed adult responsibilities early, a common occurrence.

Wendell was not one of the traders guilty of mistreating his Indian customers; indeed, the evidence suggests he was trusted and well-liked. His accounts were scrupulously kept; he made recognizable drawings to convey to his unlettered customers exactly what they owed; he carefully crossed off accounts that had been paid, and he made a note to return credit to one Indian who possibly had been overcharged. Moreover, in common with other traders, he had some debts that were never crossed off and were probably never paid. He attracted repeat Indian customers for over a decade, suggesting continued good relations. He seemed friendly to the Indians with whom he had dealings, and his descriptive phrases for identifying customers were free of malice or racial prejudice.

His sister, Susanna, had an Indian servant. Moreover, Evert Wendell, or his mother's household, where he apparently lived prior to his marriage, also had as a servant a young Mohican woman of whom the family seemed fond. She may have served as a tie to the Mohican community. Relatives of this Mohican woman obtained credit in the store and appeared frequently in the account book. Examples of the entries relating to this person include the following:

Naghnakamet, who with our native is married Debit 1703 in January a pair of stockings for one beaver. Ditto a half-worn out piece of duffel at 2 beavers, amounts to 3 beavers. 1704 May, he paid me in the country.

1705, March 1, our little native her son Debit 1 measure Indian corn @ 1 marten. 1705 June paid, so he is even.

In January 1705, Naghnakamet (also spelled Naghnakanet) obtained goods for his sister. These, too, were paid for in due time. After that, Naghnakamet borrowed a gun to go hunting. There were other entries for Naghnakamet, who seems to have been a responsible customer. Naghnakamet appeared on an Indian deed for land in Catskill in 1733.[42]

As would be expected in Albany in the early 1700s, Evert Wendell and his family members or employees kept his account book in Dutch. The account book, eight by thirteen inches in size, with its varied handwriting, blotches, and scratchouts on some pages, has proved difficult to understand and translate. A few of the entries, however, are clearly written and are easily understood. Excerpts from the account book were translated some years ago by Dingman Versteeg, a genealogist and the Librarian of the Holland Society. In addition, an unpublished translation recently was made by a Dutch researcher, Cees-Jan Waterman.

Wendell's Indian account book, sometimes described as covering the years from 1695 to 1726, in fact does not run that long. Active Indian trading occurred only for a little over a decade. One entry is dated 1691/2, with a note that the debt was paid in 1697, when it was apparently entered. A page headed "1695" contains only entries from 1697 to 1701. An entry for 1695 was inserted after a few pages from the early 1700s. There are only two entries dating to 1696.

The major activity in the book, therefore, occurs from 1697 to 1710, after which entries almost cease. Wendell kept separate pages for different Indian nations, including several pages devoted to Mohicans. There are also many Mohawk pages and a few Oneida pages. Some pages contain mixed accounts of Mohawks and Mohicans, with each Indian identified as to group or by relationship with some familiar Indian or by a note about where he or she lived. Among the Mohicans mentioned in the account book are forty-five women and sixty-eight men. Most came to Wendell's trading post more than once.

Brief descriptive identifying phrases to aid the trader in future recognition of customers were given. These include references to color: there are several mentions of white natives, such as the one on August 19, 1704, when the sister of Schekquae, who was a white female native, obtained three ells of baize for two pigs. Identifying adjectives indicate age, such as whether young or old, or appearance, such as handsome, small, male or female. Some had pocked faces or eyelids, or were toothless, or bore distinctive scars on heads or faces. One young man was described as a short, heavy native, rather an unusual figure, apparently, since the natives were usually thin and sinewy.

Although the account book is generally chronological, the entries are not entirely sequential. The writer left spaces, probably with the idea of keeping the accounts for one person together. As this system did not work, he later wrote other accounts in the blank places. Indian nations which are mentioned in the book include: Mohican, Mohawk, Oneida, Ottowa, Cayuga, Anakonkeers (Abenaki), Tuscarora, Onondaga, and Seneca. The Anakonkeers or Onagongues had been invited in 1701 to settle at Schaghticoke, north of Albany, with other New England Indians, so these individuals mentioned in the account book may have come from Schaghticoke.[43] There were Indian customers, however, including some Mohawks, who came from Canada.

Although the trader intended to keep the first part of the book for Mohican entries, the entries became mixed. He also kept a "scratch book," possibly used when he traveled, and an "Indian corn book." He was scrupulous about the accuracy of his accounts, as the quote at the beginning of this chapter attests. His occasional travels into the country and to Schenectady to meet with Indians are noted in his accounts. He was a good businessman. In addition to offering generous credit, he tried to keep his customers coming back to trade by offering small bonuses on their return. Moreover, he contracted with some of the Mohawks (although apparently none of the Mohicans) to peddle goods and alcohol to the Mohawk country and to Canada.

The book has provided useful lists for investigating Mohican debt as well as Indian debt in general, although the information is not necessarily complete. Its limitations include references to other books kept by Wendell, and a possibly restricted stock of goods, which would affect the items purchased in his store. No doubt Mohicans also obtained different items at other locations. Another distortion could be that some selection process among buyers was at work; the listed individuals possibly were not representative of the whole group. The account book nevertheless provides a stirring inside look at Mohican purchases and provides further documentation of the lives of familiar Mohicans who are known from other sources. Moreover, the account book includes many Indian family relationships and suggests the travels and locations of some of those people listed.

At the start of the account book, a list of Mohican customers is given, each with a reference to a *folio* or page section. One well-known Mohican shown was Caloolet, a sachem, who in 1708 confirmed Van Rensselaer land purchases on the east side of the Hudson. He also brought a message to Albany in 1699 about the Schaghticoke Indians being afraid to return home because they were not able to pay their debts to the traders. A translation by the author of the customer list follows:

A Register of the Mohican Natives

Jan the Native folio - - - - - - - - 1
His wife folio - - - - - - - - - - 1
His wife's sister folio - - - - - - - - 2
A woman native was with her
Nemamet his wife folio - - - - - - - 3
Jan Seeps folio - - - - - - - - - - 3
Walitgaes folio - - - - - - - - - - 4
His brother Maleck folio - - - - - - 4
Siektock folio - - - - - - - - - - - 5
Naernis folio - - - - - - - - - - - 5
Awannighqaet folio - - - - - - - - 6
Naeckae Pen folio - - - - - - - - 6
Tijoom or Rochkaeuw folio - - - - 7
Awans folio - - - - - - - - - - - - 7
Kaloolit folio - - - - - - - - - - - 8

Nannaelaemit who was with
the Grey Head   folio - - - - - - - - 9
The Grey Head is called
Wassewaencke folio - - - - - - - - - 9
Nooseewalamit folio - - - - - - - - 8
Jacob the Native folio - - - - - 10
Mackenant folio - - - - - - - - - 3
Netewakam f[olio] - - - - - - - - - 7
Wanckpaee owes 1 piece of meat
Naghnekampenit folio - - - - - - - 5
Pamolet f[olio] - - - - - - - - - - - 1
Sece Caet f[olio] - - - - - - - - - - 8
Naghnaekamet
His sister f[olio] - - - - - - - - - - 5
His wife's son - - - - - - - - - f5 - f3
Herij - - - - - - - - - - - - - - - f 12

An older Mohican with an interesting nickname was "Den Gris Cop" (the Grey Head), or Wassewaencke, mentioned above, who appears in the book several times. On another day, his wife bought one vat or keg of rum at five martens. Presumably she carried it back to the village or wigwam to peddle or for family or village use.

A sample from the account book is typical: on September 29, 1707, a young Mohican was listed; he lived with Nietewakam; his name was Magh Magh Cees (Cees is a Dutch nickname for Cornelis), and he was a handsome young native. He owed for one piece of duffels at two large beavers; for one pair of stockings at one beaver; for one lap (a piece of duffels) at two martens; for a cask of rum at two beavers; and for two little bottles together at one marten. In October one bottle of rum at one marten and also tobacco at one marten were added to his account.

The beavers, martens and otters were shown at the right side of the page, the beavers with recognizable oblong shapes, like beaver pelts. Each marten or otter was indicated by a single line. A martin was worth one guilder, while a beaver usually was worth eight guilders, but could bring a higher price if it was large or heavy.

Also shown was a sketch of the facial markings of an Ottowa man, about forty years old, named Mack Kockwas Sien. Facial tattoos were important identifiers. Unfortunately, there was no drawing of a Mohican face. Occasionally, the trader mentions a facial design or the lack of one. In addition, quite often he gives a clue to the customer's location or residence, as where he says a Mohican was from *oom Lagh*, or below, meaning this Mohican man lived south of Albany. The location had some extra connotations: it meant he was a true local Mohican, and he was not one of the group of New England Indians living at Schaghticoke. In another instance giving a residence location, Wendell listed Sanhaquisquaas as a Mohican boy who customarily lived in Catskill.

The animal furs and other items owed to the fur trader by the Mohicans included the following: many beavers and martens, some otters and raccoons, and, rarely, a bear or fisher; occasional deer skins and a few elk skins also were offered. It is interesting that occasional elk were available in the Hudson Valley in the early 1700s. Once pigs were offered as payment, noted above; corn was occasionally promised, to be paid when the crop was ripe. On a few entries, pieces of used cloth were accepted as payment. Wampum was rarely given; however, in 1706, a band of wampum was sold by Niettewapwae, a Mohican. This may have been a treasured possession; it was described in Folio 10 as 145 black wampum beads long and ten wide, with sixty-one white places on it.

The goods obtained by the Mohicans from Evert Wendell's stock included kegs and bottles of rum, beer and cider, and clothing, consisting mostly of strouds and duffels, stockings, coats, and shirts (including small shirts for children). There were also a few pairs of shoes, and one set of buckles; guns, lead, powder, gun repairs, flints, and shot. In addition, a miscellany of kettles, knives, harpoons (spears), axes, and one broadsword, and minor amounts of corn, tobacco, pipes, mirrors, boxes of paint, wire, beads, and a belt were noted.

A gun purchased from trader Wendell cost three large beavers. The wire may have been used to make "pluckers," tightly wound spirals of wire used to pull out hair by the roots from the face and other parts of the body. "To pluck out their hair, all such as have any connection with the traders make use of a pliable worm, formed of flattened brass wire. This instrument is closely applied, in its open state, to the surface of the body where the hair grows; it is then compressed by the finger and thumb; a great number of hairs are caught at once between the spiral evolutions of the wire, and by a sudden twitch they are all drawn out by the roots."[44] Wire was also used as decoration, wound around slits in the ear lobes.

Guns had long been a necessity. Without them, deer and bear now were rarely obtained. A Moravian missionary, writing of his

Inset: A tiny (under one inch) lead figure of a swallow-tailed bird or Thunderbird was found in an archeological dig at an Indian site in Lansingburgh, New York in 1894. (One wing has been broken.) Lead for bullets, obtained in trade, was occasionally used for other purposes. The site, near a seventeenth-century Mohican village called "Unuwat's Castle," is occupied by a Greek Reformed Church.

Courtesy of the New York State Museum, Albany, NY, with the permission of the Stockbridge-Munsee Band of Mohican Indians

A c.1632 map of Rensselaerswyck drawn for Kiliaen Van Rensselaer shows the fortified Mohican village called Unuwat's Castle at today's Lansingburgh, New York. In the vicinity, a large Indian site beside the Hudson River was excavated at the turn of the nineteenth century.

Map, New York State Library, Manuscripts and Special Collections experience in the mid-eighteenth century, described the Indian dependence on guns in the Ohio Valley: "Bows and arrows have fallen into disuse among those Indians that trade with whites; are, indeed, only used for small game, such as the pigeon, fox and raccoon, in order to save powder."[45] The change to European guns had occurred much earlier in the Hudson and Housatonic valleys.

Firearms, moreover, had to be repaired by European smiths using materials made by smiths or imported from Europe. Several items in the Wendell account book were for gun repairs. Sometimes, the account book shows, Indians had no guns. Possibly they had already traded them away, or their guns were out of order. In a few instances in the account book, Indians borrowed guns from the trader or took a gun on trial. In these cases, the trader's interest was involved. If his customers could not hunt, he would have no furs. Wendell did not run a pawn shop; on four or five occasions he did, however, hold a few items, such as cloth or beaded bands, for Mohawk Indians, which presumably the Indians expected to retrieve as soon as they could pay back the loan.

Other traders were less scrupulous. By 1721, which was after Wendell had ended his Indian trade, the Common Council of Albany renewed a previous ordinance forbidding the taking of guns or clothing in pawn from the Indians, ". . . by wich means they are rendered incapable to go hunting to maintain themselves and are often inveigled to drink to excesse. . . we do strictly prohibit ye buying, receiving or detaining any clothing or appearle belonging to any Indian or Indians or any of their accutrem'ts (except wampum and Indian jewells). . . ."[46] This practice was another aspect of debt and the fur trade.

Spending Patterns

Because Wendell set a value of either beavers, martens, or guilders on each item listed in his book, it is possible, by working out equivalents, to determine what percentage of payments (either on the spot or promised) was spent for certain categories of purchases. This is not so easily done with goods paid for land, because, as a rule, no values are given for the goods listed; proportions cannot be compared unless hypothetical values are obtained from other sources. However, by examining the seventeen folios or page sections in the account book devoted to the Mohicans, dating from 1696 to 1708, and adding a few Mohican entries which appear on later pages, dating mainly to 1710, it is possible to compute approximately how Mohican credit with Evert Wendell was expended between 1696 and 1710. The computation, although useful, cannot be considered perfect, as values were not entirely consistent from visit to visit.

An amazing thirty-two per cent of the Mohicans' credit was used for alcoholic products. The figure dramatizes the extent to which desire for alcohol undermined the Mohican economy and individual well-being. This expenditure is further documented by examining the lists of items paid for land, such as in the Westenhook examples listed above, in which kegs of beer and rum routinely were included as part of the desired payment. The lost buying power expended on alcohol was not unique to the Mohicans. It is clear from Wendell's account book that members of other Indian nations were obtaining alcohol in similar large proportions.

Before alcoholic beverages in value, however, came items of clothing, including pieces of cloth, for which forty-six per cent of Mohican credit was used. Clothing and alcohol were followed by guns and gun-related items, at fourteen percent. The remainder was spent for all other items, including items like mirrors and tobacco boxes.

However, almost no food items were purchased, suggesting that around 1700 the Mohicans were still relying on their own supplies of meat and fish and on the women's crops of corn, beans, pumpkins and squash. Some of these crops, according to the account book, were being raised on rented or borrowed land. For example, it was noted that a Mohican woman farmed on "the island." This island was Castle Island, also known as Van Rensselaer's Island and as the Patroon's Island. It was located close to Albany where the Port of Albany is situated today. The location was confirmed by the mention of Adriaen Janse, who was reported by Kiliaen Van Rensselaer, the Patroon, to be his farmer on that island.[47] Later, the Mohicans claimed that they had never sold half of the island, and, in the 1760s, one Mohican man, David Annahakenic, about seventy-six years of age, recalled that he was born there and had lived on the Patroon's Island until he was a man.[48] A Mohican woman kept her pigs on the island, according to the account book. This evidence suggests that one or more families of Mohicans were living on Castle Island in the 1690s and early 1700s, practically at the door to busy Albany.

It also is notable that there were no expenditures in the Wendell account book related to housing. References to wigwams in period literature, including deeds, and illustrations on maps indicate the Mohicans and other natives continued in the early 1700s to build their longhouses of saplings, bark, and mats in the traditional Indian loaf shape discussed in a previous chapter.

Summary

From the Wendell accounts, as well as from the lists of goods given for land, emerge the needs of the Indian villages of the late seventeenth and early eighteenth centuries. Blankets and items of clothing, which had long since replaced furs and leather, were the most numerous purchases. The dependence upon duffels and strouds of wool for blankets and body wraps, and on stockings, shirts and jackets for body covering, was nearly complete. Guns, powder, lead and repairs also incurred a high amount of debt at the trading post. Alcohol was draining away precious resources and undermining health and responsibility.

This look at the interaction of the Mohicans with the traders suggests the pressure which dependence on European products placed on Mohican hunters and, consequently, on Mohican communities. Needed products were obtained on credit from fur traders. Mohicans were still hunters, but their methods, locations, and purposes now were different from those of their pre-contact predecessors. Men often went on long journeys over an extended time before returning with furs to pay old debts. To pay for current needs, they took on new debts. Thus debt seemed unavoidable and was a permanent condition, but most Mohicans were still confident that they could go afield, hunt, and return with ample furs to pay what they owed. Meanwhile, family members at home, usually women, children, and older men, followed seasonal patterns of gathering, farming, and fishing, as well as occasionally working for settlers or doing craft work. They might turn to the trader to obtain items, including rum, to sell. Under these conditions native communities competed for space and resources with white settlers in the Hudson Valley and in the Housatonic Valley.

They were now part of the fabric of a mercantile society that related to natives primarily through trade and through land purchases. In this society colonial traders filled important social and economic roles for the Mohicans and other Indian nations. Although some traders were unscrupulous, others were honest and even generous. Traders who wanted to continue in the fur trade had to maintain a satisfactory relationship with their customers. The late-seventeenth century and eighteenth century traders' willingness to extend credit was essential to the Indian need for goods which affected all Mohican communities.

V.
Connecticut:
Transactions with the Mohicans

"[They] Say that if the Indians of Wawyachtenock would come to plant on Tachkanik, the other Indians who live further down will be afraid and could easily be destroyed for they have a very small heart."[1]

BELOW the Massachusetts Mohican community of Wawyachtenok at Westenhook in 1687 were other villagers to whom the Wawyachtenok natives were related. The Wawyachtenoks felt responsible for the other settlements. This mention of the Indians farther down the Housatonic River is one of the earliest references to Indian villages in northwest Connecticut. The Indian location subsequently appeared on a c. 1710 map of New England. The name given on the map was "Kiyaeck," apparently a misspelling of "Wyatiack" or Weatauk.

In 1717 a boundary line between Massachusetts and Connecticut had been finalized. By that date, Mohicans had locations both above and below the border between the two states. Accordingly, this 1717 act formally placed some Mohican villages of the Housatonic Valley community within Connecticut while others now were in Massachusetts. From the Mohican point of view, the separation from fellow Mohicans by a colony line had no meaning and conveyed no special identity. In the years to come, however, the line would determine a different history for each group.

New York Farmers in the Weatauk Area

The Indian village of Weatauk and the village of Wequadnach (Wukhquautenauk) and its neighboring smaller village, on Indian Pond and Mudge Pond north of present Sharon, may have been the communities with "a very small heart" referred to in 1687. There were also Indian wigwams situated by other lakes and streams. In 1707, Robert Livingston noted a "great Indian house" near two lakes called Wanapakaook, on a trip to the Salisbury area. It is not likely that before 1700 the residents of Weatauk, Wequadnach, or the Mudge Pond hamlet were numerous. However, a decade later, these villages were well established, and Weatauk was home to a prominent sachem, Metoxon, and a substantial Mohican population.

Long after the Indians and their villages had removed from the area, in the nineteenth and early twentieth centuries, they were remembered in local oral traditions:

"At the foot of Indian Mountain, lying partly in the town of Sharon, Connecticut, is one of those many lakes which make this region a landscape of renown. . . .As one climbs the mountain. . .he sees that there are two lakes. . . .The Indians had villages upon each of them, but seem to have preferred the western one inasmuch as their principal village was upon its shore. They called this lake and the village *Wequadnach*, but left the other nameless. . . ."[2]

The western Connecticut area included hunting ranges along the rivers and on the marshes, as well as ample fishing in lakes and streams. Fertile Indian corn lands lay near the Housatonic River. Valuable intervales also were situated along tributary creeks, such as the Salmon River, which empties into the Housatonic.

These alluring tracts had not escaped colonial notice. During a lull in English warfare with the French after 1713, it became safe for enterprising settlers to venture into the countryside. Since the Dutch farmers of Livingston Manor were close to the Westenhook area, it is not surprising that the first colonial settlers came from the Hudson River side of the Taconic hills. By 1719 a few farmers who earlier had been resident on Livingston Manor, according to a 1714 census, took up farms near Salisbury, Connecticut, on Mohican land. They settled beyond Livingston's spur of land which extended into the Lakeville and Salisbury areas, and their farms were outside the boundaries of the rest of the manor as it was shown on Livingston's survey map drawn in 1714. It is likely that they knew the limits of the Manor and wanted to have farms free of rent. Nevertheless, they maintained contact with Livingston Manor.

The first arrivals were William White and Abraham Van Deusen. Van Deusen was previously a manor farmer; William White was an Englishman with a Dutch wife. Although Van Deusen's first home site with its small burial ground was possibly on the edge of Livingston's "spur" into Connecticut, most of the large White-Van Deusen tract along the Housatonic was well east of the spur.[3]

The farmers learned that they must buy their farm locations from New England proprietors, recipients of early Connecticut country grants. In addition, the law required them to obtain Indian deeds from the native owners, who were Mohicans. The old grants had been given without regard to the Indian owners but with the understanding they would be paid when the land was occupied. Moreover, the Mohicans of the area had learned their rights and demanded that the farmers pay them for the land.

On August 22, 1719, therefore, White and Van Deusen purchased land from the local Mohicans. Their first tract was on the Housatonic River east of present Salisbury beginning at the Great Falls, north of present Falls Village, and running up the river to a little stream which comes into the river, then up that stream to a Lake called Kokonhamok, probably Lake Washinee, one of the twin lakes. From there it ran with a straight line south to the end of a hill called Weeatauwash (Wetauwanchu or Weatauk Mountain), then along the same hill to the first point at the falls on the Housatonic.[4]

The New York farmers paid the Indians thirty pounds New York money. Involved were Katrokseet (Catharickseet), Takomp, Conekamow (a woman), and Jhenem (a woman). Indian witnesses were Jhawinan, Sankoonakehek, and Mamanitiseckhan. The latter, Mamanitiseckhan, also known as Shabash, was a sachem of Shekomeko, a village a few miles to the west in Dutchess County, New York.

The following year, on August 16, 1720, compensation was given by the buyers to a woman sachem, Guttatamo, for her claim to the tract sold August 22, 1719. In addition, in the same transaction, she sold more land to White.[5] Guttatamo, a sister of Takomp, may have lived at or near Tachkanick. In 1685 she had been a witness to the sale of Tachkanick to Robert Livingston. The Tachkanick connections of Catharickseet and Guttatamo suggest that some of the Indians of Tachkanick had moved over to Salisbury after sales to Livingston. Catharickseet also had lived at Westenhook.

With their Indian deeds in hand, on August 29, 1720, William White and Abraham Van Deusen obtained from the partnership of William Gaylord and Stephen Noble the tracts bought from the Indians on the west side of the Housatonic River. Gaylord had bought up old country grants given in 1672 and 1687, and obtained additional grant land in May 1720. Gaylord sold to Van Deusen and White about 200 acres "on the Meddowes called Weataug. . .about one mile above the upper great falls."[6] The name Weataug, also spelled Weatauk, Wiataak, Wyatack, and Weatogue, was an Indian name applied to a large triangle in the present Town of Salisbury extending from the Salmon River to the Housatonic River.

Gaylord and Noble also sold 150 acres in the vicinity of the later Housatonic River crossing called Dutcher's Bridge on August 29, 1720 to Ruluff Dutcher, a farmer from Tachkanick in the Manor of Livingston. This farm was apparently covered by White's Indian deed.

Soon two more farmers arrived. On January 14, 1721, Laurence Knickerbacker and Johannes Dykeman of Dutchess County, New York, bought a fifty-acre tract west of the Housatonic River and south of the Great Falls from proprietor Thomas Welles of Woodbury. Welles had purchased an old country grant that had been awarded in 1688 to Robert Ross by the Connecticut Assembly. The deed from Welles expressly stipulated that Laurence Knickerbacker was to satisfy the Indian owners of the lands.[7]

To meet this requirement, an Indian deed for the land was acquired by the newcomers. On January 27, 1721, the Mohicans (spelled Mohokanders in the deed) of Weatauk sold a tract south of the Great Falls to Knickerbacker and Dykeman. The description placed the land on the west side of the Housatonic River, beginning at the Upper Falls to the south of Weatauk. The tract ran from there for two miles along the side of a hill called Wetawanchu by the bounds of the land which William White and Abraham Van Deusen had purchased from the Indians. The boundary continued with a straight line to a point one mile above the waterfalls in a brook called Washokastanook by the Indians. From there it ran south three miles, and then turned easterly to the Housatonic River, from where it ran up the river to the first point.[8] The precise location of the Knickerbacker-Dykeman tract has been described as "beginning at the Upper Falls running two miles along Sugar Hill, then one mile above Lime Rock Furnace and apparently including all of Lime Rock Village to the River."[9]

The Indians involved in these sales were Kennanaquen alias Corlar, Oihaekoam, Sakowenakok, Mamaqueam (a woman), Kanakanwa (a woman), and Mamaquan (a woman). Indian witnesses were Pemoto, Shuhekan, Kawetunk, and Baehus. "Corlar" elsewhere was identified as the area sachem Metoxson. He also was called by the English "Toccunuc," a shortened version of his Indian name. It is interesting that the Mohican leader in the Housatonic Valley was known by a Hudson Valley Dutch nickname, a term of respect. This name, used for the Governor at Indian conferences in Albany, was adopted from Arent Van Corlaer, who had been an important friend to the Indians. The use of a Dutch name suggests some of the Weatauk Mohicans may have come from the Hudson Valley. Metoxon was resident in the Salisbury area by 1714, when he hosted Robert Livingston and his entourage for two days while Livingston was on a surveying trip (mentioned earlier). Possibly Metoxon knew a little Dutch and was comfortable with the Livingston farmers at Weatauk, who still spoke Dutch at home.

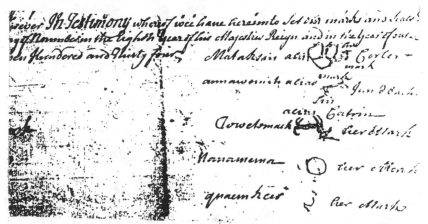

Mataksin (Metoxon), the first signer on this Greene County, New York deed, was known as Corlar. An important chief in Connecticut, he later moved to a village near Freehold, on the Catskill Creek. Three women, including Towetemack (Catrin) with her inverted deer, also signed.

New York Archives, Land Papers, 11:142

Indian locations in Salisbury may have been scattered. One historian from the area wrote that in 1720 the Indians had a village east of the Twin Lakes' North Pond (this might be a wigwam seen by Robert Livingston) and that two groups of wigwams were near Dutcher's Bridge. One site was on White's farm. The farmers with their families soon made a viable community associated with the

Indian settlement. The combined community came to be known by
the name of Weatauk, the Indian name.

The c. 1710 map noted previously placed the Indian community
at the location of today's Salisbury village on a tributary of the
Stratford (Housatonic) River. The map was derived from very old
maps of the mid-seventeenth century but had been updated along the
New England coast. It was one of the first maps to include the
Housatonic River.[10]

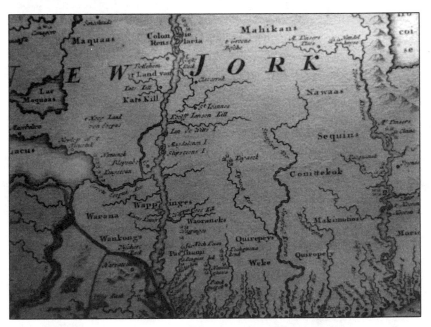

A map of c. 1710 included Kiyaeck, *a misspelling of* Weatauk, *on the Salmon
River at later Salisbury, Connecticut. Few early maps acknowledged the presence
of the Housatonic River, here called the Stratford River, as this map did. The
map was derived from old Jansson-Visscher plates of the mid-seventeenth century
but, printed by a leading German mapmaker, had been updated with new
information along the New England Coast.*

Nova Anglia Septentrionali Americae Implantata, *printed by J. B. Homann,
courtesy of James Hess, Heritage Map Museum, Lititz, Pennsylvania*

The name Weatauk, Wiataak, Wyatiak, or Weatogue was in
common use and appeared on a few eighteenth century maps.
"Wiataak" was shown east of the New York border in Connecticut

on a c. 1726 map of New York grants prepared by Cadwallader Colden, New York's Surveyor General.[11] Colden placed the hamlet on a small stream parallel to the Westenhook (Housatonic) River; he evidently knew only that Weatauk was on a small river near the Housatonic. Later the community, correctly located on the Salmon River and spelled Wyatiack, was shown on the Sautier map of 1779.

Because the Mohican chief, Metoxson, had promised to defend the farmers when they paid him for their land, the farmers evidently preferred to be close to the Indian locations for safety. It was a period when French attacks were rumored. After the initial land sales, colonial farmers and Mohican residents of Weatauk lived not far apart in the present Salisbury area. This association was recollected as peaceful, and the natives, in the old Mohican tradition, were willing to protect the settlers. Once again, the Mohicans were able to sell land without suffering serious consequences.

This comfortable arrangement, however, came to an end in the 1730s. On June 19, 1729, the Weatauk Indians, led by Metoxson, sold an L-shaped tract of land west of land they had sold earlier to speculators who had no intention of living among them. The Mohicans gave a deed to Andrew Hinman and Thomas Knowles of Woodbury, Connecticut, for a tract lying in the northwest corner of Connecticut, "at or near the place known by the name of Weatauck." The tract began at the Massachusetts line opposite a pond called Panaheconnok and ran southward to this pond and from the pond southward on the high land to a point opposite the Great Falls in the Housatonic, then turned eastward to the Great Falls. From the Falls it ran southwest with a straight line to a pond called Tautauquanock-paucok (probably Lake Wononscopomuc) and from the pond went west to wherever the dividing line between the colonies of New York and Connecticut might be set, then up that line to the Massachusetts border. According to a second description in the deed, it was bounded north by the Massachusetts line, east on the lands purchased by the people of Weatauk and the Housatonic River and southward on the lands purchased by Dykeman in part and in part on Hinman's own lands or lands purchased by Richard Sackett, and west on the place where the line might be settled between New York and Connecticut. Richard Sackett's Connecticut land was south of Salisbury and included much of neighboring Sharon. His holdings lay south of Livingston's "spur" of land, which was not mentioned in the deed.

According to the first description, the Indians would have no lands left in Salisbury except in the northeast corner. The second, more general, description of the two given above did not reserve the corner for the Mohicans and led to misunderstandings about the reserved land. The Indians received thirty pounds, or goods to that value. Those involved were Matauckson (Metoxson), Sausenauck-hege, Muckaneege, Pauqennapeet, Nanaconett, and Neshanees. All were identified as Indians of "Weatauke" in the Colony of Connecticut. They apparently expected to continue to share the land, having no way of foreseeing that within a decade their corner of Connecticut would be divided for two townships which would drastically reduce Mohican utilization of the countryside.

Although between 1719 and 1721 the farm tracts of White, Van Deusen, Dutcher, Knickerbacker and Dykeman were bought from the Indians, the Indian land purchases were never approved by the Connecticut Assembly, as required. After the farmers had been on the land for many years, their presence began to be questioned. Documents in the case give a look back into the farm community's relations with the Weatauk Mohicans over the previous decades.

In October 1736, the Dutch settlers presented a memorandum to the Connecticut General Assembly in which they detailed those relations. They noted their fear of the Indians when they first arrived. The Mohican Indians had complained angrily that the government of Connecticut had never given them any consideration for their lands; therefore, the Indians expected the farmers to pay them. According to the farmers, the Indians threatened to dispossess them if they did not "purchase the said grants of them and more lands adjoining them. . . ." The farmers stated that they had made their purchases from the Indians without Assembly approval in their "ignorance though contrary to law."[13] There was no response to their memorandum at that time.

After unsuccessfully proposing that a town be established, Hinman and Knowles reached an accommodation with the Assembly in 1737. They surrendered their Indian deed to the Assembly for a proprietor's allotment of one hundred acres in the projected township. When the new Connecticut township was being parceled out to individual proprietors, the Dutch farmers, anxious to be included, attempted again to justify why they obtained such large tracts from the Indians. Hoping to make a deal similar to Hinman's, the Dutchess County farmers made another, more extensive appeal to the General

Assembly of Connecticut. (Ruloff Dutcher was not included, presumably because he did not have to obtain his own Indian deed.)

In the new petition they described their troubles in settling at Weatauk. They stated frankly that, in the absence of any help from Connecticut, without the aid and support of the Mohicans they could not have survived:

Wetagh   May 12:1738
The Memorial of Lowranc Knikerbaker John Dikman William Whit[e] and Abraham Vanduson of Weatagh Humbly Showeth that thay Being ye First Purchasers of the [early] Grants made by this Assembly and Laid out by thair ordar...Could not posses the Same By reson of the Lands not Being purchased of ye Indian Inhabitants Hou [who] then was many in Number and we but few [We] Could not Injoy the Grants made By ye Assembly to Som [some men] for killing Indians [a reference to the early grants being given as reward for service in Indian wars] without our being killed by the Indians Except we would purches of them Such tracts as we would not have bought had it not ben to Serve the Goverment intrest and save our own Lives and thus in obtaineng four mils [miles] in Length and tow [two] in Bredth as Whits [White's] Dead [deed] Doth apear (yt is the first thair made) Cost in our Money one Hundred & twenty pounds ye othar [deed] Cost Sixty pounds our money Containing thre mils and thre Quartars in Length E [east] & W [west]: and thre in Breadth N[orth] and S[outh] as by ye Dead [deed] doth appear.[14]

The four farmers protested that now some people were laying claim to land and disposing of it without purchasing the Indian right as they had done. They pointed out that it was in the Assembly's interest to have the land purchased from the Indians, rather than to take it by force. They explained that they had purchased the land of the king or sachem of the Indians together with his heirs; as a result, he was ready to defend the right of the farmers to the land if they should desire it. The farmers reiterated that they had lived there through untold difficulty, to the advantage of the government. Moreover, they noted the aid and assistance of "our Sacham" whose influence in deterring enemies from entering his territories had safeguarded several Connecticut townships.

They added that they could not have subsisted without the Indians, having no support through all the late wars from the Connecticut Assembly. They hoped for a reasonable reward in lands for

the money which they had disbursed. In addition, they asked for one
proprietor's right to each purchaser for each deed, pointing out their
purchases from the Indians would cover twenty-five rights in the
township which were to be given out, for which they would give quit
claims. They noted also that a year earlier the Assembly had granted
one hundred acres to Captain Hinman and Captain Knowles, and
they pointed out that their farm purchases had cost more than
Hinman and Knowles' land. Therefore the farmers should have a
better reward. They hoped that the Assembly would find more reason
to consider them than Hinman and Knowles for two reasons, first
because to get rid of the Indians would have been harder than to keep
them in place, for within the farmers' purchase was the "Seat and
throne of them. . ." (the Indian village). Second, if the farmers were
not rewarded, they would have hazarded their lives and done their
work for nothing.

According to these documents, about 1720 the Mohicans around
Weatauk were "many in number." This helps substantiate later
estimates that two or three hundred Indians lived in the Salisbury-
Sharon area. The Livingston farmers claimed that the Indians threat-
ened them and insisted they take more land than they wanted.
Accordingly, the farmers bought large amounts of land to save their
own lives and for the Government's interest. In so doing, they spent
more than one hundred and eighty pounds between the two farms.
New people now were claiming land without any obligation for the
Indian title, thanks to the farmers' purchases.

While the farmers may have exaggerated the initial danger from
the peaceful Mohicans in order to make their case before the General
Assembly, it is entirely likely that the Mohicans had urged them to
take large tracts of land. The Mohicans were not without guile. They
saw in the arrival of the farmers an opportunity to obtain quantities
of much desired cloth, clothing, guns, gun supplies, and alcohol. The
Indian experience in the area, given the slow pace of settlement on
the Livingston Patent, the untouched Westenhook Patent, and Richard Sackett's undeveloped land, had led them to believe the forthcoming farms would not disturb Indian life.

It was pointed out by the farmers in their 1738 testimony that
one sale included the Indian village and settlement of sachem Metoxon. In some land sales, Indians reserved their village sites and
cornfields, but in other cases, such as in the sale of the Westenhook
Patent lands, the sale to Sackett, and here, in the sale of the Salisbury

farmlands, the Mohicans were able to sell even these vital locations and yet remain on site.

As the farmers explained, once they had purchased their land from the chief of the Indians and his heirs, the sachem was ready to defend their right to the land. This was in the nature of a subtle threat by the farmers to unleash their Indian friends against any challengers of that right, a threat that traded on the vague fear of Indian attack felt by many New Englanders. Moreover, as the farmers explained, the aid and assistance of "our sachem," with whom they became friends, had deterred Indian enemies from entering his territories. Attacks by Mohawk Indians on New England towns in the 1720s terrorized the white population. Because of the Mohican presence, it was understood that communities west of the Housatonic River would not be raided. Nevertheless, all Indians were regarded with fear and suspicion.

In 1725 and 1726, Indian wars stirred up by the French threatened. In light of the threat, in 1725 the Mohicans were told to stay on their own lands and not to have contact with any other Indian groups. Such a restriction would have prevented the Mohicans from hunting and from traveling to the Hudson Valley for interaction with traders and fellow Mohicans, and it is likely they were obliged to ignore the order.[15] This restriction was nominally to protect the Mohicans, as friendly Indians could not be distinguished from enemy Indians. It was suspected, however, that the Mohicans might be associated with the Mohawks or the Indians of Canada, and, in fact, the settlers' assertions that the sachem had prevented attacks on the area gave credence to that suspicion.

Alarmed by the prospect of New York proprietors claiming land which extended over the mountains, the Connecticut Assembly in 1702 and again in 1717 ruled that no Indian land could be bought without approval of the Assembly. The new Weatuck farmers had been ignorant of the regulation, according to their own testimony. The western boundary of the Connecticut Colony, particularly in the upper region, was still disputed with New York, and the farmers may have been gambling on New York ownership. The Connecticut Assembly, however, having resolved a jurisdictional conflict with the towns of Hartford and Windsor, took an interest in lands west of the Housatonic. Iron deposits with potential for extraction had been located in the area; in addition, water power for future mills abounded. Thomas Lamb's interest in a location called the Ore Hill south of Salisbury drew him into the area. A grant to Lamb covered part of the ten acres where Abraham Van Deusen had his first home. The cemetery reserved in Van Deusen land deeds was located at the intersection of Town Hill Road and the road to Salisbury.[16]

As the land drew more attention, speculators bought up old grants. In some cases, grants lacked defined boundaries and were intended to be laid out on any place of choice not deeded to someone else. Surveyors walked across the Indians' fields, laying out grant boundaries. Finally, following the definitive Connecticut-New York boundary settlement in 1731, the Assembly, with the intention of establishing towns, considered two townships in the northwest corner of Connecticut, on the west side of the Housatonic, and commissioned the first survey of the older country grants.

In 1732, the Survey Committee reported that the land was suitable to support towns and stated that the committee had surveyed boundaries for two adjacent townships, large rectangles which later became the towns of Salisbury and Sharon. The surveyors were hardly objective about the quality of the land; two of them already owned land in the proposed northern rectangle. Existing country grants in the northernmost town, later Salisbury, covered about 3,500 acres. In addition, several ponds accounted for 2,000 acres and waste land covered 4000 acres more; nevertheless, enough land remained to erect a self-sustaining town, according to the committee.[17] The fact that an indigenous population occupied the territory was not noted and was not a consideration for the Connecticut Assembly. Although it was understood Indians in residence must be compensated in some measure for land they farmed, all ungranted land was considered to belong to the King of England and thus was assumed to be at the disposal of the colony.

Prior New York titles such as those of Robert Livingston and Richard Sackett were not mentioned when the towns were planned, since they were considered invalid after the line with New York was established in 1731. Prior country grants made by the Connecticut Assembly, however, had to be acknowledged and could be exchanged for shares in the new town. Because the Dutch farmers had bought out country grants, they subsequently were allowed to stay in the town. In 1738, the farmers surrendered their two Indian deeds in exchange for one proprietor's right in Sharon.

The speculator, Andrew Hinman, with partners, had taken up old grants amounting to 638 acres, hoping to make a profit on the land's resale to settlers coming to a new town. The parcels were scattered around Salisbury township. As part of their land acquisition plan, Hinman and Knowles secured from the Weatauk Indian leaders, as noted above, an extensive Indian tract.[18] Within this tract, the Mohicans had reserved a corner for themselves more than two square miles in size, extending from the vicinity of the present Twin Lakes (lakes Washining and Washinee) north to the Massachusetts border and east to the Housatonic River. The section included an old burial ground and possibly an Indian fort built for the Mohicans' own protection.[9] This reserve did not include the site of Weatauk shown on the old maps and suggests that the Weatauk Indians planned to settle in a location closer to the river, to the east of their previous site.

Subsequently, Hinman petitioned the Assembly for the establishment of the projected new town. When the Assembly ignored his petitions and a town was not forthcoming, he and his associates finally surrendered their Indian deed in exchange for a 100 acre town grant, as previously noted. However, they reserved large tracts amounting to 550 acres near the south end of Taconnock Mountain, at Wenunkapaugoog (Lake Wononpakook) and adjacent to the latter tract.[20] A shrewd entrepreneur, Thomas Lamb, who was to be involved in future dealings with the Mohicans, bought up much of the Hinman and Knowles holdings. Lamb soon established an iron works in Salisbury. Other investors, preceding Lamb, had an iron works by 1733. The iron works attracted workers and increased interest in settling the town.

Although the Assembly in 1733 had devised a system for selling plots in the town, it was not until 1738 that the process was authorized to proceed. Thomas Lamb was sent on a mission to buy out any Indian claims before the "sale" of the town. In this he was not successful in the Salisbury area because he tried to cheat the Indians, and the deeds he obtained in Sharon, the township below Salisbury, caused a furor. The Indians soon complained that they did not know the contents of the deeds he obtained.

Development proceeded, nonetheless. The Salisbury township was sold off in rights which conveyed to each proprietor a percentage of the land. Many rights were immediately resold to serious settlers and several soon arrived. Roads were laid out and fences and walls around gardens and grain fields soon were erected. Those who held grants, and the Dutch farmers who had petitioned the Assembly, obtained rights in the town. By 1739, the town began to function and soon took the name of Salisbury. The name, Weatauk, however, continued to be used.

The Mohicans near Salisbury on their reserved lands were isolated in their corner and, moreover, were losing land which they believed had never been sold. They claimed that tracts in Salisbury, which had not been given to the agent Lamb in 1738, now were being built upon by the Salisbury settlers. The east side of the river, formerly theirs, was in the hands of the Town of Windsor, and they had no rights there. In 1742, the Mohicans joined with their kinsmen at Sharon in a memorial of protest to the Connecticut Assembly about the taking of their land. They stressed that the Settling Committee had sold all the land and proprietors were improving lands claimed by the Indians, who considered themselves defrauded. After an investigation, a committee appointed by the Assembly decided that all of the town of Salisbury had been purchased from the Indians except for the two-mile square tract at the northeast corner "and this seems to be generally agreed to—both the English and Indians have always understood and now believe that Corner was never intended to be sold neither was it ever honestly sold. . . ."[21]

The Committee found that "one Metoxon. . .is allowed by all to be ye Chiefe Sachem of the indians in these parts." The result was a recommendation that the Mohican chief, from whom purchases had been made in the past, should be given a gift of two blankets, and that his land and improvements in Salisbury should be bought. This was a reference to the Indian reserve. Umpachanee, the chief from Stockbridge, representing the Weatauk Mohicans, said they would sell "for Sixty pounds and not Less."[22]

The Assembly agreed with the Committee report that the Weatauk Indian tract should be purchased. Assigned to make the arrangements, in Weatauk as well as in Sharon, was an unlikely agent, Daniel Edwards, who was afraid of the Indians with whom he was to deal. Unwilling to spend time in a search for tribal representatives, he talked to colonial residents at Sharon about Indian complaints. He then traveled from Sharon north to the Mohican town of Stockbridge, where, he said, he felt safer due to the presence of the English schoolmaster. It is possible, however, that Edwards was sent to Stockbridge by natives at Sharon to find heirs to the Weatauk land, because a leading Indian family from Weatauk, possibly the family of Metoxon, already had moved there.

On his visit to Stockbridge, Edwards inquired for any Indian owners of the Weatauk reserve. He was directed to two members of a family, a woman with a boy of about fourteen in her charge, identifed by the Stockbridge Mohicans as owners of the reserved corner of Salisbury. Thereupon, Edwards drew up a deed for a five thousand acre tract, which the two Indians signed. The payment of sixty pounds he made was far less than a fair price for that amount of land in rapidly growing Salisbury, but it was the amount previously mentioned by Umpachanee. Edwards' frank account of his activity on their behalf was given to the Assembly in May 1743:

> From Sheron proceeding to Stockbridge, where whom ye claimers of ye northwestern [read northeastern] Corner of Salisbury were, and with whom most safely to transact in that affair. . .as I had before noticed [informed] them of your honours' Directions and my purpose to treat with them [I] now published among all the Indians there ye errend on which I came, to ye end I might discover whether they were agreed in allowing ye Title to be quieted [bought out] in any one person or family or whether there were not sundry opposite and contending claimers. . .on all ye Inquiry I could make by ye help of an Indian Interpreter of good report—among them together with Mr. [Timothy] Woodbridge ye Indian schoolmaster who was allso sworn an Interpreter on this occasion. . . .[23]

Finding that the corner of Salisbury belonged to certain family members, among whom was an Indian man named Tautaupusseet "who was abroad at a great distance, and allso an Indian Woman cald Shekannenooti who was present and sister to the said Tautaupusseet, together [with] a child of another brother of said Family [named] Kowannun," Edwards obtained two signatures on the deed. The deed was read in English and also interpreted in Mohican to the signers and to some elderly men of Stockbridge. Edwards thereupon "paid down" sixty pounds and got a receipt written on the deed "with a Promise to procure ye Tautaupusseet on his return (which they expected would be shortly) to execute the same allso and satisfy [pay] him. . . ." Edwards left the deed in the hands of the Rev. John Sergeant to be executed and acknowledged by Tautaupusseet when he returned.

Edwards continued: "As for Tossonee [Metoxon] ye Indian to whom two blankets were ordered I understood he was gone abroad, but would likely return in a short time, so that I neither saw nor acted any thing with him. . . ."[24] In other words, the affair was conducted without the consent of the sachem. The two Indian signers were highly suspect as owners of the Weatauk Mohicans' land. Deeds at Stockbridge identify them as Shawnee Indians living among the Stockbridges. They had appparently been given land at Weatauk (see Appendix B). Moreover, it had been noted that local Indian villages were "no longer exclusively Mohican."[25]

Rev. John Sergeant and teacher Timothy Woodbridge had the opportunity to protect their Indian associates from the loss of their lands but chose not to act. They could have advised Shekannenooti, who was probably frightened, of her right not to sign. They might have suggested she wait for a chance to consult with the Mohicans and especially with Metoxon; instead, with the aid of Umpachanee, the Stockbridge mentors seem to have assisted in the sale. Always conscious of debt, Umpachanee probably felt the Indians should get what payment they could for the land. Although to modern eyes this transaction seems hasty and unethical, Daniel Edwards considered his actions scrupulous, carefully recorded, and legal. Furthermore, he believed he carried out his mission as requested by the Assembly; the Assembly afterwards was completely satisfied with the result.

With this sudden Indian concession of 1743, Indian rights to land in Salisbury were ended in the opinion of the Assembly. It was scarcely more than twenty years since the first Indian deed to farmers White and Van Deusen had been given. The large community of wigwams at Weatauk was soon partially abandoned and resident Mohicans scattered to other villages. One researcher has noted that the houses of Benjamin and Isaac White near the Housatonic River were only four miles from the main village site of Weatauk. This suggests that, as they abandoned older sites on the Salmon River to incoming settlers, Mohicans from scattered locations around Salisbury had congregated within their reserved corner near the river, north of the White farm.[26]

Some Indian residents who left Weatauk may have moved to unsettled regions west of Catskill, New York, on the west side of the Hudson with Metoxon. A few undoubtedly moved to other locations along the Housatonic, including Stockbridge, while others went farther, to Oquaga or to other Mohican sites on the Susquehanna River, or to Pennsylvania, where they were welcome among the Shawnees. Some families and individuals did not leave, but remained quietly in remote locations and continued to make use of traditional resources, developing crafts which they could sell. The Litchfield County, Connecticut, census of 1774 included thirty-five Indians living in Salisbury.[27]

The Mohican Experience in Sharon

Not far away, a second township, to be named Sharon, was laid out south of Salisbury by the committee assigned to survey the town in 1732. The area included two Mohican villages on the lakes near Sharon as well as Mohican families in individual wigwams. Historian Charles Sedgwick wrote in 1842, "Their principal village was on the eastern border of Indian Pond, where they had made considerable clearings, and where their chief resided. There were numbers of them, too, on the borders of the other pond [Mudge Pond] and in the valley of the Oblong River [Webotuck/Ten Mile River]." According to Sedgwick, there also was a "numerous tribe" at Scaticoke (Pachgatgoch), west of Kent, and at Weatauk, in Salisbury, and "many more at Stockbridge."[28] Not far away to the west in New York was the Mohican village of Shekomeko. The area was an Indian haven.

There are few early eighteenth century mentions of the Sharon Indian communities. This was because they were located on land bought from the sachem Metoxon and other Mohicans by Richard Sackett, who made three large purchases among the Mohicans. Sackett's first tract was situated around present Wassaic and Amenia, New York, a 7,500 acre parcel obtained November 5, 1703. The boundaries of Sackett's tract were described in a February 1704 survey by Augustine Graham, Surveyor General of the Province of New York.[29]

The tract began at a place called Querapoquett at a white oak tree. The line ran northeast by the mountains six miles to a white oak tree marked by the Indians; this stood on the east side of Wesaick (Wassaic) Brook. Then the line ran northeast to the top of a mountain and then southeast to a mountain called Weputing. The line then went southwesterly by the ridge of a mountain to a pine tree, and then northwest to the place of beginning. It was bounded on the north and south by marked trees and on the east and west by mountains. Sackett presented his Indian deed and received a New York patent November 2, 1704.

Sackett settled at Kline's Corners in Amenia, where he was the first white settler. He built a house and established "Sackett's Farm";

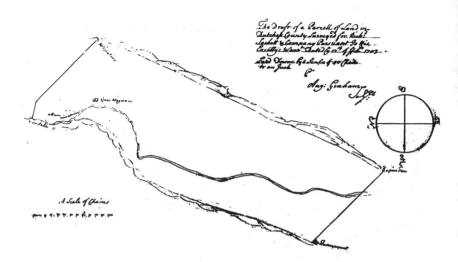

The survey done by Augustus Graham for Richard Sackett in February 1703/4 (1704) shows the Taconic Range on the east (top). Amenia, in Dutchess County, New York, where Sackett established his farm, is near the creek shown and Crays wigwam.

New York Archives, Land Papers, 4: 20

the house was about two miles west of the Connecticut-New York line established in 1731. He lived with his family among Mohican neighbors until his death in 1746. Sackett's house was near where the steel works of Amenia were later erected and his place of burial, now lost, was nearby.[30] Graham's survey of Sackett's property included a picture of the wigwam of an Indian known as Cray, located southeast of the Allum Rocks and not far east of the site of the later steel works.[31] Cray signed an Indian deed for the Little Nine Partners' nearby land on October 20, 1704.

Although the exact date of Sackett's arrival from New York City is not certain, he was well established by 1710, when, in September, Connecticut troops traveling west to the Hudson River on the way to the expedition against Canada stopped at his farm, according to the journal of a soldier. The writer noted that from Sackett's up to Dykeman's on Livingston Manor "is counted 32 miles."[32]

Other land was bought from Mohicans by the Little Nine Partners investors, including Sackett, on October 20, 1704. Sackett was one of the initial partners in the Little or Second Nine Partners Patent, which is to be distinguished from the Great Nine Partners of 1697, situated below it. The Little Nine Partners' land touched Sackett's property on three sides. According to Isaac Huntting, writing in 1897, "The little Nine Partner patent enclosed his tract on the west, north, and east. Its boundary commences on Sackett's northwest corner, which is about a half mile south of Wassaic in Amenia." From there the line went southeasterly by Sackett's north bounds to Weputing, about a mile east of Kline's Corners in South Amenia, which was the northeast corner of the 1704 Sackett grant. The two boundaries were on the same line south to the southeast corner of Sackett's land, along the ridge of mountains about six miles from Weputing. The Little Nines' boundary then turned east to the colony line of Connecticut, then north to the land of John Spragg and Company (the Westenhook Patent), then west along Livingston's Tachkanick lands, which were immediately to the north.[33]

Sackett had obtained some Little Nine Partners' lots which lay east of his original land. In 1731, these fell into a tract called the "Oblong" which was transferred to New York by Connecticut. Furthermore, Sackett later bought additional Indian land in Connecticut, east of the Little Nines' lots lying on the border. In 1726, he applied to the Assembly for a license to purchase Indian land in what was to become the west part of Sharon, with an eastern boundary two miles from the Housatonic River. Although the petition at first was denied, he became the recognized owner of the land, according to neighboring deeds, including the deed for Sharon given June 19, 1726. This deed stated that Metoxon in the year 1726 sold to Richard Sackett and company all the western part of Sharon to within about two miles of the Housatonic River and including the southwest corner of Salisbury, a sale the Indians agreed was honestly made.[34]

Sackett's holdings also were noted in Robert Livingston's Journal of 1714. The Indians with whom Livingston traveled told him Sackett's land extended into Connecticut as far as the center of a large lake called *Awankepakout*. The deed of 1729 to Andrew Hinman and Thomas Knowles notes that the south line of the tract they bought was bounded partly on land of Dyckman, partly by their own lands, and partly by lands purchased by Sackett.

As Sackett extended his holdings beyond the mountains, he apparently hoped he was within the boundary of Dutchess County, New York. In May 1731, when the Connecticut-New York boundary was fixed, the line ran north and south through the lake west of the Indian village of Wequadnach and through Sackett's property. At the fixing of the boundary, about one third of Sackett's combined tracts fell into Connecticut. All of Sackett's Connecticut lands purchased from the Indians east of the line were confiscated. He also found his right to his lots in the Oblong was challenged when New York took possession.

Despite his repeated appeals to the Assembly at Hartford for restitution, Sackett was denied his Connecticut holdings. While he petitioned, the ownership of the land remained in question for a few years. Eventually, Sackett recognized the futility of his effort to regain his possessions and abandoned the effort. Baltus Lott, a tenant Sackett had placed on the Connecticut side of the line, was told to remove from his house and farm. Lott did not obey, and later was able to remain in Connecticut by buying the tract on which he resided from the Connecticut proprietor who had obtained it.[35]

Sackett's worst blow was the discovery that his original purchase fell entirely within the Great Nine Partners Patent of 1697. This situation left Sackett without rights to his home farm. Moreover, in a survey of 1744, lots at the south end of the Little Nine Partners Patent were found to overlap the Great Nine Partners Patent, and this change also caused Sackett to lose land.[36]

Sackett was employed in 1711 by Governor Hunter as one of the Commissioners to oversee the Palatine settlers who were settled on land purchased from Robert Livingston in present-day Columbia County, then Albany County. The Palatines were to manufacture marine supplies such as tar. Although the plan went awry, leaving the Palatines in distress, Sackett remained on good terms with some of the Palatine farmers. In 1715, Sackett was appointed the first county clerk of Putnam County, and in 1730 he became an assessor for the middle ward of Dutchess County. His farm appeared regularly on county tax lists.[37] Despite his service in the county, and his years of tax payments, he never was able to clear the title to his farm. Sackett's children were left to resolve the questions of title to Sackett property remaining in Amenia.

A point two miles east "from Captain Sackett's dwelling house" marked the southwest corner of the lower Connecticut township, which became Sharon.[38] Sackett's farm in Dutchess County in New York was connected to the Sharon, Connecticut area by a well-worn path used by both settlers and Indians. Although he had placed farmer Baltus Lott on the Sackett holdings in Connecticut and had made other improvements, including building a grist mill, there was little overall development on the Sackett tract. The Mohicans in Connecticut were able to use the land sold to Sackett until Connecticut settlement began. The Little Nine Partners Patent, as well, lay dormant for many years, permitting the Mohicans there to hunt and fish as usual. Sackett's relationship with the Mohicans was friendly. He was supportive of the Indian village of Shekomeko and tried to protect the village area when a tract in the Little Nine Partners was to be sold in 1741.

Sackett's claims to Indian land gave the occupants of the various Indian settlements in Sharon considerable protection until, in 1738, the town of Sharon was established by selling proprietor's rights. After Sackett's Indian deeds were declared void, the Assembly directed Thomas Lamb (who made an offer to take on this task) to buy up the Indian lands in Sharon. Lamb was an aggressive land speculator who also ran the iron works. Considered a leading man of the area, he lived at Lime Rock in Salisbury. He had no concern for Indian welfare and was interested, instead, in acquiring land and making a profit on it.

Lamb agreed with the General Assembly that he would obtain "a good and Sufficient deed of Sale, to the Governor and company, of all the Land contained in the Township from all the indian claimers thereof always provided the sd Lamb give bond with one Sufficient Surety to the value of two thousand pounds for his procuring Said deed on or before the 15th day of January next."[39] Thus the Assembly was equally guilty of assuming that establishing the town was merely a matter of paying off the Indians and taking their land. Nothing was recorded by the members of the Assembly regarding concerns for the welfare and future of the Indian community or for the needs of the individuals in it.

Lamb contacted the Indians and they agreed to sign a deed. Once again, they were too trusting. The Indians were paid in money, supplies, and clothes for a tract of land in an agreement with limits they seem not to have understood. When the Indians saw allotments made on their cornfields and in woodlands which they had supposed were reserved for them, they knew they had been cheated. Lamb's representations to them, according to Indian complaints, were deceitful and the deed included land they never intended to sell. It is apparent he had disguised the import of the deed, "signed by the marks of many Indians, who described themselves as of the Indian nation, belonging to Muttapacuck [Muhhekunnuk]. The name of one of the signers of this deed. . .was Toccunuc [Metoxon]."[40]

Before the town was incorporated, a 1739 memorial was sent to the Assembly which notified that body that the Indians of Wequadnach claimed a tract of land in the northwestern part of the proposed township two miles square. This was their village area, which they insisted had never been bought from them.[41] It also was claimed in one of the Indian memorials that Lamb obtained other deeds from unauthorized Indians. This was a reference to a 1739 deed Lamb obtained from John Naunese for a mile wide tract across the south section of Sharon which had been reserved, as they understood, by the Indians.[42]

The Indians grew so upset and restless that the white settlers feared they would be attacked. One concerned resident was the town's minister, Peter Pratt. After listening to Indian complaints, in 1742, he, with Nathaniel Skinner and Jonathan Dunham, agents for the town of Sharon, and Stephen, Nequitimaug, Nanhoon, and other Indians, "petitioned the General Assembly for the appointment of a committee to inquire into the claim of the Indians that Lamb had taken unfair advantage of their ignorance."[43]

The petition pointed out "That many of the Proprietors of Sharon are likewise inclined to believe, that the said Indians, who were the proper owners of said land, did never, to this day sell to the said Lamb or to this government, all the lands in said Sharon or Salisbury, but that they still have an honest right to that said tract where the said Indians now live, as also to one mile in width across the south end of said town of Sharon."[44] It was clear that the intention of the Mohicans was to retain for themselves their village tract in the northwest part of the town. Unfortunately, although the proprietors of Sharon were willing that the Indians should have their land back, these proprietors expected to be paid by the Assembly for their investments or else to receive large amounts of Indian land at the south end of the town in exchange.

The petition also mentioned a supposed desire of the Indians "living at said northwest corner of said Sharon, and others not far from them, that are desirous of being instructed in the Doctrines of the Gospel; to be taught to read the Holy Scriptures. . .and that their children may be educated according to Christianity. . . ."[45] This latter request may have originated in the mind of Pratt, the town's Protestant minister, who by the early 1740s had been confronted with the

Moravian mission at Shekomeko in nearby New York. That mission was attracting Sharon Indians.

An Assembly investigative committee reviewed the known Indian deeds for Sharon, and Salisbury as well, bringing together Indians from Wukhquautenauk (Wequadnach) and Weatauk and some of the English settlers. Their report gives valuable information about the Mohicans of northwestern Connecticut:

That pursuant to your Honour's appointment on ye memorial of Peter Pratt and other agents for Sharon and Neguntemauge [Nequitimaug] and other Indians Living in or Near Sharon we (having first notifyd ye partys Concerned) Repaired to the township of Sharon and on the 13th and 14th Days of this instant October proceeded to Enquire into the several matters Referred to in said memorial and the Several partys concerned being present and having interpreters both of English and Indians we were informed by Deeds and witnesses and would humbly report to your Honours that we find that one Metoxsen alias Calloneck alias Carlow [Corlaer] is allowed by all to be ye Chiefe Sachem of the indians in these parts and that he and his tribe or Nation are the claimers of these Lands not sold and also Claimed all [lands] that have been sold there about.

That the said Metaukson [Metoxon] and other indians in ye year 1726 sold to Richard Sacket & Company all ye western part of Sharon within about two Mile of Ousatunnuk River little more or less and ye southwest Corner of Salisbury - - which sale some of ye Indians who signed ye Deed being present owned to be honestly made.

That afterwards vizt 26th of October 1738 the said Metaukson and other Indians by agreement with and for Eighty pounds Received of Thomas Lamb sold to ye Government and Company [the proprietor's association] the town ship of Sharon except one mile at ye south end which deed and bargain several witnesses Declared was fairly made and well understood by ye Indians.

That in [date illegible] 1738/39 ye said Thomas Lamb procured another Deed from an Indian of that tribe as we understood who is sometime Called John Naunese —— to ye Governor and Company for one mile across at ye south end of Sharon — for nine pounds.

That by sundry deed to Diverse persons given by some of that tribe of Indians the township of Salisbury has been purchased except about (as near as we could guess) two mile Square at ye north east Corner [a reference to the Weatauk reserve] and this seemed to be generally agreed to both by the English and Indians and Con-

cerning the said north east Corner we find that ye Deed to Knowles
and Hinman [given in 1729] describes the lands sold by Certain
Natural Monuments as ponds mountains (etc) In which Description ye said north east Corner is not contained but then the lands
are again bounded by General boundarys viz. North by Massachusetts East by the River which includes ye land at ye north east
Corner but its generally declared both by English and Indians that
they have always understood and now believe that Corner was
never intended to be sold neither was it ever honestly Sold on which
we are of opinion that its most probable that ye corner was never
intended to be sold - therefore we think the Indians who are
Generally allowed to Claim said Corner and for whom as ye Indians
say ye said corner was intended to be Left when ye other was sold
should be quieted by giving them some Consideration [payment]
to resign their claim - which Umpechenee [chief at Stockbridge] on
their behalf Declared they would do for Sixty pounds and not Less
and concerning the north east [error for northwest] corner of
Sharon we find it all to be sold and included in ye aforesaid Deed
to Sacket and that procured by Lamb. Yet from indian evidence
only we are informed that the Indians did and do now think they
might and may live there and the people of Sharon are willing they
should live there if an Equivalent [of land] is given whereupon
considering ye Circumstances of those Indians we think it might
be well to alow them about fifty acres of land to Live on which
appears to be a sufficiency and that on the proprietors of Sharon
securing the same to them an Equivalent of about two acres for one
be given Sharon at ye south end of their town they purchasing the
same of the indians if not already done. As to ye Mile at ye south
end of Sharon complained of we find little or nothing worthy of
Notice about it.

Wherefore upon the whole seeing the Indians' Desire to Live
there [at Wequadnach] and [as they] have made improvements
where they live we therefore recommend it to your Honours to
quiet and favour these indians as aforesaid and considering they are
as we are informed Disposed to be instructed in the Christian faith
we think it might be well to make some provision for that purpose
their number being 18 males fifteen females adult and 17 Children
fourty five in all and further that one Tossaunee [Metoxon] who
on some encouragement given him by ye Committee for Laying
out Lands in Salisbury that they would endeavor he should have
two blankets Resigned [to him] [and that] a Considerable improvement he had made and lived upon in Salisbury should be considered
and Made Easy [paid for] accordingly and upon the matter aforesaid
being settled we conclude the Indians will be easy and peaceable

and friendly and we hope comfortable Neighbors and friends and probably Christian Brethren.[46]

The statement about paying for Metoxon's "improvement" or village location suggests his wigwam was within the Salisbury town center bounds in 1739, near the place where he had been visited by Robert Livingston about twenty-five years before in 1714. It implies he did not live in the Indian reserve in the northeast corner of the town near the Housatonic River. Possibly he moved to Greene County, New York, west of the Hudson, about this time. Metoxon originally may have come from the Hudson Valley; in 1734, while he was still presumably at Weatauk, he had participated in a sale of land at Coxsackie, in Greene County. A deed later places him on the Catskill Creek west of Leeds. Metoxon was established there before November 1743, when Moravian representatives visited him.

The Connecticut Assembly's committee members were Thomas Fitch (later Governor), Daniel Edwards, who soon dealt again with the Mohicans on behalf of the Assembly, and Robert Walker. While the committee members' report vindicated Lamb's purchase,[47] had their recommendations been scrupulously followed, the questions of land ownership might have been resolved. That solution, however, would have left the forty-five Indians impoverished on an impossibly small fifty acres.

After receiving this report, the full Assembly agreed to establish the fifty-acre reservation requested for the Wequadnach Indians, who presumably would be joined by Indians from Weatauk. Any parcels disputed by the Indians were to be purchased from them, including the northeast corner reserve at Weatauk. Daniel Edwards of Hartford was appointed to "agree with and purchase [the land] of those Indians that have a claim to about two miles square at the north east corner of the township of Salisbury." This was a reference to the Weatauk corner tract.[48] Edwards did not attempt his commission until the following spring of 1743. He then went to Sharon, where he spoke of the Indians' concerns, not with the Indians but with Sharon residents, and from Sharon he went to Stockbridge, as related previously.

Despite these efforts and the Assembly's commitment to a fifty-acre reserve at Sharon the tensions were unchanged. The Indians felt nothing had been done. The Wequadnach Mohicans remained in their village but someone else owned it. They had unresolved claims, also, to two hundred acres of woodland on a nearby mountain. Probably a few Mohican residents of Weatauk joined the Sharon Indian population about this time, after the sale of the Weatauk corner, straining Wequadnach's limited resources even further. In 1743, Edwards reported that the Indians were not agreeable to a proposal to give colonial proprietors of Indian land two acres of land from the south part of town in exchange for each one acre in the Indian reserve.[49] Thus, despite the promise, official transfer of the fifty acres of land agreed to by the Assembly never took place. Moreover, Edwards said, the Indians complained they needed at least two hundred acres, as the ninety acres presently used was insufficient to supply firewood.[50]

There were other frictions. At a town meeting on March 25, 1745, it was voted "that Mr. John Williams shall be an agent to go to the Assembly in May next to get a taxing on our lands, and to acquaint the Assembly that the Indians are uneasy about their lands." At the same meeting, another injustice suffered by the Mohicans was noted and an attempt was made to redress the wrong. The meeting voted "That William Spencer and Garrit Winegar shall be a committee to agree with the Indians about the mare that Samuel Dunham, Jr. unjustly took from them."[51]

This latter case shows that, as the community of colonial settlers expanded at Sharon, other problems besides land appropriation arose. Especially during the war years of 1744-1748, the community was anxious to resolve these issues in order to placate the Indians. A common irritant was damage to Indian fields by roaming cattle and pigs. In colonial farming, cattle and pigs and horses were allowed loose to forage in fields and woods. Land on which corn, wheat or vegetables were cultivated was enclosed with sturdy fences of planks to keep roaming livestock from destroying the crops. The Indians, however, had never fenced their gardens. When Indian plots with their essential maize, beans and squash were savaged by roaming cattle and hogs, Indians sometimes shot the offending animals. Damage to Indian fields was occurring in Sharon. By the end of the year, the town responded again: "on December 8, 1745, William Spencer and Thomas Hamlin chosen fence viewers, both for the English and Indians, and to prize [appraise] the damage done to the Indians, in their fields, by creatures belonging to this town."[52] Payments, even when made, were not as useful as having corn stored for winter.

In spring of the following year, the problems continued: "March 6, 1746, Voted, That Messrs. Timothy Phelps and Garrit Winegar, be a committee to enquire about the damage complained of by the Indians, and if they can find just reason to suspect any particular person to have done said damages, that they, on behalf of said Indians, bring actions against him, the cost of which the town will defray, if no particular person can be convicted of it."[53] These cases of damage were recorded only after the town was established. There undoubtedly had been tensions earlier over livestock, theft, and acts of vandalism by the Christians which were not recorded. Moreover, Indian meetings, dances and the Indian manner of living frightened the conservative town population around the Indian village.

Some proprietors in the Sharon community, nevertheless, were sympathetic to the Indians and felt they had received bad treatment. On May 16, 1747, the Indians at Wequadnach petitioned for recognition of their village tract, which they claimed they had never sold, and protested incursions by proprietors and squatters. At this time they requested that a tract of 246 acres be reserved for their community. Their English lawyer, William Spencer, who donated his services in an attempt to help them, also had been named a fence viewer in order to represent the Indians.[54] Their petition follows:

To The Honourable General Assembly of This his majesties Colony of Connecticut: In New England now Siting at Hartford In May Anno Dommini 1747. The Memorial of us The Subscribers: Indians: Inhabiting In the town of Sharon In the County of Newhaven and Colony aforsd Humbly Sheweth

Whereas: Some time past upon a motion by us made to your Honours Concerning our Lands in Sharon: your Honours were then pleased to appoint and send a Comitee to Examine Into the manner of Sales of our Lands: to See wheither we had made Sale of all or not: and Ever Since we your Honours memorialists have not understood more or Less of The matter. we would once again Humbly Request of your Honors: That of your Special favour: and Goodness: to us the poor Indians Inhabiting in Sharon aforsd; That we may be allowed a Small: tract of Lands on which we have Lately built & where we have made our Improvements att a place Called the Indian ponds: in the northwest Corner of The township of Sharon aforsd: our humble Request to your Honours: is That we may be allowed About two hundred and forty six acres: if your Honours shall think fit: which Tho Small yet will be to us a suficient accomodation, and That your Honours if your wisdom Shall Think fitt to Grant That The Same may Speedely be Established unto us we being In fear of being turned off by Some person

or other: and we then must be destitute of house or home for our
Selves and families or of the means for a poor Livelyhood which
we now enjoy and further we would humbly Request that your
Honours would Consider us in our Ignorant State and Condition
for want of the means of Lerning and Education which we are
destitute of: and of your Honours Grace and favour find out: some
way That we may have a School Amongst us to Lern to read - - - -
That we may both Know our Duty and how to perform The same:
which Requests if your Honours Shall take into your wise Consideration: and Grant in some way or other as your: Honours Shall
In your wisdom Think best for us and your Honours memorialists
as in Duty Bound Ever pray ————————— Sharon, May ye 16, 1747
Quotomack *)* alias Moses (his mark)
Samuel *S C* Cockisnec (his mark)
Jannatt *L* alias Jonathan (his mark)
Ackawahanit *7* alias Bartholomew (his
mark)
Tsacoke *X* alias David (his mark)
William Spencer, Attorney
for the memorialists

Witnesses:
Sauchewawaha *)* Benjamin (his mark)
Timothy alias *)* Cowpoise (his mark)
Umpawahanit (his mark)"[55]

Quotomack was Nequitamaug, a sachem. Umpawahanit, a witness, probably was Umpachanee, chief at Stockbridge. The signers
had biblical names as a result of baptism. Moravian missionaries had
been active in the area since 1740; in 1742 a Moravian mission
officially was begun at the nearby Dutchess County Mohican village
of Shekomeko. By 1743 the Moravians had established a tiny mission
across the lake from the village of Wequadnach; members of the
Sharon Indian community became Christians through this, their own
Moravian mission, or at Shekomeko. Their Moravian connection was
another cause for friction between the Mohicans and the settlers, who
were afraid that the German Moravians would lead the Indians into
Catholicism and an alliance with Canada. At the height of war
hysteria in the 1740s, Moravians were forbidden to preach in New
York and Connecticut, and in 1745 the missions nominally ended.

No concrete results came from the Indian petition to the Connecticut Assembly, although the minister at Sharon was urged to

teach the Indian children. Although the natives now had a tacit understanding with the Assembly that they could retain ownership of their small fifty-acre village tract, the Indians were concerned that they would be turned out of their village by a Sharon proprietor. The Mohicans of Wequadnach began to consider moving away. Some members of the Wequadnach community considered following the Moravians to Pennsylvania, to which the Moravians retreated after being ejected from their missions in New York.

Meanwhile, more land was lost. "Around the periphery of the tract apportioned to them, by the Assembly, individual Wequadnach members had sold small pieces of property merely to subsist. Most of the land went to Thomas Barnes, a newly arrived investor who purchased a large tract next to Wequadnach."[56] Matters came to a head when in July 1752 Bartholomew Ackawahanit and Moses Nequitimaug, listed above on the 1747 petition, sold the reserved village tract to Thomas Barnes for fifty pounds. Other Wequadnach members protested the sale, which apparently was not approved by the community at large, many of whom were absent. Nonetheless, Barnes could now petition the Legislature for title and took possession of the village tract.

With this act, the Mohicans of Sharon were dispossessed of the last of their land by an action reflecting strong internal divisions among members of the group. The tensions were the result of the loss of tenure which had been unfolding for a decade. Although a few Mohicans reportedly remained at their Indian village on the lake, others scattered. Some "carried with them a deep sense of the wrongs they had suffered," complaining that they had been cheated and "often giving significant hints of . . .resentment which was rankling. . . ."[57] In the fall of 1754, one of the Mohicans, Timothy Cowpoise, who had gone to Pennsylvania to join the Moravians, returned to Sharon. "Timotheus complained to local farmers that the tract laid out by the Assembly's committee had never been respected or appropriately placed in the Wequadnach community's possession." Timothy supposedly cried out to one farmer, "I vow it is my land, and you know it. I swear it is my land, and I will have it."[58]

At last, Timothy, too, let go. He took "two pounds ten shillings of New York currency and eight pounds of the old tenor of Connecticut" in exchange for a quitclaim given to Thomas Barnes.[59] He moved to Stockbridge, where his name, Timothy Cowpoise, appears on several deeds.

VI.
Changing Beliefs

". . .in the morning she would be gone. . . But by night she would be back here again. Then soon after, we would hear that she had been up to Stockbridge, on the day she wasn't here. She used to visit the Indians up there, and everybody said that she was a witch."[1]

In 1720, the Mohicans from the Hudson River attended an Indian conference at Albany. They apologized for not bringing more furs to the conference and admitted their poverty. Although Indians expected gifts at conferences, there were always reciprocal Indian gifts for the Governor or Indian Commissioners. This year there would be few Indian gifts: "Wee are very glad to see You but are very poor having not been out a hunting and therefore have not much to present you withall or make proposition according to Custom--we had some presents from you Last year but they are all wore out and we are Naked and bare."[2] Peter Schuyler, acting for the Governor, scolded them for "Drinking and Laziness." Schuyler was a partner in the Westenhook Patent, a tract of undeveloped land to the east on which Mohicans had been left in peace. After advising them to be in future sober and active, he gave them the expected presents of ammunition and clothing.[3]

By the eighteenth century, Indians in the east found it difficult to pay for basic needs--the blankets and clothing, tools and utensils, alcohol and guns that they had adopted in the previous century after the Dutch arrived. Most Mohicans on the Hudson River considered themselves poor. Mohican women adapted by working for white families; others sold corn in Albany. Men also adapted: they acted as guides for travelers or as messengers, collected bounties for killing wolves, and sold deer meat, deer skins, wild fowl, and firewood.[4] These occupations, along with the family cornfields, sustained Mohican families when furs could not be found for exchange. Some natives, mostly women, married into colonial families; their descendants usually left Indian life behind.

Although they had altered their culture in many ways, few Mohican men were ready to give up hunting. Nor were they ready to give up their communal responsibilities, which included supporting old people and helping widows, or their gender-related divisions of labor. In Stockbridge deeds, Mohicans continued to refer to themselves as "hunters." While they lived at Stockbridge, they hunted and fished for their families. The women gardened. Men who tried farming were teased by members of other tribes. The general reluctance of most Indians to change their traditional life patterns was noted by observers. George Henry Loskiel, one of the Moravian missionaries of the eighteenth century, described how natives were loath to change their manner of living.[5] Indian nations across a wide spectrum had similar responses to change. David Humphreys, secretary of the Society for the Propagation of the Gospel, after the Society's Church of England mission to the Mohawks failed, wondered why the Mohawks, who had lived beside the English for many years and watched them raise ample crops, should "still refuse to till their Ground, or learn any manual Art."[6]

New Englanders, nevertheless, urged the Mohicans and their fellows to adopt English ways. The goals of reformers were to remake the Indians, first by bringing them to accept the Christian faith and second by teaching the men to be farmers and artisans and the women to be farm women skilled in women's crafts. The Christian faith involved education. To sing hymns and read the catechism as well as to fill the working roles envisaged for them, Indians needed to learn to read and write. Therefore, schools were usually proposed as part of the formula for making Indians over into Christians and for changing their lifestyles.

Most Indians in the eighteenth century, however, were still living in their world inhabited by spirits. According to Loskiel, the Indians saw reading as a magical experience. He explained that natives, when something was read to them, "believe that a spirit speaks secretly to the reader, dictating whatever he wishes to know. . .Others think, that the paper, when written upon, can speak to the reader, but so as to be heard by no one else. Therefore a letter, particularly if it be sealed, is considered a very sacred thing."[7] As a result, the prospect of engaging in the mystery of reading attracted many Indians to the Christian schools.

Reading and writing had long intrigued the Mohicans, and they had made attempts to imitate writing. Having noted that some Dutch and English placed symbols for their names on land transactions, a few Mohicans had learned to use their initials as their pictographic signature on deeds, long before there was formal teaching. Loskiel noted that after a document was read, a pictographic mark was added to signify agreement: "each puts his mark to his name, which is often nothing but a crooked line or a cross, sometimes a line in the form of a turkey's foot, a tortoise, or some other creature."[8] These marks, found on Indian deeds and treaties, began to be replaced with initials and names once the Indians began to study reading and writing.

For practical reasons, Mohicans needed to understand surveys, land deeds, treaties, and accounts. They were aware that they were being deceived in land transactions and in trade, but lacked the ability to fathom contracts and account books. In response to Indian complaints that the amount of land described in some deeds was not what they were told, a law had been passed in New York requiring that a competent interpreter fully translate every land transaction to the Indians.[9] As a result, many eighteenth century Indian deeds contain a statement that the contents of the deed have been translated to the Indian sellers and name the translator, making fraudulent presentations more difficult. Despite this improvement, the Indians remained dependant on interpreters. While most interpreters did their best, few had an extensive grasp of the Mohican language.

Religion

The general Mohican reluctance to adopt Christianity bemused English well-wishers and observers. Finding the Mohicans to be "good" people, the jump to the Christian religion seemed easy to those who had been reared in it. Christians could not resist haranguing the natives about Indian beliefs. The result was that Indian spiritual practices often were under attack. For example, the Christians took issue with the Indian belief that Manitou (a capricious spirit), rather than the Great Spirit (similar to God), caused death, while the Indians could not see why God, if good, would cause death. Indians, including the Mohican sachem Umpachanee, of Housatonic, incredulously asked why many whites lived "vicious" lives so contrary to their professed religious beliefs.[10]

In the eighteenth century, natives continued to live in a world peopled by spirits. Loskiel observed, "They know nothing of the causes of natural phenomena; nor do they desire to be informed of them. Thunder they conceive to be a spirit dwelling in the mountains and now and then sallying forth to make himself heard. Others imagine it to proceed from the crowing of a monstrous turkey cock in the heavens; others from enraged evil spirits."[11]

Although the Indians retained many of their old religious practices, their religion was evolving. The influences were many: appeals to family or village idols no longer brought ample crops and good hunting; Mohican horizons had been broadened with information about Christians, kings and complex worlds overseas; the Indian spiritual world receded as natives acquired new technical skills which replaced the handiwork of spirits with prosaic cause-and-effect knowledge. For example, when guns were first encountered, they seemed magical; once mastered, they were not perceived as very mysterious. Reading words on a page, which seemed to require the help of spirits, proved routine once letters were learned.

Traditional observances were weakened as Indian communities became scattered and less tightly controlled. For example, the old reverence for animal spirits was damaged by the pressures of the fur trade. After Europeans arrived, Indians of most nations trapped many more animals than were needed for clothing or coverings in order to obtain foreign products. Traditions stipulating selective hunting to propitiate animal spirits and to assure a future population of game for food and furs were ignored. As Hendrick Aupaumut, the Mohican historian of the 1790s noted, in the old days, his ancestors "were not to kill more than was necessary, for there was none to barter with them that would have tempted them to waste their animals, as they did after the Chuckopek or white people came. . . ."[12]

The Mohicans learned about alternate beliefs by observing the experiences of other Indian groups, particularly the Abenaki and Mohawks, with French Catholic priests. There were Protestant examples, as well. Some Mohawks who were baptized were listed in the First Church of Albany register in the 1690s. In 1704, the Rev. Thoroughgood Moore arrived to be the first English missionary to the Mohawks. Due in part to opposition from fur traders, Moore became disillusioned with the project, saying that "such Christians as the Indians saw gave them a sad notion of Christianity." He returned to New York.[13] In 1708 the Episcopal chaplain of the

Albany and Schenectady garrisons, the Rev. Thomas Barclay, was appointed to instruct the Mohawks. Barclay, who "did dayly preach good things to us the Mohawks" left for a better paying position.[14] To the Mohawk's surprise, he claimed as his own the land they had offered him for use while he was their minister, land intended to be church property.

Despite the general exposure to other faiths, many traditional Indian beliefs persisted and were practiced in the 1700s. Moravian missionary George Henry Loskiel wrote of the Delawares in the eighteenth century, "They believe the old doctrine of their ancestors, that all Indians, who have led a good life, will come to a good place after death, where they will have everything in abundance, and may dance and make merry; but that all who have lived in wickedness, will rove about without any fixed abode, and be restless, dissatisfied, and melancholy."[15] Living Indians feared these roving spirits of the dead, especially at night.

The perceived Mohican relationship with the troublesome spirit called Menutto or Manitou had been noted long before, in 1630, by Johannes de Laet, a Dutch scholar, who had heard from travelers that the Indians served the Devil and called him Menutto.[16] Similar Mohican worship was explained by Robert Livingston about 1700 in a letter to Lord Bellomont: "God, they [the Indians] say, is good and lives above. Him they love because He never do's them any harm. The devil they fear and are forced to bribe by offerings, etc., that he do them no harme."[17] By the eighteenth century, eastern natives were likely to refer to Manitou as the Great Spirit, having lost the distinction between the good spirit and the capricious one. This was probably because of exposure to Christian doctrine.

Lesser spirits helped the Mohicans cope with Menutto/Manitou. A clerical informant who visited Mohicans of Sharon, Connecticut, said, "These Indians were under the direction of five chiefs called Mughoca. They had an Idol which they worshipped as God, and committed to the care of an old squaw. This Idol, [they believed] though inferior to the great God that governed the world, was nevertheless invested with power sufficient to repel those evils brought upon them by Mutonto [Manitou], or the Devil, and in case he [the idol] refused or neglected to afford them assistance, they would severely chastise him."[18] Among the Mohicans at Shekomeko, devotion to another family idol passed down through the women proved a stumbling block to Moravian teachings. There is mention of doll or animal idols in Mohican villages in other correspondence of the eighteenth century. At Kaunaumeek, David Brainerd believed that he had weaned the Indians from idol worship but Indians who had not been converted continued the old ways.

Indians continued to practice pow wows, which were gatherings for religious or social purposes. The "Duke's Laws" promulgated by James, Duke of York, for New York in 1674 contained a prohibition against Indian gatherings for pow wows: "No Indian whatsoever shall at any time be suffered to Powaw or perform outward worship to the Devil in any Towne within this Government."[19] However, pow wows continued wherever Indians resided. Indian ceremonies included chants and dancing. "The dancing takes place either in a large house or in the open about the fire. The men lead in the dance, the women closing the circle. Such is the exultant shouting on these occasions that it can be heard two or three miles away," wrote a Moravian missionary in Ohio in the mid-eighteenth century.[20]

When it was opportune, the Indians could be encouraged by whites in their old ways. For example, Sir William Johnson, when he needed Indians to fight for him during King George's War, did not hesitate to invoke the old war customs of the natives. At a meeting of several nations with Sir William, at which they agreed to fight with the English against the French, he offered a War Belt. "A Seneca chief laid hold of it, sung the War song and danced. The Shawanese King did it next, and then the Delaware King with remarkable warmth; after that the chief Warriors of the River Indians danced and sung, and so it went round through every nation at the Meeting. . . ."[21]

Hooting, shouts, dancing, rhythmic noise, and fires during pow wows frightened white settlers of New York and Massachusetts, veterans of New England's Indian wars, who imagined attacks on their houses were about to begin. Moreover, some Protestant settlers were outraged by any exhibition of an unorthodox religion. Pow wows continued to be held, nevertheless, despite the prohibitions. Stories of noisy eighteenth century Mohican pow wows held near Great Barrington, Massachusetts, were recalled in nineteenth century history books. In 1744, the missionary David Brainerd wrote that, due to his efforts, the Mohicans of Kaunaumeek had almost abandoned their "Heathenish custom of dancing, hallooing, &c." [22] Underlying these ceremonies was a continued belief that spirits controlled every aspect of Indian fates.

Other Indian beliefs were recorded by John Heckewelder, a Moravian missionary of the second half of the eighteenth century. Heckewelder's Indian contacts included Mohicans and Delawares. He wrote about the Indian reliance on shamans or conjurers called "pow wows." (The term *pow wow*, spelled various ways, including *pauwaw*, could mean either the ceremonial leader or the ceremony itself.) John Sergeant, the Stockbridge minister, wrote in 1735 that the Mohicans "us'd to have an high opinion of these Pawaws (whose character answers pretty well to the vulgar notions of Wizards and Conjurers) and tell stories of the great feats which they can do. . .There may be something, for aught I know, in what they say; but I am apt to think they are very much impos'd upon by some kind of Pretenders, as the rest of the ignorant part of the world is."[23]

These magical persons, most natives still believed, could cure the sick or control the weather. They could contact spirits and take the forms of animals or birds. Metoxon, the important sachem of the lower Berkshires, for example, was considered to be a wizard.[24] Shamans could journey through the air. As late as 1909, an anthropologist visiting Indians of southern Connecticut (who were not Mohican) was told a story of a woman whose name was Viney Carter. "She could do a great many things that no one else could. Some evenings she would be here, and in the morning she would be gone, nobody knew where. But by night she would be back here again. Then soon after, we would hear that she had been up to Stockbridge, on the day that she wasn't here. She used to visit the Indians up there, and everybody said that she was a witch."[25] Otherwise rational Indians, Heckewelder noted, could not be talked out of this ingrained willingness to believe the physically impossible.[26] This very human trait is not so surprising considering the persistence of superstition in many modern populations, despite scientific knowledge.

Many Indians believed in witchcraft. Heckewelder recorded the Indian acceptance of the casting of a spell on a person by an unknown conjurer: "The moment that their imagination is struck with the idea that they are bewitched, they are no longer themselves. . . ."[27] Heckewelder noted that not everyone believed these things, but some felt obliged to pretend they did, to avoid trouble. Moreover, in 1734, the teacher at Stockbridge was assured that not all Mohicans had the same beliefs. Some were atheists, he was told, and did not believe in a superior being, while others believed the Sun was a God, or the residence of the Diety.[28]

Mohican religion was interwoven with history. Besides the traditional story of their origins in the west, which was recited by
Mohicans, ancient stories of creation and traditions of clan origins
were retained into the eighteenth century. Missionaries, however,
once they had the confidence of the natives, urged them to abandon
traditional ceremonies which would perpetuate their former religious
beliefs. Converted Mohicans usually put most of the old stories and
rituals behind them and substituted the rituals and ceremonies of
Christianity. For example, when Abraham of Shekomeko, became a
Christian, he was ready to burn all idols, which now seemed to him
useless. Occasionally, secret idol worship continued within family
wigwams of Christians, especially where converted Indians and non-
Christians lived together.

A London Trip for Etowaukaum

On April 19, 1710, a Mohican sachem, Etowaukaum, was one of
four Indian chiefs who rode in a coach through the streets of London
to a visit with the Queen of England. (The other three travelers were
Iroquois, and included TeYeeNeenHoGaProw or Hendrick, a Mohawk leader; SaGaYeanQuaPrakTon or Brant, a Mohawk; and Oh-
NeeYeathTonNoProw or John, of Canajoharie.) One of the goals of
the Indians' visit was to request that English missionaries be sent to
instruct the Indians in the Christian religion. Etowaukaum's willingness to ask the Queen for a missionary signaled his interest in
Christianity for the Indians. While in London, he conducted himself
with dignity, as did the others, and seems to have been a valuable
emissary to send on such an unusual mission. Some Mohawks already
had been baptized by either the Jesuits or by the Reformed ministers
at Albany and had Christian names. The Mohawks under Hendrick,
after intermittent experience with French priests and after ineffectual
English efforts extended from Albany, were anxious to admit a
permanent English missionary into their own territory.

Accompanying the Indian group was Colonel Peter Schuyler,
soldier, trader and politician. He had served as Albany's first mayor
and as an Indian Commissioner and was respected and trusted by the
Iroquois, who called him "Quidor," or Peter. Less well-known is
Peter Schuyler's long association with the Mohicans, as well. Schuyler
was familiar to the Mohicans who visited Albany for conferences. By
1688, Schuyler had obtained 800 acres near the New England path at

The "Four Indian Kings" who went to London included Etowaukaum (E Tow Oh Kaom), Sachem of the Mohicans, at bottom right. The paintings were done from life as miniatures on ivory in May 1710 by Bernard Lens, junior. The set was engraved by his father, Bernard Lens, senior.

Courtesy of the Albany Institute of History and Art

present Red Hook in Columbia County from the Mohicans. In 1690, he led a force that included Mohicans in a successful raid on Canada.[29] In 1703 and 1704, Peter Schuyler, with Dirck Wessels and others, secured land from the Mohicans at Westenhook on a long-term mortgage as a result of trade goods which he and fellow-trader Wessels had advanced to them.

In July, 1709, Lt. Governor Col. Richard Ingoldsby was among the Albany leaders who recruited the River Indians and the Mohawks for a planned expedition to attack Canada, and Peter Schuyler was one of the expedition's commanders. As a soldier, he had dealt with many Mohicans and probably knew Etowaukaum personally. The following year, in 1711, he enlisted fifty-four River Indians, as well as nineteen Indians from the Manor of Livingston, to march on another proposed expedition against Canada. In 1720, Peter Schuyler was still dealing with the Mohicans. As head of the Governor's Council, acting in the place of the absent Governor, he renewed the covenant chain with them and advised them to "behave your selfe as Dutiful Childrin and keep your selves sober and eat Drink Hunt and Plant in peace."[30]

Etowaukaum may have been included in the 1710 journey not only because he was an important sachem, but because the River Indians had participated with the Iroquois in the English campaign against Canada the summer before. This 1709 expedition against Canada had been abandoned without notice, leaving the colonies embarrassed and in debt and their Indian allies frustrated and annoyed. The trip overseas the following year was spurred by the hope Queen Anne and her advisers could be pressured to carry through on a future expedition.

In 1710 Etowaukaum already was known by the Christian name, Nicholas. He was a handsome man; the delegates were described as "within an Inch or two of six foot," with muscular, well-shaped limbs and brown complexions. Etowaukaum's portrait, painted while he was in England, showed his facial tattoos of flying birds and his dark hair.[31] He was described on the oil painting as "The King of the River Nation." John Sergeant, minister at Stockbridge, also referred to Etowaukaum as "Chief of the River Indians." Sergeant knew about Etowaukaum because a daughter of Etowaukaum was the wife of sachem Umpachanee, whose village was at Mahaiwe, on the Housatonic River. This couple, baptized as Aaron and Anna, later lived at Stockbridge and were among Sergeant's converts. Jonas Etowaukaum

of Stockbridge, Umpachanee's son, was a grandson of Etowaukaum
through his mother.

It is probable that Etowaukaum was chief sachem of the Mohicans
early in the eighteenth century, although that assumption has been
questioned. Henry Barclay, the Anglican missionary to the Mohawks, wrote that, except for the Mohawk, Hendrick, the other three
Indians who went to England were not sachems.[32] Barclay, however,
was not likely to have had much understanding of the Mohican
hierarchy. Later, the chief sachem of the Mohican nation was Ampamit, whose village was on Moesimus Island in the Hudson opposite
Schodack Landing. Ampamit was a member of the wolf clan, while
Etowaukaum belonged to the turtle clan, so the two were not the
same person.

Although one purpose of the trip to London was to request funds
for Christian missions among the Indians, the more pressing goal of
the voyage for Peter Schuyler's Albany contingent, which included
Colonel Francis Nicholson, Major David Pigeon and Captain Abraham Schuyler, was to urge the Queen and her advisers to mount
another expedition to attack French Canada. The four Indians were
schooled, probably by Peter Schuyler, to support this proposal. In a
London interview with the Queen at which they presented her with
belts of wampum, the Indian ambassadors reminded Queen Anne
"how in the late lamented campaign against the French the Indians
had put away the kettle and taken up the hatchet, but how the
expected aid from England had not arrived."[33] The conquest of
Canada was so vital to unrestricted hunting and for trade with the
English, the Indians declared (through translator Schuyler), that if the
Queen did not send help, they might be forced to become neutral,
instead of continuing their support for the English, as they preferred
to do.

The Queen listened to this warning at an audience she granted
for the voyagers. While she made no promises about an expedition
against Canada, the request for missionaries was referred to the
Archbishop of Canterbury. He, as President of the Society for the
Propagation of the Gospel in Foreign Parts, in turn referred the
request to the proper Society committee. This was tantamount to
approval. Members of the committee quickly consulted with Peter
Schuyler and the visiting sachems. The committee's recommendations were adopted by the Society before the Indians departed. Two
missionaries and an interpreter would be provided for the Indians; as

well, a chapel, a house for the missionaries, and a fort were to be built at the principal village of the Mohawks. Moreover, the missionaries were to promote the study of English by Indian children and also the education of English youth in the Indian language. Religious texts were to be translated for the Indians, and at "the earnest request of the Sachems themselves" colonial governors would be urged to enforce the laws against selling liquor to the Indians.[34]

The Indian "kings" caused a sensation in London. After being feted, banqueted, and displayed in theaters, and after sitting to have their portraits painted, the four Indians, laden with gifts, left England with the Albany men on May 7. They arrived in Boston on July 15, 1710.[35]

In the English painting done of him, Etowaukaum was depicted with a very large turtle at his feet, indicating his clan affiliation. A note of thanks for the hospitality shown them, which the Indian travelers signed with pictographic signatures, again identified Etowaukaum with the turtle clan. The note, written after the Indians' return to Boston, reminded the Society for the Propagation of the Gospel about the promises made. As a result of their trip, a fort, chapel, and missionary's house were built in 1712 at present Fort Hunter among the Mohawks. The stone house is still standing, now a remodeled private dwelling. The chapel, after over one hundred years, was torn down early in the nineteenth century to make way for the Erie Canal.

Missionary outreach in Mohican territory was not offered for many years to come, although a few opportunities for becoming Christian existed for the Mohicans. The neighboring Abenaki had resident Jesuit priests, Mohicans could visit the Fort Hunter chapel, and there was the possibility of being baptized at the Albany church. Despite this vacuum, learning about the Christian religion was weighed by numerous Indians. There were also some who wanted no part of it. The Dutch-speaking Mohicans on the Hudson had brushed aside the idea in 1720,[36] saying they could not understand a preacher who spoke English, and most of the Hudson Valley Indians remained opposed to becoming Christians. Two decades later, when a Christian teacher was offered to the Mohicans located on the Housatonic River in Massachusetts, the Mohicans there were more receptive. The proposed teacher was to be sponsored by the Society for the Propagation of Christian Knowledge, headquartered in Scotland. This was a Presbyterian group, a different denomination from the English

Queen Anne's Chapel was built at Fort Hunter in 1712, the result of the trip to London made by three Iroquois and Etowaukaum, chief of the Mohicans. The chapel, twenty-four feet square, stood within the enclosure of the fort. It was destroyed about 1820 to make way for the Erie Canal.

Drawing by Rufus Grider in *Old Fort Hunter and Queen Anne Chapel* (225th Anniversary Program), St. Johnsville, NY, 1937

group that had sponsored the Queen's chapel at Fort Hunter.[37] The Scottish group had inherited money earmarked for outreach among indigenous peoples.

The locale for the proposed missionary's work was to be in western Massachusetts rather than among the more difficult to address members of the Mohican population scattered around New York counties along the Hudson River. Moreover, it was anticipated that success with the Mohicans on the Housatonic would lead to approval from the larger Mohican population in various locations on the Hudson River and farther south on the Housatonic. For reasons then unforeseen, the mission eventually did draw many members of the Mohican nation to Massachusetts. Additionally, it was hoped the Iroquois, particularly the Mohawks, viewing what was to be a model community, would appreciate the benefits of loyalty to the English and forego defection to the French.

Within a few years, members of the Moravian sect arrived from Europe; their members were dedicated to bringing the gospel to the heathen. They began work among the Mohicans in Dutchess County, New York, and among Indians in Connecticut. Thus, finally, the scene was set for the establishment of four important Christian missions to the Mohicans.

VII.
Wnahktukook becomes Stockbridge

"Stockbridge. . .is an ancient settlement where the Indians
now live and have land of their own. . .the Indians who lived
about Sexon's swapped their lands there for those at Stockbridge for the sake of Education, they being Christianized.
The Indians informed him they had not sold some of those
lands."[1]

IN 1724, land for two Massachusetts townships at "Housatonack
alias Westonhook" was purchased by the Massachusetts General
Court from the Mohicans then associated with Indian villages
along the Housatonic River. The areas termed Housatonack and
Westonhook were interchangeable. Westonhook, usually spelled
Westenhook, had been defined in the Westenhook Patent as stretching from a falls below the Connecticut border to an undefined point
above present Stockbridge.

Rev. Samuel Hopkins wrote in 1753 of the two proposed Massachusetts towns: "The Land was purchased of the *River-Indians* who
had the native Right; but they reserv'd for themselves two small
Tracts of Land: one lying at a Place they call *Skatekook* and now falls
into the first Parish in *Sheffield* [later Great Barrington]; the other
about 8 or 10 Miles further up the river, which they call Wnahktukook, and is within the Bounds of *Stockbridge*. And at each of these
Places dwell about four or five Families of *Indians*."[2] The term
"River-Indians" in eighteenth century Massachusetts meant the Mohicans who came from the Colony of New York. Many of the River
Indians now lived in Massachusetts.

Despite Reverend Hopkins' understanding in 1753 that two
sections of land were reserved for the Indians, the 1724 deed mentions
only one reserve. It did not set aside the more northern village called
Wnahktukook. There are two possibilities for this omission: one is
that the village was beyond Monument Mountain to the north, and

Monument Mountain originally was intended as the north bounds of
the towns; the other is that Rattlesnake Mountain was intended as the
north boundary, but it was understood that the Indians near there
would remove to the Indian Reservation eventually. It is possible
there was confusion about which mountain was intended as the north
boundary, as each township was expected to be seven miles square
(i.e. a total of fourteen miles in extent, not counting the Indian
reserve), and Rattlesnake Mountain was more than fourteen miles
north of the Connecticut line. Monument Mountain, or "Mausw-
awseki," lay a few miles farther south than Rattlesnake Mountain.

Whichever the explanation, there was only one Indian reserve set
aside in the deed. In establishing the boundaries, Rattlesnake Mountain, north of Stockbridge, was interpreted as the mountain referred
to in the deed. Use of this mountain for the north boundary placed
Wnahktukook within the limits of the more northern town. After
the sale to Massachusetts, however, Konkapot did not leave his village
and the Mohicans continued to use the meadowlands. There was
apparently a verbal agreement that his village could stay in its location. John Sergeant wrote in 1736 that the lands at Wnahktukook
were comprehended in the north part of the township purchased of
the Indians "except a small Part, which Captain *Kunkapot*, and some
other Indians there, reserv'd for their own Use."[3]

The deed of 1724 did detail the bounds of land reserved for the
Indians on the west side of the Housatonic River in what is now South
Egremont and Sheffield. The deed read: "ye aforesaid Indians reserve
to themselves within the aforesaid Tract of land, described by bounds
and butments, Southardly on a Brook on ye west side Housatonack
River, known by the name of Mannanpenokcan and Northardly to
a small brook lying between ye aforesaid Brook and ye River called
Wampanikseeport allias White River [now the Green River]: viz All
ye land between ye aforesaid Brooks from said Westonook River
extending [west] unto ye patten [patent] of the Colleny of New
York—Together with a clear Meadow, between the aforesaid small
Brook extending Northwardly unto ye aforesaid White River."

Only the cleared meadow was to extend above the upper small
brook. Thus there was a jog extending above the north line as far as
the White (now Green), River. This jog sometimes is ignored on maps
reconstructing the reserve. The deed continued, ". . .the aforesaid
Indians reserve to themselves all ye land between ye Brooks running
due West [on a] line from ye mouth of sd Brooks unto ye patten of

ye Colleny of New York aforesaid. . . ."[4] The north line of this reserve, which was three quarters of a mile deep, ran through later South Egremont.

The tract conveyed by the Mohican deed in 1724 was bounded south by the Massachusetts-Connecticut boundary. The land went west to the contested line with the Colony of New York and was bounded north "on ye Great mountain known by ye name of *Manskuseehoank*." The two towns were to take in four miles east from the Housatonic River between the north and south boundaries.

The purchasers' generous allotment of land made sure they did not come out short when final boundary lines were set. The New York line was still subject to conflicting claims, and New Yorkers believed their boundary extended almost to the Housatonic River. After Connecticut set its line with New York in 1731, many assumed the New York-Massachusetts boundary would match it. To take advantage of this possibility, the Massachusetts Indian reserve and the two new towns were extended west to that point.

The list of twenty-one Mohicans who signed the deed provides a useful guide to the Mohican families in Housatunnuk (alternate spellings include Housatonack and Housatonic) at the start of formal English settlement in the area. They were divided between two Indian villages, one at latter-day Stockbridge and one north of present Great Barrington. Many of the signers' names were subject to two spellings; a first version came at the beginning of the deed, and another accompanied the signers' pictographic signatures at the end. The signers were: Conkepot (Konkapot), Poneyote, Pota wakeont (also spelled Partarwake), Naunausquan, Wanenocow (also spelled Waenenocow), Naunauquin (Naurauquin), Conconaughpeet (Cauconaughfeet), Nonaucauneet, Paunopescennot, Covconofeet, Naunhamiss, Sunkhonk, Popaqua, Taunkhonkpus, Tatakim (Tartakim), Saunkokehe, Cancanwap (Canannap), Saunkewenaugheag (Sunkiewe Nauheag), Manchewanfeet (Manchewenaugheag), John Vangilder, and Ponaskenet (Pinaskenet).

John Vangilder, also known as Toanunck, was a Mohican Indian from the Catskill area, according to his son, Joseph. Joseph Vangilder's mother told him that he was baptized in Rhinebeck as a baby. A popular tradition states that John Vangilder had been raised in a Dutch home in Rhinebeck. An educated, acculturated man, John Vangilder married a woman named Mary Karner from a Palatine German family and they were accepted in both the English and the

Indian communities, as were their children.[5] They lived on a farm west of Sheffield, near the Karner family.

Later in his life, in November 1756, during a Livingston rent disturbance, John Vangilder was accused of shooting a sheriff's deputy as settlers in the mountains west of his farm were being evicted. The Mohicans wrote in a letter to Sir William Johnson "we don't understand that the old man or his son made any attempts against any man till those people that was turning the poor families out of door undertook to make them prisoners and if the old man made not any resistance we can't see what right there was of attacking him or any others that was in the highway in the peace of the King."[6] With another man, Vangilder and son Mathew were jailed in Albany for the murder. The Mohicans, through Sir William Johnson, made strenuous efforts to have him returned to Massachusetts for trial. His release in May 1757 was intended to help keep the Mohicans on the British side during the French and Indian War. John Vangilder died about six months later, possibly as a result of his imprisonment.[7]

Konkapot, whose Indian name was Pophnehonawah, was known as the principal person among the Mohicans of Westenhook. He was the sachem of Wnahktukuk, the more northern of the two villages. Konkapot routinely signed deeds with the pictographic mark of a turkey's track, suggesting he belonged to the turkey clan. "Konkapot" appears to be a Dutch nickname brought from his days in the Hudson Valley.

According to his testimony, given before Sir William Johnson in December 1762, Konkapot was born and raised on lands lying on the Hudson River; he also stated to Johnson that he was seventy-two years old at the time.[8] Thus Konkapot was born about 1690, had lived near the Hudson until grown, and was about thirty-four years old when he signed the 1724 Massachusetts deed. Konkapot also was known as "John" after baptism. Since he had been given a commission, he was usually called Captain Konkapot. He was still alive late in December, 1763, but died before September 20, 1765.[9]

Farther down the list of 1724 signers was the Mohican later well-known as Umpachanee, whose Indian name on the list above was Saunkokehe. He was known as "Lieutenant" as a result of a commission from Massachusetts' Governor Belcher. In 1734 Rev. Stephen Williams of Springfield estimated that Umpachanee was about thirty-eight years old.[10] Upon baptism, Umpachanee took the biblical name of Aaron. In 1724, Umpachanee was a sachem of his community, called Mahaiwe and also Skatekook, which was to be within the Indian reserved land.

In 1751 Umpachanee was called "King of the Mohicans" by a Moravian friend during his long illness.[11] This may have been merely a phrase but it suggests Umpachanee was Chief Sachem of the Mohicans after the death of Ampamit of Schodack. Umpachanee, who died in August 1751, had become an admirer of the Moravians and was visited by Moravian missionaries during his final prolonged illness. During these visits he remained at Stockbridge.[12]

When the English began to settle near the Indian villages after 1724, some settlers became acquainted with Konkapot. He was described as temperate, just and upright, prudent, and industrious. Important to many of the settlers, he was inclined to embrace the Christian religion, but was concerned that if he did, his own people would reject him. Moreover, he did not approve of some so-called Christians who did not live up to their professed ideals. Konkapot was also emotional; when he listened to a sermon in July 1734, he was so overwhelmed that he wept all through it. Rev. Samuel Hopkins of Springfield heard about Konkapot from an acquaintance and was affected by the information that here was a virtuous man interested in Christianity.[13]

In 1734 Reverend Hopkins contacted John Stoddard of Northampton, active in Indian affairs, who agreed that a mission to the River Indians on the Housatonic River would be much more likely to succeed than the failed missions previously sent out to the forts on the northern frontiers of New England including Fort Dummer, Fort Richmond, and Fort George. There the Indians coming to the forts were under the influence of the French, and, in addition, Indian families were not present. Stoddard noted that the French had no influence on the River Indians. Rev. Stephen Williams of Springfield, who was consulted about the possibility of a mission at "Housatunnuk," as the area along the Housatonic River where the Indian villages were located was called, also favored the proposal. Any mission to the Indians, especially one that had a chance of success, was a popular idea of the times.[14]

Reverend Hopkins moved the proposed mission forward; the two ministers wrote to the Commissioners for Indian Affairs at Boston. In response, the Commissioners suggested that the clergymen should sound out the Indians to see if they would be interested. About this time, the Governor of Massachusetts, Jonathan Belcher, planned to honor the two principal men of the Housatonic villages, Konkapot and Umpachanee, as a means of cementing their allegiance with the English. Konkapot was to receive a Captain's commission and Umpachanee, a Lieutenant's. Since the two sachems were coming to Springfield on May 22, 1734, for the ceremony, the ministers went to the Indians' lodgings on that date and conferred with them through an interpreter, Jehoiakim Van Valkenburgh. Van Valkenburgh, a friendly trader who lived near Konkapot's village, had accompanied the two chiefs to help them by translating for them. The ministers asked the sachems if they would be interested in having a missionary come to teach them about religion.

According to Reverend Hopkins' account, Konkapot was anxious to have a missionary so the children might become literate. Umpachanee was less willing, but he agreed to the proposal. Konkapot's response reflected not only his interest in learning about the Christian religion but the strong Mohican desire to have Indian children learn to read. It was later remembered by a settler that the purpose of the Stockbridge mission was so the Indians could have a school. Religion and learning to read and write were inextricably connected.

The chiefs of the villages, Konkapot and Umpachanee, made it clear they spoke only for themselves. Two ministers, therefore, went to Housatunnuk in July 1734, to confer with Mohican residents there. For the purpose, Konkapot and Umpachanee called the villagers together to hear Rev. Nehemiah Bull of Westfield and Rev. Stephen Williams. After four days of consideration, the assembled Mohican families agreed that a minister might be sent to instruct them.

A report of their approval was presented at Boston to the Commissioners for Indian Affairs, headed by Governor Belcher. Among the Commissioners was Dr. Benjamin Coleman, whose efforts and contacts were subsequently important to the financial support of the mission. A committee of the two ministers, Rev. Bull and Rev. Williams, was set up to find a suitable missionary to instruct the Indians; they could offer a salary of one hundred pounds per year, provided by the Commissioners for Indian Affairs. The committee contacted a tutor at Yale College, John Sergeant, who had expressed a strong desire to become a missionary. The young man was committed to his Yale students for the coming winter but was willing to come when that obligation ended. The Governor and the Commissioners approved a plan which would send John Sergeant to Housatunnuk for three months in the fall, after which he would leave for the winter but return in the spring to stay.

John Sergeant was born in Newark, New Jersey in 1710 and died early in July 1749. A farming accident with a scythe during childhood had cost him the use of his left hand but this disability was seldom mentioned and did not affect his ministry. He entered Yale in 1725, was appointed a Tutor, and received a Master of Arts degree in 1732.[15] When he began work with the Mohicans, he was not yet an ordained minister.

Sergeant's journal, quoted by Hopkins, gives an account of the new missionary's first trip to the Mohicans. He was accompanied by Reverend Bull. The two travelers spent the first night in the woods. "The next Day we got to Housatunnuk a little before Night, thro' a most doleful Wilderness and the worst Road, perhaps, that ever was rid. We took Care to inform the *Indians* we were come (they had expected us some Time) and desir'd them to meet us the next Day at a Place we appointed, near the Middle between the places where the *Indians* liv'd; for one half of them liv'd near 4 Miles above, up the River, and the other about so much below."[16]

Through an interpreter, Sergeant offered a discourse the next day to twenty Indians, including Captain Kunkapot and his family, who paid strict attention. The Mohican interpreter, Ebenezer Poopoonah, spoke English surprisingly well, for he had lived among the English and, according to Sergeant, also had knowledge of the principles of the Christian religion. Because Ebenezer was very anxious for Reverand Bull to baptize him, on Thursday Ebenezer was questioned about the Christian faith and then baptized, the first of the Housatunnuk group to take this important step away from his Indian past. He afterwards served often as an interpreter for Sergeant and became an invaluable member of the Stockbridge congregation.

To accommodate their new teacher, the Mohicans met at Lieutenant Umpachanee's wigwam and agreed that during the winter they would all live together half-way between the villages where each group then lived. The half-way location was well supplied with wood and water and also was near some English families, with one of which Mr. Sergeant could live; this arrangement, however, could continue only till spring, when the Indians needed to return to their own fields to plant.

In the future Sergeant would board with David Ingersoll and his family in the vicinity of Sheffield, Massachusetts, but he also stayed with other families. About sixty English settlers already were in the area, as well as at least three Dutch-speaking families from Kinderhook, New York.[17] On Sunday, October 20, 1734, Sergeant spoke twice to the Mohicans; his sermons were interpreted for the Indians by Jehoiakim Van Valkenburgh, the Dutch trader who lived near Konkapot's village.

When he was seventy-six years old in 1768, Van Valkenburgh, in a deposition, testified that: "He has been acquainted with the Indians from his Infancey he understood their Language but not very well [although] when young understood it better than now. He knew Mr. Sergeant who kept the Indian [school] at Stockbridge he [Van Valkenburgh] was then his [Sergeant's] interpreter in his school. . . ." Several years later, when Van Valkenburgh was 84 years old, he was called to testify again. He remembered that it was some forty-six years before, about 1730, when he went to live in Massachusetts among the Indians.[18]

Now fully involved with Sergeant, the Mohicans set about building a public house half-way between the two villages to serve them as a Sunday meeting place and as a school. The large wigwam for the purpose was finished early in November. Around the school, the Indians built small houses for their families, to which they moved for the winter when the school was ready. Meanwhile, Sergeant went up to Wnahktukook, now Stockbridge, where Konkapot and some others lived, to start teaching the children there to read; he was pleased with his reception and found the children anxious to learn. He next went to Skatekook, one mile south of the base of Monument Mountain, where Umpachanee and four other families lived, and taught their children; the number of children at each place was about nine or ten.[19] This count gives an indication of the low birthrate or survival rate among the Mohicans. Five families included no more than ten children.

Mohican Customs

Sergeant fortunately requested of the Mohicans some insight into the customs of their Nation. He was rewarded with aboriginal lore that shows that as late as 1734 the Mohicans retained many native traditions. For example, at Wnahktukook in November, Sergeant attended a Mohican event. After the ceremony in which a deer was offered with prayers for food, good sleep, and safety from "Fowls that fly in the air," the old man leading the ceremony "haloow'd pretty Loud." This man was given a string of wampum to pay him for his service, "after which he halloo'd again."[20] The deer meat was boiled and all ate except the man who offered it; he abstained, to make clear the deer was a gift. The skin with the feet and some of the "inwards" were given to an old woman as an act of charity.

The participants told Sergeant that the custom was taught to their ancestors by a miraculous man who had come down from the sky to live among them. The man taught them to use snowshoes, cleared their country of monsters that infested their roads, and was held in great esteem as a hero and a prophet. Eventually he returned to the sky, leaving behind one son, who also was an extraordinary man.

In response to Sergeant's inquiries, Ebenezer Poopoonah, the interpreter, told him a few things Mohicans believed: "As that the seven Stars were so many *Indians* translated to Heaven in a Dance; that the stars in *Charles's Wain* are so many Men hunting a *Bear*; that they begin the Chace [chase] in the Spring, and hold it all Summer; by the Fall they have wounded it [the bear], and that the Blood turns the Leaves red; by the Winter they have killed it and the Snow is made of its Fat; which, being melted by the Heat of the Summer, makes the Sap of Trees."[21]

A year later, in late December 1735, the Mohicans spoke to Sergeant about attending a *keutikaw* (also spelled kentikaw), or dance. He agreed they could go when they assured him it was not a religious affair and after they promised to drink no rum, a promise they kept. Sergeant described the keutikaw ceremony: "The keutikaw is a Dance which finishes the mourning for the dead, and is celebrated about twelve months after the decease, when the guests invited make presents to the relatives of the deceas'd, to make up their loss and end their mourning. The manner of doing it is this: the presents prepar'd are deliver'd to a Speaker appointed for the purpose; who laying them upon the shoulders of some elderly persons, makes a speech showing the design of their present meeting, and of the presents prepared. Then he takes them and distributes them to the mourners, adding some words of consolation and desiring them to forget their sorrow, and accept the presents to make up their loss. After this they eat together and make merry."[22]

Sergeant continued to observe. He wrote that the parting of a man and his wife was a very common thing among the natives. He noted that it rarely used to happen that a married couple lived together until they were old. Under Mohican law, the children and all the household goods and everything but the gun belonged to the woman. The gun, however, was the man's, for his livelihood. The man, according to custom, had no right to the children. Sergeant learned also that when the Indian men went to reap in New York for the Dutch, they usually drank up all their wages. He later was proud of the great pains taken by some of the Housatunnuk Indians to cure themselves of their inclination towards drinking. They learned to refuse even a taste of rum, for they had learned that once they tasted, they couldn't stop, a wise insight.[23]

Soon Sergeant had more than twenty children attending his wigwam school on weekdays. He preached in the same large building on Sundays to about thirty listeners. Word of the mission spread. Sergeant was invited by Albany leaders to discuss the value of bringing some Mohawks to his school. On a trip to Albany, Sergeant met with Philip Livingston, who told him that there was great probability that the Protestant religion could be introduced among the Iroquois. Livingston considered it absolutely necessary to do this in order to preserve the fur trade with them and keep their friendship. Clearly, not all mission supporters were altruistic. Introducing the Protestant faith among the Iroquois was seen as keeping the Mohawks from going over to the French. In addition, a strong competition with Catholicism motivated many colonists: "And truly the infinite pains that are taken by the French. . .to make papists of the Indians should teach us to use some endeavours to make Protestants of them," wrote a supporter to Sergeant in 1748.[24]

When Sergeant returned from sounding out Albany leaders about the Mohawks, he found that a young assistant, Timothy Woodbridge of Springfield, had been obtained by Rev. Stephen Williams to teach the Indians in the school and instruct them in religion while Sergeant returned to New Haven for the winter of 1734. Woodbridge proved to be a competent partner for Sergeant and outlived him. He taught alternately with Sergeant at separate Mohican locations until the school was built. After that, he became the teacher for the central mission school. He continued to teach the school after Sergeant's death and was an influential adviser to the Mohicans for many years. He later was named a special Justice of the Peace for the Mohican community at Stockbridge.

Early Days of the Mission

There were set-backs even as the mission was under consideration. On Sunday, December 8, 1734, few Indians came to hear
Sergeant's sermon, although this was the day before he left to return
to Yale. Traders from the Hudson Valley had sold a large quantity of
rum to the Indians from the two Mohican villages, Skatekook and
Wnahktukook, which together were known as Housatunnuk. Some
of the villagers had become drunk and continued to drink for several
days, in violation of their pledges. They were not sober by Sunday.
"This was the most discouraging week I had," wrote Sergeant, "For
the Dutch traders. . . make vast Profit by selling them *Rum*, and
making Bargains with them when they are drunk. . . . These Traders
tell them, that the *Religion* we are about to teach them, is not a good
one; that we design in the End to serve ourselves by them, to make
Slaves of them and their Children, and the like."[25]

This same story about slavery would be told to the Mohicans at
Shekomeko when the Moravians came; it must have been perceived
by traders as an effective way to influence Indian behavior. The
Mohicans knew the traders from Albany well, for they often went
among them for business and while visiting their relatives. An Indian
village near Dutch-speaking Kinderhook was a location where Indians
from the Housatonic Valley could trade as well as at Albany. Sergeant
noted that the Dutch had great influence over the Indians. He longed
to counteract that influence. Before he left for New Haven, Sergeant
tried to convince Umpachanee and Konkapot that it was the traders
who wanted to prey on the Indians and their children, rather than
the English. Captain Konkapot was satisfied; Lieutenant Umpachanee, as usual, was less easily convinced.

The warning by the traders frightened the Mohicans into recon-
sideration of the missionary's presence. A Massachusetts law against
private individuals selling alcohol to the Indians was in effect. The
traders from the Hudson (heavy drinkers themselves, according to
Hopkins' account) resented this law as an arbitrary restriction on the
Indian trade and tried to encourage the Indians to consider the rule a
limitation on their freedom. To evade the law, the traders left rum at
New York Mohican villages not far from the border, from where the
Indians themselves could carry it back to their Massachusetts villages.

Despite the fiasco caused by the traders, when Sergeant returned
to New Haven for the winter of 1734, he took with him two Indian

boys. He hoped to teach them the English language and way of life and also to practice the Mohican language with them. Relations with the chiefs were intact: Captain Konkapot could be depended upon to keep clear of drinking events, and Lieutenant Umpachanee had remained sober during the drinking. When Sergeant asked the chiefs if they would let two Mohican boys live with him at New Haven for the winter, "they agreed that the Captain's only Son, Nungkowwat, and the Lieutenant's oldest Son, Etowaukaum. . .should be the children."[26]

The boys were young, Nungkowwat about nine years old, Etowaukaum only eight, but both were brave enough to go to New Haven with a stranger who did not speak their language. Young Etowaukaum, according to John Sergeant, was a grandson through his mother of Etowaukaum, the chief of the River Indians who had gone to England during Queen Anne's reign. Etowaukaum and his parents lived at Skatekook (also known as Mahaiwee), where the first meeting with Sergeant had been held. At New Haven, Sergeant took the boys into his own lodgings at the College and sent them to the New Haven Town School while he attended to his other duties. The two boys were very intelligent, especially Umpachanee's son, and did well. They received much attention during their stay. Etowaukaum later took the name Jonas, and as an adult fought bravely in the Seven Years War on the side of the English.[27]

While Sergeant and the boys were away for the winter of 1734-1735, a great meeting including the Mohicans from the Hudson Valley was held at Housatunnuk. Sergeant was not present because the gathering had been postponed from the fall to winter, to accommodate the Indian hunting season. At this important meeting, the whole Mohican nation was to consider whether the mission at Housatunnuk should be allowed. This assembly was by way of a reckoning, for the Indians at Housatunnuk had proceeded on the controversial mission project without the advice of the other villages and without the necessary consent of their relatives and fellow tribesmen. Because there was strong opposition to Christianity among Mohicans along the Hudson, the so-called "birds of rumor" flew. The Housatunnuk Mohican families heard that the Hudson River Indians resented the Housatunnuk chiefs' actions; they heard there was envy of Konkapot and Umpachanee because of their commissions from Governor Belcher; whispers warned of a plan to poison the chiefs.

Alarmed, the Indians of Housatunnuk quickly sent for help from some of the ministers planning the mission. On January 15, 1735, therefore, Rev. Stephen Williams, Rev. Samuel Hopkins, and John Ashley of Westfield came to Housatunnuk to offer moral support. The Mohican representatives from the Hudson River arrived on Saturday, January 19. The next day, through an interpreter, Reverend Williams preached a sermon to the Indians, "in Number about 150, or 200, great and small."[28] It is likely Mohicans from northwest Connecticut also were present as well as those from Dutchess County. This was probably as large an aggregation of Mohicans as had been called out in many years and harked back to assemblages of the seventeenth century; the number of Mohicans who chose to make the trip indicates that controversy over the religious issue was intense. The get-together dramatically emphasized the underlying unity of the Mohican nation.

The ministers had conferences with the listeners, read an encouraging letter from John Stoddard to them, and attempted to answer their objections. The visiting Mohicans were convinced; they thanked the ministers and expressed a desire that the teacher, Timothy Woodbridge, might continue at Housatunnuk and that John Sergeant would return. They promised to give an account of the meeting to their several towns. Moreover, they gave hope to the speakers that they would as a nation agree to religious instruction. Although many were in attendance, others were waiting at home in the villages to hear the results of the meeting. The opposition was overwhelmed.

Despite the Mohican concessions, the conference did not end well. A drunken frolic which included dancing concluded the affair, after which several Massachusetts Indians became ill, and two men were seized with a fever and died suddenly. These events, in light of the rumors about poisoning before the meeting, made the alarmed Housatunnuk Indians suspect that the pair who died had been poisoned. A month later, Konkapot and Umpachanee decided to hold a pow wow so they could "apply to some *Invisible Power*" to find out if the two men were poisoned, "for they expected that those who did the Fact would appear to their *Priests*."[29]

The February 21 "Pawwaw" site was Umpachanee's large wigwam at Skatekook, which, Rev. Samuel Hopkins explained, was about fifty or sixty feet in length. Timothy Woodbridge, who attended the evening ceremony, found forty Indians in the longhouse, which had been swept clean. Indians were seated on each side of good fires, from end to end, except for a space at one end reserved for the pow wow leaders. Each Indian had two sticks about a foot and a half long, one of them split at the end, which they held under their legs as they sat. The ceremony began with a rapping of their sticks and with singing, their eldest religious leader sitting and talking, taking a different role from the rest. After an hour, the leader threw off all his robes except his breech clout and began to dance from one end of the wigwam to the other with his eyes shut, using distorted gestures and grimaces. After an hour, a second leader succeeded him, and then a third and a fourth continued the ceremony. "*This* continued all Night, without any Intermission except some short intervals in which they smoak'd a Pipe, and some Times, for a short Space, they all got up and danc'd."[30]

Woodbridge, although an outsider, had the rare experience of witnessing a timeless Mohican ceremony, but he did not appreciate it. Outraged, Woodbridge afterward scolded the participants for this form of worship and they agreed never to do it again. As a result, the occasion may have been the last pow wow performed by the Mohicans at Housatunnuk.

About the middle of February, the Mohican families left their villages and went into the woods to make their year's stock of maple sugar. They promised to return when the sugaring season was over at the end of March or in the middle of April. The process of making sap into sugar involved collecting the sap into pots from a channel cut into maple trees, after which the sap was boiled well and then stirred. The work was time-consuming. It is unlikely that the Mohicans were able to boil sap for long periods in prehistoric times before the advent of metal pots, but it is known that some eastern Indians collected fresh sap to drink.[31] The vast forest between the Housatonic and the Hudson, according to Hopkins, contained many maple trees. By the 1730s, the practice of making maple sugar was widespread among Mohicans. Those at the village of Shekomeko in Dutchess County also went into the woods to make maple sugar in the spring.

Since the children were going with their parents, school was canceled for the month, permitting Timothy Woodbridge time to visit friends in Springfield. In early May, while Sergeant was still at Yale, Konkapot, Umpachanee, Umpachanee's brother, named To-htohkuhkoonaunt[32], and Ebenezer Poopoonah, the translator, came to New Haven to retrieve the two boys and accompany Sergeant back to Housatunnuk for a visit. The Indian visitors responded with poise to a tour of the college. Sergeant reported that Etowaukaum and Nungkowwat were learning satisfactorily, considering the brief time they had been studying. Moreover, Nungkowwat, Konkapot's son, soon returned to New Haven for the summer, after which he was reported to be able to speak and read English.

Not surprisingly, the various visitors to Sergeant's quarters, and especially the boys' winter visit, put a strain on the missionary's limited finances. He soon was writing to Dr. Benjamin Coleman, one of the Commissioners at Boston, making it clear to this benefactor that he was short of funds and would need more than the allotted one hundred pounds a year to support the mission. Coleman in turn contacted a London gentleman who had offered money for missions. He also sent copies of Sergeant's Indian sermons to potential contributors in England. From these contacts he received gifts which he forwarded to Sergeant and Woodbridge.

On May 10, Sergeant returned to Housatunnuk with the Indian men and boys for a visit and on Sunday, May 11, 1735, he preached to about twenty people. Some of his listeners were much affected. Umpachanee's wife, the daughter of Etowaukaum, wept during the sermon. Konkapot wiped away tears. Sergeant happily noted that the Indians seemed more friendly to him than in the fall, a reminder of the considerable resistance existing when he first arrived. Feeling himself truly welcome, Sergeant made a final decision to devote his life to the Indians at Housatunnuk.

Combining the Villages

The Mohicans were at this time "parted again from the School-House; and liv'd some of them at *Wnahktukook* and some at *Skatekook*; for at those Places they planted their Corn and Beans, which is all the Husbandry they carry on. For the Rest of their living, they depend upon *Hunting*."[33] The need of members of his congregation for a summer dispersal to their permanent locations was an impediment to the functioning of the mission. To cope with the division at the time of his sixteen-day spring visit, Sergeant spent one week at Konkapot's house, while Woodbridge stayed with the Indians at Skatekook, and then they exchanged places.

In July, having completed his duties at college, Sergeant returned to the Mohicans, some of whom, including Konkapot, wanted to be baptized. To perform baptisms and to act as their minister for the future, Sergeant needed to be ordained. The ceremony was arranged for August 1735 at Deerfield. All Massachusetts Indian nations had been called to Deerfield by Governor Belcher for a treaty (conference). On August 31, therefore, after the business of the Indian meeting was concluded, the Housatunnuk group attended Sergeant's ordination. Asked by the Rev. Stephen Williams if they were willing to receive Sergeant as their teacher, the Mohicans indicated their willingness. Sergeant's mission thus was continued with the approbation of many of the Mohicans of Housatunnuk. That there were still some pockets of opposition was shown by later events.

While enthusiasm for the new religion, the school, and the mission ran high, Sergeant was kept busy. The leaders of the community were anxious to be baptized: November 2, 1735, Sergeant baptized Konkapot with the name of John and his wife, reportedly a very sober and good woman, as Mary, and also baptized their oldest daughter. A week later, he baptized the rest of Konkapot's family and Ebenezer Poopoonah's son. Besides Konkapot's oldest son, Nungkowwwat, mentioned above, who took the name Abraham, Konkapot had two daughters, Katherine, the eldest, and Matherene, who appear in the Stockbridge records. The couple had at least three more sons, John, Jacob, and Robert. (Mary, Konkapot's wife, died of consumption March 29, 1741, while Katherine died during the week of January 19, 1746; Matherene also died in the 1740s.)[34]

On November 7, 1735, in an English-style ceremony conducted at their request, Sergeant had married the faithful Ebenezer Poopoonah and his Indian wife. On November 16, he baptized Ebenezer's wife and named her Sarah. The same day, he baptized Lieutenant Umpachanee, as well as his wife, who was called Hannah, and the rest of his family, including his wife's sister; the total was eleven persons. At the time, Sergeant was enthusiastic about Umpachanee, whom he described as clear-headed, smart, pleasant, and a good speaker. Sergeant noted with pleasure that Lieutenant Umpachanee had given up drinking. This temperance was not to last. In the course of the next few years, Umpachanee regressed and drank to excess. His later overt hostility became a hindrance to the success of the mission and Umpachanee was threatened with expulsion. However, that time had not yet come. By November 18, 1735, Sergeant had baptized nearly forty Indians.

Wnampee and his wife and family were among those baptized. Wnampee (Wenaumpeh, Weananumpee, Wnaupey) took the name

Isaac. Wnampee may be the same man as Wunnupee, who signed important deeds around Shekomeko, an Indian village in Dutchess County, New York in 1703 and 1704, as well as much later at Stockbridge. Umpachanee's brother, Tohtohkhoonaut, and others also were baptized. Sergeant had written in the spring, "Johtohkoonaunt had been a very vicious Fellow, and a bitter Enemy of the Gospel; but. . .he came strangely about, and was much in Favour of the Christian Religion; undertook to learn to read, and made extraordinary Proficiency in it."[35] Early in December, Sergeant baptized David Naunauneckaunuk, an important man among the Mohicans, described as honest, faithful and obliging. By December 1735, the Stockbridge Mohicans were so inspired that they agreed to have no further trading in rum.

Unnuquuunut, a visiting Susquehannah Indian, who spoke a little Dutch and who had given up drinking, was representative of strangers who began to come to Housatunnuk. By January 18, 1736, Sergeant was preaching at the Lieutenant's house to a group of eighty or ninety persons, about half of whom were strangers. Two new families among this group, encompassing eight people, decided to remain at Housatunnok. Unnuquuunut left two sons at the Indian school, one of whom was especially bright.

Because they lived apart, it was difficult for all of the mission Indians to attend Sunday worship together, except in winter. With Sergeant's concurrence, a plan was proposed by Governor Belcher to move the Mohicans from Umpachanee's village of Skatehook north to Konkapot's village of Wnahktukook. This change would not be simple, as there were some English and Dutch settlers in the area who in the past decade had obtained farms on both Mohican land and on the land sold to the province in 1724.

The plan proposed to have the Mohicans give up the strip of land which they had reserved for themselves in 1724, within which Umpachanee's village sat, in exchange for a new location to the north. On Konkapot's meadows beside the Housatonic all the Indians were to live together. This land had been conveyed to the committee of the General Court by the Indians in the 1724 deed. The Mohicans would be giving away their reserved lands at Great Barrington in exchange for return of a part of the land they had sold in 1724. The newly defined Indian tract would surround Wnahktukook, Konkapot's village, and would become a new town. This meant it would be run along the lines of the English towns around the

Massachusetts countryside. It is unlikely the Mohicans had a concept
of the administration of an English town.

The farmers already settled on the land would be asked to move
south to the former Indian reservation strip. These settlers would be
rewarded by being assigned so-called equivalent holdings. An incentive for them to move had to be provided. As a result of the inclusion
of this incentive, so-called equivalent lands, both at Stockbridge and
on Mohican land in Connecticut, unfailingly proved to be larger and
more valuable than the original farm being given up. The difference
usually came from Indian land.

The plan had been suggested by Governor Belcher to the Mohicans at the fall 1734 treaty at Deerfield. He had noted that they lived
far from one another and that they lacked land enough to support
their families, and he promised to take up the matter with the General
Court at its fall meeting, which he did. A committee including Col.
John Stoddard was appointed to look into the matter. Stoddard knew
the Mohicans; he had been on the General Court's committee in 1724
which bought the two townships from the Mohicans and he was
well-known for his interest in Indian affairs.

The Mohicans received a letter from Stoddard in January 1735
telling them of the plan to sell the reserved land and combine the
Indian villages. "There is a projection," he wrote, "to get the most
of the great Meadow above the Mountain of Housatunnuk for the
Indians, so that they may live together." Not surprisingly, the Mohicans were startled and unhappy that such a scheme was already in
progress. Although the idea had been mentioned to them, the preliminary steps taken by the General Court were made without asking
their permission. Even though supposedly there was still time for the
Mohicans to decide whether or not to accept this resettling of their
villages, they were warned by Stoddard that "These Things are great
Tokens of Kindness towards the Indians; and they [the Indians]
should be very careful how they put a slight upon them."[36]

The Indians remained suspicious about the land transfer. They
were concerned that the English had some hidden intentions to take
advantage of them and had several meetings among themselves, to
decide what answer they should give. Sergeant attributed this lack of
enthusiasm to the Indians' caution and self-interest, as well as to
warnings given to the Mohicans that the English planned to enslave
them. Enemies of the mission, Sergeant believed, were not only
Indians in other places but also false Christians, the people who

wished to make money by selling goods and rum to the Indians. Sergeant, however, prior to their meeting with the committee, was able to satisfy his Indian parishoners of the good intentions of the English.

The committee headed by Stoddard was charged with making the arrangements for the exchange of land. However, Stoddard had illness in his family. In early February 1736, as a result, Major Seth Pomeroy and Capt. David Ingersoll, two other members, came to the meeting house at Housatunnuk to ask whether the Mohicans were willing to live together in one village and give up their land below the mountain. In exchange, the Indians were to have a township above Monument Mountain, where they were promised good meadowland. They were offered a town of six miles square, which would include Konkapot's location known as the Great Meadow.

Once again, the Mohicans allowed themselves to be persuaded to do something which their first instinct had distrusted. The assembled Mohicans agreed to the plan, and they agreed also to set aside lots in the new town for the minister and the schoolmaster. The Indians requested that they be settled in the new location by planting time, late spring.

The committee, foreseeing success in obtaining the land from the several settlers who already had farms in the Upper Township, promised to report to the General Court.[37] If the members approved of the steps taken so far, the General Court would appoint another committee to continue the process. Most of the English and Dutch people who held land above the mountain were willing to move, although two or three Dutchmen held back.

On the 25th and 26th of March 1736, the General Court gave the new committee (composed of the same three men) complete authority to dispose of the lands that were reserved to the Housatunnuk Indians in the Town of Sheffield, in order to satisfy the owners already situated on the land now granted to the Indians above Monument Mountain.[38] The Mohicans were expected to give up their rights to the land which was set aside for them when they sold the towns in 1724.

There was reluctance to do this. In February 1736, when asked if they were willing to resign the reserved land, Konkapot demurred. The Indians had sold land east of Taconic Mountain, on the west end of the reserve, to three Dutch farmers, families he did not want to unseat. Moreover, John Vangilder, a respected Mohican, lived on the reserved land west of Sheffield. It was the Indians' intention to keep him at that location, and on October 24, 1737, they issued a deed "out of love and esteem" to him for the south half of the reserved land west of Sheffield, despite the rights granted to the General Court's committee. The signers were Konkapot, Skannop, and Poniote (Poneyote).[39]

Among the persons unwilling to move from above was the trader Joachim Van Valkenburgh, Konkapot's friend and interpreter, who had been given a tract of forty acres of meadowland as well as about 250 acres of upland by the Indians about 1730. Van Valkenburgh had been useful to the new mission. He had interpreted for John Sergeant, as well as for Konkapot, and had spent time in teaching Sergeant the Mohican language. As late as June 1736, when he was still serving as Sergeant's interpreter, he expressed surprise at how sensibly some of the natives talked about religion. He was reluctant to lose his home and Indian connections by participating in the village exchange. Having lost much of his income as a trader, however, he finally agreed to sell his land to John Sergeant and Ephraim Williams, who turned over the land to the Indian town in exchange for equivalent land.[40] Van Valkenburgh moved to a farm in New York colony.

The General Court approved the plan to grant a township and appointed the same three men to be a committee to lay out the land, to apportion the meadow lands to the Indians, and to do whatever was necessary to put the Indians into possession of the tract. Had Konkapot not been so enthusiastic about the mission, he never could have agreed to this, as it was his own fertile meadow land which was taken for the new township. According to the deed of 1724, however, he had no hold on the area except that which might be conceded by the English as a result of an unwritten understanding. The land soon was to be divided English-style into individual plots.

By October 1736, a deed noted that the committee was authorized by the General Court to dispose of the lands that formerly were reserved to the Housatunnuk Indians in the Town of Sheffield and mentioned in the committee's report, in order to satisfy the colonial owners of land granted to the Indians north of Monument Mountain. Aaron Gardenier from Kinderhook was one of the first whose land north of Monument Mountain was traded for Indian reserved land at Sheffield. In exchange for his former four hundred acres, he received a fourth part of the Indian reserved land, described as sixteen acres of the meadow land in the reserve together with the swamp lying between the meadow and the road from John Vangilder's to Captain Van Alstyne's, as well as one fourth part of the upland.[41]

As noted, the next year, in October 1737, Konkapot, Skannop, and Poniote gave a deed to ensure John Vangilder would not be turned off his farm. Matthew Vangilder, when he later was jailed with his father after the murder in 1756, also was granted land. Matthew's land came from a Mohican woman named Noch Namos, possibly the mother of John Vangilder, who offered all her rights to the whole of the land in and near the township of Sheffield, "for the love and affection I have and Do bear unto John Vanguilder. . ." and for other good causes and sums of money and other presents. She identified herself as an Indian woman then living in the Fishkills of Dutchess County; she was formerly of Housatunnuk.[42]

In 1736, while the exchange was under consideration, the Indians moved out as usual at the beginning of March to tap trees and make maple sugar. It took them only two days to prepare houses for themselves among the maple groves. Half were with Umpachanee and half with Konkapot, and, as soon as the dwellings were ready, John Sergeant and Timothy Woodbridge each joined a group. After the first three weeks, as usual, the two teachers exchanged locations. Snow still lay in the woods. They slept on spruce boughs covered with a warm deerskin with the hair on, with blankets under and over them, and were fed a simple diet prepared by the chiefs' wives. Sergeant reported he was in good health the whole time in the woods. Sergeant was already saying prayers composed, with the help of an interpreter, with his hosts in the Mohican language.

The visit gave Sergeant a welcome chance to learn more about their language and society. He observed they were without special courtesies in their relationships with each other; moreover, children showed no special respect or deference to parents. Yet the members of the group were modest and women and children were bashful. They all were kind to one another, and they made everyone welcome who came to their houses. According to Indian custom, a visitor who entered a Mohican house did not disclose his business until he was served food and had eaten it.[43]

Sergeant noted some Mohican words: the oldest child called all the younger children, whether boys or girls, *Nheesumuk*. Their elder sisters were called by the younger children *Nmesuk*. The elder brothers were called by the younger brothers and sisters *Netokhaunut*. There were other terms for relatives for which there were no synonyms in English. He noted also that girls, at the time of their first menstruation, left the group and went alone into the woods, where they were to do no work at all, and where they remained from fourteen to forty days. They cut off their hair, and, during their time apart, they were not to be seen by a man, as it was bad luck.[44]

Upon the Housatunnuk families' return from sugar making, the Mohicans began final arrangements for their proposed move. Umpachanee was still uneasy. At a meeting of the Mohicans with the committee on April 20, Umpachanee, after expressing thanks graciously and stating his commitment to the Christian religion, had some serious questions to ask. He wondered why they had been neglected so long and was wary of the questions of the committee about ownership of the land. He pointed out that the Indians lacked documents to prove they owned the land and would have to depend on witnesses for proof. He noted that if anyone should insist upon more than the testimony of witnesses, the Indians could prove no title at all. "However, their Titles were good, according to their [Indian] Law and Custom in such Cases," he explained.[45] He was concerned that the English would secure some hold over them as a result of all these favors and asked what security the natives had that their children would be free. The Mohicans took seriously rumors spread by the traders that the English intended to make slaves of the Indians and their children. It was not too preposterous a threat; both the English and the Dutch held people as slaves.

John Stoddard and Major Pomeroy were persuasive. Various previous efforts made on behalf of the Indians of New England were listed, and Pomeroy assured them that they would hold their titles in the same manner as all other owners did. Moreover, the Indians were promised that they would not lose their liberty. The Mohicans were satisfied with the explanations offered by their advisers. They agreed to the plan, now unfolding, to unite the villages. In late April, the Committee again conferred with the Mohicans. By May 1736, the Indians had removed to their new town and appeared pleased with it. Two new families joined them. The Indians were enthusiastic about their gardening, Sergeant wrote, and they had planted at least three times more than previously. Near the end of the month of May, Sergeant preached to the Indians in their new settlement.

While Timothy Woodbridge lived with Konkapot, Sergeant continued to board with an English family five miles below Wnahktuhkook. Sergeant noted how hard Woodbridge worked, and how lonesome he was at Captain Konkapot's house. By January 1737, the lonely Woodbridge had built a house near the Indian village and had married. This allowed Sergeant to move up to the Indian town, now called Housatunnuk, to live with Woodbridge and his wife.

At Sergeant's request, four English families were invited to the new town; they were to set an example for the Indians and be company for the minister and teacher. In the future, as the English families multiplied, their offspring would require tracts of land in the town. At the time, however, it was not anticipated that English families would compete with the Indians for their land. Moreover, as businessmen and investors also moved into the town over the next decades, the English population soared. The long-range plan of the mission's minister and teacher was for the natives to make appropriate cultural and social changes learned from the English. Neither of these early idealistic planners nor the Mohicans could foresee that allowing English residents into the Indian town eventually would force the Indians to leave after five decades.

Umpachanee and Konkapot, with others, visited the Mohicans on the Hudson River in June 1736 to resolve a murder there. They reported on their return that the Mohicans of Schodack were persuaded that they should become Christians; several promised to come to the mission with their families to be instructed and apparently some did. Although his son went to Stockbridge, Ampamit remained at his Hudson River island village in Schodack.

By June 1736, Sergeant had baptized almost fifty-two Indians. The number of Indians residing around the Housatunnuk mission had risen to ninety. Now that the two groups were combined, the enlarged village at Wnahktukook was informally called Housatunnuk or the Indian Town; the Stockbridge name was adopted in 1739. Sergeant was pleased with the progress he saw among the Indians. "A very remarkable Reformation appears, more and more, in their Manners; their Hearts seem really to be engag'd."[46] Drunkenness was now a disgrace. Sergeant was diligently studying the Mohican language but was not yet able to converse with the natives, although he could understand some things they said.

Meanwhile, a boarding school for Indian boys had been proposed by a donor in England, who had been contacted by Dr. Benjamin Coleman. Twelve boys were to be supported. When another donor offered to help the mission, Dr. Coleman proposed using this second gift for support of some girls in a school. At this time, the Mohicans reported in a letter of thanks how glad they were to be living together, how thankful they were to be new Christians, and how appreciative they were of all the gifts they were receiving.

The signers' names provided a roll call of the leaders of the village in 1736. They were: Isaac Wnaumpee, James Wohquanbekomeek, Abraham Maukutehewant, John Touwoonaunt, Nicholas Ubwaunmut (Etowaukaum?), John Pohpnehaonnuwot (Konkapot), Aaron Sankewenaukbeek (Umpachanee), David Naunaunekennuk, Ebenezer Poohpoonah (the translator), Abraham Tohtaunkuhkconaunt (Umpachanee's brother), and Ephraim Woonaunnuhqueen. This period was a high point in the Housatunnuk mission experience for the Mohicans.[47]

In July 1736, Governor Belcher invited the Mohicans to an audience at Boston, requesting that they bring "Corslar their chief Sachem." The name commonly was applied to Metoxson, widely recognized as the leader among the Connecticut Mohicans of Weatauk and Wequadnach. This reference suggests he served briefly as the Mohicans' chief sachem after Ampamit retired or died. By 1743 Metoxon was living in Greene County, New York.[48]

A group of Mohicans from Housatunnuk, accompanied by an equal number of Mohicans from the Hudson Valley, visited the Massachusetts Governor and Council on August 5, 1736. At the Indian audience with the Governor, Umpachanee made a speech, offering thanks for the township and for the convenience the Indians found in living together. He asked for the assistance of the Government in building a meeting house and a school house. Since they had received so much, and he was asking for additional favors, Umpachanee probably felt, in the Indian way, that it was necessary to return some gifts so the two sides would be even.

He offered land and furs, traditional Indian gifts. Umpachanee announced that the Mohicans would give up their claim to land which extended a mile on each side of the road from Housatunnuk to Westfield. Next the Mohicans made the Governor a present of skins. The Governor in response spoke of their progress and expressed hope they would continue to meet the government's expectations. He accepted their gesture of giving up their challenge to the land bordering the road to Westfield, where apparently the road had been improved and settled without benefit of Indian deeds, and promised to report to the General Court their requests for a meeting house and a school house. The furs he ordered to be sold; the money was to be spent for books for John Sergeant, a gesture appreciated by Sergeant.

Rev. Samuel Hopkins noted that from Westfield to the outskirts of Sheffield, where the road ran, was about twenty-six miles. The land to which the Indians gave up their challenge "should be esteemed no inconsiderable Return for the Favour bestowed."[49] Perhaps the Mohicans had been overly generous. However, subsequently the General Court ordered that a meeting house thirty feet broad and forty feet long, as well as a school house, should be built for the Indians, at the expense of the Province. John Stoddard, as well as Sergeant and Woodbridge, were to see the buildings erected.

Although most difficulties in obtaining the land for the Indian Town had been overcome, one of the Dutch farmers had not yet given up his land in the Indian territory, and, worse, supplied the Indians with rum, so that some of them drank to excess. Probably this was Van Valkenburgh, who did not remove until 1739, as Konkapot had asked that he be allowed to stay.[50] Umpachanee and Kónkapot, however, now tried to limit drinking.

New Indian families arrived from time to time. In the spring of 1737, although the Indians went to make maple sugar, they returned every week for Sunday services. One couple, Naukuckewat and Wauwoonemeen, followed the English custom of publishing their bans and then were married in an English ceremony translated into the Mohican language. In August 1737, Sergeant began to preach to the Indians in their own language, for which they flattered him, claiming that he now spoke their languge better than they themselves did.

To encourage the settlement of land, with General Court approval townships began to be sold around Stockbridge. In June 1737, Nahun Ward and Ephraim Williams bought land for four townships to the east of Sheffield. The General Court on May 28, 1735, had granted to the town of Boston three tracts of land for towns, each to be six miles square, to be laid out in the unappropriated land of the Province of Massachusetts. In June, 1737, Jacob Wendell of Boston purchased one of these township rights at auction and a year later came to see the Mohicans at Housatunnuk. For 120 pounds, he obtained a deed from Masinamake, alias Solomon, the owner of the land Wendell wanted. This was a large tract "To ye Northward of ye upper Town at Housatonnik at ye Distance of Ten Miles Above ye Hoplands," extending six miles on both sides of the Westenhook

River. Konkapot and Sankewengeeh (Umpachanee) witnessed the sale, as well as Timothy Woodbridge and A. Van Dyke, who were required to approve it. This tract for "Wendell's Town" became Pittsfield.[51] The purchase of townships around Stockbridge continued until the towns of Stockbridge and later West Stockbridge were all that remained in Indian hands.

In May 1737, Governor Belcher gave a charter for the Indian town to the Housatunnuk Indians, and in 1739, at the instigation of one of the new English settlers, Ephraim Williams, the Legislature incorporated the Indian town as Stockbridge. Ephraim Williams, as justice of the peace in Hampshire County, became the principal manager of Indian affairs in the town. Consequently, Williams and the two chiefs, Konkapot and Umpachanee, were delegated to assemble the town's property owners, in order to organize the town by choosing a town clerk. The sudden imposition of an English-style town government confused the Indians, wrote John Sergeant in the segment of his journal which survives.[52] Clearly, the Indians would have to be educated about the political organization and the responsibilities involved.

Mission Life to Change

On August 21, 1737, Sergeant baptized Yokun and his wife and their three children. Yokun was described as a reformed drinker. He was the grandson of Ampamit, the chief sachem of the Mohicans. The same week, the son of Ampamit desired baptism. Ampamit's son had been at Stockbridge for a short time; his name was Pmaupausoo, apparently from the Mohican word *penumpausoo*, meaning "a boy."[53] Also desiring baptism was Nomshoos, who had come from the Shawnees' country a year before. Because both were young, Sergeant deferred baptism in order to have longer to impress them with the seriousness of their decision to become Christians. The following week he had another candidate, a young man named Ukhihnauwequn. On September 14, 1737, he baptized the three men.

On September 11, 1737, following their invitation, Sergeant preached at the Mohican village of Kaunaumeek, eighteen miles to the west on the Kinderhook Creek. Kaunaumeek, which subsequently became an independent mission, is detailed in the following chapter.

In the summer of 1737, John Sergeant began to build himself a modest house. This first house was not on the hill, but on the road across the meadow, not far from the church.[54] Sergeant had been allowed only fifty pounds toward the house by the Indian Commissioners. As a result, he sent a petition by way of John Stoddard to Governor Belcher, who supported his request in the General Court; this body voted Sergeant one hundred pounds. Although delayed by the lack of funds, his house was completed in late fall. It was Sergeant's plan to take into his house on the meadow the boys who were to be sent to school, for which the money had been promised by an English donor. Time in the fall was used for getting cloth from Boston and making up clothes for the boys. Sergeant hired as housekeeper Weenkeesquoh, an Indian woman who lived at Stockbridge. She also kept house for Timothy Woodbridge.

Finally, on January 11, 1738, Sergeant took twelve Indian boys into his small house, under his own instruction. By the end of 1738, however, the burden of teaching and supervising twelve boys proved too great, and Sergeant made other arrangements. Those of the boys he could persuade to it, he boarded with English families, from where they went to school to improve their reading and writing. Those who refused to be boarded lived with their own Indian families and attended Timothy Woodbridge's Indian school at Stockbridge, wearing clothing supplied from the donated school funds. Not surprisingly, the boys who lived with English families made better progress in learning and in speaking English than those who attended Woodbridge's school from their Mohican-speaking homes.

By the time Sergeant administered his first Communion service in June 1738, Umpachanee had begun to slip back into occasional bouts of drunkenness. He had always retained some hostility to English ideas. When Sergeant proposed to use some donated funds to board girls as well as boys with English families, Umpachanee strongly opposed it. Since Konkapot, on the contrary, was in favor of the proposal, Konkapot's oldest daughter and one other girl went to board with an English family during the summer. They did not remain very long. "Thro' a childish Fondness for Home, they would not be contented to stay long enough where I sent them, to obtain any good of it," wrote Sergeant.[55]

As the project to educate girls had failed, Sergeant received the money allotted for girls to assist him in his work. Sergeant also received money from the Corporation in London, as well as occa-

sional private gifts, channeled through Dr. Coleman. Without this
extra support, reported Rev. Samuel Hopkins, Sergeant could not
have continued the mission. At the end of 1738, three hundred pounds
was sent from the Society in England, part of which was used for
buying ploughs, axes, and hoes for the Indians to use in their farming
and gardens. Such extras were luxuries which Sergeant's yearly sti-
pend would not cover.

It was in June 1738 that Ephraim Williams and Josiah Jones
brought their families to Stockbridge. They were two of the English
families who had been asked to settle among the Indians to provide
Sergeant with company and as examples of civilized living. Two more
families, those of Samuel Brown and Joseph Woodbridge, followed
later. The Williams family, at several levels, was to have a profound
influence on the future of Stockbridge.

By 1739, delegations from various settlements of the River Indians (Mohicans) began to appear at Stockbridge to hear John Sergeant's
preaching. Others asked Sergeant to come to them to preach. In April,
one of the visitors was Maumauntissekun (later known as Abraham),
a Mohican of some importance, from the Mohican village of Shekomeko, in Dutchess County, where a Moravian mission was begun
a year later. On June 17, Maumauntissekun returned to Stockbridge
from Shekomeko. He indicated he was inclined to come to live there
but instead remained at Shekomeko. In May, Sergeant's acquaintances
from Kaunaumeek invited him to speak to the Indians at Mohican
sachem Ampamit's village, on Moesimus (Menanoke) Island in the
Hudson River, opposite Schodack Landing. In June, ten Mohicans
from Wukhquautenauk (Wequadnach), in Connecticut, about
twenty-eight miles to the south, came to hear Sergeant. On July 1,
seventeen men, women and children (including the ten who had
previously visited) arrived from Wukhquautenauk. They stayed for
the week, and seemed to think well of Christianity; the Stockbridge
mission introduced a favorable attitude toward Christianity among
some of the Mohicans from villages in Connecticut and Dutchess
County, New York. This introduction paved the way for the
Moravian missionaries when they arrived at these villages a year later.

Sergeant reported a May 1739 meeting with Jeremy Aunauwauneckheek, chief at Kaunaumeek, who had returned from a visit
to the Shawnees with three belts and a string of wampum. The
Stockbridge Mohicans had been advising the Shawnees to become
Christians. Jeremy, already a knowledgable Christian, first explained

his absence: "Brother Netohkum (which in our Dialect signifies my elder Brother) don't think your brother Keshum (or younger brother) has hid himself somewhere in the Woods. I design to live where I am, so long as the Lord our God shall spare me. . . ."[56] He identified the place he had been as Mukhauwaumuk (the Shawnee town) and brought greetings from the Shawnees who lived on the great island and at the river called Spunnauweh (Susquehanna), as well as from the Delawares. He also brought the promise of the Shawnees that, since the Mohicans had advised them that drinking was not good, they would not get drunk any more. The Shawnees, he reported, had made a law against buying any rum of the traders and had broken some kegs of rum which traders had brought to those who wanted rum. This report illustrates the determined attempts among the Indians to overcome the ill effects of rum, the most commonly available alcoholic beverage.

Similar efforts were made by Sergeant at Stockbridge, when he and others proposed to the Indians that they should take measures to restrain those Indians who were bringing rum into the town and selling it. A penalty of forty pounds New York money as a fine was agreed on to penalize those Indians who brought in rum. There was an appeal to the nearby tavern keepers not to sell drink to Indians inclined to excess, but this effort was met with derision.

It is likely that Sergeant's desire for marriage had something to do with his decision to end the boarding school in his home late in 1738. He was openly looking for a suitable wife.[57] On August 16, 1739, he married Abigail Williams, oldest daughter of Ephraim Williams, who had brought his family to Stockbridge in 1738. In so doing, Sergeant, after five years of devotion to the Indian mission, took a necessary and human step away from his Indian obligations. His dedication to the mission from that point was tempered by family responsibilities and by his connection to the Williams family.

The effect on Sergeant's life's work was probably more negative than he anticipated. Although Sergeant considered her his greatest joy and a gift from Heaven, his wife avoided contact with the Indians. Jonathan Edwards later heard from the Indians that "Mr. Sergeant did very well till he married her; but that afterwards there was a great alteration in him and he became quite another man." Mrs. Sergeant was regarded as "proud and covetous and not to be trusted."[58] Moreover, about this time Sergeant stopped keeping the extensive journal entries which had recorded the history of the mission in detail for the first five years. He and his wife in time built a stylish house on the hill, possibly because she did not care to live in his small house or close to the Indians on the meadow. At his death, Sergeant owed over 700 pounds, a debt possibly incurred in part by the second house.[59] The second Sergeant manse, now moved from the hill to a new location on Stockbridge's Main Street, has been preserved and is open to visitors.

Sergeant now found it difficult to live on his salary, even with the occasional gifts he received. Dr. Coleman sent him fifty pounds from the English donations which Coleman managed, and advised Sergeant that if his salary would not support his family, he must tell the Indian Commissioners. Coleman further advised him not to mention the occasional assistance Sergeant received through Coleman. Unfortunately, in September 1740, Sergeant's English benefactor died. Dr. Coleman sent Sergeant and Woodbridge money from the amount remaining in the fund, as well as some books for Sergeant.

In 1739, Stockbridge was incorporated as a town, with rights to form a parish. Sheffield objected to this step, as the Town of Sheffield had exercised some jurisdiction over the Upper Township, including collecting some taxes. Sheffield's efforts delayed organization of the Town of Stockbridge for two years. Early in 1741, the General Court issued orders for the organization of a meeting house and parish for the township lying north of the former Indian reserve. The area included later Great Barrington and area grants, including one made by the Indians to Captain John Spoor about 1731.[60]

By January 1740, a war between England and France was already anticipated. This would open hostilities between the English colonies and French Canada. Canada already threatened Indian relationships in New York and New England. Sergeant preached to a large gathering of Indians who were promoting a league of neutrality among Indian tribes of North America. The Stockbridge Mohicans had heard from the Indians at Schaghticoke in Rensselaer County, New York that both the French and English Mohawks would remain neutral. The Schaghticokes, who had French connections, urged the Stockbridges to remain neutral, as well. The Mohicans, Schaghticokes and Highland Indians presented belts and gave speeches to persuade friendly eastern Indian nations to do the same.[61] However, groups already closely associated with the French planned to fight the English.

To avoid allowing his Indian parishioners to relapse into a drunken celebration on New Year's day 1740 (which was celebrated that way, according to Sergeant, by their influential Dutch neighbors across the border), he planned a public worship for New Year's. As a result, the Indians were at Meeting, and there was little drinking, despite the availability of rum. Sergeant admitted that among the population there were some disorderly Indians, who were too free with strong drink, but he was pleased that drunkenness was lamented by the greater part of the Indian population. The change to temperance was a primary contribution of the mission to the health of the native population.

The number of residents at Stockbridge continued to increase. By March 1740, the Indian population was up to 120. The influx was necessary to make up the losses from death. "Our Number is increas'd by the addition of new Families, but reckoning by Births and Deaths, the Number is somewhat lessened," Sergeant wrote. This negative rate had been the case ever since Sergeant had known the Mohicans, and, he speculated, seemed to be the case among the Indians in general who lived in contact with the English, as ". . .in some places [the Indians] are diminished and come almost to Nothing."[62]

Sergeant blamed drinking, by both men and women, and irregular eating, for the number of deaths. He noted the Indians might go two or three days without a meal, but, when food was available, they would eat a great deal. He reported they also took no special care when they were sick and walked around while ill in all weather, if they were able to stay on their feet. In summer 1741, Umpachanee's wife, (Etowaukaum's daughter), was among Indians who died of consumption (tuberculosis). Konkapot's wife, Mary, also died of this disease March 29, 1742. Consumption, a communicable disease, was rampant among both the Indian and the English populations.

Early in 1740, John Sergeant planned a visit to the Shawnees, to discuss the possibility of a mission to be sponsored by the Edinburgh, Scotland, Society for Propogating Christian Knowledge. He had promised to send a report to the Society, but he could not get free to go to Pennsylvania until spring of 1741. He did, however, write a journal describing the religious success of the Stockbridge mission for George Drummond, who had contacted him on behalf of the Society for Propogating Christian Knowledge. This journal has not been found in any archive by researchers.

In a letter accompanying his account, Sergeant explained to Drummond, chairman of the Society, that "You will easily perceive. . .that the *Indians* are a very difficult People to deal with; whoever undertakes to have much to do with them, had need to fortify himself with an obstinate Patience. Opposition I always expected, but met with it in Instances where I dreamt not of it, and least expected it. The Devil has always his Temptations and Instruments to promote his Cause. A Number [of Indians] we have, I hope, that are truly converted." He continued, "Our affairs are now in a good and flourishing State, considering the Opposition the Gospel has met with, especially from some professed Christians."[63]

In June 1741, he wrote again to Drummond. He had just returned from the Susquehanna River, where he had gone with some Stockbridge Indians to "open the Way for the Propagation of the Gospel among the Showanoos." He hoped a mission similar to the one at Stockbridge could be established among them. The Shawnees called the Mohicans their elder brother, thanks to help from the Mohicans in the past, and the Mohicans called the Shawnees their younger brother.[64] The Shawnees were located at Mukhhauwaumuk in Pennsylvania about fifty miles from any English inhabitants, over a difficult path.

At Mukhhauwaumuk, Sergeant found that the Shawnees claimed not to understand him and would not pay attention to what he had to say. He learned they had strong and invincible prejudices against the Protestant religion, derived, he believed, from the French traders but also from some Christians who did not treat them well. Moreover, they held land by permission of the Senecas, strongly under French influence, who had charged them never to receive Christianity from the English. Under these conditions, the Shawnees probably did not dare to listen to Sergeant. Sergeant had made the trip of about 220 miles with little effect, even though the two Indian groups were friends and even though Jeremy Aunauwauneckheek of Kaunaumeek had paved the way. The Shawnees pointed out that Christianity need not be the bond of union between them. Some Shawnees, despite this, proposed sending two or three of their children to Stockbridge to be instructed in Christianity, and soon there were several Shawnees at Stockbridge.

When he visited the Delawares as he made his return, Sergeant preached to them in the Mohican dialect, which they, ancient relatives of the Mohicans, could understand without an interpreter. Here he had more success. About thirty Delawares listened to him attentively and desired further instruction, with the result that he preached to them a second time. Sergeant wrote to Drummond that there was a prospect of a successful mission among them. With this report the Drummond correspondence ended. Later, Sergeant wrote to the Society in Scotland asking that they assist with a proposed boarding school; he received no answer. Possibly his letter was lost along the way.

In March 1741, John Sergeant first mentioned to his sponsor, Dr. Coleman, his desire for an Indian boarding school in which the students would study a trade as well as learn reading, writing and religion. The Indian customs and way of living had led the men to let the women do the heavy work of getting wood, planting and weeding, even on their farm plots in Stockbridge. The demanding life left the women no time to learn the arts of housekeeping. The men still saw themselves as hunters, and, indeed, they still went hunting and fishing from time to time. Sergeant felt that the way to break the chain of traditional gender divisions would be to train children in the arts of industry and good living.

In 1742, Dr. Coleman had found another benefactor, the Rev. Isaac Hollis, who promised to lend a helping hand to Sergeant's boarding school. Hollis was offended that the people of New England did so little toward spreading Christian knowledge among the heathen, and suggested they might give up a few luxuries for so worthy a cause as saving heathen souls. Hollis' generosity, amounting to over 846 pounds sterling, caused Dr. Coleman to reflect on the lack of helping hands from his New England compatriots. He understood Mr. Hollis's anger with the New England populace.

Sergeant felt that the Indians now were ready to put their children in a boarding school where they could learn manual skills as well as reading and writing. In spring 1743 he had placed two young Indian women with English families at Northampton at the girls' own request; they were willing to work for their keep in order to learn the English language. When this venture proved successful, he proposed the boarding school to the Indians.

Sergeant drew up a plan for which he hoped Dr. Coleman would find financial support. Sergeant expected also to acquire a gift of two hundred acres of land from the Indians on which to erect a house for the school and to maintain there children and youth between the ages of ten and twenty years, under the care of two masters. The students were to have their time divided between hours of work and hours of study. They would help support themselves by their efforts, but might obtain some small rewards for their work, to encourage further industry. He hoped to have some cattle and other farm animals on hand. Eventually, he planned to take in girls as well as boys. Girls, as Dr. Coleman noted in a letter, not only were precious in their own right, but were influential because they raised the children for the first seven or eight years.

Sergeant wished to include children from neighboring Indian tribes, in hopes they would bring Christianity to their villages. He expected as much disipline to be used as the free-spirited Indians would stand for, noting that the Indian children and families "know *nothing like Government* among themselves, and have an *Aversion* to every Thing that *restrains* their Liberty."[65] Sergeant's concern was the large amount of money that must be raised to begin such a project. He also could foresee that the public might think there was some self-interest or ulterior motive behind the plan. He declared solemnly that he had no other aim than rendering the Indians a more happy society by cultivating humanity and virtue among them.

His growing disenchantment with his Indian charges and his feeling that he had not been able to mold them as he wished in almost a decade of trying was reflected in his assessment that "the Indians, in general, are a People *difficult* to be reformed from their own *foolish*, barbarous, and wicked Customs. . . ." In desperation, he was willing to try this new, boarding school approach and hoped for its success. At the same time, he wrote, "I do not *flatter* myself with any Romantick *Expectations* of accomplishing *all* the Ends proposed at once."[66] He noted the costs and pains involved and even suspected the plan might not work. Sergeant's dark discouragement came not from religion, but, apparently, from the Indians' inability, in his eyes, to cope with private land ownership, farming English style, town affairs, debt, and alcohol. He conceded to Coleman that the Indians were a base, ungrateful people. Yet, in another letter, and in a better mood, he described them as agreeable and a naturally ingenious and good-tempered people.[67]

His early idealism seems to have given way to the reality that Indian habits and culture were deeply ingrained and that the Indian town, with its conflicts, was not leading to the enlightenment he had expected. He could point only to some good effects which had attended his long labors at Stockbridge. Perhaps one reason for

Sergeant's depression was that he was overworked and underpaid. He was ministering to a colonial congregation as well as an Indian one. On Sundays he preached two sermons twice a day, one in English and one in Mohican—double the work, in his estimation. At times he paid an Indian interpreter two days a week to help him prepare his sermons, and also spent time privately instructing Indians. In addition, he had family responsibilities.

Sergeant needed a committee to collect and disburse the money for the proposed manual-arts boarding school. Dr. Coleman, although old and feeble, wrote an impassioned plea for the project and had copies printed of a letter from Sergeant and of Coleman's own letter. These he circulated among benefactors, interested clergymen, friends and government officials. Mr. Hollis asked that some of his money should be used for support of twelve boys of the age of nine through twelve years. He stipulated, however, that girls should be supported out of the funds of others. The English members of the congregation at Stockbridge made modest contributions. The Indians offered to help clear the land for the building. Despite this support, major contributions from wealthy donors were few and no committee to take charge emerged. Of four promised large gifts, none made their way to Sergeant. No other subscriptions were forthcoming. Despite strenuous efforts in England, which included getting royal sponsors, the project failed—from lack of Christian generosity, according to its proponents. At the last minute, the Society in London offered to contribute, but by that time the project had been delayed by the war.

King George's French War

By 1743, the attentions of colonial New York and New England turned to the French in Canada. "The *War* with France falls out unhappily for this Design [the boarding school project]. We are situated on the Borders of the *Massachusetts Province*, open to the *French* settlements, and in the road where the French and Indians us'd to make their Irruptions."[68] For the present, wrote Sergeant, it would not be prudent to spend any money for the boarding school. When money that a benefactor sent for the education of twelve boys was set aside due to the war, the donor protested that if his money was not used until the war ended, it might be a long time, indeed!

When war was imminent in 1744, the Mohicans tried to avoid becoming involved. While the Mohawks previously had agreed to stay neutral, in 1744 they considered joining the French. They demanded that the Mohicans join with them. In response, the Mohicans at Stockbridge built a fort for protection from the Mohawks as well as the French and invited other neutral Indians to take refuge there. In April 1744, Mohican sachems and their Indian advisers from Wequadnach, Weatauk, Stockbridge and Pachgatgoch attended a war council at Shekomeko. This alarmed the English.[69]

On June 2, 1744, Massachusetts Governor William Shirley received King George's Declaration of War against the French. The same month, John Stoddard and others met at Albany with forty-seven Mohicans and Schaghticokes (of New York), who reaffirmed their alliance with the Mohawks and the English. Just before the formal notice of war with Canada, the Mohicans and the Mohawks had a friendly meeting.[70] At the time, the Mohawks still planned to stay neutral.

Sergeant wrote, "My House is garrisoned: a Number of Soldiers are sent into the Town;—and Provisions are scarce."[71] Raiding parties of soldiers and Indians from Canada, killing farmers in their fields and taking family members captive, terrified New York and New England. The conflict with Canada, known as King George's War, which was to eject the Moravian missions to the south, also altered the Indian experience at Stockbridge. As Stockbridge fortified itself, outlying Indians moved into the safety of Stockbridge village. The Mohicans were frightened as much as the English.

Because French attacks on settlers in New York and Massachusetts escalated in 1746, the Mohicans were invited to another conference at Albany. A delegation from Stockbridge attended the Albany meeting, although they had been ignored at similar conferences in the past. Just as the conference began, a French force successfully attacked Fort Massachusetts, located at present North Adams. When this news was carried to Albany, the Mohicans received the New York Governor's respectful attention. On August 21, 1746, they were invited to participate with the Iroquois, now committed to the English side, in a concerted attack by the colonies on Canada. The River Indians were promised "Arms, Ammunition, Clothing, Provisions and everything necessary for the War."[72] Present were New York Governor George Clinton, his Council, Commissioners from the Government of the

Massachusetts Bay Colony, the Commissioners for Indian Affairs at Albany, and the Mayor and other representatives of Albany.

On August 26, the River Indians responded: "You have told us what mischief the French have done and what Murders they have Committed upon the Christians therefore we declare from our hearts and not from our Lips that as you have ordered us to shed the Enemies Blood in return for what they have done we are Resolved to do it and we will live and Dye with you in the Common Cause." The Mohican speaker then gave this pessimistic addendum, which illustrates the great reluctance of the Mohicans to become involved with the persistent English-French wars: "When you Christians are at War You make Peace with one another but it is not so with us therefore we depend upon you to take care of us[,] in Confidence of which we now take up the Hatchet and will make use of it against the French and their Indians."[73] Since the French wars involved some of their Indian friends to the north, who would hold a grudge for a long time, Indian alliances would shift. The fighting would leave the Mohicans with fewer Canadian friends after the war's end. They were aware that they could not count on future government interest and support once the war was over.

French Indians were regularly ambushing travelers and farmers across New England and New York, often scalping them. In 1746, in order to return barbarity with barbarity (justifiable, in English eyes, for self-preservation only), Massachusetts reluctantly agreed to employ Indians against the French and their Indians. English-allied Indian warriors were to be paid forty pounds for any male prisoner or thirty-eight pounds for a male scalp brought in. Women and children brought less for capture or scalp, but nevertheless were to be taken. Any Indian setting out on such an expedition was to be allowed five pounds.[74]

Consequently, in April 1747, John Stoddard, writing from North Hampton, mentioned he had sent for "10 or 12" Stockbridge Indians.[75] A list of officers and men serving in the garrison company under Major Ephraim Williams, Jr. at Fort Massachusetts on June 26, 1747 included the following: Ensign John Pohpnehonnuwoh [probably Konkapot's son], Lt. Samuel Brown, Lt. Samuel Elmore, Sgt. David Whitney, John Pebble, Drummer, Samuel Brian, John Lebourvou, Felix Powel, Wautaunkummeet, Robin, Shouwunnokhok, Wauwaumpequunnaunt, Waumehewi, Pauuqunusmookhhoh, Ummcheekhheek, Wauwootummuwoh, Yokun, Wautaunquun-

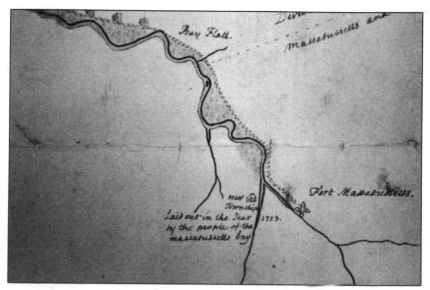

Fort Massachusetts, attacked during King George's French War of 1744-1748,
was located on the Hoosic River, part of a natural pathway from Canada. Several
Mohicans under Col. Ephraim Williams served there in 1747. The fort was at
present North Adams, Massachusetts.

Annonymous "Map of the Northern Parts of New York," c. 1758,
from the Peter Force Collection, Library of Congress

naunt, Chaunehwaus, Muttohkummun, Nukhhikenuuwequun, Naunees, Sam Frank, Nicholas Claus, and Pauponkseet. There were three illegible names.[76]

The Indians were to assemble at Fort Massachusetts to prepare for an expedition to Canada. While waiting for action, men under Col. William Williams worked at rebuilding Fort Massachusetts, burned the previous year. French Indians in the woods near the fort harassed the English men and Stockbridge Indians who were passing back and forth to Albany for supplies, while scouts tried to protect them. One party of scouts was under Ensign John Pohpnehonnuwoh.

A 1750 narrative gives the following account of one day's events: On May 25, 1747, "Major [Ephraim] Williams of Stockbridge had been to Albany for stores, and was now on his Return with a number of Waggons near the Fort. He sent a few Men this Morning to mend the Way and give Notice to the Fort that they were a-coming. When they had got within fifty or sixty Rods of the Fort, they saw the

Part of a list of the settlers and proprietors of Stockbridge, with the acres assigned to each, dates to Monday, June 11, 1750.

Stockbridge Library Historical Collection

enemy creeping towards the Fort. They fired upon them, which made them [the enemy] discover themselves and fire at our Men who were on the Guard, and at work, and pursue those who were coming with Major Williams. Our Men fired from the Fort and pursued them at some distance from the Fort, till the Enemy seemed to aim to get between them and the Fort, and then they retreated. The Enemy kill'd one Stockbridge Indian, and wounded three more of our Men, who are since recovered."[77]

The dead Stockbridge had been scalped. The enemy had taken note of the caravan when it left for Albany and had sent a force to ambush the wagons. This force, frightened by the size of the caravan, quickly withdrew after the encounter.[78] Through the summer, however, soldiers working near Fort Massachusetts and the other forts along the northern line of defense were regularly ambushed.[79]

The Mohawks also had losses while fighting on the side of the English. Some Mohicans met with them at the home of Sir William Johnson to commiserate with them and to reinforce the Mohawk commitment to the war. After wiping away the tears of their "Unkle", loyal Mohicans reminded the Mohawks that the friendship they had made long ago with the English should be maintained and that Johnson represented the King of England, saying "Let us Gether about him and Stand around him and if he falls let us fall with him."[80]

When the war drew to a close in 1748, Indians expressed regret at having been drawn into the conflict, which had accomplished so little. Their distrust of English motives in wartime was reinforced. English leadership was also suspect. The expected expedition to Canada, for which they had been recruited, never occurred and they had little reward for their involvement except their daily rations, although the following year they received some gifts.[81]

Community life resumed its importance. To resolve land ownership questions, late in 1749 the Housatunnuk Indians had been declared a "distinct proprietory" by the General Court. Col. Timothy Dwight, ordered to Stockbridge, called a May 26, 1750, meeting of the Indian proprietors, "at which meeting the sd Proprietors are Impowered by the sd Great & Gen'l Court by A majority vote to ascertain the number of the Proprietors & what each Proprietors proportion Shall be & to choose a proprietors Clerk to be Under Oath to Record all Legal votes, Grants & orders of the sd Proprietors & all Lands heretofore Laid out by order of the Committee formerly Appointed by the Gen'l Court for that purpose."[82]

The proprietors were to keep a record book of the land which they assigned to each Indian. Moreover, land could be sold or parceled out by the Indian proprietors as needed, but Timothy Woodbridge was supposed to ensure that each sale was fair and essential. The Indian proprietors met June 11, 1750, and assigned shares ranging from 10 to 80 acres to fifty-five members of the tribe. One half of the remaining land was reserved for future Indian residents. House lots for Indian homes along the main street and meadow lots on both sides of the Housatonic River were laid out. Ephraim Williams, however, continued brazenly to appropriate large acreages, much of which he managed to keep.[83]

The Boarding School

In part because of pressure from a donor who was waiting for the boarding school so he could support some of the students, Sergeant had obtained from the Mohicans two hundred acres of their land for the postponed boarding school; the land was situated about a mile from the meeting house. Sergeant continued to work on the project but was unable to organize a group of trustees to supervise the school. Nevertheless, he resolved to erect the necessary building, so that he could begin the education and maintenance of the twelve boys for whom money was available. Because of the war and a shortage of funds for the building, however, Sergeant temporarily provided the boys with a teacher, Captain Martin Kellogg, and boarded them out. Kellogg was to instruct them "both in learning and hard labour."[84] Twelve boys were chosen, and the school began under those arrangements at Newington in May 1747.

In 1749, Sergeant again tried fund-raising for a boarding school for girls as well as boys, with little success. By 1748, nevertheless, a building was almost ready for the boys. His plan was that the Indian children at the school, under the care of their teacher, who would work with them and supervise them, should clear and cultivate the two hundred acres of land on which they lived. He expected them to keep a farm stocked with cattle, sheep, and hogs. The girls, under a mistress, were to be in charge of the wool, flax and milk, and to learn work suitable for women. It was expected that the school would support itself, and that the young people would learn the English language and manners, so that, at about the age of twenty, they would be ready to set up farms of their own. This regime was designed to cure the Indian youths of idleness, a major vice in English eyes. The plan ignored their native culture entirely, much as later ill-conceived Indian schools did.

The twelve boys boarding out under the care of Captain Kellogg made progress in reading and writing and, in general, behaved well. It was learned later, however, that they were not well-fed or well-cared for. At Sergeant's request, Kellogg brought the boys to Stockbridge in April 1749. He now asked Kellogg to spend a year with them in Stockbridge.

Kellogg agreed; after the school began in a private house, Kellogg moved with them into the boarding school building, which was nearing completion. The school was thirty-eight by thirty-six feet, with three rooms with fireplaces on one floor, and two additional rooms above. There was a large cellar under it. According to a writer of 1890, the school was a little south of the then residence of Lucius Tuckerman.[85]

It was Sergeant's plan, in the summer of 1749, to invite children of the Iroquois to come to Stockbridge to receive an education in the boarding school, and to open the doors to other interested Indian tribes. Before he could set his boarding school in motion, John Sergeant died on July 27, 1749, at age 39, after a few weeks of illness. Those with whom he had been dealing were shocked. Governor Belcher, who had now become governor of New Jersey, was truly fond of him and admired his devotion to the Indians. The Indian population of Stockbridge was stunned and sad. They assembled in the church and spent a day in fasting and prayer. Sergeant's wife, Abigail, reported that "Sergeant's poor bereaved flock. . .are incessantly lamenting this judgment upon them."[86] The Indians considered Sergeant's death payment for their sins.

Sergeant had three children, Electa, about eight or nine years old; Erastus, the middle child, who became a doctor at Stockbridge; and John, an infant. In 1752, Sergeant's widow married Col. Joseph Dwight; the couple remained in the Sergeant house for several years.[87] In this circumstance, John Sergeant's young son, John Sergeant, Jr., who never knew his father, nevertheless grew up among Indian companions, learned the Mohican language, and developed an empathy for the Indians. As a result of this experience, he later served as the minister to the Mohicans, both at Stockbridge and at New Stockbridge in the colony of New York.

At the time of Sergeant's death, there were 218 Indians living at Stockbridge, in fifty-three families, of whom 129 Indians had been baptized. Forty-two (eighteen men and twenty-four women) were members of the church in good standing. Twenty of the families lived in frame houses and there were some well-fenced, relatively productive farms. In all, Sergeant had baptized a total of 182 Indians, many of whom by then were dead. Woodbridge had about fifty-five scholars in his school, with about forty attending at any one time. The students could read their bibles well and some spoke English freely.[88] By 1749, there were about twelve or thirteen English families at Stockbridge. Land had been set off for them.

In December of that year, the Indian property in the Town was turned over to the Indian proprietors and/or Indian residents, as noted above, although the official proprietors' meeting was not held until the following summer. The Indians were to divide and dispose of their land among themselves as they judged necessary; they could admit Indians of other tribes to live among them, who could not, however, sell the land entrusted to them. The Indian residents, moreover, could not directly sell their assigned land to pay debts, no matter how desperate the situation, without the permission of the General Court. The law restricting sale of land remained on the books until 1765. In the interim, many subterfuges were adopted to permit Indian land to be transferred to colonial hands.[89]

With the death of John Sergeant in 1749, only Timothy Woodbridge was directly charged with the welfare of the Mohicans at Stockbridge. The Indians became increasingly dependant upon his counsel, although they had had some differences with him over his acquisition of land in the past. For over a year, the Indians managed with substitute ministers in their pulpit. Their first choice for a replacement, Samuel Hopkins, son of the minister who had helped initiate the Indian mission, preferred not to come. The minister Hopkins recommended was his mentor, the controversial Jonathan Edwards, ousted by his Northampton congregation for his conservative religious views. Edwards did not know the Indian language and was considered old-fashioned, but he was willing to come. He was not the choice of the prominent English faction at Stockbridge, made up of Ephraim Williams and his connections; they complained that besides not knowing the language, Edwards was not sociable and was too old.[90]

Timothy Woodbridge, however, was suspicious of the connections of an alternate minister proposed by the Williams clan and supported Edwards. After Edwards spoke to the Stockbridge congregation of both English and Indian families, he was approved. Although he was deemed an impractical theologian and had strict points of view on religion, Edwards attempted to tailor his sermons to his Indian listeners, with some success. After he arrived in summer 1751, he purchased, on the street that lead through the plain to the meetinghouse, a plot of eight acres and Sergeant's original house. He added to this structure to make room for his wife and six children,[91] who arrived by winter. He also bought fifty acres for a future home site, and soon began to buy timbered land from the Mohicans, ostensibly for firewood, without the approval of the General Court, but with the approval of the Indian proprietors and Timothy Woodbridge.[92]

Since he did not speak the Mohican language, Jonathan Edwards availed himself of John Wauwaumpequunaunt as translator. Edwards felt "no other educated American Indian better understood divinity and the scriptures."[93] In addition to his Stockbridge obligations, Edwards spent long hours in his study writing papers defending theological positions and paid little attention to mundane affairs. He left early in 1758 to head the University at Princeton, New Jersey, but died soon after he arrived there. Rev. Dr. Stephen West, who succeeded Jonathan Edwards at Stockbridge after more than a year's hiatus, remained as missionary minister until 1775. He, in turn, was succeeded by John Sergeant, son of the original missionary, who followed the Mohicans to New Stockbridge, New York.

The invitation to send sons to the boarding school brought Mohawks, Oneidas, and Tuscaroras to Stockbridge. They were offered land; many considered moving to Stockbridge, and some came in February 1752. Soon Mohawk parents and children in the village numbered close to ninety. Families stayed in wigwams near the school.[94] Among the visitors was the noted Mohawk chief, Hendrick, of the Upper Castle on the Mohawk River.

Timothy Woodbridge obtained an English-speaking Indian assistant, in order to take into his existing school all the resident Stockbridge Indian children as well as children of the English families. The Iroquois children were to attend the new boarding school, where their teacher was to be Gideon Hawley, a fresh Yale graduate; Hawley was to replace the unsatisfactory Captain Kellogg. Kellogg, although his contract was up, refused to give up his position.[95]

The demise of the boarding school can be traced to interference by Colonel Ephraim Williams, "the most conspicuous of the first English settlers." Because he was so anxious to obtain land by any method and to get control over Indian affairs, Williams was disliked by the Indians and by Timothy Woodbridge. Colonel Williams, nevertheless, due to his connections, had been appointed resident Commissioner of the Indian Board of the Province of Massachusetts. In this position, he was able to collect donations intended for the Stockbridge mission and was charged with not providing records of how the money was spent.[96]

The Williams clan grasped at the school. Williams' daughter, Abigail Sergeant, was to begin an Indian girls' school in her home but had few students as she was not popular with the Indians. Her prospective husband, Joseph Dwight, was appointed manager of the boarding school project. Dwight also was in line to profit from completion of the boarding school building for which John Sergeant had gone into debt. Other Williams relatives were selling goods to the visiting Iroquois. To harass Jonathan Edwards, Joseph Dwight refused to attend church when Edwards preached, a bad example set before the Indians which upset the English families of the congregation.

In addition, Ephraim Williams arrogantly interfered with Gideon Hawley's appointment by backing Kellogg. As a result of the discord, the Oneida parents removed their sons from the school and left, on Gideon Hawley's advice, rather than have their children taught by Kellogg. Most Mohawks, discontented, left in 1753 and the remainder were ordered home by spring 1754 because of impending war. Although Williams' scheme to take over Indian affairs was exposed by Rev. Jonathan Edwards, the boarding school did not revive. Soon the building suspiciously burned. Gideon Hawley left to be with the Oneidas in their homeland, where he taught until the Revolutionary War began. Some of the remaining boarding school endowment was used in 1755 to send a few Stockbridge Indian children to board with Dr. Bellamy, in Bethlehem, Connecticut.[97]

Challenges

Despite their difficulties, the Stockbridge Mohicans, with some adopted friends including Shawnees and a large group of Wappingers, remained at Stockbridge for over thirty years following the death of John Sergeant. There were unique challenges for these Mohican residents. The Indians in the 1750s and 1760s were faced with competition for town offices and for land within their own town. By the mid-1750s, they were complaining at Indian conferences that they had no land. A new war effectively lasting from 1755 to 1760 drew away their young men, who hoped to earn a soldier's pay with Rogers Rangers or with Sir William Johnson's troops. Meanwhile the community's elders continued to press land claims both in Massachusetts and New York, hoping to obtain payments on which to live. As part of their land policy, they sold land which fueled the "Anti-Rent" disturbances on the Livingston patent; they also disagreed with the Van Rensselaers over patent boundaries. They became increasingly reliant on counsel and supplies from Sir William Johnson, Superintendent of Indian Affairs. In 1774, West Stockbridge was separated

Know all men by these Presents, that we Robert
Naunghawaut and Jacob Scautcaw both of Stockbridge
in the County of Berkshire and Province of the Massachusetts Bay
in New England Indian Hunters, In Consideration of Twenty
Pounds worth of Good Merchantable Goods, to me in Hand paid by
Benjamin Willard of Stockbridge in the County and Province aforesaid Yeoman. We the said Robert & Jacob have Delivered over
and Put into the Possession of the said Benjamin a Certain Grant
of Land to be laid out within the Town of Stockbridge Containing Sixty
Acres which Grant was Granted to the above Named Jacob at a
meeting of the Proprietors of the said Town of Stockbridge and is part
of the Right that belonged to Capt. Kunkapot Deceased: all which
said Grant we the said Robert & Jacob for our selves and our heirs
Deliver over and into the Possession of the said Benjamin his heirs
and Assigns for Security of said Sum of Twenty Pounds, hereby
Engaging the Possession and Improvement of the Premises to him
the said Benjamin and his Heirs free and Clear without Molestation
or Demands from the said Robert & Jacob and their Heirs untill
the said Sum of Twenty Pounds, be well and Truly paid by us
or Our Heirs to the said Benjamin or his Heirs, with the
Lawful Interest of the same! And we the said Robert & Jacob
hereby Promise and Engage whenever the way can or may be
made Lawful To Execute a good Deed of Sale To the said
Benjamin and his Heirs, of the above said Grant of Land in
Case the above said Sum be not well and Truly paid as above-
said within the space of two years, from the Date of these
Presents. As witness our hands and Seals this Twentieth day
of September Anno Dom 1765 and in the fifth year
of His Majesty's Reign ————

Signed Sealed and   Robert Naunghawaut
Delivered in Presence of
                                                  his
                              Jacob   ⨁   Scautcaw
Jacob Cheekjannkun   mark
Nathaniel Palmer

from Stockbridge and incorporated, another loss of land and income for the Indians. The Williams family and Williams cohorts, by devious methods, obtained the largest share of Stockbridge area land. Some merchants deliberately overcharged the Indians or threatened them with jail to get their land. Beginning in 1765, Indians were allowed to sell their land to pay debts. Much of the Mohicans' remaining Stockbridge land was sold to pay for living expenses and for debts.[98]

The Indians' old adviser, Timothy Woodbridge, after an illness, died in 1774. Mohicans served in the Revolution, but lost many men. Despite their valorous war service, their land was not protected and they were denied benefits that went to white veterans. Finally, Mohican leaders acknowledged that they could not survive in the English town. Although most now were firm Christians, they longed to rejoin Indian society. In the 1780s, groups of Stockbridge Indian residents moved away from Stockbridge to a new location among the Oneidas in western New York, in response to an invitation first proffered to them in the 1750s.[99] Some individuals and families, mostly people who were old or those with special ties to the area, remained behind.[100] Of course, there were other Mohicans in the Housatonic valley who had never moved to Stockbridge and who also did not move away.

The central figures of Mohican society, however, including the chief sachem and his counselors and relatives, were part of the move to New Stockbridge. Strong new leaders arose. At New Stockbridge, despite a split into two factions, the Stockbridge emigrants would be in control of their own affairs and could combine old ways with the new as they chose. They had not imitated the English as the missionaries had hoped, yet they now were experienced in English ways and at New Stockbridge they replicated their Stockbridge town. Most were Christians. At the same time they retained their language and Indian mores. Their evolving Mohican identity was still rooted in traditions of the past.

Facing page: *Robert Nungkauwaut and Jacob Scawtcauw signed a deed in 1765. Jacob, of the turtle clan, was a son of Captain Konkapot. Robert was either Jacob's brother or his son. The two men, who had mortgaged Jacob's portion of the land inherited from Konkapot, deceased, in order to pay debts, promised a future deed to the buyer. They were not allowed to make an outright sale of the land.*
Stockbridge Library Historical Collection

VIII.
The Kaunaumeek Mission

" 'We do not want this white man here; let us make away with him.' But others said, "No, we will not kill him.' " —Mohicans at Kaunaumeek.

"He was a lovely man. He was a staff to walk with." —Mohican woman from Kaunaumeek, speaking of David Brainerd.[1]

A S THE STOCKBRIDGE MISSION became well-established, Mohicans from villages around New York and Connecticut were attracted there. In addition, the Shawnees of Pennsylvania had expressed interest, although Sergeant was rebuffed on a visit to them. Indians from Kaunaumeek, too, had visited Stockbridge and had invited Sergeant to speak to them. The Mohican community of Kaunaumeek was located on the Kinderhook Creek, near the present Columbia-Rensselaer County line.

In late summer 1737, John Sergeant had been informed that ten families of Indians living at Kaunaumeek wanted him to come to preach to them. Consequently, on Sunday, September 11, he traveled through the forest to the village eighteen miles from Stockbridge, accompanied by some of the more important Stockbridge Indians. He had prepared a sermon in Mohican for the occasion. For his talk, he had about thirty Indians in attendance, although not all belonged to the village. The residents of Kaunaumeek had spread the word of his coming to others who lived nearby, "so that a considerable Number were got together." His audience listened carefully and assured him they understood him. "We were entertain'd very kindly: The chief Man there whose name was Aunauwauneekhheek, appear'd to be a rational, judicious Man," Sergeant noted.[2] Aunauwauneekhheek could speak a little English, carried on some farming, and lived well, according to Sergeant's account.

Aunauwauneekhheek, although interested in the new religion, was not ready to accept it. He promised to come to hear Sergeant at

Housatonic. The chiefs from Stockbridge urged their fellows at Kaunaumeek to accept the Christian religion. Another Indian present, who seems to have been Wautaunkumeet, second in importance at Kaunaumeek, reported he "had been baptiz'd in his infancy by some priest, was well-inclined to religion and purpos'd to come and live with us," wrote Sergeant.[3] In February 1740, Sergeant, with some reservations, baptized him in the Protestant religion. Sergeant noted: "Baptised Waunaubauquus, a grave & Sober man of good behaviour; a Kinswoman and her child. . .Waunaubauquus about two years ago came hither from Kaunaumeek with his family for the Sake of being instructed in Religion. He was baptised in his Infancy by a Popish priest; but as he had lived altogether in heathenism, he was willing to be baptised by me; which perhaps I Should not have insisted on, had he been averse to it."[4]

Soon the Kaunaumeek leader came to Stockbridge to hear Sergeant and discuss religion. His associate, Wautaunkumeet, had already decided to move to Stockbridge and in February left his son with Sergeant. Between late February and early April, Wautaunkumeet moved to Stockbridge. He was a man of about forty, good tempered, and knowledgeable, and a reformed drinker. On April 16, 1738, Wautaunkumeet and two of his children were baptized. He took the new name of "John."

In mid-October, Aunauwauneekhheek came from Kaunaumeek to spend several days at the Stockbridge mission, but Sergeant was away. A few months later, in January 1738, Sergeant preached again at Kaunaumeek. Aunauwauneekhheek was by then anxious to be baptized. He sent his only child, a daughter, to learn to read, and came himself again for a week's visit to the mission. Sergeant baptized him and his daughter.[5] Once converted, Aunauwauneekhheek actively recruited new adherents.

On June 10, 1739, at Stockbridge, Sergeant wrote in his journal, "Present seven new Hearers from Kaunaumeek and the Neighborhood, with Aunauwauneekhheek at the head of them. At the same Time they told me that the Indians of the Island were very desirous that I would come and preach to them." The island was Moesimus Island in the Hudson River at Schodack, called Menanoke by the Mohicans. Here in a village of four houses, Ampamit, the chief sachem, lived with his entourage.

Two weeks later, Sergeant made the long ride to Moesimus Island, which lay in sight of the dock at the Dutch-speaking hamlet of

Schodack Landing. On the island, he addressed a crowd of about "thirty intelligent hearers, who gave good attention. . . ." The Indians from Kaunaumeek were present and Aunanwauneekhheek, particularly, urged Sergeant to lodge with the Indians on the island rather than with the Dutch-speaking people on the mainland.[6]

In May 1739, Aunauwauneekhheek, who was also known as Jeremy, had returned from a visit to the Shawnees of Pennsylvania. He had brought messages and belts of wampum from these associates. The Mohicans, with the Wappingers (their traditional allies), and the New York Schaghticokes were at the time trying to persuade the other eastern nations to remain neutral if war between the English and the French broke out, as seemed likely.

Thus Aunauwauneekhheek, although he lived at Kaunaumeek, was well-traveled. He acted as a messenger between the Mohicans at Stockbridge and the Shawnees and was also well-connected with the Mohican chief sachem, Ampamit, and with other Mohicans living on Moesimus Island at Schodack. Kaunaumeek, morcover, was a nucleus for scattered Mohican families along the Kinderhook Creek and the Valatie Kill. The Mohican residents had close ties to both the Indians' island village at Schodack and to Stockbridge. These associations may have caused the Kaunaumeek residents some anguish, as the Mohican population at Moesimus Island had resisted the pull of Stockbridge. However, after Sergeant's visit in 1739, the opposition of the Mohicans on the island began to crumble, in part due to Aunauwauneekhheek's efforts.

John Sergeant, unable to fully serve the Indian group at Kaunaumeek, appealed for another missionary. He wrote to Scotland's Society for Propagating Christian Knowledge not only about the likelihood of success of a mission among the Delaware Indians, but also about the Indians at Kaunaumeek and the prospect of success which a missionary might have among them.[7] As a delayed result, in 1743 a young missionary, David Brainerd, came to stay for a year with the villagers at Kaunaumeek. Aunauwauneekhheek and his family paved the way for Brainerd's reception among them, but some Mohicans of the village resented his presence.

Brainerd was born April 20, 1718, at Haddam, Connecticut, of respectable parents and was one of nine children. His mother, Dorothy Hobart, a minister's daughter, died when he was fourteen; his father had died four years before. They were a religious family in a religious time; three of the family's sons became ministers. A devout, self-centered, and melancholy young man, David Brainerd kept a journal in which he recorded his struggles to overcome feelings of religious unworthiness and also his physical travail. As he attended college, he was already ill with consumption, a communicable disease.

Although a leading scholar, Brainerd had been expelled from Yale in his third year, after an unfortunate incident in which a private remark he made was held against him. Next he pursued private studies for the ministry. In 1742, he was invited to consult in New York "in reference to evangelizing of the Indians" with local representatives of the Society for Propagating Christian Knowledge. Soon, with their encouragement, he agreed to become a missionary to the Indians.[8]

In August 1742, David Brainerd traveled through the Kent, Connecticut area. In the morning, while he was stopped, New England Indians from Pachgatgoch (Scaticoke) came to him and he felt forced to preach. At the time, they were curious about the Moravians at Shekomeko and were evaluating what response to Christian overtures would be to their benefit. The Indians were greatly moved by Brainerd's preaching, and he urged them to hire an English woman to keep a small school among them. However, nothing was done. In 1743, an English-speaking teacher, Joseph Shaw, was sent to the Indians of Pachgatgoch by the Moravians, much to the alarm of the Connecticut settlers. To counteract the Moravian influence, Rev. Cyrus March, of Kent, sent a delegation from his church in August to promise Gideon Mauwehu, the sachem, that Connecticut would open a school among them. Mauwehu turned the offer away because it would have meant ousting the Moravian teacher.[9]

Brainerd was inspired by the experience at Pachgatgoch and visited again in March 1743. "He stopped in New Milford on a Saturday and the following Sunday rode five or six miles to Schaticoke [Pachgatgoch] to hold divine services. But by then the die had been cast in favor of the Moravians."[10] Nevertheless, Moravian Bishop Cammerhoff wrote later that Brainerd's visits had had a dramatic effect. "Almost all our Pachgatgoch Indians were awakened by his preaching," Cammerhoff said.[11] Brainerd was resentful of the Moravians' appeal to the Indians, although he later came to admire them.

The American committee of the Society which employed Brainerd originally planned to send him to the Indians living near the Forks of the Delaware, as proposed by Sergeant. Instead, due to danger and tensions on the Delaware and in consideration of the suggestions of John Sergeant, they directed Brainerd to Kaunaumeek. After a stop at Stockbridge, early in 1743 he moved to the Kaunaumeek area. On April 1, Brainerd wrote in his journal, "I rode to Kaunaumeek, in the wilderness, near twenty miles from Stockbridge, and about an equal distance from Albany, where the Indians live with whom I am concerned; and lodged with a poor Scotchman about a mile and a half distant from them. . . ."[12] There, for two months, he slept on straw in a shared log room with a dirt floor.

Brainerd's diary says almost nothing about the Mohican society in which he worked. It can be regretted that the names, personalities and habits of his Indian contacts were not recorded. The Indians recognized his sincere devotion to their religious welfare, and, after some hostility, accepted his presence. He began to preach to them through an interpreter by April 10, 1743 and soon attracted Indians and some isolated European settlers, as well, to his services. Neither the settlers nor the Indians spoke English as Brainerd knew it. On May 18, he wrote, "I live in the most lonesome wilderness; have but one single person to converse with that can speak English. Most of the talk I hear is either Highland Scotch or Indian."[13]

The Scot with whom he lived in 1743 was apparently John McCagg, whose wife was Lyntjie Van Deusen; their son was baptized at Kinderhook. The McCaggs lived near the military road from Pontoosuc (Pittsfield) to Albany. A burned cabin, thought to be McCagg's, was found at Kaunaumeek in 1758 during the last French and Indian War by soldiers traveling to Albany. A soldier's diary also mentions a cleared place at Kaunaumeek, where a company camped. A few days later, other troops stopped at Kaunaumeek.[14] A map of 1767 indicates McCagg returned after the war and erected a new dwelling, probably west of his earlier location.

Jonathan Edwards' *Life of Brainerd* states that the person at Kaunaumeek who could speak English was an Indian. "This person was Brainerd's interpreter, an ingenious young Indian belonging to Stockbridge, whose name was John Wauwaumpequunnaunt. He had been instructed in the Christian religion by Mr. Sergeant; had lived with the Rev. Mr. Williams, of Long-Meadow; had been further instructed by him, at the charge of Mr. Hollis, of London; and understood both English and Indian very well, and wrote a good hand." [15]

Brainerd found his existence at Kaunaumeek trying. He often had no bread and, although he had a horse, it was frequently lost in the woods. He had to send someone, or go himself, ten or fifteen miles for a supply of bread, which grew moldy before he finished it. He wrote, ". . .most of my diet consists of boiled corn, hasty pudding, etc. I lodge on a bundle of straw, my labor is hard and extremely difficult, and I have little appearance of success to comfort me."[16] This last comment was a reference to the resistence of some of the villagers to his presence among them. Before they learned to trust him, some told him to go away. Brainerd, however, took brief note of the pressures on the Mohicans of Kaunaumeek as a result of the hostility of some colonial settlers. "The Indians have no land to live on but what the Dutch lay claim to; and these threaten to drive them off. They have no regard to the *souls* of the poor Indians; and by what I can learn, they hate me because I come to preach to them."[17] Although what he said was true, Brainerd's attitude reflected the strong feelings against the Dutch-speaking residents of Rensselaerswyck and Kinderhook, prevalent among Stockbridge's English leaders and New Englanders in general.

However, the land was, according to colonial records, Van Rensselaer land. Under terms of the 1685 charter obtained by Van Rensselaer family members from the King's representatives, their manor land extended twenty-four miles east of the Hudson River. In 1707 and 1708, deeds had been signed by the Mohican chiefs at the Hudson River confirming earlier Van Rensselaer Indian purchases.[18] The initial grants had been along the river, with vague references to interior distances, often containing terms such as "inland as far as their [the signing Indians] rights extend." The early eighteenth-century confirmations, however, were specific. The 1707 and 1708 deeds included all land from a south point opposite Beeren Island beside present Coeymans north to a point opposite the Cohoes Falls, and extended twenty-four miles to the east of the Hudson River. The confirmation deeds were requested of the Indians by Kiliaen Van Rensselaer in response to the elevation of Queen Anne to the throne. The Queen's agents required landowners to produce their proofs of ownership.

Due to the recurring French wars, little settlement occurred on the eastern lands of Rensselaerswyck until the 1760s. In the 1730s, a time between wars, farms established by settlers of Dutch and German stock were creeping up from the south along the Kinderhook

Creek, south of the Rensselaerswyck line. In 1732, four Indians from Keekameek (presumably a misspelling of Kaunaumeek), named Wanneeck (a shortened version of Aunauwauneekhheek), Claes, Onnosies (a woman), and Nackavina had sold land along the Kinderhook south of Kaunaumeek to Johann Casper Roush of Kinderhook.[19] Roush was already on the seventy-acre site, so the twelve pounds they received was a formality for an occupation already in progress, given because they complained. Much of the area below eastern Rensselaerswyck the Indians later claimed never to have sold. As noted above, however, Kaunaumeek sat squarely on land conveyed by the Mohicans to the Van Rensselaers.

One signer, Claes, seems to have been Etowaukaum, known as Nicholas, who went to London in 1710 with the Indian delegation to meet Queen Anne. Claes is the Dutch nickname for Nicholas. Twenty-four years after his voyage, Etowaukaum apparently was a member of the Mohican community at Kaunaumeek. He died by 1736 (before the Kaunaumeek mission began), according to a mention in a letter.[20] His daughter's sons, through her marriage to Umpachanee, perpetuated Etowaukaum's line in Stockbridge. Etowaukaum's grandson, Jonas Etowaukaum, was well-known and later descendants were prominent Mohican leaders in the nineteenth century.[21]

It seems strange that the older Mohicans were not aware that Ampamit, his brothers, as well as the respected leader, Caloolett, his son, Camela, and others had signed the early eighteenth century confirmation deeds granting Rensselaerswyck possession twenty-four miles inland. It is possible that a poor interpreting job was done for the Indian signers, and that they did not know they were granting so much land. It is also possible that the early Indian grants and their eighteenth-century confirmations were forgotten or ignored by 1743. Sir William Johnson claimed in 1754, after explaining that an Indian deed was necessary before any patent was issued, ". . .most of the lands concerning which you complain were patented when you were children, some before any of you were born."[22] Johnson's was the English way of looking at property sales as permanent transactions.

In any event, as the land had been left largely unsettled, here was another instance where the Mohicans had sold land and yet continued for years to live on it and use it as their own for hunting and fishing. In the course of doing so, they regarded it as their own. In recognition of this situation, often the colonial landowner or the settler who leased a farm or mill paid the resident Indians a token amount when it came time to settle the land. For example, in 1760, within the tract sold in 1708, a small Indian village of Stockbridge Indians was situated near present Nassau Village, New York, a few miles to the west of Kaunaumeek. It is likely that the Indians had a connection to the former Kaunaumeek village. In that year, two separate tracts were sold by these Indians to Rensselaerswyck lease holders. One tract was at present Nassau Village, the second was beside an adjacent marsh, which became Hoag's Pond, now Nassau Lake.[23] Both sites were within the earlier grants.

By May 1743, Brainerd made a trip to New Jersey to consult with the correspondents of the Society for Propagating Knowledge. He wished to obtain permission to set up a school among the Indians, and desired that his interpreter, John Wauwaumpequunnaunt, might be appointed as schoolmaster. Both objectives were approved, although the school never materialized, due to the early dissolution of the mission. Brainerd quickly returned to Kaunaumeek.

Recognizing that the distance between his rented lodgings and the Indian village denied him contact with his charges, Brainerd moved to the village and lived with the Indians in one of their wigwams for a month. While he shared a village wigwam, he erected a small house for himself, into which he moved on July 30, 1743. He had few belongings, but did not complain. "Just at night, moved into my own house, and lodged there that night; found it much better spending the time alone than in the wigwam where I was before."[24]

Brainard's method of approaching the villagers was described years later by a granddaughter of one of the Indians at the Kaunaumeek mission. When asked what her grandmother said about David Brainard, she gave this interesting response: "He was a young man—he was a lovely man; he was a staff to walk with. He went about from house to house to talk about religion; that was his way. He slept on a deer-skin or a bear-skin. He ate bear-meat and samp; then we knew he was not proud. He would come to my grandmother's and say, 'I am hungry,—make haste!' Then she would take down the kettle, and he would eat. But some of the people did not like him, and said, 'What has this white man come here for? we don't want him here' and they told him to go off. When the Indians assembled to dance and have a feast, he would go there also, and go away in the bushes and pray for them; and then some said, 'We do not want this white man here; let us make away with him.' But others said, 'No, we will not kill him.' After a while they found he was an honest man, and then they would do anything he said."[25]

This description presents a different side of the man who agonized over his unworthiness in his private diary. He was apparently successful in conveying the faith he felt. Despite the hours Brainerd spent in solitary prayer and in writing, his absence in travel, and his bouts with illness, the Kaunaumeek Indians began to regard him with affection. By October 4, on his return to Kaunaumeek from New Jersey, he could write, "This day rode home to my own house and people. The poor Indians appeared very glad of my return. Found my house and all things in safety."[26]

The committee who employed him had directed him to spend some time during the winter with John Sergeant, to learn the Mohican language. Beginning November 29 he began to ride his horse back and forth to Stockbridge for this purpose, a hardship during the severe days of winter. He soon began to use his budding knowledge of the Mohican language. He wrote, "After I had been with the Indians several months, I composed sundry *forms* of *prayer*, adapted to their circumstances and capacities, which, with the help of my interpreter, I translated into the Indian language; and soon learned to pronounce their words, so as to pray with them in their own tongue. I also translated sundry psalms into their language, and soon after we were able to sing in the worship of God."[27] In a letter Brainard related that the Indians had abandoned idol worship and had almost given up dancing and "hallooing." He felt they were improving in the matter of drunkenness.[28]

By March 11, 1744, however, Brainard was preaching his last sermon to the Indians of Kaunaumeek. As Jonathan Edwards wrote, "The Indians at Kaunaumeek being but few in number and Brainerd having been laboring among them about a year, and having prevailed on them to be willing to leave Kaunaumeek, and remove to Stockbridge, to live constantly under Mr. Sergeant's ministry; he thought he might do more service for Christ among the Indians elsewhere."[29] The war between England and France was not mentioned but raids by Canadian Indians along the frontier had begun in 1743. The raids probably entered into Brainerd's decision to leave this unprotected location. The Mohicans of Kaunaumeek, by virtue of their alliance with the English, were as vulnerable to attack by the French as colonial farms and communities and probably felt safer at Stockbridge than at Kaunaumeek.

When Brainerd requested a new assignment from the commissioners of the Society, they agreed he should leave Kaunaumeek. After returning from his interview with the commissioners by way of Stockbridge, where he preached, he rode back to his little house near the Kinderhook Creek. On May 1, 1744, Brainerd wrote, "Having received new orders to go to a number of Indians on Delaware River, in Pennsylvania, and my people here being mostly removed to Mr. Sergeant's, I this day took all my clothes, books, etc. and disposed of them, and set out for Delaware River, but made it my way to return to Mr. Sergeant's, which I did this day, just at night."[30] The departure of many of its converted Indian residents to the presumed safety of Stockbridge ended the mission at Kaunaumeek.

Brainerd next served at intervals for almost two years at the Forks of the Delaware in Pennsylvania and then at Crossweeksung (Cranberry) in New Jersey, where he was well received and later fondly remembered. Bethrothed to the daughter of Jonathan Edwards, David Brainerd died in 1747 at the Edwards home in Northampton, Massachusetts of the consumption from which he had been ill for more than five years. The Indians believed that David Brainerd died at such a young age because he "was not used to our way of living, -

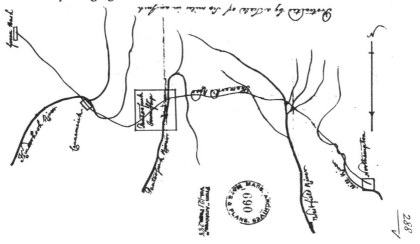

In 1752, surveyor Elisha Hawley drew this map which shows the location of Kaunaumeek on the Kinderhook Creek. Assisted by two Indians from Stockbridge, he marked a road intended for horse travel from Caunemeick (Kaunaumeek) east to Northampton.

Massachusetts Archives, Maps and Plans, Vol. 21, Page 288

so cold in the winter, sleeping on skins and on the ground."[31] He was succeeded in his work among Indians in New Jersey by a younger brother, John Brainerd.

According to David Brainerd's words, the Indian village was one and one half miles from the house of the Scot with whom he briefly lived. McCagg's house was located not far from a military path to Albany opened during the last French war; soldiers during that war saw its burned remains. A military path for horses and riders was laid out in 1752 by surveyor Elisha Hawley with the assistance of two Indians from Stockbridge. Hawley's map shows the proposed path from Northampton going through "Caunemeick" on the way to Greenbush (the City of Rensselaer) on the Hudson River. The former mission location of Kaunaumeek in 1752 may have been occupied by a few Mohicans. It still retained its Indian name, known to the Stockbridge Indians. Once the Seven Years' War ended, it appears the marked military road through Kaunaumeek was abandoned.[32]

In the mid-nineteenth century, the Indian village location was remembered to be at a curve in the creek near where a bridge crossed the Kinderhook Creek. In 1854 Electa Jones wrote, "Some remains of the little hut built by Brainard [sic] at Kaunaumeek are still to be seen, and a pine is growing up in the center of what was once his only room." A letter of 1864 mentioned that a few foundation stones were all that remained of Brainerd's house and noted that a huge apple tree thought to have been planted by the Indians stood in the rear of an ample farmhouse near the spot. This same letter recounted that the name *Kaunaumeek* came from a sound coming from the top of the mountain, a sound the Indians believed told them that deer were around to be hunted. [33]

In 1865, a "remote kinsman" named John Brainerd undertook to trace the life and service of his namesake, John Brainerd. In so doing, he wrote, as well, of his ancestor's brother, David, the missionary. The kinsman-biographer firmly believed that David Brainerd had served his first mission at the site of Brainerd's Bridge, today known simply as Brainard. In a footnote, he explained that Kaunaumeek "is now the site of a village about sixteen miles east of Albany. . .The village is now called Brainerd's Bridge; not from the missionary but from Jeremiah Brainerd, Esq., afterwards of Rome, Oneida county, N.Y., who early settled on the spot, and built the bridge over Kinderhook Creek. . .No remembrance of the Indian occupants remains except the apple-trees which they planted, some of which measure four feet in diameter. On the plain, in a bend of the creek girdled all round by hills, tradition locates the cabin of the missionary. In the vicinity Indian graves, arrow-heads, and hatchets have been found. . . ."[34]

Indians liked to plant apple trees near their wigwams; the villagers of Kaunaumeek (at later Brainard, New York), were no exception. The trunk of a surviving Indian apple tree there measured thirteen feet four inches in circumference in 1864 and still produced a "fair, sweet apple, some years in great abundance."

Brainerd, *The Life of John Brainerd*, p. 76

IX.

Moravian Missions to the Mohicans

"O! we have never in our life heard that, we only hear always, you must keep the Sabbath, not get drunk, and if we don't do them, God would be angry with us, now we hear that we can get all for nothing, when we only learn to believe and get Jesus's Blood in our Hearts."[1]

THE UNITED BRETHREN or Moravians were a Protestant religious sect based in Germany, with a long history in Europe. Missions around the world were undertakings of great importance to them, and many Moravians spent their lives in this service. In the eighteenth century, Moravian representatives came to America hoping to preach to Indians far from white settlements. The Moravians settled in Pennsylvania, where some spent the following years among the Delawares. Beginning in the 1740s, Moravians contacted Mohicans in Dutchess County, New York, and in Connecticut's Housatonic Valley.

The Moravians provided a contrast with many of the traders and settlers with whom the Mohicans had contact. Moravians at a mission aimed to lead a life without blame, as an example to their converts. Moreover, they were to take all means to learn the language of the people with whom they were working and they were to treat the Indians as they would wish to be treated themselves. Moravian missionaries were expected to marry and to avoid being alone with Indian women. Moravian wives were to accompany their husbands as helpers among the females in congregations. After baptism, adult Indian converts were expected to continue learning. Children of baptized parents could be baptized and thereafter were of special concern; schools were begun in which children were taught to read and write. Some Moravian schools taught German; others taught English, according to the needs of the area. Children were to learn fundamental articles of the Christian Doctrine "with enjoyment of them in their hearts."[2]

The Moravian headquarters in the colonies was at Bethlehem, Pennsylvania. Since most Moravian missionaries had little formal training, there were deacons who visited the missionaries at new outposts to perform the sacraments. Moravian sermons centered around the sacrifice of Jesus for mankind and emphasized his blood, his wounds, and his sufferings. Missionaries and ministers used hymns to evoke emotions and love. Music was ever present in Moravian communities, which were noted for their happy people. "Every religious service, every celebration, every form of work, had its special lyrics, accompanied by musical instruments."[3] Even a knock on the door might bring an outburst of song announcing the presence of visitors.

The missionaries were self-sufficient craftsmen and gardeners, although supported as needed by workers at Bethlehem and, initially, by funds from Europe. At Bethlehem, two groups were formed, "one to go into the forests as teachers and evangelists, the other to stay in the settlements to earn support for those who went out."[4] The Moravians led an active communal life among their congregations. The same rigorous lifestyle was expected of baptized converts, who the missionaries regarded as equal in importance to themselves.

Despite this equality, the missionaries recognized themselves as the initial teachers and trainers: "the Baptized must be trained to regular Labour, vizt: to plant, hunt, fish and do every thing on the right Season—to keep good House with everything they have, to tend their Corn well and to make provision for their Families and also their Cattle in the right Season."[5] If achieved, a successful mission would bring not only religious changes but welcome order to any Mohican village involved. Rather than teaching Indians to improve their behavior, the Moravians started by urging the natives to achieve salvation by identifying with the sufferings of Christ, whose blood would wash away sin. Faith gave the necessary prompting for an individual to put his life in order.

A Moravian mission was initiated in summer 1740 at Shekomeko by a newly arrived German, Christian Henry Rauch, who was looking for a place to begin his work. Shekomeko was a Mohican village in Dutchess County south of present Pine Plains. Rauch's appearance was well-timed to meet Indian needs. Most Hudson Valley natives of the period, overwhelmed and outnumbered after a century of colonial settlement, were discouraged and poor. Reduction of the spatial environment to which they were so finely tuned and which they had so effectively managed in the past meant they now had to devise new management and social systems. It also was a time of evolving belief systems, as old ceremonies had ceased to serve them. To find new, satisfying ways to support themselves and relate to the world around them, they needed a bridge to a new way of life. Native Americans found various bridges; converting to the Christian religion was a way for many Mohicans.

The story of the beginnings of the Moravian mission at Shekomeko is well-known. Rauch observed drunken Mohicans in New York City when he first arrived from overseas in early summer 1740. When two Mohican leaders, Maumauntissekun, also known as Shabash, and Wassamapah, were sober, he was able to converse with them because they understood the Dutch which Rauch had learned during a stay in the Netherlands. Wassamapah was lame from a drunken accident; Maumauntissekun was identified by a snake tattooed on each cheek.[6] They had some familiarity with the work of missionaries through Stockbridge contacts and had heard sermons at Stockbridge. The two native leaders regretted their drinking bouts and expressed a little knowledge of the Christian religion. After recovering from another bout of drunkenness in New York, they agreed to take Rauch back to Shekomeko, their village, and named him their new religious teacher. They were ready to hear about the gospel.

Maumauntissekun had visited Stockbridge in 1739 to receive some instruction in religion. While there, he had related a frightening vision which he had during a drinking bout. In his waking dream, Indians lay cold and distressed in the woods, unable to escape nasty water being pumped over them, and a voice advised him to take notice and avoid such wickedness. A strong light shone about him, until a blast of wind dispersed the Indians into the air.[7] He considered the event a spiritual warning, and began to entertain serious thoughts of religion. Since then, he had nearly given up drinking, with the notable exception of binges on his visit to New York City.

Rauch followed the men from New York to Shekomeko, where, despite their invitation, the missionary found himself unwelcome. Self-respect in this Indian village was low. The Shekomeko Mohicans were accorded "the worst in all this part of the Country."[8] A deceitful property transaction had embittered them, and they knew the proprietors all around them were anxiously waiting to obtain their land. They were literally afraid to leave their village unattended for fear it would be confiscated in their absence. The land claim influenced the actions of Maumauntissekun for the next several years.

The Shekomeko residents, moreover, had declined previous opportunities to become Christians through the Stockbridge mission. By reopening the question of accepting Christianity, Rauch's presence now posed a threat to the village social order. To make matters worse, traders told the Mohicans that Rauch would take their children and make them slaves. Consequently, the Mohicans' response to him fluctuated wildly. One drunken Indian nearly killed Rauch with a hatchet. The lame Indian, Wassamapah, threatened to shoot him and wanted him to leave. Yet it was Wassamapah who, according to an account of the Shekomeko mission, on observing an exhausted Rauch asleep in the wigwam, said "This man cannot be a bad man, for he fears no evil, not even from us, who are so savage, but sleeps comfortably, and places his life in our hands."[9]

Rauch Takes a Hand

Palatine immigrant Johannes Rau, farming near the Shekomeko village, considered the Indians beyond help. Nevertheless, he was friendly to missionary Rauch and offered him a place to stay. Rauch retreated to the home of this farmer. He earned board by teaching Rau's children but visited the Indian village often. Rauch also walked to the Connecticut Mohican village of Wequadnach, north of present Sharon, and made the acquaintance of other Mohicans. Some of them began to come to Shekomeko to hear his sermons.

In addition, Rauch's presence at Shekomeko attracted the attention of a displaced Pequot leader, Mauwehu (Gideon), also known as Ammawassamon, who had gathered followers at Pachgatgoch (Skaticoke) near the Housatonic River west of present Kent, Connecticut. Some of his people began to come to Shekomeko to hear Rauch's teachings. Over time, the promise in Rauch's sermons at Shekomeko won listeners, even as his affection for them and his frugality convinced the Mohicans that he would never covet their land nor enslave their children. The Mohicans appreciated the additional contributions of Rauch, who, besides preaching, offered to teach interested Indians to read and tried to heal them when they were sick. His audiences became more thoughtful. There was less drinking. Shekomeko noticeably improved its image. By the end of the second year, their longer Indian names were little used. Shabash, formerly Maumauntissekun, as well as Tschoop, formerly Wassamapah, and others had found a new spiritual view and new self-esteem through Rauch's teachings.

A transformed and repentant Tschoop (a form of his first Christian name, Job) remembered himself in a letter as formerly a great drunkard and a wild savage. When he began to accept Moravian teachings, he noted that it was his nearest friends and his family members, including his wife and children, who were the greatest enemies to his reformation. Tschoop's account detailing this family conflict gives a rare glimpse into a Mohican family in transition. Although he was a respected sachem, Tschoop was challenged by his wife's mother for having allowed the Moravian missionary into the village. She was the keeper of a leather talisman, stitched with wampum, in the shape of a man. This doll-like figure had been passed down from her grandmother. As the oldest person, her role was to ensure that the family would venerate the figure. No doubt, in her mind, the family's future depended on the intervention of spirits reached through the talisman. Tschoop now refused to pray to any idols; he was anxious to cast them all into the fire.[10] His wife's mother resisted the sachem's frightening disrespect to the spirit world. Meanwhile, Tschoop was full of excitement at his opportunity to embrace a new spiritual view which brought worth to his life and promised more power than the old pantheon of spirits.

Another Moravian, Gotlob Buettner, with his wife, came in January 1742, to help Rauch in his endeavors. In February 1742, Martin Mack was appointed as Rauch's assistant and also came to Shekomeko. In the Moravian way, the missionaries patiently encouraged those who showed interest in learning about the faith. By winter, they had won their first converts, but no one was authorized to perform baptism. Early in 1742, therefore, Shabash and two New England Indians, Seim and Kiop, husbands of Mohican women belonging to the village of Shekomeko, set out with Rauch for Pennsylvania, where Rauch was to be ordained a deacon. After Rauch's ordination, the three Indians from Shekomeko were baptized on February 11, 1742 in John de Turk's barn at Oley, Pennsylvania, not far from Bethlehem, along with a large party of Delawares.[11]

Thus Shabash was the first Mohican at Shekomeko to adopt the Christian religion and, as a chief with important family connections, by example he opened the door for many others. His Christian name became Abraham, the name by which he was thereafter known. Seim and Kiop, the other two Indians from Shekomeko, were named respectively Isaac and Jacob. The Moravians were aware that converting an influential man was a way to break into a new family and, indeed, into a family-oriented village. If a man made a change, his wife and younger children usually soon followed. Abraham's wife, Sarah, was baptized at Shekomeko on August 11, 1742 by Rauch. Older children and grandparents were harder to persuade. Mohicans subsequently found difficulty in sustaining any marriage in which one partner was Christian and one was not.[12]

Abraham of Shekomeko later served as an influential chief among the Mohicans who moved to Gnadenhutten, Pennsylvania. Although he had stated that the new Christian faith "had deliver'd me & many of my Friends,"[13] his faith occasionally wavered and he had family troubles. He nevertheless was elevated to an influential position as a negotiator for the Mohican nation. While he was in the Shekomeko area, Abraham was particularly close to Umpachanee, of Stockbridge, who admired his temperance. (It is possible, although not stated, that the two were related.) While at Gnadenhutten, Abraham helped the missionary Pyrlacus with his Mohican translations, and, to survive, made and sold twig brooms. He died in December 1762.[14]

The Land Troubles

Shabash, formerly known as Maumauntissekun, appears to be the same person as Mamanitiseekhan, who in 1720 approved and witnessed a Mohican sale to William White of land called Weatauk, near present Salisbury, Connecticut, about twenty miles from Shekomeko. Land also had been sold in the past for the Little Nine Partners Patent but the patent was not promptly occupied by non-Indians. (This patent was variously called the Second Nine Partners patent and the Upper Nine Partners patent.) When the patentees became active and began to divide the property, Abraham protested that payment was due to him, as owner of the tract. The affair was not resolved, but settlement seems to have ceased. As a consequence, until the 1740s Indian land around Shekomeko was not disturbed by many settlers. When surveying began, Abraham protested.

Abraham was willing to sell some land, but expected to decide where settlement would be allowed, and he expected to be paid for the land. The affair impacted the Moravian mission. The missionaries did not wish to become involved in the land troubles, as it was their goal never to become embroiled in political or legal affairs. Out of compassion for their new Indian brethren, nevertheless, they could not forebear writing out some appeals for them. They also discussed the affair in letters among themselves and tried to offer advice to Abraham.

One account of these troubles was recorded in a memorandum written to the Governor for Abraham by an unnamed missionary in September 1743. In the memorandum, Abraham related that the Indians went to New York in 1724 and made an agreement with the Governor to sell him their lands. The Indians arranged with the Governor that they would keep one square mile for their own village and fields "which is Shecomakes." The Governor promised to send payment in goods for the land to Red Hook for them within four weeks. Some Indians went to Red Hook and waited, but, having received no goods, they finally went home, thinking that the bargain made with the Governor had fallen through. Richard Sackett, an honest man and a friend to the Mohicans, who had earlier bought and paid for Mohican land near present Amenia for his own patent, was appointed to receive the payment on the Indians' behalf. He, too, was at Red Hook. He spent the value of about five pounds on the Indians during the long wait for a payment that did not arrive. [15]

South of the Little Nine Partners lay an earlier patent of 1697 titled the Great Nine Partners Purchase. In 1730 and again in 1737, Abraham was able to share with the Highland (Wappinger) Indians payments resulting from negotiations with the Great Nine Partners owners. The payments related to unpurchased Indian land within the expanded bounds of the Great Nine Partners patent; the Great Nine Partners tract included some Mohican territory as well as Wappinger territory.[16] No doubt, this success encouraged Abraham with regard to his rights on the Shekomeko lands.

About 1738, on a visit to New York, the Mohicans spoke again with the Governor concerning their land near Shekomeko. He "entreated them with Civility and called them his Beloved Children" and promised they would be paid as soon as the lands were surveyed. He suggested that for their own security they should mark off the square mile of land they wished to reserve as their own possession. He then presented them with ten shillings for the expense and trouble of coming to New York. He promised they would not be wronged and said he would endeavor to help them. They believed him, although his words were empty promises.[17] The Shekomeko natives would have been wise to take his advice, however, and stake out the land they wished to retain, but apparently they did not do this.

On the Little Nine Partners' land nothing was paid to the Mohicans until spring 1743, when Martinus Hoffman gave them five pounds in money and thirty five pounds in credit for Hoffman's ninth part of the patent. Hoffman, one of the partners, occupied a site on the Hudson River south of the Livingston Patent line and west of the Little Nine Partners patent. After this payment by Hoffman, Capt. Isaiah Ross, another partner, several times came to Shekomeko and told the Indians repeatedly that they had sold all their land without exception and that they had been paid for it all, but they protested to him that was not true.

In September 1743, the land finally was surveyed and divided into lots. One of the lots ran through the land which the Indians reserved for themselves. The disturbed Indians decided they would not interrupt the surveyors measuring their land, but that instead they would acquaint the Governor with the proceedings so that they might retain their rights. It was then, with Moravian help, that Abraham sent his memorandum to the Governor. In closing he wrote, "Now they first Desire for the Future that they might not be interrupted in the said possession and Secondly that they might be paid for the remainder of the Land Which they hope the Gov'r and the Partners will satisfye them for as it is not otherways than Reasonable."[18]

Faith in the Governor's help proved unfounded. Abraham and his cohorts heard nothing from him. The Indians soon learned that the plot of land which was run across their reserved square mile had been sold to a proprietor. On October 17, 1743, with a missionary's help, Abraham wrote directly to the Little Nine Partners. He produced Indian witnesses to prove he was the rightful owner of the land. Tschoop was among the attestors who signed the petition.

Abraham addressed his complaint to the "Honorable Committee of the Second Nine Partners or to any of the Partners therein Concerned" reminding them that he, Abraham or Shabash, was always allowed by them to be the true and lawful owner of lands now patented and called the Second Nine Partners, and that they had promised to pay him for the lands. He had learned the partners now were not inclined to pay Abraham because they had "formerly Bought the Same from an Indian who called himself the owner thereof." That no other Indian was the owner, the five witnesses could attest. Abraham reminded the patentees that when the land first began to be settled, Mr. Van Dam and Mr. Lurting and others told a certain man who still lived there that the Little Nine partners might take a farm at any place within the patent provided that they "should pay and agree With mee Shawas [Shabash] for the same and as for the Liberty to Settle the Same but not without my Consent. . . ."[19]

The unnamed man who still lived there was Richard Sackett. Sackett, a farmer, and a Livingston Patent official in 1711, lived on a large tract which lay across the Connecticut border. In addition, Sackett was a proprietor in the Little Nine Partners patent. The Indians had earlier talked to Sackett, who agreed that he had never heard of any owner of the land other than Abraham. Since Abraham at several different times with other Indians had obtained goods from Sackett totaling the value of sixteen pounds, it had been agreed that the sum owed to Sackett was to be deducted when Sackett paid Abraham for his one-ninth part of the land. Both Richard Sackett and his son acknowledged that they took Abraham for the right owner; they promised to help him as much as possible when Sackett next went to New York. Sackett also said that the Governor himself told him, Sackett, that he had promised Abraham a mile square for himself out of the land.

Armed with this information, Abraham circulated his petition and tried to get his white neighbors to sign it, but without success. Each had a reason. Only fellow Mohicans were willing to sign. The story was told in a letter from a Moravian at Shekomeko to Brother Noble, dated October 16, 1743.

The Indians first went to Johannes Rau, an old friend of the mission, whose daughter Janette spoke Mohican; she had married one of the missionaries, Martin Mack. Rau reluctantly refused to sign the petition, through fear of displeasing Rip Van Dam, a principal in the Nine Partners. Rau had not paid Van Dam for his land and feared that Van Dam "would Directly thro him in prison for the said Dept [debt]."[20]

Next the Indians went to Martinus Hoffman, who also acknowledged Abraham to be the owner of the land. Hoffman had never heard of any other owner and seemed astonished that the partners would wrong Abraham. Hoffman was the only partner who had paid the Indians for his one-ninth section of land. Being a partner, however, he did not care to "appear publick" on the petition which Abraham was trying to get his white neighbors to sign.

The Indians went back to Sackett, who agreed the petition contained the truth. Sackett remembered receiving a letter nineteen years earlier in which he was ordered to call the Indians together at Fulling Brook, apparently Red Hook, where he was to receive their payment for the land. As noted above, the Indian entourage waited about three weeks in company with Sackett before dispersing, having received no payment, while Sackett sustained them. Sackett felt he could not sign because of his connection to the Nine Partners.

Next Abraham acquainted Martinus Hoffman with Sackett's information and asked his advice in the matter. Hoffman then wrote a letter which was sent to Bethlehem on October 17. The missionaries who had written this account for the Indians were also unwilling to sign the petition, as they had been advised "not to appear in it," and wished not to cause any controversy for their mission. In the end, on October 17, 1743, the petition was signed by six of the oldest Indians, including Tschoop. Four had been baptized, so both Indian and baptismal names were given. The Indians who signed were: Katonocksack (Catharickseet) now Cornelis; Shawwonock now Jeptha; Naakottow; Kockanont; Job, now Johannes (Tschoop); and Ammawasamon now Gideon.[21]

Brother Buettner wrote, "We Apprehend by the Partners themselves that there is a Difference between them in so much that they are one against the other. . . ." He also noted that Hoffman, Sackett and Van Dam "is of one Partie but each seems afraid of the other." The missionary believed the matter would be fairly resolved, as its merits were so clear. When Abraham's right was proved, as the missionaries were confident it would be, they advised that he make a "fresh assignment" of the deed. Then followed an enigmatic note about another tract of land sold by the Indians. "The Deed signed 1714 they say is a tract of land which is by [near] Mr. Sackett: but not the Second Nine Partners."[22]

Meanwhile, the missionaries had forbidden Abraham from signing anything without Brother Noble's advice or that of someone Noble delegated. Thomas Noble, a merchant in New York, had joined the Moravian Society there. A postscript on Buettner's letter reminds Noble to keep Mr. Hoffman's name private as much as possible, because he had been upright and acted responsibly in the affair with Abraham.

Despite Abraham's appeals, his persistence, and the Moravians' help, the matter was never resolved in Abraham's favor. The New

York Governor's 1724 false promise to the Mohicans of Shekomeko, telling them to wait for their payment by the river at Red Hook, was cruel and dishonest, and his pretense of friendship to the Indians patently hypocritical. Successive governors obviously knew little of the real facts in the case, but wished to appease the Indians. Yet, despite Abraham's anguish and the genuine astonishment of Richard Sackett and Martin Hoffman that Abraham's ownership should be questioned, earlier Indian deeds had been given for the Little Nine Partner's area, and Abraham knew about them. Richard Sackett also knew that the Little Nine Partners' land had been purchased from other Mohicans; such a purchase was necessary in order to obtain the patent. Abraham considered the early deeds fraudulent, however, since he, the present and rightful owner, had not been paid.

Richard Sackett, moreover, recognized Abraham's claim and tried to protect the Indian settlement. When he and his sons sold 300 acres of Little Nine Partners' land in October 1741 to Johan Tise Smith in Lot 12, the Sacketts and Smith inserted a clause in the lease reserving the right of "some Native Indians . . .there residing [who] lay claim to some part of the above demised and granted premises." The Indians were to retain for themselves and their heirs any land which they could lawfully hold by "their title which they now have and their present claim."[23] Unfortunately, Smith took other lands as a substitute for the three hundred acres, as there was an earlier claimant for Lot 12.

The earlier deeds reflect the complexity of purchases in the area. The Little Nine Partners Patent dated to April 10, 1706. The original partnership included a land speculator named Sampson Sheldon Broughton, who, with various partners, also obtained land north of the Mohawk River and tracts on Staten Island. Broughton had asked for a license to purchase land in Dutchess County as early as 1689.[24]

Facing page: *A 1779 map shows the Little Nine Partners Patent above the Great Nine Partners Patent; note Stissig Hill, which was near the Mohican village of Shekomeko. Also indicated are the east line of the Manor of Livingston and Mr. Hoffman's location on the Hudson. The stone heaps identified by Catharickseet in 1712 were at Nawanagquasick on the Livingston line. The new townships east of Kinderhook were on land sold by the Mohicans. Richard Sackett's patent, not shown, overlaid the northeast corner of the Great Nine Partners Patent; his land also lay in the narrow rectangle called the Oblong as well as in Connecticut. Weatauk (Wiyatiack) at Salisbury, Connecticut, right, was on the Salmon River.*

Sautier, "A Chorographic Map," from O'Callaghan, *Documentary History* 1: 774

Even before this, in 1686, Henry Pauling and Michael Vaughton had agreed to make a purchase from the Wappinger Indians in order to obtain a vast parcel of land lying at the Crum Elboogh, in Dutchess County. Michael Vaughton duly obtained the license for the pair to buy land from the Indians. With the license, Pauling proceeded to buy several thousand acres from the natives, probably Wappinger Indians. Although this land was located far to the south of Shekomeko, its boundaries were vague. As Vaughton was at sea on a voyage, Pauling chose not to notify Vaughton's wife when the Indian purchase was made. Vaughton died before returning from his voyage. Pauling also died. Pauling's widow in 1691 obtained a patent for her 4,000-acre share of the land.[25]

Vaughton's widow learned with surprise of the Pauling patent. In vain, she sued for her share of the "thousands of acres" purchased from the Indians. However, she was unable to obtain any land. Thereupon, a company composed of Leigh, Atwood, and others, petitioned Lieutenant Governor Nanfan in April 15, 1702 to have the whole Pauling purchase surveyed, asking for the remainder aside from the Pauling share to be assigned to them. Their license to buy land of the Indians soon expired.

Following this, a petition for a license to buy some of this same land of the Indians was submitted in November 1702 by Broughton and a partner, Robert Lurting. As the license was not acted upon, Broughton, in 1704, was granted a renewal of the license. Shortly thereafter, he and Lurting asked permission to do the required survey, indicating an Indian deed had been acquired in 1704. Broughton died in February 1705; early in 1705, Broughton's widow, Mary, requested, on behalf of herself and the company, the patent for the Little Nine Partners tract "bordering on branches of the Ten Mile and Wiantomick rivers, lying to the northward of the land lately patented to Richard Sackett, in Dutchess County, purchased of the Indians by her husband, in his lifetime."[26] The following spring, April 10, 1706, the Little Nine Partners patent was issued.

Earlier, the Great Nine Partners purchase had been made to the south. The land obtained by the Little Nine Partners was not the land left over from the Pawling purchase, but a tract farther north. A document titled "Indian Land Sales with Marks in Shekomeko" included with the Moravian archives' copies of Abraham's memorandum and his petition gives a list of names of Indians who signed deeds for lands at or around Shekomeko early in the century. The deeds themselves are not included in the list. The years given are 1704, 1705, 1706, 1706 and 1714. There is no explanation for the inclusion of this list of names, but it is titled in German and written in a Moravian hand, and thus apparently dates to the 1740s. Perhaps the names of the Indians were copied off deeds or were dictated from the memory of old Indians. The 1704 part of the list, dated October 20, may represent the Mohican signers for the Little Nine Partners' tract, who were not the rightful owners, according to Abraham. The Indians who signed were Nopamukgno, Wunnupee, Tisqueake and Donowoactum. Among the witnesses were Crays, whose wigwam was drawn on Sackett's survey, and Promish, the father of Ampamit.[27]

Abraham eventually left his village site, moving first to Wequadnach. Once he and the others left Shekomeko, the land was taken over by a waiting proprietor and the mission village was torn down. In December 1748, Moravian visitors from Bethlehem found everything destroyed except the burying ground. Later, after Abraham had moved to Pennsylvania, Stockbridge Mohicans petitioned the New York Governor in 1754 about various lands which had never been purchased from them. The list included "A considerable tract. . .at a place called Wohnockkaumechkuk lying east of Mr. Hoffmans and running south some miles." This description meant the Little Nine Partners land, lying east and south of Martin Hoffman's location on the Hudson River. The signers of the appeal were Stockbridge Indians John Pophnehonnohcook (Konkapot), Solomon Waunumpaugus, and six others. [28]

Abraham died in December 1762 in Pennsylvania. His sons took up the cause. On September 20, 1763 they appeared before Sir William Johnson with an old friend, Mohican Abraham, known as Keeperdo, to plead their case. Sir William wrote an account of the interview: "*Abraham* alias Assergo [Keeperdo] with two sons of Old Abraham came & made Complaint, that the Pattentees of the Nine Partners near to the Highlands in Dutchess County, never paid for Said Tract, & when demanded by their late Father [he] was always trifled with, & told that as ye Partners were liveing in different parts of the Countrey, they could not make up the Money before they were all together, on being asked what consideration would satisfy them, they [the Indians] Sayed they would be content with L100, altho they were sensible that many Farms therein had been Sold for five times that sum." The sons of Abraham presented Sir William with a belt of wampum.[29]

Sir William told the sons that he had, on an application formerly made to him by their deceased father, written to John Sackett (a son of Richard Sackett) concerning this land, and that John Sackett and Capt. Isaiah Ross, representing the patent, denied the charge that they had not paid. However on Abraham's sons being "very pressing" Sir William promised them he would write again to Mr. Sackett and that he would let them know Sackett's answer. "He then with 2 Black Strowds [pieces of blanket cloth] covered ye Grave of Old Abraham their late Father—for wh. they returned Sir Wm many thanks." The term "covered the grave" was a euphemism for giving a gift to ease their sorrow.

The claims of Abraham in the 1720s arose because the land was not used or occupied by any colonial proprietors after they had patented it. For over two decades the natives were able to use the fields and woods as usual. The Mohicans continued to think of these isolated lands as their own. In turn, by the 1740s, some of the partners of the company knew little of the original Indian owners decades earlier. For the natives, it was more than a matter of deeds. Unoccupied land, in Indian eyes, returned to Mohican use. They expected to be paid when the land was taken again after such a hiatus. The incident shows that as late as the 1740s, even for these relatively acculturated Mohicans, the chasm between white and native land customs still opened wide in some respects.

The incident also illustrates that sometimes statements by Mohicans that certain lands had never been sold to Europeans were incorrect by European standards. Indian assurances that tracts of land had never been sold led unsuspecting settlers into purchasing Indian deeds for land patented at an earlier date. Sir William Johnson had occasion to remind the Mohicans of early deeds on more than one occasion.

Abraham's Story

Shekomeko, near the southern edge of Mohican territory, was a thoroughly Mohican village in the 1740s, despite the presence of several outsiders. A Moravian list of the Shekomeko natives baptized in 1742 and 1743 identified twenty-one people as Mohicans.[30] Mortality was high in the village; several widows and widowers were listed. Many children died. As a result, Shekomeko baptisms after 1744 were frequently for children of the couples baptized in the first few years; often children died shortly after baptism. The loving Indians feared that if their endangered children were not baptized, the parents would not meet them again in the afterlife.

Some parents sent their children to the Moravians at Bethlehem to be adopted and raised, fearful that the children might not survive if kept at home. In 1747, John Sergeant, minister at Stockbridge, wrote of the Mohicans in Massachusetts in a letter to England: "The Families indeed are but small, as is common among the Natives. Near half that are born die in Infancy or Childhood. . . ."[31] Conditions at Shekomeko probably paralleled those of Stockbridge.

High mortality had plagued Mohican populations in the past. The story of Abraham's forebears gives an example of the toll of disease and war on family life; Abraham's family's sad record of untimely death was typical of both Indians' and settlers' families late in the seventeenth century and in the eighteenth century. The frequent wars made matters worse; besides causing death in battle and disrupting living cycles, wars spread epidemics which swept through villages and killed young warriors assembled for expeditions.

Abraham dictated a unique Mohican family history to a missionary friend while he was fighting to prove his right to the land in the 1740s. His grandmother, Mannanockqua, who had control of the land around Shekomeko, died in an epidemic, "about Sixty Years ago," probably about 1684.[32] She may be the woman named Mamanequanaskqua who signed a deed of 1684 for land on the Kinderhook Creek east of present Stuyvesant Landing. Mamanequanaskqua was among the heirs of Sauwachquanent, the son of Aepjen, chief sachem in the mid-seventeenth century.

Abraham's grandmother left two children, a boy and a girl, but her son died shortly after she did. Sensing death, she had nominated two men, Tathemshon (Tataemshatt) and Wompapawockom, to take care of her children and act for them with regard to the land until they were of age. Mannanockqua's daughter, Manhaet (Manhagh), soon to be Shabash's mother, married Argoche (Agotach), also called Nawonnaequageck. From this couple issued "Shaveous [Shabash] now Aberham [Abraham] and Annimapaw and a Daughter." Argoche, Abraham's father, died of sickness, and "in the War between the French & English Indians Manhaet was taken prisoner and killed at the Same time[;] Aberham was 11 years Old being the eldest son."[33]

It is likely the parents' deaths occurred near the end of the French War, about 1698. According to this hypothesis, Abraham was born about 1687.

A deed for a tract of land in the Livingston Patent near the south line was given to Robert Livingston by two Mohican women, My Lady and Manhagh, in July 1697. Each signed the deed with a box-like human figure, a sign usually reserved for sachems or persons with special standing. Manhagh was Manhaet, Abraham's mother, mentioned in his story. The deed indicates she was still alive in 1697, but she apparently died soon after. In the transaction with Livingston, a payment of two fathoms of duffels, some powder, shot, and rum were included for her two sons, Tsioas and Winnigh Po. Winnigh Po was clearly Annimapaw, and Abraham or Shaveous therefore was Tsioas. Abraham may have been about ten years old in 1697, as his mother died when he was eleven. This information fits with his known maturity; he was functioning as a sachem by 1720. Gifts for male children in deeds were not unique; they were intended to include men who might have future claims. English law saw the mother merely as a guardian for her son.

Appended to the deed was an attestation that Goose, the Indian, was present at the sale, and that the land extended as far as the high hills. Goose said he was employed by the two women to dispose of the land. Goose was Tataemshatt, one of the two men who had been designated by Abraham's grandmother to act for her children with regard to the land until they were of age. Although Manhagh was of age, he was apparently still helping her. Tataemshatt was involved in other deeds in Columbia County in the 1680s.

A few decades later, Abraham learned that Livingston intended to rent the land to a farmer. In 1725, a memordandum written by Robert Livingston noted that Tsioas, Indian son of Manhagh, one of two women who sold the land on the south side of Livingston Manor to him in July 1697, "complains that he nor his brother never had a farthings worth of anything that his brother received for the said land, being then infants. . . ."[34] They requested a gift from Livingston and promised that if they received it, they would never make a claim to any part of the land in the Manor of Livingston. Livingston gave Tsioas/Shabash and his brother Winnigh Po two fathoms of duffels, some powder, shot, and rum, with which, Livingston said, they were well contented. Abraham thereafter never claimed any land in Livingston Manor. His action illustrates the native feeling that the land was theirs and that from time to time, they could receive gifts from succeeding owners. Livingston understood this. In at least one other early instance, Livingston had paid an Indian family within his bounds when he wanted to place a farmer on their wigwam site in the later Town of Gallatin.[35]

Abraham's sister died at the age of sixteen, and his brother died, as well. Annimapaw, his brother, however, left two children, both still living in the 1740s. Moravian records mention two "brothers" who came to visit Abraham in his later years. As Indian kinship terminology was often more inclusive than English, it is likely these were his two nephews, named White Walnut and Blackfish. [36]

Abraham's troubles with the Little Nine Partners continued. As an undated memorandum by Abraham dictated about 1743 pointed out, "Shaveos otherwise Aberham remained without Interruption owner of the Land which is well know[n] here for 20 Miles around that they never heard of any other possessor of the Land than now Aberham which is well known by writings now in the hands of Mr. Sackett Appraiser as also [by] the Inhabitants settled thereon by the Leave of Mr Van Dam & Mr. Lurting who [the inhabitants] was first ordered to have his [Abraham's] consent thereto."[37]

Abraham married a woman baptized as Sarah. Sarah died in June 1764 at the Philadelphia Barracks, where Pennsylvania Indians were being protected. While at Shekomeko, they had a large family by Indian standards. Five sons are mentioned in Moravian records: Friederich (Tschekanai) eighteen years old in August 1749; Joachim, an infant who died; Jonathan; David; and Tobias (Kajosch), fifteen years of age when baptized in September 1749. Tobias died in an accident near Gnadenhutten, Pennsylvania and was buried at Gnadenhutten February 7, 1750. There also was a daughter named Sara.[38]

It seems likely, based on his family's land holdings, that Abraham had lived as a child along the Roelof Jansen Kill not far from Shekomeko, and that the family had shifted south to the Shekomeko area, perhaps after the 1697 deed was given to Livingston by his mother and certainly before the 1725 payment was requested.

Tschoop's Contributions

Abraham's Shekomeko was a village of Mohican families related to him or to Tschoop. Tschoop, after baptism known as Johannes, was the second sachem at Shekomeko. In 1733, as Wassamapah, he signed a deed for Mohican land east of Kinderhook in conjunction with Ampamit, the Mohican chief sachem, and others.[39]

Count Ludwig Zinzendorf, the Moravian leader, had heard about "all the machinations of his mother-in-law, who sought to perplex him." He noted the mother-in-law's objections caused Tschoop's wife and daughter to vacillate. Zinzendorf exulted, "This brand snatched from the fire is no longer Tschoop, but *John*, and is an esteemed teacher among his people."[40] Since he had been unable to travel to Olney with Abraham in February, Tschoop was baptized at Shekomeko on April 16, 1742. Despite her initial opposition to the new religion, Tschoop's wife, Martha, followed Tschoop's lead and was baptized on December 12, 1742. Tschoop and Martha's children were sons Ampowachnant, who was friendly to the mission but resisted baptism, Papenoha, and a daughter, Techtonoah. Martha had a son, Simon, from a previous marriage. Tschoop also had a brother, Wompecom.[41]

Tschoop or Johannes, often referred to as John, became an enthusiastic advocate for his new faith, frequently visiting Wequadnoch and Pachgatgoch (Scaticoke) to explain that he now understood that Jesus had died and given his blood so that even the Indians could be saved. He was valuable at the Shekomeko mission as an interpreter; in 1744 a missionary wrote "John is grown better. He gave us hopes the next day if possible to come to our House, which we were glad of because we can't translate without him."[42] He became a skilled craftsman in the workshop used by the Moravians and the Indians at Shekomeko. Soon after moving from Shekomeko to Pennsylvania, Tschoop died at Bethlehem during a smallpox epidemic on August 27, 1746 at about forty-nine years of age.[43]

The Mission Becomes Official

The Indians listed by the Moravians in the Mohican village of Shekomeko who were not Mohicans can easily be accounted for. One man, Thomas, was an Esopus Indian (the son of Shawwonnock, baptized as Jeptha) whose wife, Esther, was a New England Indian, baptized at Shekomeko in 1742; Esther's mother was from Potatik, an Indian village on the Housatonic, below Mohican territory. Esther very likely had come by way of Pachgatgoch, as she had close connections there. Moreover, she was a daughter of Jacob (Kiop). Three men at Shekomeko, Isaac, Jacob, and Zacheus, were New

England Indians, probably also from Pachgatgoch; they were husbands of Mohican women Rebecca, Rachel, and Magdelena. Isaac and Jacob were among the first converts. Isaac died of smallpox in Bethlehem in 1746.[44]

One Highland (Wappinger) Indian, Abel, a widower, was listed; he had since married a second Mohican woman of Shekomeko, Elizabeth, the sister of his deceased wife. Michel, a Minnisink Indian identified as a widower, also may have been the husband of a deceased Shekomeko Mohican woman. The attraction of the mission may have brought the men to the Mohican village, where they married in order to stay, as the Moravians did not encourage the presence of unattached men or women. The seven outsiders also demonstrate the older tradition that an Indian man often lived in his wife's village, and these examples of marriage indicate the wide range of marriage choices for Mohican women.[45]

The mission was formalized in summer 1742. On August 16, Count Ludwig Zinzendorf, a leader and financial supporter of the Moravians, arrived at Shekomeko after a difficult journey from Bethlehem, with his daughter, Benigna, a devout Moravian, and an entourage. Brother Rauch lodged the visitors the first night in his hut. After that, they happily occupied a bark house which had been built for them. There was delight among the Moravian visitors at Rauch's success with the Indian villagers. A ceremony was arranged at which six Indians, Kaubus, Kermelok, Harris and the wives of Abraham, Isaac and Harris were baptized. Their new names became: Timothy, Jonas, Thomas, Sarah, Rebecca and Esther. After "internal conflicts" among the Moravians, it was decided by Zinzendorf and the missionaries to organize the baptized Mohicans into a congregation, the earliest Moravian church of converted Indians in North America.[46]

As affairs of the mission were settled, Rauch was to be sent on a new assignment. No doubt he was considered a superb first-contact person. Perhaps one of the internal conflicts was that he did not want to leave. Gotlob Buettner was to return to serve the Mohicans at Shekomeko; he left Bethlehem for Shekomeko October 4, 1742. In addition, the marriage between missionary Martin Mack, who had been in the area for six months, and Janette Rau, daughter of farmer Johannes Rau, was arranged. Janette, who had grown up in close contact with the Mohicans of Shekomeko, was known for her ability to speak Mohican. She was an ideal wife for a missionary to the Indians and well-loved for her warm personality, as well. Zinzendorf and his entourage also were to take one of Abraham's sons back to Bethlehem. A young woman, Techtanoah, the daughter of Johannes (Tschoop), decided not to leave, as she was considering a marriage proposal. The departing group also took converts Gabriel, alias Wanab, and Nahan, alias Tassawachamen. These men were baptized at Bethlehem on September 15, 1742 in the first baptism of Indians at Bethlehem proper.[47]

Zinzendorf left Shekomeko after a public farewell, "with sadness and regret, though with mutual assurances of tenderest love." He noted his experience among the "Mohicans, a confessedly worthless tribe of Indians" in his journal. This was probably a reference to comments such as Tschoop had made, that he formerly had been a wild, drunken man.[48]

A small dwelling with a German-style stove and a cellar was built for the missionaries. It was gradually improved between 1742 and 1744. Indian winter dwellings were built in fall 1742, arranged according to the Moravian recommendations for the layout of missions. By July 1743 the bark-covered church was nearly finished.[49] The Moravians purposely tried to use materials familiar to the Indians, rather than imposing alien styles of building. The reconstituted village of eighteen Indian residences is shown on a birds-eye view of the village and surroundings drawn in 1745 by Brother Hagen. Only one house, the house of Joseph, is recognizable as a small Indian wigwam. The other structures have European-style gabled roofs, but they are elongated, in imitation of the familiar long wigwam of the Mohicans. Abraham's house was somewhat apart on the east, and Isaac's was outside the fence on the west. In the distance was K'takanatschan, "the big mountain."[50]

A European-style hay barrack, a stable and "John's workshop" where Tschoop worked had been erected. The mission did have a horse to keep in the stable, but it was stolen. Other livestock occasionally were noted; in her will of 1745, a woman named Ruth left, besides mats, wooden dishes, spoons, kettles and hatchets, a mare and a yearling calf.[51] Fields around the village held large and small gardens. The creek on the mission land was straightened out. As Moravians and village Indians worked together, the natives learned to raise turnips and eat sauerkraut, sang hymns, attended "love feasts," (celebratory communal dinners held after a religious service) and, at least once, some were baptized by moonlight. In 1744, the Indians were advised to pursue home industry instead of going away from

A rude sketch of the Mohican mission village of Shekomeko was made in 1745. In the foreground is the mission house (1) attached to the church (24). Close by is a Dutch-style hay barrack with a moveable roof for storing grain (3). Abraham's house was on the right at (6) and John's house at (7). Joseph's wigwam was at (13). The square at (14) was a graveyard.

Moravian Archives, Box 112, Folder 17

home to hunt or work; they had begun to learn broom and basket-making, as well as other crafts. In 1743 one missionary, Frederick Post, married an Indian woman, Rachel, from Pachgatgoch. She had been taught by David Brainerd, probably during Brainerd's two visits to Pachgatgoch.[52]

At the onset of the mission, hunger was common in the village; malnutrition was one reason so many children died. As usual, the Mohicans owed money to the traders. The Indian villagers were urged by the Moravians to remain aloof from the traders, who were excluded from the village. In early 1743, the residents were advised by Buettner to get rid of debt and support themselves. On occasion, even after the missionaries arrived, the group was short of corn for a love feast. In winter, Sarah, Abraham's wife, went to the Hudson River to find work in order to obtain corn.[53] On occasion, the missionaries gave from their own supplies to feed the Indians.

As the love feasts had grown to include many people, larger gatherings were held on a potluck basis; guests brought food. At one, the meat of five deer was served. December 1743 was a high-point. Following an evening in which "Christmas Eve was celebrated in the simplest form," a feast was held on Christmas Day for ninety-one guests. The next day, one hundred guests were present. Despite contributions, the tide of visitors strained the Indians' resources. Finally, in 1744, there was a good corn crop, but by winter, the corn was gone and the Indians dispersed to find work.[54]

Villagers of Shekomeko, like their relatives at Stockbridge, tapped maple trees in March. The missionaries built a hut among the trees during the sugaring operation in the spring, so they could stay in touch with converts and help them avoid drunken frolics. Missionary couples did not stay long at a mission. Each couple came on a temporary basis, according to the sect's regulations. In time, several missionaries and their wives, in turn, had been resident at Shekomeko village. With the missionaries' influential presence and strict rules of abstinence, sobriety was the norm. It was reported that drunken Indians were occasionally tied up by their fellow Indians and the missionaries until they were sober, to keep them from causing trouble.[55] This was surely a new experience for the residents of Shekomeko.

The official organization of the mission and erection of buildings aroused curiosity. In October 1742 about twenty Indians traveled to Shekomeko from Stockbridge. They were accompanied by John Sergeant, as well as by the minister from Sharon, who had been charged by the Connecticut Assembly with teaching the Sharon Mohicans. [56] After the English ministers left, the Stockbridge Mohicans stayed to hear and evaluate a sermon from the Moravians. A subtle rivalry for the allegiance of unattached Mohicans developed between the two missions.

By 1743 Shekomeko served as a base for Moravian excursions into western Connecticut and other parts of New York. Moravians Mack, Rauch and Buettner traveled from Shekomeko to wherever unconverted heathens were located, including Wequadnach and a satellite

village which were located at the foot of Indian Mountain near present
Sharon, Connecticut. The main village was on the east end of Indian
Lake, while the smaller village was on present Mudge Pond. Moravian
missionaries also visited Indians at Stockbridge, as well as at Weatauk
near Salisbury, at Pachgatgoch in Kent, and at Potatik, a Paugusset
village in present Newtown, Connecticut.[57]

Exceptions were the nearest neighbors of the Mohicans, the
Highland Indians, or Wappingers. Missionary Gotlob Buettner wrote
in spring 1744 that the Highland chief, Nimham, was a sorcerer. Very
few Highland Indians responded to Moravian advances. Later in the
year, Buettner reported that Nimham had tried to entice residents
away from Shekomeko and had forbidden his people from attending
Moravian meetings.[58]

Soon more serious trouble arose for the villagers. As the Mohicans of Shekomeko became noticeably more temperate and better fed,
they tried to stay out of debt and avoided contact with white traders.
Some anxious traders tried to turn the Indians against the missionaries; Indian self-sufficiency preached by the Moravians threatened the
traders' sales of alcohol and goods as well as their supply of furs from
the Indians, however reduced. Moreover, a proprietor who had title
to the Indians' land was waiting for them to leave, thus ending the
Indian occupation. Nearby farmers and residents of hamlets springing
up on the Hudson were suspicious of the Moravian attachment to the
Indians. It was hinted that the Moravians had Papist connections, as
they lived with the Indians as the Jesuits did. This was ironic, since
the sect's troubles in Europe had been largely the result of their
opposition to Catholicism, as countries changed official religions.

Moravians at Wequadnach

The Shekomeko mission had attracted Mohicans from nearby
Wequadnach and Pachgatgoch, who attended their services. For
example, in February 1743, twenty-seven visitors from Pachgatgoch
and Potatik were at Shekomeko. Wequadnach Indian residents were
baptized at Shekomeko in 1742.[59] Once additional missionaries arrived to help at Shekomeko, Moravians considered missions at
Wequadnach and Weatauk. While their visits did not result in a
mission at Weatauk, regular Moravian services did begin for Wequadnach. Mohicans at Wequadach, led by Moses Nequitimaug, were
traumatized by the loss of their land and by colonial pressures as the

Town of Sharon was developed. The Moravian promise of self-sufficiency and future hope was helpful to them. By October 1743, a
Moravian mission had been established on the New York shore at
the west end of Indian Lake, in Dutchess County (in the present
Town of Northeast), opposite Wequadnach. The Moravian missionaries changed the name of the lake to Gnadensee (Lake of Grace) and
erected a small wooden chapel combined with a room for living
quarters.

The first baptism held at Wequadnach was that of the second wife
of Gideon Mauwehu, sachem at the village of Pachgatgoch. Mauwehu
had been given his Christian name and baptized by the Moravian
missionary, Martin Mack, in 1743. Not a Mohican, Mauwehu, probably a displaced Pequot with a few followers, is thought to have settled
at a tiny Paugusset (Weantinock) village in the Housatonic Valley
west of Kent, Connecticut. Mauwehu's village, under pressure from
English settlers, had moved west of the Housatonic River to land
which was supposed to be reserved for them.[60] In listing their converts
from this village, the Moravians identified individuals as *Wom-
panosch*, meaning "easterners." This was an Algonquian word and, as
used by the Moravians, usually meant a person from Pachgatgoch.
Occasionally, the term was applied to Paugusset residents from the
village of Potatik.

With Mauwehu's encouragement, a formal mission was established by the Moravians at his village by October 1742. Martin Mack
was sent there. Although each of the three locations, Shekomeko,
Wequadnach and Pachgatgoch, had its assigned Moravian missionary,
Moravian visits to each location were frequent and the missionaries
and Indians became a closely-knit community. Consequently, Mohicans of the Wequadnach area adopted a form of Christianity that was
thoroughly Moravian. Moravian practices were somewhat outside
the pale of settled church practices in New England. This set the
Moravians and their converts apart. The church at Stockbridge, in
contrast, was conducted in the traditional New England mode, although it included extra instruction geared to the Indians.

Demise of the Missions

Despite the Moravian success in improving Indian self-sufficiency, sobriety, and health, opposition to Moravian activities gained
momentum. Through no fault of their own, the Moravians soon

became the center of a storm of attention which would damage their missions to the Mohicans of Dutchess County and Connecticut and cause the missionaries to retreat to their Pennsylvania locations, drawing with them as many converts as they could persuade to go. There were several reasons for these developments: Traders and settlers resented the Moravians; there was prejudice against all Indians; the missionaries were suspected of Catholic leanings and the Indians were suspected of ties to Canada. Most importantly, the impending war with Canada posed the threat of Indian incursions from the north. Settlers retained vivid memories of atrocities and captivities only a few decades previous. By association, they feared the Mohicans. The likelihood of an approaching war made settlers uneasy.

Raids by Indians from the St. Lawrence Valley began as early as 1743, and rumors flew suggesting Canadian connections with Shekomeko. The Moravians were accused of being Canadian supporters; a story circulated that the Moravians were going to lead an Indian uprising.[61] Isolated settlers formed a night watch for protection.

Abraham of Shekomeko pressed his case against the Little Nine Partners. His repeated appeals to the proprietors, to the Governor, and to Sir William Johnson, Indian Commissioner, held the proprietors at bay and added to the criticism of the mission. The precipitating factor in the local distrust of the Moravian missions, however, was the deterioration in relations between the colonies and Canada, followed by King George's War, which lasted from 1744 to 1748.

As raids from Canada occurred in New York and Massachusetts, Mohicans of Wequadnach and Weatauk were feared to be planning attacks on settlers. Sharon settlers prepared for a pre-emptive attack on Shekomeko. Area colonial communities, including Stockbridge in 1741, put up palisades or built blockhouses for defense against all Indians. What most of the aroused settlers did not appreciate was that the scattered Mohican villages—one or more in Schodack, locations in Greene County west of the Hudson River, a village near Kinderhook[62] and those at Shekomeko, Wequadnach, Weatauk, and Stockbridge—were in as much danger from the French as were the settlers on outlying farms in New York and Massachusetts.

Accusations of Disloyalty

The Moravians' refusal in 1744 to serve in the militia was regarded as proof of their potential disloyalty. Rumors related that they were supplying mission Indians with weapons for an attack on English settlements. In June 1744, on receiving the Governor's orders to do so, a sheriff's posse led by Col. Henry Beekman searched Shekomeko for stored weapons and ammunition, but found nothing out of the ordinary. A local posse previously had interviewed four Moravians and many Indians at Shekomeko. They found "All the Indians at work on their plantations Who seemed in a Consternation at the approach of the Sherif and his Company but received them Civilly."[63] The interrogators accused the Moravians of being disaffected from the Crown, but the innocent Moravians denied this, saying they, too, were afraid of the French and their Indians.

The Moravians explained that their "business is meerly to Gain Souls among the Heathens and that they had a Commission from the Archbishop of Canterbury and were ready to Shew their Credentials." The Moravian refusal on "Scruple of Conscience against Swearing" to take an oath of loyalty to the King was regarded as another sign of likely disloyalty. The principal missionary at Shekomeko at the time, Gotlob Buettner, expressed his allegiance to the English king, but explained that the Moravians could not swear oaths. Although Buettner assured the posse that the Mohicans intended no evil, the Moravian ministers were charged and subsequently ordered to face the Governor and Council. In July the Moravians, on the charge that they "Endeavoured to seduce the Indians from their Allegiance which in this Time of Warr would be of most dangerous Consequence. . ." were ordered to New York to be examined.[64]

Thanks to the accusations against the Moravians, brief descriptions of Shekomeko in 1744 exist. In July the Dutchess County Sheriff reported that Shekomeko was a place "in the remotest part of the County inhabited Chiefly by Indians where also live Gudlop Bynder [Buettner], Hendrick Joachim Senseman and Joseph Shaw three Moravian priests with their Familyes in a Block House [i.e., a cabin made of logs] and Sixteen Indian Wigwams round about it." The drawing by Hagen done in 1745 corroborates this information, with the addition of two houses.[65]

Further, Brother Senseman, a baker earlier in his life, reported that he preached to the Indians through an interpreter named Johannes (Tschoop) and "that he and his Brethren work for their Livelihood and plant Indian Corn and Wheat (which they Enjoy in Common) on some Land whereon the Indians remain & that they built themselves a House wherein they all three live." Senseman had a wife who had come with him from Germany.[66]

The Moravian missionaries from Dutchess County appeared before the Governor and his Council on August 1, 1744. Joseph Shaw, after giving his life story, explained that he was the schoolmaster. He reported that although the missionaries had no settled salary from the Moravian Church, they "work as much as they Can and the Church supports them in what Else they want." At Shekomeko, he said, "they are Settled on a Small Tract of Land which they plant with Corn and that he has taught some of the Indians to read English." He mentioned that he understood little of the Indian language but an Indian whose name was John (Tschoop) and another called Isaac interpreted for him. Isaac was the Indian from Pachgatgoch named Seim; Seim and his wife were baptized members of the Shekomeko community. Gotlob Buettner added to the interview the information that besides the sixteen Indian families "there are others that come 12 or 20 miles to hear them [the Moravians] and there are about 30 Indian men at Schacomico."[67]

In response to being told they might be ordered to leave the Indians, Joseph Shaw warned that if the Moravians removed (to their headquarters in Pennsylvania), the Indians would follow and the Mohawks would be unhappy if this happened. Interestingly, the Mohawks had made a pact of friendship with Count Zinzendorf when he visited them.[68] In addition, pressure continued on the Mohicans to fight on the side of the Mohawks, who were still undecided as to which side they would support in the war. Thus the potential support of the Mohawks for the French, and the possible alliance of the Mohicans with the Mohawks, were considerations underlying the settlers' distrust of the Mohicans.

Although in August the Moravians were allowed to return home to Shekomeko, in September 1744, missionary activities were ordered to be discontinued. By the end of November an act had been passed in New York requiring "Moravian and vagrant Teachers among the Indians" to desist from further teaching or preaching and to leave the province. Count Ludwig Zinzendorf, leader of the sect, who had been so impressed when he visited Shekomeko, angrily petitioned the London Board of Trade requesting freedom from petty restrictions and asking for the right of Indians to join the Protestant Church in the colonies.[69]

The New York ordinance ended the work of the missionaries at Shekomeko, but the devoted Moravians were unwilling to leave the Indians. When they were ordered to depart, two who did not leave were imprisoned in February and March 1745. Other Moravians came to Shekomeko in defiance of the ban, although they did not preach. On February 23, 1745 missionary Buettner died of consumption and was buried by the saddened Indians in the Mohican cemetery at Shekomeko.[70]

When bands of New York settlers seized Indian land, blocked travel, and forbade Moravian services, some Shekomeko Indians moved over the colony line to Wequadnach in 1745.[71] However, Connecticut was evicting the Moravians, as well. The Moravians finally reluctantly returned to their headquarters in Bethlehem, Pennsylvania. As there was little room there, a new home for the Mohicans was already planned not far from Bethlehem. Some Shekomeko Indian residents immediately followed the Moravians in 1745. Tschoop (John) and Isaac, for example, were already at Bethlehem in 1746. As more Mohicans moved to Bethlehem, a settlement for them called Gnadenhutten, near the mouth of the Mahoning Creek in the Lehigh Valley, was begun in the spring of 1746. Intended to be temporary, it grew in size and was not abandoned until November 1755, when the missionaries there were massacred by the Shawnees.[72] The Indians fled to Bethlehem and eventually some, including Sarah, Abraham's wife, were given shelter in Philadelphia.

Although some resident Indians already had departed from Shekomeko to join the Moravians at the new Pennsylvania mission, Abraham (Shabash) was reluctant to leave until his land claim was resolved. To leave would be to abandon not only his payment but the mile square tract on which the mission village was situated. Abraham, moreover, did not wish his family to leave the isolation of Shekomeko for the temptations and danger of the Wyoming Valley; he also correctly feared that any Indians who went to Bethlehem might be attacked by the English there. English and Indian tensions were high in Pennsylvania at the time.

Meanwhile, King George's War brought changes in Indian relations. The Stockbridge Indians had built a fort and their chief invited neighboring groups to assemble there for safety and to repulse the Mohawks, should they actually side with the French. Some Shekomeko Mohicans wanted to move to Stockbridge. An April 1745 council with chiefs from Stockbridge, Wequadnach, and Pachgatgoch was held at Shekomeko.[73]

A conference at New York with the governor produced no changes; the governor made false representations to the Indians about the Moravians, which the Mohicans surely did not believe, and gave the Mohicans some coins which were supposed to help them preserve their land. While in New York the Mohicans boarded with some Moravian brethren and were treated well. Abraham was recognized as an influential leader. This support for his claims encouraged Abraham to remain on his land at Shekomeko.

With the advent of war, the Massachusetts government was anxious to retain Mohican good will. In June, when Stockbridge chiefs visited Boston to pay respects to Governor William Shirley, they promised, as always, to remain friends of the English. Later, representatives from Shekomeko, Stockbridge, Wequadnach and Pachgatgoch, totaling some forty or fifty Indians, were ignored at a conference held with the New York governor and Six Nations in Albany in October 1745, although the Housatonic groups had been invited to attend. At the conference, the Six Nations were scolded by the New York governor; he had heard rumors circulating the previous winter that the Iroquois were going over to the French. Their response was that the English were "to think no more of it."[74]

Since the allegiance of the Mohicans was assured, the Iroquois, sitting on the fence, were the players of importance. Although Mohawk loyalty had wavered, at this conference the Mohawks agreed that they would fight for the English if there were more French attacks. For the moment, however, they were not ready to take up arms. They needed time to notify "far nations" and to call in their scattered members.[75]

As the war escalated, the Stockbridge Mohicans declared war on the French. The Moravians were pacifists and taught their converts to avoid war. In contrast, John Sergeant and Ephraim Williams at Stockbridge endorsed the use of Indian fighters, with the result that sixteen Stockbridge Indians agreed to fight. Abraham and Johannes (Shabash and Tschoop), who did not wish to kill anyone, decided to stay at Shekomeko as long as possible, planning to retreat to Stockbridge only if war actually came to the area. Fighting was against their new principles. Although a few men from Shekomeko agreed to enlist, they soon returned home, but some unbaptized Shekomeko residents did volunteer.[76] Thus there was an ideological separation of the Moravian Indian converts from the Indians at Stockbridge as well as from unbaptized Indians.

Around Shekomeko, fear of the Mohicans still ran high. When visiting Indians and a Moravian minister came to the community for a church service, settlers in Rhinebeck thought the Indians were assembling for an outbreak. Colonials made ready to strike. Frightened by threats made by local residents to kill the Indians of Shekomeko, about half of the Indian residents left for Pennsylvania and, in summer 1746, all missionaries left as well. Not every Mohican went directly to Gnadenhutten; some went to Bethlehem; Abraham and his family dispersed temporarily to Wequadnach. Some Mohicans from Shekomeko went to Stockbridge and some to Pachgatgoch. When the Mohicans visiting Stockbridge, in turn, set out for the new mission of Gnadenhutten, they took some of the Stockbridge Mohicans with them to Pennsylvania; these may have been Shekomeko relatives who had gone to Stockbridge during the war.

Without the Moravian presence, the small remaining Shekomeko community was adrift. By 1748, some Indians began to consider

A few Mohican families remained in Dutchess County through the first half of the nineteenth century. The memorial to Chief Crow is located on Turkey Hill Road, off Jackson Corners Road, near Pine Plains, New York.

Photograph by Melinda Camardella

A marker on Silvernails Road near Pine Plains, New York honors Mannessah. A descendant of the Shekomeko Mohicans, he lived in Gallatin, Dutchess County, New York.

Photograph by Melinda Camardella

selling everything and following other Mohicans to Gnadenhutten, Pennsylvania, but "not yet this year" they said.[77] They were tenacious in retaining their hold on the small tract left to them.

Some Shekomeko Mohican families, probably those who had rejected close ties with the Moravians, remained in the vicinity for the next century. Indian descendants survived into the mid-nineteenth century near the village of Shekomeko. Others intermarried with local colonial families.[78]

Moravians Return

In 1749, after the war was over, the English Parliament established the right of missionaries to work with the Indians. The Moravians prepared to return to the Mohicans. However, war and land loss had done the work of disrupting the villages. Shekomeko was obliterated; Pachgatgoch village was intact but lacking in spiritual leadership; the Wequadnach community had lost its land and its members were demoralized. Mohican Christians drifted back and forth between the Pennsylvania missions and their Mohican home base in Connecticut.

Wequadnach, however, experienced a brief reawakening. On February 10, 1749, Abraham (Shabash), Moses Nequitimaug, and Jacob, rejoiced in the arrival of a new missionary, David Bruce. Abraham and his family were at Wequadnach. The group wrote to Bethlehem, "We, Abraham, Moses and Jacob, and all the brethren and sisters, salute the whole Church, and are very glad and thankful that the Church has cared for us again, visited us, forgiven us all that has hitherto passed and sent somebody to instruct and teach us. . .for we thought we should never more, in all our lives, have any one from the Brethren's church among us. . . ."

After promising to remain steadfast in their faith, the writers conveyed greetings and concerns to family members at Bethlehem: "Joshua's grandmother salutes him heartily, and is very glad that his sister was baptized at Bethlehem. . .and I salute Brother Joseph and Mother Spangenberg; and we brethren and sisters wish that where the Brethren live we may live also; for, so long as we had no teachers, we could not say that we loved the Brethren; but now we feel that we love them. Sarah [Abraham's wife] salutes Brother Joseph and Mother Spangenberg, Brother Cammerhoff and Sister Cammerhoff, and all the brethren and sisters at Bethlehem, Gnadenhuetten, Nazareth, and in all the churches. Our Sister Rachel does the like; our sister Abigail the like; Bartholomew's mother the like; our sister Miriam the like, our sister Esther the like. . . ."

As well, the writer, Abraham, asked that his son, Jonathan, ". . .may see this letter that he may know what we have made out." Sarah, Abraham's wife, saluted her son Jonathan and his wife, Anna; "and we shall be glad if he comes back again; and Sarah is glad that Jonathan again stands on a good ground [with the church]." Moreover, Esther saluted Jonathan and Anna, and all the sisters, "and is sorry that she could not go with them, for her mother hindered her." Sad news was included, "Brother Jephthah's daughter, who is sick, salutes her sister in Gnadenheutten, and thinks she will not live; prays, therefore heartily to be baptized."[79]

In this affectionate letter, twelve converts, some from Shekomeko, who remained in the Wequadnach community are mentioned, as well as others who had removed to Bethlehem. The fragmentation of the families is clear. Although Brother David Bruce may have put the words on paper for them, the Christian Mohicans spoke from their hearts. They had made many adaptations and had moved far from the Indian outlook of the previous century. They were probably more changed than the Indians at Stockbridge. Yet, they would still identify themselves as Mohicans for years to come.

In a separate letter written by David Bruce, Wequadnach residents Magdalenah, Martha, and Old Cornelius and his wife were mentioned, bringing the total of known converts remaining at the Wequadnach mission at sixteen.[80] "Old Cornelius" was Catharickseet, whose father had helped Abraham's mother sell her land. Catharickseet was probably a relative of Abraham. Bruce's letter conveys a picture of a loving group of relatives and friends. Other Indians not mentioned in the letters, most as yet unbaptized, still resided in Wequadnach village, despite the appropriation and sale of their land.

After the war, sentiment against the Moravians subsided. Although Shekomeko was lost, the missions at Wequadnach and Pachgatgoch once again could be staffed by Moravians from Bethlehem. Brother Bruce was now appointed to the care of the Christian Indians at Pachgatgoch and Wequadnach. Bruce resided chiefly in a house at Wequadnach, belonging to the brethren, but he sometimes resided at Pachgatgoch, from where he paid visits to Stockbridge by invitation of the chief of the Mohicans, "sowing the seeds of the gospel wherever he came. . . ."[81]

The Mohicans of Wequadnach were being pressed by claims of a Sharon proprietor, Joseph Skinner. Missionary David Bruce reported that Skinner was making a pretense that he had bought the Indian land. Skinner claimed that he had tried to help the Indians by buying their land, but, as he now had to sell it, he was willing to sell it back to them. David Bruce reported Skinner wanted one hundred pounds for a hundred acres, an exorbitant amount. Skinner was trying to involve the Moravians in assisting the Indians with payment.[82] Well aware the Mohicans did not have one hundred pounds, Skinner seemingly was trying to extort money from their Moravian connections. Skinner's claim to the land may have been fraudulent, but other proprietors were eyeing the Indian land and would willingly pay for his claim. Although the Indians continued to live on the land, they feared that their hold was tenuous and they would soon be evicted by a new buyer for the land Skinner wanted to sell.

In April 1749, the few Indians left at Wequadnach again considered leaving. Missionary David Bruce believed it was God's will they should all go, but he was trying not to interfere. He spoke with Moses Nequitimaug, one of the community's leaders, "about what he [Moses] now thought in regard to the land, since the white people are intent on taking it away. He [Moses] said he knew nothing. . . ."[83]

Bruce, however, helped thwart Skinner's machinations temporarily. When Skinner and the sheriff came to Bruce to tell him that the Indians should get off the land, he responded that it was not his affair to advise the Indians in such matters. He suggested the sheriff could discuss Skinner's claim against the Mohicans with other people. Thus he turned away Skinner's hopes that the Moravians would be blackmailed into paying for the Indian land. This incident illustrates that the white community fully understood the Moravian commitment to the Indians.

Another threat arose when a Dutch farmer named Van Aernem claimed some Indian land was his. His deed, if he had one, would have been illegal, as land assigned to the Indian group by the Connecticut Assembly could not be sold by individual Indians.[84] The overlapping claims led to a dispute between Skinner and Van Aernem. Van Aernem's deeds may have been for some small parcels of land which had been sold by individual Mohicans in order to obtain desperately needed food, clothing and guns. Some parcels also went to a newcomer, Thomas Barnes. Soon Barnes obtained the large tract south of Wequadnach held by Skinner.[85] With this, Barnes became the major player in obtaining the last tract held by the Mohicans at Sharon.

The Wequadnach Indians were thoroughly frightened. Moses reported to David Bruce "that their land was now entirely gone and that they will have to get off it." Convinced they had lost their rights, the Indians evaluated the worth of their houses, fields, and land. They "went to become reconciled with the man who has purchased the land. The man dealt very honestly with them, and wanted to give them around 220 pounds New England money for their work," wrote Bruce.[86] Whom they went to is not certain, but it was probably Barnes, who had obtained the land from Skinner.

The Wequadnach Mohicans considered several options: they could linger in Connecticut or wander in the Housatonnic Valley, as some Indians not connected to the mission did; they could move up to Stockbridge; they could join friends and relatives in Pennsylvania; or they could go to Pachgatgoch, nearby, where Gideon Mauwehu had offered them the opportunity to join his community. "Gideon sent word. . .those who were not inclined to going to Bethl., he would prefer it if they had a mind to come to him instead of going to Wanachquategog [Stockbridge]. For he believed t'would be better for their soul at his [place]. . .and he would take them in with love."[87] The mutual dependence on the shared Moravian ministers had led to very close social as well as religious ties between residents of Pachgatgoch and Wequadnach. Stockbridge, where the English reigned, was regarded by both David Bruce and Gideon Mauwehu as not a good place for Christian Indians. The mission at Pachgatgoch survived until 1762.

An old resident of Pachgatgoch, incensed with the treatment of the Sharon Indians, joined with Moses Nequitimaug in protesting to the Governor about the illegal actions of some people in Sharon. Although the Governor sent for the Indians, the meeting produced no change in the situation.[88]

Late in April 1749 some Wequadnach residents left for Pennsylvania, including, finally, Abraham of Shekomeko. Those left behind were angry because so many went away. David Bruce described the pain brought by the decision to leave. Unwilling to part, Indians who would remain at Wequadnach walked beside the departees for a distance: "We left at 9 o'clock and all of Wechquatenach accompanied us a stretch and when taking leave many tears were shed on both sides. . ." "Martha's son changed his mind and stayed behind. . . ."[89] Those who departed in groups over the course of three days included Jephtha; "Old Cornelius" (Catharickseet) and his wife; Abraham and his sons; Jacob and his wife and three children; Johannes and Lorellu's sister, and his brother and their little daughter; and Joachim's wife and her son.

Although David Bruce accompanied Jephtha and old Cornelius and his wife to Pennsylvania, Bruce soon returned. David Bruce invigorated the missions at Wequadnach and Pachgatgoch. After a few weeks, Bishop Cammerhof arrived from Bethlehem with Brother Beyold to baptize "no less than twenty new converts" and to administer the sacraments. Cammerhof's journal reports that Abraham's wife, Sarah, hurried out to meet the Bishop's entourage. Others in residence at Wequadnach were John, "who had recently visited Bethlehem," Miriam, Abigail, Jephthah, Jacob, and several others. [90] It appears that Jephthah and Jacob, as well as some others, had returned from Pennsylvania; clearly there was considerable movement between the two locations. The John mentioned was not Tschoop, who was already dead.

Unexpectedly, David Bruce's time at Wequadnach was cut short. He had arrived in January. In July news was carried to Bethlehem from Pachgatgoch that Bruce was ill "in the mission house at Wechquadnach. . . ." Bruce died there on July 9, 1749, before Frederick Post, a fellow missionary, could hurry to his side from Bethlehem. Post reported that Bruce had returned from "Westenhuc, or Wannaquatiksk," that is, Stockbridge, on the sixth of July. Moses Nequitimaug of Wequadnach and Joshua, the son of Gideon Mauwehu of Pachgatgoch, tended Bruce with devotion in his illness. After a funeral service at the mission on the west end of the lake, Bruce's body was carried by canoe to the large Indian burial ground at the east end of Indian Pond.[91]

The exact location of the Wequadnach mission chapel and house, located in New York across the lake from the Indian village, was described in Newton Reed's *Early History of Amenia*, published in 1875, as "on the farm of Col. Hiram Clark, in the present town of Northeast, not far east of his [Clark's] house and on the west side of Indian Pond."

The remaining Mohicans of the Wequadnach congregation were crushed by the loss of their new religious guide and teacher. As the mission now lacked a resident missionary, the Indians drifted away. Bruce was succeeded after a few years by a traveling Moravian missionary, Abraham Reinke, who visited the area for eight weeks in summer 1752. Ironically, he was welcomed and asked to preach by the local settlers. The Moravian preachers found their audience from that time forward among the unchurched white settlers of Connecticut and Dutchess County. The Indian mission at Wequadnach on Indian Pond was dissolved in 1753, "a step rendered inevitable by the sale of the Indian lands and the consequent dispersion of the tribe."[92]

In July 1752, Moses Nequitimaug and Bartholomew sold the fifty-acre tract on which the Mohican village of Wequadnach was located to Thomas Barnes for fifty pounds. This was far less than the 220 pounds discussed with "the man" about 1749. To the south of the tract sold by Moses and Bartholomew was the land that Barnes had bought from Joseph Skinner, north was the town of Salisbury line, and west was Indian Pond. Included in their 1752 sale was "all Our improvements in said Township of Sharon, it being the whole of what Land We claim in said Township. . . ."[93]

Other members of the Indian community were surprised and angry to learn of the close-out sale of their village land to Barnes in their absence. Although it was contrary to law to obtain deeds from individual Indians without prior legislative approval, the Assembly as usual approved Barnes' title to the land. The Indians remained deeply grieved, and "some of them were often back among the inhabitants [of Sharon] complaining that they had been overreached [taken advantage of], and often giving significant hints of. . . resentment. . . ."[94]

As a result, a few would not leave. According to Moravian records, a remnant of the Wequadnach Indians continued to live in their settlement by Indian Pond after the land transfer to Barnes. Some went back and forth to Pachgatgoch. Later a small population of Indians, probably Mohicans, was reported in the Sharon area.

The Moravians continued the mission at Pachgatgoch for another decade. Even as late as 1770 missionaries continued "to visit such Christian remnants as preferred persecution to exile, and so lingered behind."[95] Wequadnach Indians kept up contacts there. A letter reported in September 1752 that the Indians of Pachgatgoch, "were all busy going about their work of making *Canuh* [canoes] and baskets. Sister Susana and Magdelena arrived here from *wegquatnach*. Gotlieb had shot a bear of which they also sent us a piece."[96] Soon Timothy and two unbaptized Indians arrived from "Wegquatnach." They stayed for four days.

A missionary in November 1752 found several Indian members of the Wequadnach congregation still living in their village, including Esther, Augustus' wife with her little daughter, Hanna, and Jonathan's son. The missionary, Brother Senseman, wrote that they were planning to visit Pachgatgoch, and Susana was hoping to live at Pachgatgoch for the winter. Two other Wequadnach residents, Timothy and young Moses, had gone to Wanachquaticock (Stockbridge). Joshua, now a resident of Pachgatgoch, reported in February that the Indians of Wanachquaticock had sent a string of wampum to Wequadnach "and had with it said that their gate would always be open for them if they wanted to move to them. . . ."[97] The few remaining Indians at Wequadnach, however, had not yet made a decision.

A messenger, Nathaniel, informed the Indians of an alliance between the Nanticock Indians and the Moravian brothers at Gnadenhutten. Nathaniel also carried this news to Stockbridge. A week later he returned, carrying a belt of wampum from upriver, and carrying as well the news that Abraham/Shabash would be installed as an officer to give out belts of wampum in the name of the Mohican nation. This important diplomatic appointment for Abraham pleased the Mohicans at Pachgatgoch, who sent their approval to Bethlehem in the form of a wampum belt. The appointment meant Abraham was to act as an important liason with other groups. In 1757 Abraham was described at a conference of the Indians with Sir William Johnson as "one of the Chief of the Mohikanders (who destitute of Land or Habitation) went to live at Wyoming on Susquahannah." The Iroquois desired Abraham to carry a belt among all the Mohican Indians, to advise them to collect themselves at Otsiningo (a Mohawk village on the Chenango River near its confluence with the Susquehanna River), or in some fixed place and not wander about, as "their continuing in that Dispersed Manner might be fatal to them."[98] The statement indicates the Nation's dispersal had not been fatal to that point. The appointment of Abraham as messenger demonstrated that the Mohicans' sense of national unity, their identity, and their traditional political organization had managed to survive the war's fragmentation.

Clearly, the hostility of colonial neighbors during King George's War proved a critical element for the missions in the Housatonic Valley. Although the fighting ended by 1747, the Shekomeko and Wequadnach missions did not survive. Many of their residents moved to Pennsylvania with their Moravian teachers. By drawing the Indians to their missions in Pennsylvania, the Moravians carried away a substantial segment of the disenfranchised Mohican population of Dutchess County in New York and Litchfield County in Connecticut.

In the few years they existed, the Moravian missions had effected profound changes among some Mohicans of Dutchess County, New York and northern Connecticut. The teachers helped the Mohicans to new, positive beliefs; finding new spiritual connections brought the Mohican world view closer to that of their English neighbors, although at the cost of an ancient lifestyle. Some Mohicans learned skills that allowed them to stay at home rather than to wander in search of game or furs. They were able to produce items which could be exchanged for goods, as furs once were. Some developed new attitudes toward war. A number learned to read and write. As many moved away from the valleys and hills of their homeland, they took new abilities and Christian beliefs with them, while retaining their Mohican identity.

X.

Clans, Chiefs, and Close-out Deeds

"Then I ask'd them if they would let two of their Children go and live with me at *New-Haven* the Rest of the Winter; and they agreed that the *Captain's* only Son *Nungkowwat*, and the *Lieutenant's* oldest Son *Etowokaum*, (who by the Way is grandson by his Mother to *Etowaukaum*, Chief of the *River-Indians*, who was in *England* in Queen *Ann's* reign) should be the Children." —John Sergeant, December 1734.

Clans

MORAVIAN MISSIONARIES as late as the 1780s were told by their Indian contacts that the three clans of the Delawares and the Mohicans were the turkey, wolf, and turtle. Rev. George Henry Loskiel, a German Moravian, for example, wrote, "Most [Indian] nations are divided into tribes [clans], each forming a separate republic within the state. The first tribe of the Delawares is called the *large tortoise*; the second, the *Turkey*; and the third, the *Wolf*."[1] In the seventeenth century, turtles, turkeys, and wolves were depicted on Mohican deeds, confirming the presence of these three clans among the Hudson Valley Mohicans. Since deer also appear on deeds, there may have been a deer clan or sub-clan among the Mohicans, and undoubtedly there were other sub-clans. No depictions of bears appear on any of the many known Mohican deeds prior to 1730, although recognizable bears appear on Mohawk deeds through the period. The Mohawk clans in deeds were the bear, wolf and turtle. The Mohawk turtle was often drawn as the mud turtle or snapping turtle, which has a long neck and substantial tail. The Mohican turtle seems to represent a more generic turtle, similar to the turtle called the red slider which suns itself in freshwater ponds.

Mohicans of the twentieth century believe there was a bear clan among the Stockbridge Mohicans. About 1792, Hendrick Aupaumut wrote in his Mohican history that the three clans of the Mohicans were the wolf, the bear, and the turtle. The turkey clan and any deer or other sub-clans were not mentioned. This omission of the turkey clan is hard to understand, and could be an error, as the turkey clan was recognized at Stockbridge. However, there may have been a local bear clan among the Stockbridges.

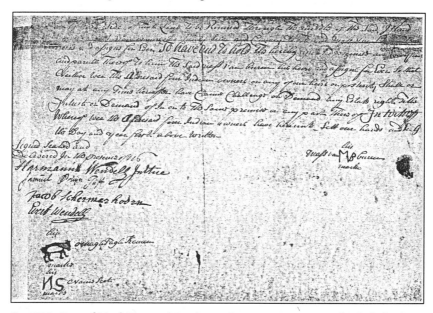

In 1730, OmaghTaghKemen (Matakemen) was a witness to a Schodack deed. He drew a bear for his mark, the only bear pictograph found as yet on a Mohican deed. Evert Wendell, also a witness, possibly was the Indian trader whose account book is discussed in Chapter 4.

New York Genealogical and Biographical Society, Mss. Maas Van Buren

There is a pictographic signature drawn on a deed in 1730 by an Indian from the island in Schodack that may represent a bear. The possible bear drawing was made by a man named OmaghTaghKemen, witness to a 1730 deed for part of Moesimus Island, on which chief sachem Ampamit had his village. OmaghTaghKemen moved to Stockbridge from this island in the Hudson. With his name shortened, he was the person called Matakeamin who a few years later took part in a sale of a tract six miles square on the Housatonic River.[2] Matakeamin's previous location was confirmed in the 1737 deed written at Stockbridge which describes him as formerly of Menanoke, the island in the Hudson below Albany. That the first letter of Matakeamin's name was dropped was not unusual; the first syllable of an Indian word frequently was lost or changed from one document to another, especially if it was a soft *a, o, m, n* or *w*.

What were Matakeamin's origins? Unless his wife or possible sisters belonged to the bear clan, Matakeamin could not have carried the bear clan to Stockbridge, since clan affiliations descended through the women's line. Mohicans of the eighteenth century may have introduced the bear clan by marrying Iroquois, however, although no other eighteenth century Mohican deed has been located that carries a bear pictograph. Perhaps some exist which have not been found.

Another pictograph which did not appear on Mohican deeds until the mid-eighteenth century was the snapping turtle, a well-represented Mohawk icon. This again suggests Iroquois clans may have made their way into eighteenth-century Mohican family stocks through marriages between Mohican men and Iroquois women. Mohicans and Mohawks became more closely associated in the eighteenth century than they had been in the previous century, when they were enemies. Associations with Iroquois, for example, came at Stockbridge and in emigrant locations where Mohicans lived near Mohawks, such as at Schoharie and in villages along the Susquehanna. In these locations opportunities for marriage greatly increased as the eighteenth century progressed.

Within a few years after 1734, the use of clan symbols by Christianized Mohicans became uncommon. Clans represented stories of human origins and belief in animal spirits contrary to Christian tenets and, as symbols of connections to the old spirit world, were discarded. Undoubtedly ancient ceremonies relating to reciprocal clan obligations also were abandoned. Indians who did not become Christians were free to use animal symbols on deeds, but, among both groups, initials on deeds began to substitute for clan or personal symbols.

Some Mohicans possibly were related to Hendrick, mid-eighteenth century sachem of the Mohawks, who reputedly was part Mohican. John Konkapot, Jr., a "young and intelligent Indian of the Stockbridge tribe," claimed to be part Mohawk. He stated in 1804 that he was a grandson of the famous Mohawk chief and warrior, Hendrick. The account follows:

> John Konkapot, jun. Nhu'h kekit Ochuch Anquiquoi you, mactshenaunetatseh, austou Ich nastkmuch." "Such are his name and titles, as lately given by himself at Cambridge, in the Moheagan tongue. He is, by his own account, a grandson of the famous old warrior, Hendrick, the Chief of the Mohawks, who was killed in the French war, 1758 [read 1755]. This young Indian says, that his grandfather Hendrick was the son of a Moheagan Chief (called the Wolf), by a Mohawk woman; and that Hendrick also married a Mohawk woman, Hunnis, a daughter of the Chief of the Mohawks."

This information is contained in a footnote to an article published in 1804, written by James Haughton, who was described as one of the Overseers of the Moheagan tribe situated between Norwich and New London, Connecticut. The Moheagans were a tribe separate from the Mohicans. The footnote, however, which applies to the Mohicans, not the Moheagans, seems to have been written by a different man, A. Holmes, who submitted the article.[3]

Since Konkapot was identified as a Mohican from the Hudson Valley, this account by John Konkapot hints that a son of Konkapot married a Mohawk woman, a daughter of Hendrick. These two would be the parents of John, Jr., a young man in 1804. The use of the term "Junior" need not cause confusion. Many New England families of the time included three generations with the same name, each called "Junior." Nephews who bore an uncle's name also were called "Junior."

Some Little-known Mohicans

Particularly persistent in retaining clan symbols were Mohican contingents in present-day counties of New York, especially Greene and Washington counties. While many of them drew turtles on deeds, among these Indians was Kagewap, who drew a graceful dog, Pissicks, who drew a horse, Thomas, who drew a snapping turtle, and Tapapeet, who drew a horse. Their delay in becoming Christian can probably be traced to the leadership of Metoxon.

In the 1740s, Metoxon, a sachem who had removed from Connecticut to Freehold, Greene County, welcomed and then rejected overtures of the Moravians. As he was seventy years old in 1743, he had encountered great changes in his long life and by then had lost the land he commanded in Connecticut. When Metoxon changed his mind about welcoming the missionaries, he knew enough about the vocabulary of the Christian faith to warn one Indian woman that missionary Rauch and his wife would go to hell "together with all ye Indians yt hear them."[4] Metoxon may have died within a few years, since land sales in the area after 1745 do not include his name.

The Mohicans hidden in the back country of Greene County in the eighteenth century are little known. There may have been a population of one hundred, according to the fragments of information which exist. For example, Mohicans from a Greene County group were anxious to fight on behalf of Sir William Johnson during the Seven Years War. In 1757, River Indians described as residing along the Schoharie and Catkill creeks were camped opposite Fort Johnson waiting to be called to fight.[5] The Schoharie Creek was Mohawk territory, but a group of Mohicans, by invitation, lived on the Schoharie Creek among the Mohawks at this time.

There were also young Mohicans from the area who turned rogue during the same war and preyed on war-time couriers who were carrying important letters between Sir William Johnson's officers. The first recorded attack on a messenger occurred in September 1757. Sir William sent for the heads of the River Indians. Johnson told the Indians that three of their people had attacked and wounded a messenger and robbed him of dispatches sent from Captain Lotteridge of the New York Regiment at Fort Hunter to the commanding officer at Albany.

The Mohicans were scolded by the Oneidas for permitting the attack on the courier on the road between Albany and Schenectady. The Mohican response came the next day. The River Indians apologized for the actions of their young men who had attacked the messenger, "as there are several of their People who live a wandering unsettled Life & will pay no regard to the Advice or Directions of their Wise & Elderly People."[6] However, they added that they were totally ignorant of whom the persons were who did it and were themselves innocent. They hoped that the incident would not destroy the friendship which all the chiefs and wise people of their nation wished to preserve with their brothers, the English. Johnson later promised to say no more about the affair.

On June 10, 1760, information was sent to Sir William Johnson that twelve "Mohickanders" were out intending to take prisoners or scalps along the Mohawk River between Albany and Schenectady. General Jeffrey Amherst took charge and the Mohican raiders were quickly traced. By June 12, Amherst noted in a letter to Johnson that Lt. Colonel Massey had sent out a "good party either to Overtake or waylay them, and in Which he thinks they will prove Successful; if they do, it will certainly put an end to all those Scalping parties, and make the Communication very safe."[7] The implication was that there had been other attacks. Johnson did not make the mistake of confusing the loyal Mohicans with the small outlaw group, and, in fact, some of the perpetrators probably went on to fight in his army. Mohicans both from Stockbridge and from Greene County helped the English defeat the French in the 1750s.[8]

By June 4, 1760, Sir William was wishing he could find Indians to act as battoemen, to help transport army supplies by boat. Had any of his Indian officers been available, he would have sent them down into the "country below Albany" (i.e., into Mohican territory in southern Albany County, now Greene County) where some men might be found; however, no Indian officer was available to go.[9]

In August 1760, Johnson noted he had a total of twelve Mohicans among his Indian troops. Shortly after, on an August list, sixteen Mohicans were among Indians who went with the Army under General Amherst from Fort William Augustus to Montreal. The Mohicans were: Paghkenaont, Honamauckh, Mughaghkehandy, Tsiksakan, Maquamopogh, Magdoghk, Kose, Aneweemot, Oscawaghkamen, Mahose, Tankalkel, Naghkaweemet, Eaidon, Knamhickan, Wosanek, and Songose.[10] It is likely that some of these men lived along the western reaches of the Catskill Creek or among the Mohawks at Schoharie.

Names

In the eighteenth century, some Mohicans took Christian first names even when they were not Christians. When Mohicans began to attend English schools and to become literate, and as the necessity of signing documents continued, they adopted surnames to go with their Christian names. Some families used the familiar name of their patriarch, such as the Metoxon and Konkapot families. Some used a shortened form of the parent's Indian name, such as Quinney for

Quinnauquaunt. Others took the father's first name, in the Dutch way, as the sons of Hendrick Aupaumut did. One observer noted, "Capt. Hendrick Aupaumut, according to a common custom in the Tribe, dropped the Indian name, Aupaumut, and was known as Capt. Hendrick. Since then, *Hendrick* has been the Sur-name of the family."[11] The name thereafter was also spelled Hendricks.

An emphasis on adopting the father's name was European; it helped undermine the Mohican traditions of matriarchy. Women, once Christianity took hold, lost their tribal prominence in land transactions. This was encouraged particularly by the English, who were uncomfortable with women as landholders unless they were widows holding land in trust for male heirs. Colonial administrators (all men) emphasized the male role. Even Timothy Woodbridge, the teacher and adviser to the Mohicans, in giving the genealogy of Mohican sachems, stressed male heirs, as if they were the ones who transmitted the lineage. Although he was well acquainted with former Mohican practice, now that the Mohicans were Christians no doubt he assumed only males would be future sachems and landowners.

The Indian custom was strong, however. George Loskiel, a Moravian missionary among the Delawares and Mohicans, wrote in the 1780s that "the sons of chiefs cannot inherit their father's dignity, being considered as strangers on account of their mothers; but a grandchild, great grand-child, or nephew, may succeed him."[12] Despite such traditions, New England viewpoints served to put pressure on the Mohicans to change their matriarchal traditions in which a woman's line was the source for future sachems, and in which women transmitted family rights to certain parcels of land.

An example of the change in emphasis was a deed of 1766 in which the Catskill Mohicans sold a tract of land and released their rights to all other parcels belonging to the Catskill Indians in the County of Albany. (This was before Greene County was separated from Albany County.) All of the signers were men, who were described as the "whole residue or remainder of the Tribe of Kats Kill Indians."[13] This was an egregious statement. The whole residue of the tribe surely consisted not only of men, but women and children, as well. In contrast, early deeds from Greene County included prominent Indian women as signers. The first Greene County land sale, in 1649, featured a woman as sachem.

Setting Boundaries

As early as the 1660s, when Aepjen was called into the Albany court to testify about the rightfulness of the claim of Jacob Gardenier to a piece of Schodack Island and to land along the Muitzeskill, Mohican authority for old boundaries was sought and the recollections of senior Indians were needed to interpret boundary lines. The impetus to resolve disputed patent lines continued through the eighteenth century; respected Mohican chiefs frequently were called to help settle disputes. The use of authoritative Indian testimony in resolving land claims in New York colony is an overlooked part of county and state histories.

One of the most detailed and valuable instances of Indian testimony on old land grants was that given on August 22, 1709 by Mohicans from Schodack and Catskill. Ampamit (a future chief, who lived at Schodack), his brothers Penonaemp and Tonwehees, and six other people, including Ampamit's mother, Wananagkea (Wanenagkela), gave an account of the sale of land to Barent Pieterse Coeymans thirty-seven years before. The other 1709 Mohican signers of this deposition were: Nawanaqugheet, Anehehoes, and Koewama and two women, Annalesem and Nanaquogqut.

The land, they recounted, was sold by Maghah, also called Maghshapeet or Magakemmena, sachem of Catskill, on December 26, 1672. He was widely known as Machackniminaw and also was called Joris, a Dutch nickname. Maghshapeet was an influential Mohican chief who served for over two decades and reportedly was chief sachem of the Mohicans for a few years.

In 1709, Barent Pieterse Coeymans and then patroon Kiliaen Van Rensselaer, son of Jeremias Van Rensselaer, formerly Director of Rensselaerswyck, were in dispute over the rights of the Coeymans Patent. Van Rensselaer was certain the Coeymans purchase intruded into Rensselaerswyck's territory. Indian testimony about the land sold to Coeymans was requested by the Coeymans' representatives with regard to the contested boundary line.

Coeymans' land began on the Hudson River at Jan Bronk's creek north of Coxsackie, according to the 1709 document which recited the bounds given in the Coeymans Patent. The tract extended north to a small creek by a marked tree at about the middle of John Reyersen's Island and went westward into the woods as far as the right of sachem Maghshapeet extended. This westward boundary line in

1709 was described using both Dutch and Indian landmarks. For example, John Reyersen's Island, also known as Smack's Island, was called Sietpaghack, and a creek northward into the woods was called Kakekoin, possibly the origin of the name Hannicroix Creek. The farthest point was a hill which the Indians called Maamkatuk.[14]

While the locations given in the Mohican tongue were meaningless to most readers, the document did mention the creek of Daniel Winne, a settler; his location would have been known to the Dutch. To clarify the western extent of the tract, the 1709 confirmation stated that the north and south lines went into the woods twelve English miles from the river.

The Mohicans testified that their deceased relatives were the true owners at the time of sale, and they were sure the land had never before been sold to any Christian. The 1709 document again confirmed the land to Barent Pieterse Coeymans and his heirs, and in it the Indians declared that neither Kiliaen Van Rensselaer nor his parents had any claim to the land in question. This statement was misleading. In fact, much of the land had been contained long before in a Van Rensselaer Indian purchase of 1631 from their ancestors. This early purchase underlying the Van Rensselaer claim had been made by agents for Kiliaen Van Rensselaer's grandfather, the first patroon, also named Kiliaen.

In 1632, Patroon Kiliaen Van Rensselaer wrote of this event, "Director Minuijt [Peter Minuit] has given me a map of the land lately purchased, situated between Beeren Island and Smax Island...stretching towards the woods and inland two day's journey."[15] Smack's Island of 1709 was the old Smax Island of 1631 and it was the same as John Reyersen's Island or the Sietpaghack of the Indians. The 1631 boundaries echoed those of 1672. Within a few years after 1709, the dispute between the Coeymans family and the Van Rensselaers was settled by a compromise. The Coeymans were given title to the land but had to pay a yearly sum to the Van Rensselaers.

The Mohicans testifying in 1709 stated they were the children and relations of the deceased original signer, Maghshapeet. In 1672, Maghshapeet, the chief, had signed on behalf of several others: Brownis, Cackonapit, Nahont Narmoes, Janaman, and Tielheysem. Names, as usual, were spelled two or more ways within the document. The 1709 signers traced out their relationships to the deceased family members listed in the 1672 deed: Ampamit (Ambamet, Aembamit) was the son of Brownis; Wananagkea (Wawaghakea, Mananagkea) was the widow

of Brownis; Annabesem was the sister of Maghshapeet; Onakekoes
(Anekehoes) was the brother of Maghshapeet; Nanaquogkat was the
grandchild of Maghshapeet; Koewamo was a cousin to Maghshapeet;
and Tonwehees (Tawahees) was a brother of Ampamit. The widow
of Brownis, who was the mother of Ampamit, Penonamp and
Tonwehees, given above as Wawaghakea or Wananagkea, was identified in a different deed as Wanenagkela.

Also interesting were the pictographic signatures. Ampamit
signed with a wolf, as he had on other deeds. This implies that his
mother, Wanenagkela, was of the wolf clan. Nawanaqugheet also
signed with a wolf, while Nanaquogqut, a woman, the grandaughter
of Maghshapeet, signed with a turtle. This suggests that Maghshapeet's wife had belonged to the turtle clan. Ampamit's mother,
made a half-circle mark. Koewamo drew a pictographic man with an
animal head, possibly a sign he was a shaman.

Van Rensselaer and Livingston

On the east side of the Hudson River, other Van Rensselaers
engaged in a different boundary dispute, this one with Robert Livingston. The 1712 dispute involved Hendrick Van Rensselaer, who had
received the "Lower Manor" as the result of a settlement among
members of the Van Rensselaer family in 1696. The land was formally
deeded to him in 1704 by his brother, Kiliaen, who became the Lord
of the Manor (known as the patroon) under the family agreement of
1696.[16]

Based on Indian sales of 1649 and 1670 to Rensselaerswyck's
managers, the Van Rensselaer Lower Manor adjoined the Livingston
Patent on the west end. Hendrick Van Rensselaer claimed a "gore"
or elongated triangle of land extending below what Livingston believed to be his line. To resolve the controversy, Mohicans were called
in 1712 to identify a point along the border where there was a
well-known Indian stone heap, Wawanaquasick. Kiliaen and Hendrick Van Rensselaer brought an old chief, father-in-law to Ampamit,
with them. Robert Livingston brought some Indians with him, as
well. After identifying the names of some unrelated stone heaps, the
Indians agreed that a certain stone heap was Wawanaquasick, the
boundary mark in question. The Mohicans stated that the significance
of the word Wawanaquasick "is a great Lord of whom they are afraid
to whom they offer stones to appease him."

In Robert Livingston's handwriting appears a statement from the Indians that on "ye 8th day of April 1712 [we] were desired by Rt. Livingston owner of ye manor of Livingston to accompany him and ye Sachem with seven Indians to ye place called Wawwanaquasick from where ye said Livingston could run his line. . . ."[17] Kiliaen Van Rensselaer and his brother, Hendrick, with the Indians, hiked to the stone heaps, which the Indians identified, confirming Livingston's line, to the Van Rensselaers' chagrin. According to the account, Catharickseet, a Tachkanick Mohican, and Hendrick Van Rensselaer argued about the location.[18]

In a later case, in 1768 Johannes Van Rensselaer was brought to trial on an information filed, on behalf of the King, for a suspected intrusion on some lands claimed to be vacant east of Kinderhook. As with the Livingston patent, the boundaries of the Lower Manor Van Rensselaers became controversial when their large holdings were scrutinized by Lord Bellomont and succeeding governors. Particularly involved was Cadwallader Colden, official surveyor for the colony and eventually Lieutenant Governor of New York. Colden pursued his campaign against the large landholders for many years. The Van Rensselaer family was accused of stretching their patent's eastern boundaries to include much more land than was intended in the original patent by altering the distance to the Indian landmarks written in the deed.

At issue was a definition of the head of the Kinderhook Creek and the location of a place called Patkook. Various men testified that there was a waterfall called Patenhook in a little creek which emptied into Claverack Creek. The area called Patkook or Patenhook lay at the intersection of the Claverack Creek and the tributary creek. This little creek was called Cornelis's Kill, for Keesiewey, a Mohican who lived near there in the seventeenth century. "Kees" was a nickname for Cornelis. Keesiewey sold land to the Van Rensselaers in 1649. The tributary stream was alternately called Gose's Kill, for Tataemshatt or Goose, the father of Catharickseet.

"Paten," or "Patenos," Mohican for waterfall, was the basis for the word Patkook (also spelled Patenhook and Poghtecocke). The term was used for the area near the falls as well as for the actual waterfall, according to testimony of area residents, and was described by one deponent as a little piece of land near Captain Hogeboom's. Hogeboom lived near the Claverack Church, built in 1767. Another man said that the settlements at Claverack were called Patkook.[19] The

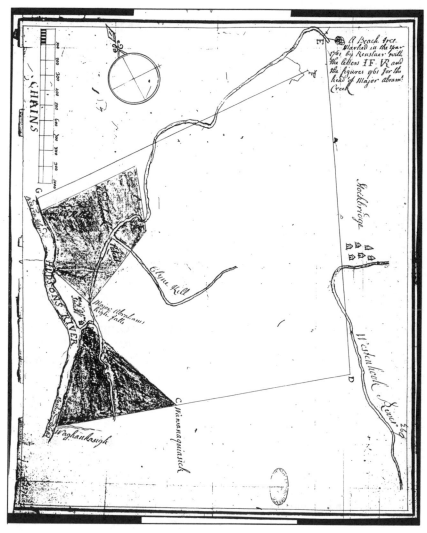

Lt. Governor Cadwallader Colden disputed the boundaries of the Van Rensselaer "Lower Manor" and other large estates. This map of 1762 showed the Kinderhook Patent on the left; below it was the Van Rensselaer Patent as Colden believed it should be. John Van Rensselaer, however, claimed his land extended to letters D. and E. He stated the stone heap called Wawanaquasick was twenty-four miles inland, although it was less than ten miles from the river. The Mohicans claimed land in the light-colored triangle east of the two patents.

"Map of Van Ranslaer's Pattent" at British Archives, MPG 376 Columbia County designation "Patkook" figured in several Indian deeds in later Columbia County and in the Westenhook deeds.

Patkook lay at the intersection of the Claverack Creek and a tributary Creek; whether territory east of Patkook had originally been included in the Van Rensselaer grant was questioned. Indian testimony was vital and, moreover, the Indians had their own interest in the boundary line. The Indian brothers Tataemshatt and Michiel (Waquassamo) stated in the 1712 Livingston document noted above that the small creek which ran southerly into the large creek of Patkook (the Claverack Creek) was the division line between their land and Van Rensselaer's. On this basis, the Mohicans continued to lay claim to land east of Kinderhook and Patkook.

The Livingston Patent lay to the south, and the Westenhook Patent lay vaguely to the east of Patkook and Kinderhook, leaving a large tract in limbo. Van Rensselaer already had a few tenants in the area. This was the crux of the confusion: whether the tract to the east of Patkook was available for sale by the Indians or whether it belonged to the Van Rensselaers.

On July 27, 1755, at Albany "John, Cornelius & Joe, Three River Indians" (possibly Konkapot, Catharickseet and Shawquethqueat) set before Col. William Johnson, Superintendent of Indian Affairs, a paper signed by several of the sachems contending that certain Mohican lands were never sold by the true owners, but had been taken up and occupied by some persons without payment. The greatest part, they explained, was in possession of Col. John Van Rensselaer. The Mohicans asked to be paid for this land. The tract in question was the triangle east of Kinderhook and Claverack. On some maps, the tract had been represented as belonging to the Westenhook Patent, on others as belonging to Johannes Van Rensselaer. Col. Johannes Van Rensselaer, who had inherited the Lower Manor from his father, Hendrick, was sent for and declared ambiguously that not one foot of the lands in question were in his possession. Yet, several farmers were living around Kinderhook and Claverack.[20] As the Indians were certain some of the farmers on the land were Van Rensselaer tenants, this left the situation confused.

The Indians asked William Johnson's advice about the matter. They wondered whether, if they could sell their title to any white persons, they should do it. Johnson gave them the answer they wanted to hear; he said that while he could not determine the justice of their claim, if any persons who checked into the matter were willing to purchase the Indian title, and the Indians were willing to dispose of it, he thought they were at liberty to do it. He noted that the white people could settle the dispute better among themselves than the Indians could.

Mohicans as Neighbors

There is strong evidence in testimony detailing the disputes over boundaries between Hendrick Van Rensselaer and Robert Livingston that some Mohican families remained on land close to Dutch and English settlements in the first half of the eighteenth century. For example, in 1768, Indians still living in eastern Albany County (later Columbia County) testified about events which occurred in the early 1700s. One Indian, David Annahakenic, recounted that he had grown up on Van Rensselaer Island, near Albany, and had hunted across the area between Westenhook and the Hudson River. A settler, Johannes Dykeman, who lived in the southeast part of the Manor of Livingston, in 1768 recalled a Mohican Indian named *Tackleroukeck*, (undoubtedly Catharickseet), who lived at Tachkanick some fifty or sixty years earlier.[21]

In the 1790s, a visitor to Livingston Manor, William Strickland, noted "Upon a swamp near Clermont, [in today's Germantown] some families of the Stockbridge Indians have resided till within this twelvemonth, but they are gone to join the Chiugas [Cayugas], with all their tribes, the Chiugas having invited them and given them lands. They were civilized as much as Indians are capable of civilization. They frequently worked for Mr. L[ivingston]; and he says one Indian was capable of executing as much work as three white people; but their tempers being fickle and inconstant, they were never to be relied upon, as they would quit their work suddenly and without previous notice; they got their subsistence chiefly by making baskets, besoms [twig brooms], and such like articles."[22]

Most of the information about locations and home sites comes from colonial documents, but some Mohicans made reference to their lives before coming to Stockbridge. Aupaumut wrote in his 1790s history that the chief seat of the Mohicans was on Hudson's River. It is true that the wellspring of the nation was the Hudson Valley, although, as this book has shown, there was Mohican settlement in the Housatonic Valley in the 1650s. The chief sachems of the Mohican nation resided in the Hudson Valley in the seventeenth century. After much land was acquired by Mohawks and Dutch investors along the Hudson, there was movement of Mohicans inland to locations in Connecticut's northwest corner. This transition was accelerated when missions at Stockbridge and Shekomeko were established.

A Berkshire County deed of October 25, 1737 describes some Stockbridge Mohican leaders as formerly of Menanoke "or the Island in the Hudson below Albany" (Moesimus Island), who were now "planters in the Indian Town on Housatonic River." Stockbridge at the time was known as the Indian Town. The men identified as Hudson Valley natives were: Jacobus Coocheecomeek (Cohquahegameek), Mahtookamin (Matakeamin, from Schodack), and Wampanon (Wampenum) from Shekomeko. As noted previously, Konkapot had declared that he, too, had grown up in the Hudson Valley.

Many Indian lines at Stockbridge, according to a letter written to Sir William Johnson by Timothy Woodbridge in 1772, descended from Mohicans living on the Hudson River at Schodack. Woodbridge explained that the descendants of Humpaumit (Ampamit, former chief sachem) and "Old Paumaumpausoo" (Ampamit's son) shared large rights to unsold Mohican lands. Captain Solomon Uhhaunauwaunmut, he explained, was the head of Ampamit's family at Stockbridge, and Timothy Yokun was the first male heir and grandson to Paumaumpausoo. Woodbridge added that there were many others (at Stockbridge) whose lineal descent was from those Indians.[23]

Chief Sachems

Through the first half of the eighteenth century, the Mohicans kept up the traditional system of choosing a sachem from among those who had inherited the right. However, John W. Quinney (Waunnaucon), speaking in 1854, said that chief sachem Benjamin Kokhkewenaunaut was the last of the hereditary chiefs of the Mohican nation.[24] After Benjamin, Solomon Uhhaunauwaunmut became Chief Sachem of the Mohicans in 1771. Solomon, in succeeding Benjamin, may have been selected without consideration of his mother's line.

It is not always clear who the chief sachems of the Mohican nation were, due to absence of documentary evidence and confusion in colonial reports about the status of chiefs. The following appear to

In 1924, Harriet Quinney, a Mohican, was photographed in Wisconsin at the age of eighty, wearing her prized wampum necklaces. Her father was Chief Austin E. Quinney. She was born along the Hudson River below Albany.
Skinner, "Notes on Mahikan Ethnology," 1925

have been some of the probable chief sachems beginning with Aepjen
in the mid-seventeenth century:

Aepjen (*Skiwias*): He was acknowledged as chief sachem from c.1640
to c.1670.[25] His clan was the wolf.

Maghshapeet (*Machackniminaw*): Usually identified with Catskill,
he very likely had succeeded Aepjen by 1677, although there
could have been an intermediate sachem. Maghshapeet, also
known as Joris, was an effective mediator during the Esopus
Wars, helping preserve the Mohicans' neutrality and protect-
ing the isolated farms of Rensselaerswyck and Catskill from
Esopus warriors. He was active in four large land transactions
and, as chief sachem, signed a treaty of 1679 in which the
Mohicans promised not to attack Indians and settlers in Maryland and Virginia. This treaty noted that two years earlier Joris
was chosen Sachem of the Mohicans who lived below Albany.[26] At the time, that was a specific reference to the Mohican nation, as opposed to the New England Indians of
Schaghticoke living to the north of Albany. Maghsapeet or
Joris did not appear in documents after 1682 and may have died
close to that time.

Wattawit: He was the son of Pepewitsie and uncle of Onackhaeska.
Onackhaeska, a daughter of Wattawit's sister, acted for her
uncle at the end of the century, implying he was dead by 1697.
A Westenhook deed of 1685 had identified him as "sachem of
the Mahikanders."

Etowaukaum: There was a chief sachem after Wattawit, before the
term of Ampamit. The probability that Etowaukaum was this
person for a period in the early 1700s has been discussed earlier.
The likelihood is further supported by a 1736 letter written by
Rev. Stephen Williams in which he states that the River
Indians' "Prince, or Chief Sagamore was the late *Etou-
coam*. . . ."[27] Etowaukaum's clan was the turtle.

Ampamit: He was chief sachem in the 1730s, when his village was
on Moesimus Island in the Hudson River, opposite Schodack
Landing, a Dutch hamlet. The names of Ampamit's mother,
father, and brothers are given above. His wife was a daughter
of Catharickseet, a Mohican who has appeared frequently in
these pages. Ampamit's clan was the wolf.

Metoxon: He probably functioned as chief sachem after Ampamit.
In 1736 Massachusetts Governor Belcher requested that the
Mohicans bring Corslar, their chief sachem, to a meeting.
Corslar was a name for Metoxon.

Umpachanee: A card in the index to the Moravian Records, carrying
entries dated 1751, is headed "Aaron, Captain, Westenhuc
'King of the Mohicans.' " (Aaron or Umpachanee was called
Lieutenant, not Captain). In 1768 testimony, in the case against
John Van Rensselaer, mentioned above, Joseph Vangilder recalled that nearly thirty years ago, Umpachanee, whose name
also was Sankenakeke, was the *Sachem* of the Mohicans.[28]
Umpachanee's interventions at Weatauk in 1742 and 1743
when he served as negotiator for the sale of Indian land suggest
he was chief sachem. Although Umpachanee died in 1751, he
may have relinquished the post of chief sachem by 1750,
possibly because of failing health.

Benjamin Kokhkewenaunaut: A resident of Stockbridge, he was
chief sachem by 1750, according to a deed of June 9, 1750 in
which Benjamin was described as "ye Indian King."[29] According to testimony given in the case of the Crown against John
Van Rensselaer, previously noted, David Nannakchin was the
father of Benjamin Kohkewenaunaut. Nannakchin, whose
name was also spelled "Annachin" and "Nannahacken," was
about seventy years old in 1738.

Solomon Uhhaunauwaunmut: he was chosen chief sachem in 1771.
Solomon Uhhaunauwaunmut fought for the British during the
Seven Years War in the 1750s and was named an officer. It is
likely he had two sons, Hendrick Aupaumut and Solomon I.
Identified as Captain Solomon Unhaurinauwaussmut, early in
1773 he petitioned, on behalf of himself and other officers,
sergeants, and soldiers who had served during that French war,
for two tracts of land in Albany County never sold by the
Mohicans, which the petitioners claimed as officers.

In an attempt to help the Indians with their claim, on
February 9, 1773 a sympathetic Asa Douglas, whose family had
obtained land at New Lebanon and at Stephentown, New
York, submitted a petition on behalf of five Indians who served
as captains and subaltern officers in the war, for a grant of
12,000 acres in two tracts of land in Albany County, later
Columbia County. The first tract lay south of the manor of
Rensselaerswyck and to the north of lands granted Cornelius
Van Schaack and others; the other tract lay to the west of New
Canaan and "to the south of Manwigginnunck."[30]

These locations were in the lands east of Kinderhook and
Patkook claimed by the Stockbridge Indians. The Indians
were, in effect, asking for land which they believed was their
own. However, the Indian applicants were not given the

consideration of other veterans and did not receive land. Solomon died in 1777.

Joseph Shawquethqueat: A deed of March 10, 1781 identifies Joseph Shawquethqueat as "Chief of the Stockbridge Indians." He was the eldest son of Benjamin Kokhkewenaunaut. As sachem, Joseph sent delegates to George Washington regarding land claims.[31] His counselors over the years included Hendrick Aupaumut, John Konkapot, Jr., and Joseph Quinnauquaunt (Quinney). (Joseph Shawquethqueat is not the same person as Joseph Quinnauquaunt, as there are instances where both appear as signers on the same document.)[32]

Hendrick Aupaumut: He was the chief of the Mohicans, according to Col. Timothy Pickering, writing in 1826, but no indication of the time Aupaumut was appointed was given. In 1791, a Troy, New York newspaper, noting his presence with some eastern Indians, referred to him as their chief, but probably he was merely the leader of a delegation.[33] Aupaumut signed two treaties in 1794 in the name of the Stockbridge Indians; again, he probably was not chief sachem at the time. By 1818, however, a deed notes he was chief sachem. More information about Aupaumut appears below.

John Metoxen: John Metoxen served the Mohican nation for many years. According to an account in the *Wisconsin Historical Collections* of 1858, he was born at Stockbridge in 1770. He attended the Moravian School at Bethlehem, Pennsylvania, but returned to New Stockbridge before completion of his studies. He was a descendant of the powerful sachem, Metoxon.

Overleaf, top: *Solomon Uhhaunauwaunmut and other Stockbridge Indians fought for Sir William Johnson and for Rogers Rangers during the Seven Years' War. Solomon's elaborately carved powder horn reads "Soloman Mak[e] He Horn For March and Go Ondeero: 1761." Ondeero meant Ontario. A decade later, Solomon became chief sachem of the Mohican nation.* Middle: *The reverse of Solomon's powder horn showed "Albony" and forts and locations along the Mohawk and Hudson Rivers. It included a scene from the City of New York and an intricately carved sailing ship.* Bottom: *Ebenezer Maunauseet, who probably owned this powder horn, belonged to the turtle clan. He fought in the Seven Years War against Canada; his powder horn records an expedition to Lake George in 1756.*

Facing page: *Rendering by Douglas E. Skiff.* From the collection of David Wolfe

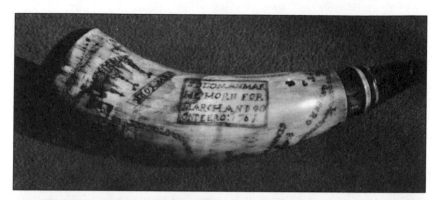

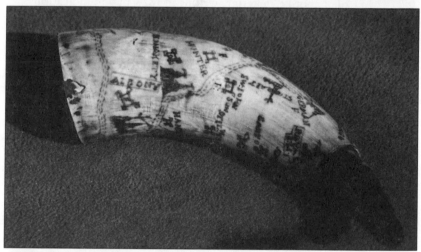

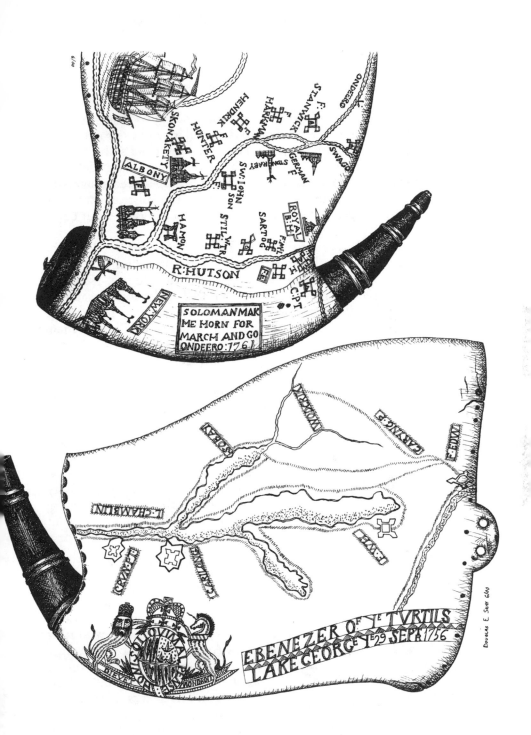

Capt. Hendrick Aupaumut

One of the Mohicans' most notable statesmen was Hendrick Aupaumut, born in 1757.[34] Due to the similarity of their names, he has been confused with the person of Ampamit, chief sachem of the Mohicans in the 1730s. Ampamit, however, died before Hendrick Aupaumut was born. John W. Quinney, in his 1854 speech, suggested that Hendrick Aupaumut was educated in the mission school in Stockbridge. Aupaumut's service to the Mohicans as an adult could have begun late in the 1770s.

Aupaumut had at least one brother, Solomon, and at least one sister, Elizabeth, who became the wife of Joseph Quinney, Aupaumut's close associate. When he fought in the Revolution, Hendrick Aupaumut used the name Captain Hendrick Solomon. Because of this, it can be speculated that Hendrick Aupaumut, his brother Solomon, and sister Elizabeth were the children of Chief Sachem Solomon Uhhaunauwaunmut. This would make Hendrick Aupaumut a member of a respected Mohican lineage.

Interestingly, the *Berkshire County History* hazards the assertion that Hendrick Aupaumut grew up among the Mohawks.[35] No documents are cited and the claim remains mythical. It is refuted by John Quinney's assertion that Aupaumut went to school in Stockbridge. After he fought in the Revolution, Aupaumut returned to Stockbridge.

Hendrick Aupaumut's wife was Lydia Quinney and they had at least three children who took "Hendrick" as their last name. They were Abner W., John, and Solomon U. According to Jones, writing in *Stockbridge, Past and Present*, John was murdered.[36] Abner went west with his father in 1818. Solomon, according to Jones' history, was Aupaumut's youngest son.

A deed of 1818, conveying a tract of property left behind in Stockbridge, was signed by Hendrick Aupaumut, as sachem, and by David Neshoonhuk, Solomon I. Hendrick, Abner W. Hendrick, and Solomon U. Hendrick, "counselors of the Muhheeconnuck tribe of Indians, formerly proprietors of the town of Stockbridge, who now reside in New Stockbridge." Hendrick Aupaumut was by then chief sachem. It appears that the first Solomon named in the deed, Solomon I., was Aupaumut's brother. Solomon traveled with him in 1791 on Aupaumut's mission to the western Indians. The next two counselors given in the 1818 deed, Abner and Solomon U., were Aupaumut's sons.

Chief sachem Solomon Uhhaunauwaunmut was reported by Timothy Woodbridge, the school teacher of the Stockbridge Indians, to be the head of the family of sachem Ampamit of Schodack. Ampamit's son, who came to Stockbridge to be baptized and to live, was named Paumaumpausoo and was known as Paumaumpausoo Aumpaumut. This suggests that Aupaumut and Ampamit were variations of the same Indian word. Hendrick may have chosen the name "Aupaumut" to carry on the family name.

According to testimony by Joachim Van Valkenburgh, sachem Benjamin Kokhkewnaunaunt's father was David Nannakchin; he may have been Hendrick Aupaumut's grandfather. David Nannakchin appears to be one of three Naunaunekennuks listed in church records. In 1854, John W. Quinney named a David Naunauneeknuk as his grandfather, on his mother's side.[37]

As noted previously, traditionally sachems became eligible for appointment through the female line. Hendrick Aupaumut wrote of this in the history of the Mohicans: "Our ancestors' Government was a Democratical [one]. They had Wi-gow-wauw or Chief Sachem successively. . .And this office was hereditary by the lineage of a woman's offspring, but not on male's line, but on woman's part. That is—when Wi-gow-wauw is fallen by death, one of his Nephews (if he has any) will be appointed to succeed his Uncle as a Sachem, and not any of his sons."[37] By the time Aupaumut wrote these words, the old rules of succession had been set aside. The prominent families still retained influence, however.

During the American Revolution the Mohicans supported the patriot cause. Aupaumut, known as Hendrick Solomon, was a member of George Washington's Indian Brigade. Washington had hoped that having a body of Indians at hand, joined by some woodsmen, would strike terror into the British troops. The Indians, including a large group of Stockbridge men commanded by Daniel Nimham, the Wappinger sachem who had moved with some of his people to Stockbridge, were assigned to Huntington's Brigade. They were known as excellent marksmen. Stationed near the British lines around New York, they were ambushed on Van Cortland Manor, in today's Kingsbridge section of the Bronx, on August 31, 1778, by British troops and cavalry. Outnumbered, many Indians, including at least fifteen Mohicans, were massacred on the field. In this battle, Daniel Nimham was killed, along with his son, Abraham.

Lt. Hendrick Solomon (Aupaumut), only twenty-one, was next in the line of command. He was assigned to take charge of the Indian Brigade. On September 11, 1778 he sent a note to General Washington requesting relief for a few Mohicans who had survived the fight. "Lt. Solomon, who commands the remaining part of the Stockbridge Indians, has requested His Excellency to discharge four of their tribe who are in your Brigade. As they behaved well and were unfortunate in a late action. . . ." The same day, Washington passed a request to General Huntington to release and discharge the four Stockbridge Mohicans still in Huntington's Brigade.[38] In 1783, Joseph Shawquethqueat sent Capt. Hendrick Aupaumut, with four others, to George Washington's headquarters at Newburgh to confer about land claims.

Hendrick Aupaumut left Stockbridge, Massachusetts, later than some other Stockbridges, but by 1791 he had a house at New Stockbridge in Madison County, New York.[39] About 1792, he, with another man, wrote a short history of the Mohican nation as the two men had learned it from their older relations. The two recited a history well-known to most members of the Mohican nation. Through the seventeenth century, the Mohicans had frequently made reference to the fact that when the Dutch arrived, they were a large nation. They had grown small since the Europeans came. They also made references to an early treaty at which they had agreed to allow the Mohawks to trade with the Dutch. However, nothing was recorded at conferences about Mohican history previous to the arrival of the Dutch on the Hudson River.

That a traditional story did exist is revealed in a brief statement at a 1757 meeting with Sir William Johnson, at which a Mohican recited a part of the history on which Aupaumut was to enlarge in the 1790s. The Mohican speaker recounted, "We are sprung from those Indians who antiently lived near the Sea shoar,"[40] an interesting preliminary to Aupaumut's more detailed version. As Aupaumut explained, "Our forefathers asserted, that their ancestors were emigrated from west by north of another country; they passed over the great waters, where this and the other country is nearly connected, called Ukhkopeck; it signifies snake water, or water where snakes abounded; and that they lived by side of great water or sea, from which they derive the name of Muhheakunnuk nation."[41]

Aupaumut's history was shared with John Sergeant, Jr., minister to the Stockbridges at New Stockbridge, who was so familiar with it that he was able to to paraphrase a missing part of the history from memory. Sergeant passed the history to Rev. J. Morse. An extract was published by the Massachusetts Historical Society in 1804, and other versions surfaced afterwards. In 1854, Electa Jones published a nearly complete text in her *Stockbridge Past and Present*. Anthropologist Alanson Skinner found a version of the history "in a rare and age-yellowed pamphlet," probably Jones' work, and printed the contents, considerably edited, in 1925. Another version of the nation's history was presented by John W. Quinney (born in 1797) in an 1854 speech.[42] Quinney believed that Hendrick Aupaumut's written history had been lost.

On May 10, 1791, Capt. Hendrick Aupaumut set out from Philadelphia with his brother, Solomon, and his son, Abner, on an official mission for the United States government. He was to make the rounds of the western tribes who were carrying on a war against the frontier settlements in the midwest. His intent was to persuade them to cease their war against the new country.

Capt. Hendrick Aupaumut began his crusade at an Indian conference at Tioga Point, an Indian location between present-day Waverly and Owego. From there, he sent his brother "cross the woods" to Oneida (New Stockbridge) to fetch Aupaumut's bag of peace, in which there was "ancient wompom" and to get two of his best counselors and a young man, so that the western nations would understand that his mission was serious. In addition, the five members of the party could help each other if they were attacked, and there would be a young man to escape with the news if they were overwhelmed.[43]

A newspaper, *The American Spy*, published in Troy on July 22, 1791, noted Aupaumut's peace mission. Reporting the Indian treaty held "at Newtown, twenty miles above Tioga Point, June 23," the newspaper correspondent noted, "We alighted at Col. Pickering's [headquarters] and found him conferring with some Oneida and other eastern Indians, who came down with a view to mediate peace. Their chief, Hendrick Aupaumut . . . was speaking."[44]

On this mission, Aupaumut wrote a journal. As a prologue, he explained the ancient connections of the Mohicans with some of the western tribes and the Delawares. He outlined the relationship of the Mohicans with the Delawares or *Wenaumeeu*, the grandfathers "to which we adhere without any devi[a]tion in these near two hundred years past." He next described the Shawnees, or *Weshauwonnoow*, as the "younger brothers" who were rescued by the Mohicans "near 200 years past" from the "mouth of many nations" including the Five Nations. These are rare references to events occurring before 1600, preceding the arrival of Europeans on the Hudson. The successful fight to rescue the Shawnees from the Five Nations confirms the ancient emnity of the Mohicans with the Iroquois, a rivalry which several Mohicans had described to Moravian missionaries.

Aupaumut went on to list past aid given to the Miamis, the Monthees, the Wyandots, and the Ottowas by the Mohicans, obligations which made them all friends in the west, and therefore amenable to his influence.[45]. The friendship between the Mohicans and the Ottowas is illustrated by the visit to the Ottowas of a large body of Mohicans in the 1680s, noted in an earlier chapter.

Hendrick Aupaumut had written previously about these western connections in his Mohican history of c. 1792. In this history, Aupaumut also noted that members of the "Muhhcakunnuk" nation were formerly considered to be the best warriors in the field and were truly formidable to any nation. This, he said, was still acknowledged by the western tribes. He explained, also, that his forefathers were distinguished in peacemaking, which had won them allies even among the most remote nations. As a result of their past importance and power, the Mohicans, therefore, had considerable influence with western tribes.

Col. Timothy Pickering wrote that Hendrick Aupaumut lived in New Stockbridge, the township given to the Mohicans by the Oneidas; Pickering dined with Aupaumut at his house there in 1794. Aupaumut's house also was mentioned in 1791 in the accounts of a trader, Peter Smith. In 1808 or 1809, Colonel Pickering again met Hendrick Aupaumut at Washington, D.C. when Aupaumut and Nicholas Cusick, a Tuscarora Indian, were on their way to North Carolina to petition for payment for the land lost by the Tuscaroras, driven from North Carolina a century before.[46]

Capt. Hendrick Aupaumut was a leader of that segment of the New Stockbridge population that wished to have a town which excluded whites. He emphasized Indian ways and preferred an Indian Christian minister. In this, he opposed the faction that favored John Sergeant, Jr. In 1810, Aupaumut was on the White River, with his son, Abner, where he was influential in countering the influence of

Tecumseh, a Shawnee who was leading a movement to gather the mid-west Indians and resist white influence.

In the War of 1812, Captain Hendrick, although no longer young, received a commission. Soon after that war, he become restless at New Stockbridge, and, in 1818, he led some of the residents from New Stockbridge west to Indiana.[47] Although they found the promised tract of land to which they were headed had been sold, Aupaumut had a home in Indiana before removing to Wisconsin with other Mohicans. Hendrick visited Congress in Washington, DC, to ask for reimbursement for the Stockbridges after the group found it necessary to leave the Oneidas and proceed west. In 1830, Mohican statesman Hendrick Aupaumut died in Green Bay, Wisconsin, where he had moved in 1829.[48]

Words from Mohican Speakers

Several Mohican terms were included by Hendrick Aupaumut in his history of the Mohican nation written in the 1790s. Since the Mohican language is no longer spoken, the terms are of interest. Because his history was printed in several versions, certain words vary in spelling. The initial spellings given here are from an incomplete but early "extract" printed in the Collections of the Massachusetts Historical Society in 1804. The rest of the spellings are from the version given by Electa Jones in Stockbridge Past and Present, 1854. Hyphens, which appear in her version, have been eliminated. Aupaumut noted the following Mohican words:

skommonun (also spelled skommon) = Indian corn
tupohquaun = beans
uhnunnekuthkoatkun = Indian squashes
Pempotowwuthut or Muhhecanneuw = the fire place of the nation, in the vicinity of Albany, where allies used to come on any business
Muhhaakunnuk = (also spelled Muhheakunnuk) great waters or sea, constantly in motion, flowing or ebbing
Ukhkokpeck = snake waters or waters where snakes abounded
Muhheakunneuw = a man of the Muhheakunnuk tribe
Muhhekunneyuk = the plural number of Mohican
uthonnetmuhheakun = a stone axe, "something like the shape of a metal axe, with a helve [stick] made for that purpose fastened to it"

Chuckopek = white people (The letter *p* probably should have been read as *s*; John Sergeant wrote the word as *Chohkoosuk* in his 1739 journal on page 13.)

puhwy = a weapon for war, made of a wooden knot with a helve to it

quennehtuhheakun = long cut, knife

tkuttekun = a spear made of bone or horn or of flinty stone, with a long helve to it

quiver = a container for forty or fifty arrows, often of otter skin

Wauntheet Monnittoow = the Great, Good Spirit

Mtontoow = a wicked spirit that loves to do mischief

Uhwutheet = hard-hearted

Wigowwauw = Chief Sachem

Wohweetquanpechee = the sachem's Counselors

Moquaupauw = a Hero, the war leader of courage and prudence, who takes over the business of fighting

Mkhoohquethoth = the Owl (an appointed office); has a strong memory, is a good speaker, wakes the people, proclaims the duties for the day

Unnuhkaukun = the messenger or runner for the sachem, lights the sachem's pipe at conferences

Wekowohm = wigwam or house; the sachem had a long wigwam

Mkithnon (Muksens) = moccasins

Mnotti = peace bag, for strings and belts of wampum

Weethkuhnpauk = bitter sort of hemp used for bags

Wauponneppauk = white hemp used for bags

Squauthowon = belts of wampum

Nemauwoneh Mnoti = bag which contains nourishment for a journey

mauwpeen = the business of getting wampum from their women

Another Mohican, the Rev. Jeremiah Slingerland of Keshena, Wisconsin, "himself a Stockbridge Indian of pure blood, and the minister of the Stockbridges residing there"[49] in the nineteenth century supplied historian Charles J. Taylor with the following Mohican words:

Ou-thot-ton-ook = over the mountain; applied to the part of the Housatonic Valley near Great Barrington (The first syllable had the sound of *ou* in *out*.)

Mas-wa-se-hi = a nest standing upright, the Mohican name for Monument Mountain

Scot-koak = the pronunciation for Skatekook, the Indian village
   in Sheffield, located where the Green River formerly emptied
   into the Housatonic River
Wnokh-tuq-kook = head of the stream, referring to Konkapot's
   village
Neh-hai-we (Mahaiwe) = place down stream; it was located a mile
   or two north of the Great Wigwam at the ford above later
   Great Barrington, and one mile south of the base of Monument
   Mountain[50]

Close-out Deeds

Colonial settlers were happy to obtain deeds which ended Indian
ownership of a certain territory. It meant to them that the Indians on
the land would now disappear, although, in fact, Indians usually
remained in an area after final deeds were given. A deed in Washington
County, however, reflects the 1754 departure of most of the Schaghticoke Indians from the land set aside for them almost a century before.
At White Creek, Washington County, on May 20, 1761, land on both
sides of a brook or rivulet "Called by the Indians Tightillijagtihook,
by the white People the South Branch of Batten Kill, Bounded on the
south by the Pattent of Wallomsack; on the West by Sawyers and
Lansings Purchase, on the north by Batten Kill and on the East the
high mountains," was sold.[51] The land was purchased by Arent
Corlaer (a trader, grandson of Arent Van Corlaer) and Nicholas Lake
for fifty Spanish dollars, from Jacob, alias Schenk, who was, according
to the deed, "the only remaining Indian of the tribe of Schacktihook
Indians who Have all Deserted to Canada."
   At Catskill, as noted above, a deed of March 25, 1766, ended
Catskill Indian ownership in Albany County, which, at the time,
included later Greene County. Catskill area Indians did not necessarily leave. For Weatauk, Connecticut, the final deed was negotiated by
Thomas Fitch at Stockbridge in spring 1743. At Wequadnach, Connecticut, the close-out deed was given July 24, 1752, although, unhappy with the sale, some members remained at the village site or
nearby for several years.
   On September 2, 1783, the Stockbridge Indians notified the
Massachusetts Legislature that they were going to leave. Gracious and
generous as always, they wrote, in part:

We the Chiefs of the Moheakonnuk Tribe of Indians residing in Stockbridge this day met together beg you to listen to us a few Words—

Brothers. We remember We were once great, and you were small when you first came on this Island, and now We are very small and You are very great. We also remember that our Forefathers have often looked to you for Protection, Advice and Assistance. We with Pleasure look back and consider you have always heard us, when we have Spoken to you. Now brothers since We are small We look to you as Children do their Fathers We wish you would always remember as Parents do their Children Brothers, We will put You in mind that ever since We first see You, We were always true Friends to you in all the Wars, until this present Day. In this late War [the Revolution] we have suffered much, Our blood has been spilled by the Side of your Warriors, almost all those Places where your Warriors have left their Bones, there our Bones are seen also—Now We who remain are become very poor Now Brothers, We will let you know We have been invited by our Brothers the Oniadas, to go and live with them. We have accepted their Invitation. . . ."[52]

The letter asked for a committee to take care of the little interest of land they had left in the town, and requested that the Mohicans not be sued for debts. It was signed by Johoiakim Matoksin, Joseph Shawquethqueat, Hendrick Aupaumud (sic), Jehoiakim Nannuphtonk, and Joseph Quonmikant (Quinnauquant).

The Stockbridge residents had previously signed deeds which disposed of much of their land in Stockbridge; they began to leave for New Stockbridge in Madison County, New York, in 1783 and 1784. Other Stockbridge families moved to New Stockbridge over the next few years. A few old people would not go. Sales of small parcels of land at Stockbridge were made in the next few decades by Mohicans visiting or corresponding from their New York location.

Before and after these final sales of land in New York, Massachusetts and Connecticut, Mohicans scattered to many places; Mohican locations were in Pennsylvania, in Indian towns along the Susquehanna River, in the Ohio country, at New Stockbridge in New York, and in Indiana, Wisconsin, Canada and other retreats. A few successful Indian farmers remained behind in Sheffield. Some families stayed in remote sites in Hudson Valley counties and in the Housatonic Valley. Lacking formal leadership and without tribal inspiration, families and individuals survived by combining traditional Indian skills in hunting, fishing and farming with the sale of craft items. Their Indian history was never forgotten.

Remarkably, Mohicans kept a sense of tribal identity through the nineteenth century not only while sojourning on their Wisconsin reservation but when among other Indian groups and even when they married into colonial families. This tribal identity survives to the present.

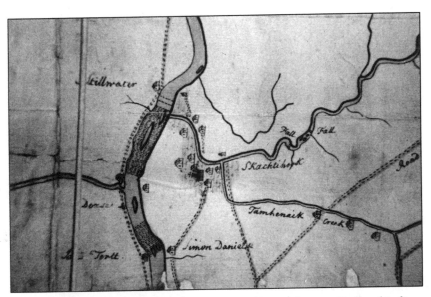

Schaghticoke, north of Albany, was set aside as a haven for New England Indians in 1676. Like Stockbridge, it had become an English town by the time the Schaghticoke Indians left the area in 1754.

Annonymous, "Map of the Northern Parts of New York," c. 1758,
from the Peter Force Collection, Library of Congress

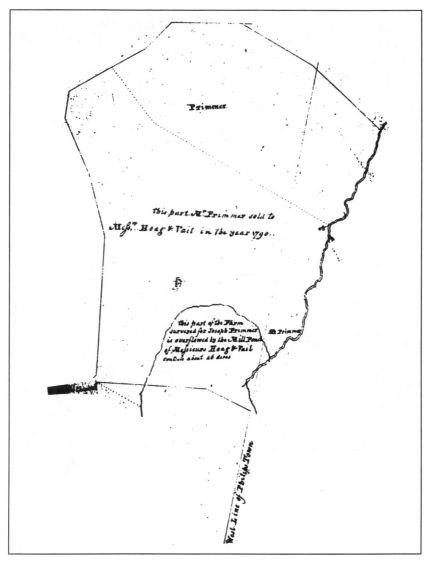

The south end of a farm bought by Joseph Primmer from the Mohicans in 1760 included a beaver pond which later was dammed for a mill. Mohican descendants returned to visit the farm in the nineteenth century. The pond became Nassau Lake.

New York State Library, Manuscripts and Special Collections,
Van Rensselaer Manor Papers, Stephentown-Nassau Surveys, p. 64

Notes

Abbreviations of Frequently Repeated Sources

BHS   Brooklyn Historical Society
CONN   State Archives, Connecticut State Library, Hartford
ERA   Pearson and/or Van Laer, *Early Records of the City and County of Albany and Colony of Rensselaerswyck*
JP   Johnson, *Sir William Johnson Papers*
LIR   Leder, *Livingston Indian Records*
LP   O'Callaghan, *Calendar of N.Y. Colonial Manuscripts Indorsed Land Papers 1643-1803*
MOA   Moravian Archives, Bethlehem, Pennsylvania; microfilm at New York State Library
NARR   Jameson, *Narratives of New Netherland, 1609-1664*
NYCD   O'Callaghan and others, *Documents Relative/Relating to the Colonial History of the State of New York*
NYHS   The New-York Historical Society
NYSL   New York State Library, Albany, New York

Chapter 1: Managing the Environment

1. *NARR*, p. 71.
2. Moeller, *Journal of Middle Atlantic Archeology*, 12: 63.
3. Johnson, *Discovering the Ancient Past at Kampoosa Bog*, p. 15.
4. Van der Donck, *A Description of the New Netherlands*, pp. 20-21.
5. *Ibid.*, p. 37.
6. *NARR*, p. 49.
7. Van Laer, *Van Rensselaer Bowier Manuscripts*, p. 197.
8. Hopkins, *Historical Memoirs Relating to the Housatonic Indians* (1911), p. 57.
9. Denton, *A Brief Description of New-York: Formerly Called New-Netherlands*, p. 7.
10. Van der Donck, *A Description of the New Netherlands*, p. 82.
11. Champlain, *The Voyages and Explorations of Samuel de Champlain (1604-1616)*, 2: 139-140.
12. Hart, *Current Northeast Paleoethnobotany*, pp. 91-93; Moeller, *Journal of Middle Atlantic Archeology*, 12: 62, 123.
13. Van der Donck, *A Description of the New Netherlands*, p. 71.
14. *Ibid.*, p. 67.
15. Champlain, *The Voyages and Explorations of Samuel de Champlain (1604-1616)*, 2: 125.
16. *Ibid.*, pp. 121, 122.
17. *Ibid.*, pp. 139-140.
18. Butzer (1992) quoted in Moeller, *Journal of Middle Atlantic Archeology*, p. 64.
19. Champlain, *The Voyages and Explorations of Samuel de Champlain (1604-1616)*, 2: 120.
20. Moeller, *Journal of Middle Atlantic Archeology*, 12: 62.
21. Wolley, *A Two Years' Journal in New York*, pp. 62-63.
22. Gibbons, *Stalking the Wild Asparagus*, pp. 172-173; Van der Donck, *A Description of the New Netherlands*, p. 38.
23. O'Callaghan, *Documentary History of the State of New York*, 1: 721.
24. Denton, *A Brief Description of New-York*, p. 4.
25. Gibbons, *Stalking the Wild Asparagus*, pp. 107-108.
26. Moeller, *Journal of Middle Atlantic Archeology*, 12: 63.
27. Hart, *Current Northeast Paleoethnobotany*, pp. 124-131.
28. Van der Donck, *A Description of the New Netherlands*, pp. 28, 34, 57.

29. *Ibid.*, p. 34.
30. *Ibid.*, p. 22.
31. Wood, *New England's Prospect*, p. 107.
32. Thursday, October 21, 1714, in Robert Livingston's "Trip Journal," Livingston Family Papers, Clermont State Historic Site. See page 95.
33. Champlain, *The Voyages and Explorations of Samuel de Champlain*, 2: 92; Wood, *New England's Prospect*, p. 106.
34. *ERA* 1: 74.
35. Denton, *A Brief Description of New-York*, p. 7.
36. Van der Donck, *A Description of the New Netherlands*, pp. 5-6, 53.
37. Kaufman, *Lives of North American Birds*, p. 154. The heath hen became extinct in 1932, the passenger pigeon in 1914.
38. Van der Donck, *A Description of the New Netherlands*, p. 50.
39. Champlain, *The Voyages and Explorations of Samuel de Champlain*, 2: 159.
40. Zeisberger, *History of the North American Indians*, p. 31.
41. LeBrun, Fred, "Wolf issue an equation for science," *Times Union*, Albany, NY, December 19, 1999.
42. "Hudson River Recovers," *Times Union*, Albany, New York, December 23, 1998.
43. Champlain, *The Voyages and Explorations of Samuel de Champlain*, 2: 143.
44. Wood, *New England's Prospect*, p. 107.
45. Aupaumut, "Extract from an Indian History," 9: 101.
46. Hopkins, *Historical Memoirs Relating to the Housatonic Indians*, (1911), p. 36.
47. The author made this discovery with the assistance of Janny Venema of the New Netherland Project. The 1624 document is held in Manuscripts and Special Collections, NYSL.
48. Dunn, *The Mohicans and Their Land 1609-1730*, p. 47.
49. Jackson, *American Colonial Architecture*, p. 23.
50. Snow, *Northeast Anthropology*, 53: 61-84; Hopkins, *Historical Memoirs Relating to the Housatonic Indians* (1911), p. 25; Denys, *Description and Natural History of Acadia*, p. 404.
51. Denys, *Description and Natural History of Acadia*, p. 404.
52. Williams, *What Cheer, Netop!*, p. 22.
53. Dankaerts, *Journal of Jasper Dankaerts*, p. 55.
54. *Ibid.*
55. *NARR*, p. 57.
56. Van der Donck, *A Description of the New Netherlands*, p. 80.

Chapter 2: The Mohican Network

1. *NYCD* 13: 496.
2. Dunn, *The Mohicans and Their Land 1609-1730*, pp. 192-197.
3. *Ibid.*, 208; *NYCD* 13: 460.
4. Johnson, Eric S. "Coercion and Warfare in Native New England," *Northeast Anthropology*, no. 55 (Spring 1988): 1-14.
5. *NYCD* 13: 345.
6. *Ibid.*, 5: 663-664.
7. *NYCD*: 13: 345.
8. Hubbard, *The History of the Indian Wars in New England*.
9. Stokes, *The Iconography of Manhattan Island*, Plate 27.
10. Hopkins, *Historical Memoirs Relating to the Housatonic Indians* (1911), p. 152.
11. Campbell, "New Light on the Jansson-Visscher Maps of New England," *The Map Collectors' Circle*, Plates IV, VIII, X, XI, XII, XIII.
12. This map is discussed and illustrated in Chapter III.
13. Munsell, *The Annals of Albany*, 4: 48.

14. *LIR*, pp. 30-33.
15. Dunn, *The Mohicans and Their Land 1609-1730*, p. 120.
16. *LIR*, p. 36; Dunn, *The Mohicans and Their Land 1609-1730*, p. 185.
17. *LIR*, pp. 37-38.
18. *NYCD* 13: 440
19. *Ibid.*, p. 460.
20. *Ibid.*, pp. 546, 571-572.
21. Quinney, "Celebration of the Fourth of July, 1854," *Wisconsin Historical Society Collections*, p. 316.
22. Champlain, *The Works of Samuel de Champlain*, 5: 214-229.
23. Dunn, *The Mohicans and Their Land 1609-1730*, Appendix A: Recorded Land Transactions.
24. Brodhead, *History of the State of New York*. 2: 295.
25. Taylor, *History of Great Barrington, Berkshire County, Massachusetts*, p. 9.
26. Brodhead, *History of the State of New York*, 2: 295.
27. *ERA* 2: 19; see also *ERA* 3: 509; *NYCD* 13: 545.
28. Orenstein, David, "Wal-Mart abandons 4-year plan to build store in Leeds," *Times Union*, Albany, November 6, 1996.
29. Taylor, *History of Great Barrington*, p. 53; Collier, *History of Columbia County*, p. 15.
30. *NYCD* 13: 494, 496.
31. *ERA* 2: 63, 179.
32. *Ibid.* p. 282.
33. Livingston Family Papers, BHS, Indian Deeds F. 9.
34. Dunn, *The Mohicans and Their Land 1609-1730*, p. 176.
35. *LIR*, p. 108.
36. Taylor, *History of Great Barrington*, p. 53.
37. Preiss, *Sheffield, Frontier Town*, p. 11.
38. Taylor, *History of Great Barrington*, p. 17.
39. *Ibid.*, p. 61.
40. *Calendar of Land Papers*, p. 58.
41. Albany County Hall of Records, Deeds, Book 4, pp. 272, 273.
42. Ruttenber, *History of the Indian Tribes of Hudson's River*, p. 177.
43. Collier, *A History of Old Kinderhook*, pp. 14-15.
44. Wraxall, *An Abridgement of the Indian Affairs*, p. 14.
45. "Letter from Lt. Gov. Jacob Leisler to the Governor of Boston, Simon Bradstreet," Massachusetts Archives, Vol. 36, p. 48.
46. *NYCD* 3: 808.
47. *NYCD* 3: 653.
48. Taylor, *History of Great Barrington*, 55.
49. Hopkins, *Historical Memoirs, Relating to the Housatunnuk Indians* (1753), p. 26.
50. Wadsworth, "Wadsworth's Journal," pp. 102-110.
51. From *The Talcott Papers* (Vol. 2 Hartford: Connecticut Historical Society, 1896, p. 402), quoted in Colee, *The Housatonic-Stockbridge Indians: 1734-1749*, p. 93.
52. Pettee, *The Rev. Jonathan Lee and His Eighteenth Century Salisbury Parish*, p. 49.
53. Dyer, *Gnadensee, The Lake of Grace*, pp. 18-19.
54. Taylor, *History of Great Barrington*, pp. 17, 61.
55. *Ibid.*, pp. 59-61.
56. *Ibid.*, p. 54.
57. Wright, *Indian Deeds of Hampdon County*, pp. 184, 185.
58. Taylor, *History of Great Barrington*, p. 64; Pope, *The Western Boundary of Massachusetts*, p. 6.
59. Indian Deeds, Item 117, Feb. 1950, The Stockbridge Library Historical Collection.
60. Dyer, *Gnadensee, The Lake of Grace*, p. 19.
61. Church, *Historical Addresses*, p. 7.

62. *The Book of Berkshire*, p. 247.
63. *Ibid.*
64. Taylor, *History of Great Barrington*, p. 52.
65. *Ibid.*, p. 3.
66. *Ibid.*, p. 51.
67. *Ibid.*, p. 52.
68. *The Book of Berkshire*, p. 67.
69. Johnson, *Data Recovery Operations at the Chassell 2 and Kampoosa Bog Sites, Stockbridge, Massachusetts*, pp. 2, 8-13.

Chapter 3: Westenhook

1. Smith, *History of Dutchess County, New York*, p. 52.
2. Pope, *The Western Boundary of Massachusetts*, p. 4.
3. Pettee, *The Rev. Jonathan Lee and His Eighteenth Century Salisbury Parish*, pp. 19, 31.
4. Pope, *The Western Boundary of Massachusetts*, pp. 19, 26, 31.
5. Albany County Hall of Records, Deeds, Book 4, pp. 272-273.
6. *ERA* 2: 189-192.
7. Taylor, *History of Great Barrington, Berkshire County, Massachusetts*, p. 3.
8. *ERA* 2: 260-261.
9. *Ibid.*, pp. 268-269.
10. Dunn, *The Mohicans and Their Land, 1609-1730*, p. 292.
11. *LP*, p. 45.
12. Albany County Hall of Records, Deeds, Book 4, pp. 272-273.
13. "Map of Manorial Grants along the Hudson River," HM 15440, c. 1726, Huntington Library, San Marino, Calif.
14. Albany County Hall of Records, Deeds, Book 4, pp. 273-274; Misc. Mss. "Schuyler, Peter," NYHS.
15. Collier, *A History of Old Kinderhook*, p. 82.
16. Secretary of State, Book No. 7 of Patents, p. 290, quoted in Taylor, *History of Great Barrington*, p. 7; Misc. Mss. " Schuyler, Peter," NYHS.
17. Albany County Hall of Records, Deeds, Book 4, p. 311; see Taylor, *History of Great Barrington*, p. 4.
18. Pope, *The Western Boundary of Massachusetts*, p. 14; *Calendar of Land Papers*, p. 79; Taylor, *History of Great Barrington*, p. 2.
19. Taylor, *History of Great Barrington*, pp. 4-5.
20. New York Council Minutes, quoted in Pope, *The Western Boundary of Massachusetts*, p. 26.
21. Taylor, *History of Great Barrington*, p. 6; *History of Berkshire County*, 1: 53.
22. *History of Berkshire County*, 1: 54; *LP*, p. 182.
23. *NYCD* 13: 546.
24. Referenced in Livingston Family Papers, 18: 31 (microfilm), NYSL.
25. O'Callaghan, *Documentary History*, 3: 612.
26. *Ibid.*, p. 613.
27. *Ibid.*, p. 615-616.
28. *ERA* 2: 189-192.
29. O'Callaghan, *Documentary History*, 3: 615.
30. *ERA* 2:281-283; O'Callaghan, *Documentary History*, 3: 618. Tachkanick, now the Copake and West Copake area in Columbia County, also included (in Livingston's interpretation) arable valley land lying within the hills east of Copake.
31. Keith, *History of Taconic and Mount Washington from 1692 to 1892*, p. 15.
32. O'Callaghan, *Documentary History*, 3: 620.
33. Morrill, "The Spur at the Heel of the Manor," p. 39.

34. Robert R. Livingston Papers, Roll 1, (microfilm) quoted in Morrill, "The Spur at the Heel of the Manor," pp. 39-40.
35. *ERA* 2: 269.
36. O'Callaghan, *Documentary History*, 3: 628; Livingston Family Papers, Indian Deeds F 13, BHS; Collier, *A History of Old Kinderhook*, pp. 100, 534.
37. *LP*, p. 38.
38. Piwonka, *A Portrait of Livingston Manor*, p. 27.
39. Miscellaneous Papers, Columbia County, NYHS.
40. Piwonka, *A Portrait of Livingston Manor*, p. 28.
41. Wadsworth, "Wadsworth's Journal," pp. 107-108.
42. O'Callaghan, *Documentary History*, 3: 690.
43. *Ibid.*, p. 629.
44. Pope, *The Western Boundary of Massachusetts*; the map is at the back of the book.
45. Livingston Family Papers, Indian Deeds F.19, BHS; see also Livingston-Redmond Mss., Roll 10 (microfilm), NYSL.
46. Livingston Family Papers, Robert Livingston's Trip Journal, 1714, Clermont State Historic Site, NYSOPRHP, Taconic Region.
47. "Notes of Evidence on Trial. The King ag't John Van Rensselaer, Esq'r," Misc. Mss. Van Rensselaer, John, NYHS. Courtesy the New-York Historical Society.
48. *Ibid.*
49. Livingston Family Papers, Clermont State Historic Site.
50. "Notes of Evidence on Trial. The King ag't John Van Rensselaer, Esq'r," Misc. MSS. Van Rensselaer, John, NYHS.
51. Livingston Family Papers, Indian Deeds, BHS.
52. Livingston Family Papers, Clermont State Historic Site. This rock and tree featured prominently in the Van Rensselaer boundary dispute of 1712.
53. Binzen, *Mohican Lands and Colonial Corners*, p. 25.
54. Livingston Family Papers, Clermont State Historic Site.
55. *Ibid.*
56. Identification of the Bayless property is in Morrill, "The Spur at the Heel of the Manor," p. 42.
57. Huntting, *History of Little Nine Partners of North East Precinct and Pine Plains, New York*, p. 28.
58. Livingston-Redmond Mss., Roll 7, (microfilm), quoted in Morrill, "The Spur at the Heel of the Manor," p. 42.
59. Referenced in Robert R. Livingston Papers, 18: 27 (microfilm), NYSL; Livingston Family Papers, 1974, 18.F.15, BHS. Pictured in Grumet, *The Lenapes*, p. 46.
60. Robert R. Livingston Papers, Roll 28 (microfilm), NYSL.
61. Livingston Family Papers, 1974, 18.F.15, BHS.

Chapter 4: The Mohican Indians and the Albany Traders

1. Notes of Dingman Versteeg, BV Wendell, Evert. Account book, 1695-1726, NYHS. Material from the Wendell account book is used courtesy of the New-York Historical Society.
2. Seaver, *A Narrative of the Life of Mrs. Mary Jemison*, p. 48.
3. Collier, *A History of Old Kinderhook*, p. 20.
4. Hopkins, *Historical Memoirs Relating to the Housatonic Indians* (1911), p.87.
5. *ERA* 2: 376.
6. *NYCD* 4: 576.
7. Livingston Family Papers, F. 19, BHS.
8. *ERA* 1: 106; see Dunn, *The Mohicans and Their Land 1609-1730*, pp. 292, 303.
9. Munsell, *The Annals of Albany*, (1852) 3: 30.

10. *NYCD*, 5: 662, 663.
11. McFarling, Usha Lee (Knight Ridder), "Research Links Brain Chemical to Alcoholism," *Times Union* (Albany, NY), November 26, 1998.
12. Van Laer, *Court Minutes of Fort Orange, Albany, Rensselaerswyck and Schenectady 1652-56* (1920), pp. 89, 106, 288.
13. *NYCD*, 13: 268.
14. For a discussion of the problem, see Dunn, *The Mohicans and Their Land*, pp. 142-145.
15. BV Wendell, Evert. Account book, 1695-1726, NYHS. In Dutch. Text given is in part from an unpublished translation done by Cees-Jan Waterman, a Dutch scholar. The author used a microfilm copy of the original account book for study and translation and for comparison with the translation by Waterman.
16. "Expenses Incurred during Negotiations for the Purchase of Paponikack," from the Van Slichtenhorst Court proceedings, translated by Charles Gehring, New Netherland Project.
17. *NYCD*, 4: 577.
18. A. J. F. van Laer, "Albany Wills and Other Documents 1668-1687," *Dutch Settlers Yearbook*, (Vol. X., 1934-1935), p. 4; Dunn, *The Mohicans and Their Land 1609-1730*, pp. 193, 199-201, 204.
19. *ERA* 1: 107; Beers, *History of Greene County, New York*, pp. 25, 94.
20. Jones, Paul, *Our Yesteryears, A Narrative History of the Town of White Creek, Washington County*, n.d., n.p. [1959], p. 21.
21. Van Laer, *Van Rensselaer Bowier Manuscripts*, pp. 483-484.
22. Innes, *Labor in a New Land*, p. 25.
23. *NARR*, p. 305.
24. Innes, *Labor in a New Land*, p. 24.
25. *LIR*, p. 39.
26. Grumet, "The Selling of Lenapehoking," p. 22.
27. Brasser, *Riding on the Frontier's Crest*, p. 24.
28. *Ibid.*, pp. 24, 25, see note #97.
29. *NYCD* 13: 564.
30. *NYCD* 4:59-63.
31. New York State Archives, *Indorsed Land Papers*, 3:38, 45.
32. *ERA*, 1: 74, 161.
33. Joseph, "The Yorker, Van Valkenburgh," pp. 4-8.
34. Jones, *Stockbridge Past and Present*, p. 39.
35. Hopkins, *Historical Memoirs Relating to the Housatonic Indians*, (1911), p. 15.
36. "Notes of Evidence on Trial. The King ag't John Van Rensselaer, Esq'r," pp. 52-55, Misc. Mss. Van Rensselaer, John, NYHS. Used courtesy The New-York Historical Society.
37. *ERA* 2, pp. 269-70.
38. *Ibid.*, 259-61.
39. *Ibid.*, 268-69.
40. Cooke, Rollin Hillyer, ed., *Historic Homes and Institutions and Genealogical and Personal Memoirs of Berkshire County, Massachusetts*, 2 vols. (Lewis Publishing Co. 1906) I: 68; II: 332.
41. *Albany Institute of History and Art: 200 Years of Collecting*, p. 50. In addition, the Albany mill run by Evert Wendell's son, Abraham, is illustrated in a painting in the collections of the Albany Institute of History and Art.
42. From the translation of the account book by Cees-Jan Waterman, with alterations by the author. The deed is given in Dunn, *The Mohicans and Their Land 1609-1730*, p. 322.
43. *NYCD*, 3:482; *NYCD*, 4:834.
44. Isaac Weld, in his 1795-1797 travels in America, quoted in *Native American Portrayals*, the National Newsletter for Reenactors of 18th & Early 19th Century Eastern American Indians, Vol. 1, No. 1, Spring, 1997.

45. Zeisberger, *History of the Northern American Indians*, p. 29.
46. Munsell, *The Annals of Albany*, (1857), 3: 268.
47. Dunn, "Settlement Patterns in Rensselaerswijck," p. 17.
48. "Notes of Evidence on Trial. The King ag't John Van Rensselaer, Esq'r," p. 61, Misc. Mss. Van Rensselaer, John, NYHS.

Chapter 5: Connecticut: Transactions with the Mohicans

1. *LIR*, p. 108.
2. Dyer, *Gnadensee: The Lake of Grace*, p. 17.
3. Pettee, *The Rev. Jonathan Lee and his Eighteenth Century Salisbury Parish*, p. 53.
4. Salisbury, Connecticut, Deeds 3, p. 504; State Archives, Conn. State Library: Patents, Deeds and Surveys of Land, Vol. 4: 441.
5. Salisbury Deeds, Book 3, p. 504; Dunn, *The Mohicans and Their Land 1609-1730*, p. 306.
6. Pettee, *The Rev. Jonathan Lee and His Eighteenth Century Salisbury Parish*, pp. 31-32.
7. State Archives, Conn. State Library: Patents, Deeds and Surveys of Land, Vol. 3 (1710-1724), pp. 376-379.
8. State Archives, Conn. State Library: Towns and and Lands, First Series, Vol. 7, Doc. 245a.
9. Pettee, *The Rev. Jonathan Lee and His Eighteenth Century Salisbury Parish*, p. 51.
10. Map at Heritage Map Museum, Lititz, Pennsylvania, courtesy James Hess.
11. Map HM #15440, Huntington Library, San Marino, CA.
12. State Archives, Conn. State Library: Colonial Land Records, Vol. 4-5: 440; see Binzen, 110, 111.
13. State Archives, Conn. State Library: Towns and Lands, First Series, Vol. 7, Doc. 239a.
14. *Ibid.*, Doc. 243 a-b.
15. Binzen, *Mohican Lands and Colonial Corners*, pp. 34-35.
16. Pettee, *The Rev. Jonathan Lee and his Eighteenth Century Salisbury Parish*, pp. 45-48.
17. Binzen, *Mohican Lands and Colonial Corners*, pp. 37, 38.
18. Pettee, *Rev. Jonathan Lee and his Eighteenth Century Salisbury Parish*, p. 32.
19. Binzen, *Mohican Lands and Colonial Corners*, p. 43-44, 52.
20. State Archives, Conn. State Library: Land Records, Vols. 4-5, p. 441.
21. State Archives, Conn. State Library: Indian Papers, Series 1, Vol. 1, Doc. 244; Sedgwick, *General History of the Town of Sharon* (1877), pp. 32-33.
22. State Archives, Conn. State Library: Indian Papers, Series 1, Vol. 1, Doc. 244.
23. *Ibid.*, Doc. 246.
24. *Ibid.*
25. Binzen, *Mohican Lands and Colonial Corners*, p. 114.
26. Pettee, *Rev. Jonathan Lee and His Eighteenth Century Salisbury Parish*, p. 51; Binzen, *Mohican Lands and Colonial Corners*, p. 73..
27. Hoadley (1880), referenced in Binzen, *Mohican Lands and Colonial Corners*, p. 52.
28. Sedgwick, *A History of the Town of Sharon* (1842), pp. 10-11.
29. *LP*, pp 74-75.
30. Huntting, *History of Little Nine Partners*, pp. 17-19; Reed, *Early History of Amenia*, p. 15.
31. Huntting, *History of Little Nine Partners*, p. 18; New York State Archives, *Land Papers*, Vol. IV, p. 20.
32. Buckingham, *The Private Journals*, p. 31.
33. Huntting, *History of Little Nine Partners*, p. 19; see also Robert R. Livingston Papers, Reel 28, NYSL.
34. Reed, *Early History of Amenia*, p. 15.
35. Sedgwick, *General History of the Town of Sharon* (1877), pp. 14-15.
36. Reed, *Early History of Amenia*, p. 15; Huntting, *History of Little Nine Partners*, pp. 5-7, 20.
37. *Old Miscellaneous Records of Dutchess County*, Vassar Brothers' Institute, Poughkeepsie, 1909.
38. Sedgwick, *General History of the Town of Sharon* (1877), p. 11.

39. State Archives, Conn. State Library: Towns and Lands, 1st Series, Vol. 7, Doc. 248.
40. Sedgwick, *General History of the Town of Sharon* (1877), pp. 15, 31; Church, *Historical Addresses*, p.7.
41. Binzen, *Mohican Lands and Colonial Corners*, p. 114; Connecticut Archives: Towns and Lands, Series 1, Vol. 7, Doc. 249.
42. State Archives, Conn. State Library: Indian Papers, Series 1, Vol. 1, Doc. 244.
43. Pettee, *The Rev. Jonathan Lee and His Eighteenth Century Salisbury Parish*, p.62.
44. Sedgwick, *General History of the Town of Sharon* (1877), pp. 32-33.
45. Sedgwick, *General History of the Town of Sharon* (1877), pp. 32-33.
46. State Archives, Conn. State Library: Indian Papers, Series 1, Vol. 1, Doc. 244.
47. Sedgwick, *General History of the Town of Sharon* (1877), p. 34.
48. State Archives, Conn. State Library: Indian Papers, Series 1, Vol. 1, Doc. 245.
49. Binzen, *Mohican Lands and Colonial Corners*, p. 65, 66.
50. State Archives, Conn. State Library: Indian Papers, Series 1, Vol. 1, Doc. 246.
51. Sedgwick, *A History of the Town of Sharon* (1842), p. 12; Sedgwick, *General History of the Town of Sharon* (1877), p. 34.
52. Town Records, quoted in Sedgwick, *A History of the Town of Sharon* (1842), p. 12.
53. *Ibid.*
54. State Archives, Conn. State Library: Indians, 2nd Series, Vols. 1 & 2, Doc. 103a.
55. *Ibid.*
56. Binzen, *Mohican Lands and Colonial Corners*, p. 83; Sedgwick, *General History of the Town of Sharon* (1877), p. 35.
57. *Ibid.*
58. Quoted in Binzen, *Mohican Lands and Colonial Quarters*, p. 86.
59. *Ibid.*, p. 87.

Chapter 6: Changing Beliefs

1. Speck, "The Mohegan Indians," p. 199.
2. *NYCD* 5: 562, 563.
3. Hopkins, *Historical Memoirs, Relating to the Housatunnuk Indians* (1753) p. 46.
4. Bunninger, quoted in Binzen, *Mohican Lands and Colonial Corners*, p. 69.
5. Loskiel, *History of the Mission of the United Brethren Among the North American Indians*, p. 17.
6. Bond, *Queen Anne's American Kings*, p. 63.
7. Loskiel, *History of the Mission of the United Brethren Among the North American Indians*, p. 23.
8. *Ibid.*, p. 23.
9. *NYCD* 5: 663.
10. Hopkins, *Historical Memoirs, Relating to the Housatunnuk Indians* (1753), p. 49.
11. Loskiel, *History of the Mission of the United Brethren Among the North American Indians*, p. 30.
12. Aupaumut, *Collections of the Massachusetts Historical Society*, p. 101.
13. O'Callaghan, *Documentary History* 3: 1151.
14. *NYCD* 6: 314-315.
15. Loskiel, *History of the Mission of the United Brethren Among the North American Indians*, p. 36.
16. *NARR*, p. 49.
17. Collier, *A History of Old Kinderhook*, p. 13.
18. Dyer, *Gnadensee, The Lake of Grace*, p. 21.
19. Collier, *A History of Old Kinderhook*, p. 12.
20. Zeisberger, *History of the North American Indians*, p. 18.
21. *NYCD* 7: 159.
22. Frazier, *The Mohicans of Stockbridge*, p. 59.

23. Hopkins, *Historical Memoirs, Relating to the Housatunnuk Indians* (1753), p. 24.
24. Westmeier, *The Evacuation of Shekomeko and the Early Moravian Missions to Native North Americans*, p. 219.
25. Speck, "The Mohegan Indians," p. 199.
26. Heckewelder, *History, Manners, and Customs of the Indian Nations*, p. 241.
27. *Ibid.*, p. 239.
28. Hopkins, *Historical Memoirs Relating to the Housatonic Indians.* (1911), p. 24.
29. *Calendar of Land Papers*, pp. 35-36, 747.
30. Wraxall, *An Abridgment of the Indian Affairs*, pp. 69, 91; *NYCD* 5: 563.
31. Bond, *Queen Anne's American Kings*, p. 2.
32. Colee, *The Housatonic-Stockbridge Indians: 1734-1739*, pp. 132, 168; Hopkins, *Historical Memoirs, Relating to the Housatunnuk Indians* (1753), p. 16.
33. Bond, *Queen Anne's American Kings*, p. 1. (Bond, in error, called all four Indian delegates Mohawks.)
34. *Ibid.*, pp. 7-8.
35. *Ibid.*, pp. 13-15.
36. *NYCD* 5: 562.
37. Colee, *The Housatonic-Stockbridge Indians: 1734-1739*, pp. 76-77.

Chapter 7: Wnahktukook Becomes Stockbridge

1. "Notes of Evidence on Trial. The King ag't John Van Rensselaer, Esq'r." Misc. Mss. Van Rensselaer, John, NYHS. Courtesy the New-York Historical Society.
2. Hopkins, *Historical Memoirs, Relating to the Housatunnuk Indians* (1753), p. 2.
3. Wright, *Indian Deeds of Hampden County*, pp. 116-117; Taylor, *History of Great Barrington, Berkshire County, Massachusetts*, pp. 16, 61.
4. Wright, *Indian Deeds of Hampden County*, pp. 116-117.
5. *The Karner Brook Watershed, A Proposal for Nomination as An Area of Critical Environmental Concern*, Egremont, Massachusetts, October, 1991, p. 33 (Appendix G). Also testimony of Joseph Van Gilder, found in "Notes of Evidence on Trial, The King ag't John Van Rensselaer, Esq'r.," Van Rensselaer, John, NYHS. See also this book, Appendix A, Deeds, June 1, 1756 and May 25, 1757.
6. Stockbridge Library Historical Collection: handwritten copy in Loudon Collection, No. 5026 (m. 73-1.30).
7. Information from Debbie Winchell, a descendant; see *JP* 9: 632, 686-687.
8. *JP* 10: 599-601.
9. Stockbridge Library Historical Collection, deed, September 20, 1765.
10. Appleton, 1736, quoted in Colee, *The Housatonic-Stockbridge Indians: 1734-1749*, p. 130.
11. Fliegel, *Index*, 2: 49.
12. *Ibid.*, 2:49.
13. Hopkins, *Historical Memoirs, Relating to the Housatunnuk Indians* (1753), p. 2.
14. Hunter, 1795, in Colee, *The Housatonic-Stockbridge Indians: 1743-1749*, pp. 83-85.
15. Colee, *The Housatonic-Stockbridge Indians*, p. 15.
16. Hopkins, *Historical Memoirs, Relating to the Housatunnuk Indians* (1753), p. 8.
17. Sheffield, Connecticut, Town Hall Records, Book 1722-1762, pp. 178-179, quoted in Colee, *The Housatonic-Stockbridge Indians*, pp. 72.
18. "Notes of Evidence on Trial. The King ag't John Van Rensselaer, Esq'r." Misc. Mss., Van Rensselaer, John, NYHS.
19. Hopkins, *Historical Memoirs, Relating to the Housatunnuk Indians* (1753), p. 10.
20. *Ibid.*, p. 12.
21. *Ibid.*, p. 11.
22. *Ibid.*, p. 38.
23. *Ibid.*, p. 31.
24. Hopkins, *Historical Memoirs Relating to the Housatonic Indians* (1911), pp. 27, 150.

25. Hopkins, *Historical Memoirs, Relating to the Housatunnuk Indians* (1753), p. 15.
26. *Ibid.*, p. 16. Konkapot later had other sons.
27. Frazier, *The Mohicans of Stockbridge*, p. 125.
28. Hopkins, *Historical Memoirs* (1753), p. 22.
29. *Ibid.*, pp. 22-23.
30. *Ibid.*, p. 24.
31. Denys, *Description and Natural History of Acadia*, p. 381.
32. Colee, *The Housatonic-Stockbridge Indians*, p. 132.
33. Hopkins, *Historical Memoirs* (1753), p. 28.
34. Konkapot's son Robert was mentioned in a deed noted by E. W. B. Canning. See "Indian Land Grants in Stockbridge," *Berkshire Historical and Scientific Society*, p. 51; other sons are named in Jones, *Stockbridge, Past and Present*, p. 34, 117; the daughters' deaths are noted in Colee, *The Housatonic-Stockbridge Indians: 1734-1749*, p. 125.
35. Hopkins, *Historical Memoirs* (1753), p. 27.
36. *Ibid.*, p. 44.
37. Taylor, *History of Great Barrington*, p. 26.
38. Wright, *Indian Deeds of Hampden County*, pp. 134-135.
39. From General Court Records, quoted in Taylor, *History of Great Barrington*, pp. 63-64; the deed is in Wright, *Indian Deeds of Hampden County*, pp. 141-142.
40. Elias Van Schaack, the other hold-out, was the last to leave.
41. See Appendix A, October 22, 1736; Wright, *Indian Deeds of Hampden County*, pp. 134-135.
42. See Appendix A, June 1, 1756; Wright, *Indian Deeds of Hampden County*, pp. 155-156.
43. Hopkins, *Historical Memoirs* (1753), p. 52-53.
44. *Ibid.*, p. 52.
45. *Ibid.*, p. 49.
46. *Ibid.*, p. 54.
47. *Ibid.*, p. 57.
48. Dunn, *The Mohicans and Their Land*, p. 321; a grandson of Arent Van Curler, bearing the same name, maintained a trading post in (later) Washington County.
49. Hopkins, *Historical Memoirs* (1753), p. 58.
50. Taylor, *History of Great Barrington*, p. 66.
51. See deeds of June 2, 1737 and September 11, 1738 in Appendix A.
52. Frazier, *The Mohicans of Stockbridge*, p. 47; John Sergeant "Journal," Yale Library, p. 7.
53. Jones, *Stockbridge, Past and Present*, p. 32.
54. *Ibid.*, p. 77.
55. *Ibid.*, 71.
56. *Ibid.*, p. 76.
57. Frazier, *The Mohicans of Stockbridge*, p. 45.
58. Wheeler, *Living Upon Hope: Mahicans and Missionaries, 1730-1760*, p. 141.
59. Frazier, *The Mohicans of Stockbridge*, p. 99.
60. Taylor, *History of Great Barrington*, pp. 79, 80, 86.
61. Hopkins, *Historical Memoirs* (1753), pp. 77-78.
62. *Ibid.*, p. 82.
63. *Ibid.*, p. 88.
64. Jones, *Stockbridge, Past and Present*, p. 17.
65. Hopkins, *Historical Memoirs* (1753), pp. 99, 106.
66. *Ibid.*, p. 99.
67. *Ibid.*, p. 130.
68. *Ibid.*, p. 131.
69. Frazier, *The Mohicans of Stockbridge*, p. 70.
70. Hopkins, *Historical Memoirs Relating to the Housatonic Indians* (1911), p. 87.
71. Hopkins, *Historical Memoirs, Relating to the Housatunnuk Indians* (1753), p. 115.
72. *NYCD* 6: 319, 321.

73. *Ibid.*, p. 323.
74. Drake, *A Particular History of the Five Years French and Indian War*, pp. 133-134.
75. *New England Historical and Genealogical Register* XX (1866), p. 134.
76. The list is from the collection of Lion Miles.
77. *New England Historical and Genealogical Register* XX (1866), p. 134.
78. Drake, *A Particular History of the Five Years French and Indian War*, p. 146.
79. *Magazine of History*, Extra Numbers 5-8, Vol II, 1909, pp. 16-19.
80. *JP* 1: 125-126.
81. Frazier, *The Mohicans of Stockbridge*, p. 81.
82. Proprietors' List, Stockbridge Library Historical Collection.
83. Miles, "The Red Man Dispossessed," pp. 52-53.
84. Hopkins, *Historical Memoirs, Relating to the Housatunnuk Indians* (1753), p. 136.
85. Canning, "The Indian Mission in Stockbridge," pp. 240-241.
86. Frazier, *The Mohicans of Stockbridge*, p. 83.
87. Jones, *Stockbridge, Past and Present*, p. 79.
88. Canning, *The Indian Mission in Stockbridge*, pp. 240-241. (Field, Rev. D. D.) *An Historical Sketch of the Stockbridge Congregational Church*, Stockbridge, Berkshire County, Mass., 1888, p. 10.
89. For the text of the document, see Canning, "Indian Land Grants in Stockbridge," pp. 47-48. For discussion of the 1765 law and the problems of Indian debt, see Miles, "The Red Man Dispossessed," pp. 65-67.
90. Frazier, *The Mohicans of Stockbridge*, pp. 82, 83.
91. See Appendix A, deed of December 5, 1751; Jones, *Stockbridge, Past and Present*, p. 156.
92. Frazier, *The Mohicans of Stockbridge*, pp. 91-92.
93. *Ibid.*, pp. 94-95.
94. Jones, *Stockbridge, Past and Present*, p. 74; Frazier, *The Mohicans of Stockbridge*, p. 99.
95. Frazier, *The Mohicans of Stockbridge*, p. 101.
96. Canning, "The Indian Mission in Stockbridge," p. 244.
97. Frazier, *The Mohicans of Stockbridge*, pp. 101-102; Jones, *Stockbridge, Past and Present*, p. 75; Canning, "The Indian Mission in Stockbridge," p. 245.
98. Miles, "The Red Man Dispossessed," p. 72.
99. *JP* 9: 847.
100. Brasser, *Riding the Frontier's Crest*, p. 38; Strickland, *Journal of a Tour in the United States of America*, p. 116.

Chapter 8: The Kaunaumeek Mission

1. Brainerd, *The Life of John Brainerd, the Brother of David Brainerd*, p. 465.
2. Hopkins, *Historical Memoirs* (1753), p. 61.
3. *Ibid.*, p. 61.
4. Sergeant, John, "Journal," Yale Library, p. 14.
5. Hopkins, *Historical Memoirs* (1753), p. 63.
6. *Ibid.*, pp. 85, 86; Dunn, *The Mohicans and Their Land*, pp. 221-222.
7. Sergeant, "Journal," Yale Library, p. 14; Edwards, *The Life of David Brainerd*, pp. 52, 60, 61.
8. *Ibid.*, pp. 32, 51, 53.
9. Westmeier, *The Evacuation of Shekomeco and the Early Moravian Missions*, pp. 96, 98-100.
10. *Ibid*, p. 99.
11. Reichel, *Memorials of the Moravian Church*, p. 28.
12. Edwards, *The Life of David Brainerd*, p. 61.
13. *Ibid.*, p. 64.
14. *Diary of William Sweat*, quoted in Huey, *The Early History of Nassau Village*, pp. 2, 4.
15. Edwards, *The Life of David Brainerd*, p. 64.
16. *Ibid.*, p. 65, 69.

17. *Ibid,*. pp. 64-65.
18. Dunn, *The Mohicans and Their Land*, pp. 305, 306.
19. *Ibid.*, p. 308.
20. From Appleton, 1736, quoted in Colee, *The Housatonic-Stockbridge Indians*, p. 168.
21. Frazier, *The Mohicans of Stockbridge*, pp. 107, 125. Apparently through marriages with Wappingers at Stockbridge, Etowaukaum had descendants among both the Stockbridges and the Wappingers.
22. Dunn, *The Mohicans and Their Land*, p. 306; O'Callaghan, *Documentary History* 2: 605.
23. See Deeds, Appendix A.
24. Edwards, *The Life of David Brainerd*, p. 67.
25. Brainerd, *The Life of John Brainerd, the Brother of David Brainerd*, p. 465.
26. Edwards, *The Life of David Brainerd*, p. 76.
27. *Ibid.*, pp. 79, 87.
28. Frazier, *The Mohicans of Stockbridge*, p. 59.
29. Edwards, *The Life of David Brainerd*, p. 89.
30. *Ibid.*, p. 91.
31. Brainerd, *The Life of John Brainerd, the Brother of David Brainerd*, p. 465.
32. *Berkshire Book: by Its Historical and Scientific Society*, Pittsfield Mass., Vol. 1, 1892, p. 122; the map is at Massachusetts Archives, Maps and Plans: Item 690.
33. Jones, *Stockbridge, Past and Present*, pp. 68-69; Brainerd, *The Life of John Brainerd*, p. 75.
34. Brainerd, *The Life of John Brainerd*, pp. 59-60.

Chapter 9: Moravian Missions to the Mohicans

1.   MOA, Box 11, Folder 3, Item 3.
2.   MOA, Box 315, Folder 3, Item 7.
3.   Gray, *Wilderness Christians*, p. 29.
4.   *Ibid.*, p. 26.
5.   MOA, Box 315, Folder 3, Item 7.
6.   Frazier, *Mohicans of Stockbridge*, pp. 60-62.
7.   "Journal of Rev. John Sergeant," 1739, 1-2, Stiles MSS., Yale College Library. A transcription can be found in Colee, *The Housatonic-Stockbridge Indians, 1734-1749*, Appendix A. A photocopy is in the Stockbridge Library Historical Collection.
8.   MOA, Box 111, Folder 3, Item 4.
9.   Loskiel, *History of the Mission*, Part 2: 13.
10. MOA, Box 319, Folder 1, Item 1.
11. Reichel, *Memorials of the Moravian Church*, p. 55; MOA Box 3191, Folder 1; Hasbrouck, *History of Dutchess County*, p. 26.
12. Wheeler, *Living Upon Hope*, pp. 222-223, 229.
13. *Ibid.*, p. 129; MOA, Box 112, Folder 19, Item 5.
14. Reichel, *Memorials of the Moravian Church* 1: 147; Fliegel *Index*, 6-10; Wheeler, *Living Upon Hope*, Appendix B, p. 313.
15. MOA, Box 113, Folder 5, Items 2 and 6.
16. Smith, *Wappinger Land Transfers*, unpaged; McDermott, *Eighteenth Century Documents of the Nine Partners Patent*, pp. 5, 15, 110-113.
17. MOA, Box 113, Folder 5, Item 2.
18. *Ibid.*
19. *Ibid.*, Items 8 and 9.
20. *Ibid.*, Items 6 and 11.
21. *Ibid.*, Item 6.
22. *Ibid.*
23. Huntting, *History of the Little Nine*, pp. 22, 23.
24. *LP*, p. 62.
25. Huntting, *History of the Little Nine*, pp. 6-8.

26. *LP*, pp. 63, 69-70, 78.
27. MOA, Box 113, Folder 5, Item 1.
28. *LP*, p. 283.
29. *JP* 10: 853-854.
30. MOA, Box 3191, Folder 1.
31. Hopkins, *Historical Memoirs* (1753), p. 127.
32. MOA, Box 113, Folder 5, Item 5.
33. *Ibid.*
34. Livingston Family Papers, 18.F.15 (1974), BHS.
35. Ellis, *History of Columbia County*, p. 412.
36. Fliegel, *Index to the Records*, p. 8.
37. MOA Box 113, Folder 5, Item 5.
38. MOA, Box 3191, Folder 1; Wheeler, *Living Upon Hope*, Appendix B, p. 313.
39. Dunn, *The Mohicans and Their Land*, pp. 132, 308.
40. Reichel, *Memorials of the Moravian Church*, p.55.
41. Wheeler, *Living Upon Hope*, p. 314.
42. MOA, Box 112, F 1.
43. MOA, Box 3191, Folder 1.
44. MOA, Box 3191, Folder 1.
45. Wheeler, *Living Upon Hope*, 315.
46. Reichel, *Memorials of the Moravian Church*, pp. 54, 55; Dyer, *Gnadensee*, pp. 46-47.
47. Reichel, *Memorials of the Moravian Church*, pp. 56, 57, 77.
48. *Ibid.*
49. Fliegel, *Index to the Records*, p. 1342.
50. MOA, Box 112, Folder 17.
51. Wheeler, *Living Upon Hope*, p. 315.
52. O'Callaghan, *Documentary History* 3: 1616; Westmeier, *The Evacuation of Shekomeko*, pp. 98-99.
53. MOA, Box 11, Folder 4: Fliegel, *Index to the Records*, p. 1342.
54. Wheeler, *Living Upon Hope*, p. 250.
55. *Ibid.*, p. 127.
56. Binzen, *Mohican Lands and Colonial Corners*, pp. 64-65.
57. Dyer, *Gnadensee*, p. 51.
58. MOA, Box 112, Folder 2, Item 3; Smith, J. M., *Wappinger Land Transfers, 1680-1737*, unpaged, see Demographic Profile, "Nimhammaw."
59. Dyer, *Gnadensee The Lake of Grace*, p. 52.
60. Ruttenber, *History of the Indian Tribes of Hudson's River*, p. 195; Westmeier, *Evacuation of Shekomeko*, p. 93; Smith, *General History of Dutchess County*, p. 20.
61. Frazier, *Mohicans of Stockbridge*, p. 65.
62. O'Callaghan, *Documentary History* 3: 1034.
63. *Ibid.*, p. 1013.
64. *Ibid.*, pp. 1012-1013.
65. *Ibid.*, p. 1015.
66. *Ibid.*, p. 1016.
67. *Ibid.*, pp. 1015-1019.
68. Reichel, *Memorials of the Moravian Church*, p. 32.
69. Fliegel, *Index to the Records*, p. 1343; O'Callaghan, *Documentary History*, 3: 1021-1030.
70. Loskiel, *History of the Mission*, Part 2, p. 13; Frazier, *The Mohicans of Stockbridge*, pp. 72-73.
71. Orcutt, *Indians of the Housatonic and Naugatuck Valleys*, p. 181.
72. Reichel, *Memorials of the Moravian Church*, p. 72.
73. Frazier, *Mohicans of Stockbridge*, pp. 73-74.
74. *NYCD* 6: 298.
75. *Ibid.*, p. 304.

76. Frazier, *Mohicans of Stockbridge*, p. 77.
77. DeForest, *History of the Indians of Connecticut*, pp. 402-403.
78. Huntting, *History of Little Nine Partners*, p. 336.
79. Dyer, *Gnadensee*, pp. 65-66.
80. Binzen, *Mohican Lands and Colonial Corners*, pp. 81-82.
81. Dyer, *Gnadensee*, p. 78.
82. David Bruce manuscript, trans. and ed. Corrina Dally-Starna, at Mashantucket Pequot Museum and Research Center, quoted in Binzen, *Mohican Lands and Colonial Corners*, pp. 77-78. Used with permission.
83. *Ibid.*, p. 79.
84. Bruce manuscript, trans. and ed. Corrina Dally-Starna, quoted in Binzen, *Mohican Lands and Colonial Corners*, pp. 79, 80.
85. Sedgwick, *General History of the Town of Sharon* (1877) p. 35.
86. Bruce manuscript, trans. and ed. Corrina Dally-Starna, at Mashantucket Pequot Museum and Research Center, quoted in Binzen, *Mohican Lands and Colonial Corners*, p. 80.
87. *Ibid.*, p. 81.
88. *Ibid.*
89. *Ibid.*, p. 82.
90. Dyer, *Gnadensee*, 73-74.
91. *Ibid.*, pp. 75, 93.
92. *Ibid.*, p. 81.
93. Sedgwick, *General History of the Town of Sharon* (1877), pp. 188-189.
94. *Ibid.*, p 35.
95. *Moravian Missions: Twelve Lectures*, p. 286.
96. Joachim Senseman manuscript, trans. and ed. Corrina Dally-Starna, at Mashantucket Museum and Research Center, quoted in Binzen, *Mohican Lands and Colonial Corners*, p. 85.
97. *Ibid.*, p. 86.
98. *JP* 9: 846.

Chapter 10: Clans, Chiefs, and Close-out Deeds

1. Loskiel, *History of the Mission*, p. 129.
2. Wright, *Indian Deeds of Hampden County*, p. 136; Dunn, *Mohicans and Their Land*, pp. 307, 321.
3. Aupaumut, "Extract from an Indian History,", p. 97.
4. From Appleton, quoted in Wheeler, *Living Upon Hope: Mahicans and Missionaries*, p. 219; see notes of Buettner, Nov. 6, 1743, MOA, Box 111, Folder 2, item 7.
5. *JP* 9: 833.
6. *Ibid.*, pp. 833, 837, 843-844.
7. *JP* 10: 171, 173.
8. Frazier, *Mohicans of Stockbridge*, pp. 114-145.
9. *JP* 10: 167.
10. *Ibid.*, pp. 175, 182-183.
11. Jones, *Stockbridge, Past and Present*, p. 119.
12. Loskiel, *History of the Mission*, p. 130.
13. Van Bergen Family Papers, Item 14665, Manuscripts and Special Collections, NYSL; see Dunn, *The Mohicans and Their Land*, pp. 249-250.
14. Van Rensselaer, Killiaen K., Manuscripts and Special Collections, NYHS.
15. Van Laer, *Van Rensselaer Bowier Manuscripts*, p. 197.
16. For an explanation of this agreement, see Dunn, "Settlement Patterns in Rensselaerswyck," *de Halve Maen*, vol. IXX, Spring 1997, No. 1, pp. 7-18.
17. Both quotations are from "Ruff draft of Testimony about ye north line," in Livingston Family Papers, Clermont State Historic Site.

18. "Notes of Evidence on Trial. The King ag't John Van Rensselaer, Esq'r." Misc. Mss. Van Rensselaer, John, NYHS.
19. *Ibid*, see Van Valkenburgh testimony.
20. *JP* 9: 211-212.
21. "Notes of Evidence on Trial. The King ag't John Van Rensselaer, Esq'r." Misc. Mss. Van Rensselaer, John, NYHS.
22. Strickland, *Journal of a Tour*, p. 116.
23. *JP* 12: 975-76.
24. Quinney, *Wisconsin Historical Society, Collections*, p. 315.
25. Dunn, *Mohicans and Their Land*, pp. 164-184.
26. Richter, "Rediscovered Links in the Covenant Chain," p. 61; *LIR* p. 67.
27. See testimony of Joseph van Gilder in "Notes of Evidence on Trial. The King ag't John Van Rensselaer, Esq'r" Mss. Mss. Van Rensselaer, John, NYHS; Dunn, *The Mohicans and Their Land*, p. 313.
28. Fliegel, *Index to the Records*, vol. 1, p. 49; "Notes of Evidence on Trial." Misc. Mss. Van Rensselaer, John, NYHS.
29. Wright, *Indian Deeds of Hampden County*, pp. 149-150; see also deeds, Appendix A.
30. *LP*, pp. 590, 591.
31. Personal communication about Shawquethqueat from Lion Miles; Frazier, *The Mohicans of Stockbridge*, p. 237.
32. Jones, *Stockbridge, Past and Present*, p. 119.
33. Troy Newspaper Collection, Troy Public Library.
34. Wyss, "Historical Memoirs: Stockbridge, New Stockbridge, and the Nostalgia of Conversion," p. 36.
35. *History of Berkshire County*, Vol. 1, p. 28.
36. Jones, *Stockbridge Past and Present*, pp. 119, 122.
37. Aupaumut, "Extract from an Indian History," pp. 99-102.
38. Walling, *Death in the Bronx*, unpaged; Miles, "The Stockbridge Indian Massacre Continued," unpaged; Frazier, *The Mohicans of Stockbridge*, p. 237.
39. Smith, Peter, "Indian Personal Name Entries in Peter Smith's Indian Blotter," pp. 467-468.
40. *JP* 9: 845
41. Aupaumut, "Extract from an Indian History," p. 100.
42. Skinner, "Notes on Mahikan Ethnology," pp. 101-105; Quinney, *Wisconsin Historical Society, Collections*, p. 325.
43. Aupaumut, "A Narrative of an Embassy to the Western Indians," p. 78.
44. *The American Spy*, Newspaper Collection, Troy, New York Public Library.
45. Aupaumut, "A Narrative of an Embassy to the Western Indians," p. 77.
46. *Ibid.*, pp. 70-71; Quinney, *Wisconsin Historical Society Collections*, p. 310;
47. *Census of the State of New York for 1855*, p. 516.
48. Ruttenber, *History of the Indian Tribes of Hudson's River*, p. 325.
49. Taylor, *History of Great Barrington*, pp. 12-13.
50. *Ibid.*, pp. 44, 55, 61, 62
51. *LP*, p. 303.
52. Indian Letter of September 2, 1783, The Stockbridge Library Historical Collection.

Bibliography

Unpublished Sources

Collections. Albany Institute of History and Art, Albany, New York.

Connecticut Archives. Connecticut State Library, Hartford, Connecticut.

Deeds. Albany County Hall of Records, Albany, New York.

Deeds. Hampden County Registry of Deeds, Springfield, Massachusetts.

Deeds. Massachusetts Middle Registry of Deeds, Pittsfield, Massachusetts.

Indorsed Land Papers. Secretary of State, New York State Archives, Albany, New York.

"Journal of Rev. John Sergeant." Manuscript in the President Stiles Papers. Beineke Library, Yale University.

Livingston Family Papers. Brooklyn Historical Society, Brooklyn, New York

Livingston Family Papers. Clermont State Historic Site, Clermont, New York.

Livingston-Redmond Papers and Robert R. Livingston Papers Microfilm. New York State Library, Albany, New York.

Manuscript Collections. New-York Historical Society, New York City.

Manuscript Collections. Connecticut State Archives, Hartford, Connecticut.

Maps of New Netherland. Manuscripts and Special Collections, New York State Library.

Moravian Records Microfilm. New York State Library

Moravian Records. Moravian Archives and Library, Bethlehem, Pennsylvania.

Newspaper Collection. Troy Public Library, Troy, New York.

Sir William Johnson Manuscripts. Manuscripts and Special Collections, New York State Library.

Stockbridge Library Historical Collection. Stockbridge, Massachusetts.

Published Sources

A Field Guide to Wild Flowers. The Peterson Field Guide Series. New York: Houghton Mifflin, 1968.

Albany Institute of History and Art: 200 Years of Collecting. New York: Hudson Hills Press, 1998.

(Aupaumut, Hendrick). "Extract from an Indian History," *Collections of the Massachusetts Historical Society,* Vol. IX. Boston, Mass., 1804, pp. 99-102.

_____. "A Narrative of an Embassy to the Western Indians, from the Original Manuscript of Hendrick Aupaumut, with Prefatory Remarks by Dr. R. H. Coates." *Memoirs of the Historical Society of Pennsylvania.* Vol. II. Philadelphia: Carey, Lea & Carey, 1827.

Binzen, Timothy. *Mohican Lands and Colonial Corners: Weataug, Wechquadnach and the Connecticut Colony 1675-1750.* Thesis Submitted for the Degree of Master of Anthropology. University of Connecticut, 1997.

Bond, Richmond P. *Queen Anne's American Kings.* Oxford: Clarendon Press, 1952.

Book of the Supervisors of Dutchess County, N.Y. (A.D. 1718-1722) Poughkeepsie, NY: Vassar Brothers' Institute, no date.

Brainerd, Rev. Thomas. *The Life of John Brainerd, the Brother of David Brainerd.* New York: Presbyterian Publication Committee, 1865.

Brasser, Ted J. *Riding on the Frontier's Crest: Mahican Indian Culture and Culture Change.* Ottowa: National Museums of Canada, 1974.

Brodhead, John Romeyn. *History of the State of New York.* 2 vols. New York: Harper & Brothers, Publishers, 1853, 1871.

Buckingham, John. *The Private Journals Kept by Rev. John Buckingham of the Expedition Against Canada in the Years 1710 & 1711, From the Original Manuscripts.* New York: Wilder and Campbell, 1825 (Roll and Journal of Connecticut Service in Queen Anne's War 1710-1711. Edited for the Acorn Club, 1916.)

Calendar of N.Y. Colonial Manuscripts, Indorsed Land Papers in the Office of the Secretary of State of New York 1643-1808. Comp. E. B. O'Callaghan. Revised reprint. Harrison, NY: Harbor Hill Books. 1987.

Canning, E. W. B. "The Indian Mission in Stockbridge" in *Book of Berkshire: Papers by its Historical and Scientific Society.* Pittsfield, Mass., 1890.

_____. "Indian Land Grants in Stockbridge." *Collections of the Berkshire Historical and Scientific Society.* Berkshire, Mass., 1894.

The Book of Berkshire, Describing and Illustrating its Hills and Homes for the Season of 1887. Great Barrington, Mass.: Clark W. Bryan & Co., 1887.

Campbell, Tony. "New Light on the Jansson-Visscher Maps of New England." *The Map Collectors' Circle.* No. 24. London: Durant House, 1965.

Champlain, Samuel de. *The Voyages and Explorations of Samuel de Champlain (1604-1616).* Trans. Annie Nettleton Bourne. 2 vols. New York: A. S. Barnes and Company, 1906.

_____. *The Works of Samuel de Champlain.* Ed. H. P. Biggar. 6 vols. Toronto: The Champlain Society, 1933.

Church, Samuel. *Historical Addresses Delivered by Hon. Samuel Church and Ex-Governor A. H. Holley.* Pittsfield: Chickering & Axtell, 1876.

Colee, Philip S. *The Housatonic-Stockbridge Indians: 1734-1749.* UMI Dissertation Services, 1977.

Collier, Edward A. *A History of Old Kinderhook.* New York: G. P. Putnam's Sons, 1914.

Dankaerts, Jasper. *Journal of Jasper Dankaerts.* Ed. B. James and F. J. Jameson. New York: Charles J. Scribner's Sons, 1913.

DeForest, John W. *History of the Indians of Connecticut.* 1851.

Denton, Daniel. *A Brief Description of New-York: Formerly Called New Netherlands.* [1670] (Readex Microprint Corp., 1966)

Denys, Nicholas. *Description and Natural History of Acadia.* Vol. 2. Toronto: Champlain Society, 1908.

Drake, Samuel G. *Particular History of the Five Years French and Indian War.* 1870. Reprint. Freeport, New York: Books for Libraries Press, 1970.

Dunn, Shirley W. *The Mohicans and Their Land 1609-1730.* Fleischmanns, NY: Purple Mountain Press, 1994.

Dunton, Anna Mary. *Reflections: Canaan, New York Bicentennial 1976.* Canaan Historical Society, 1976.

Dyer, Edward O. *Gnadensee The Lake of Grace.* Boston: The Pilgrim Press, 1903.

Edwards, President (Jonathan). *The Life of David Brainerd*. New York: American Tract Society, (no date, c. 1822).

Ellis, Captain Franklin. *History of Columbia County, New York*. Philadelphia: Everts & Ensign, 1878.

Fliegel, Rev. Carl John, comp. *Index to the Records of the Moravian Mission Among the Indians of North America*. New Haven, Connecticut: Research Publications, Inc., 1970.

Frazier, Patrick. *The Mohicans of Stockbridge*. Lincoln, University of Nebraska Press, 1992.

French, J. H. *Gazeteer of the State of New York*. Syracuse: R. Pearsall Smith, 1861.

Garnet, Edna Bailey. *West Stockbridge Massachusetts 1774-1794*. Bicentennial Committee, 1976.

Gibbons, Euell. *Stalking the Wild Asparagus*. Field Guide Edition. New York: David McKay Company, 1962.

Gray, Elma E. *Wilderness Christians*. Cornell University Press, Ithaca, NY, 1956.

Grumet, Robert S. *The Lenapes*. New York: Chelsea House Publishers, 1989.

_____. "The Selling of Lenapehoking," *Proceedings of the 1992 People to People Conference*. Rochester Museum and Science Center: Research Records No. 23, 1994, pp. 19-24.

Hart, John P., ed. *Current Northeast Paleoethnobotany*. New York State Museum Bulletin No. 494. University of the State of New York, 1999.

Hasbrouck, Frank, ed. *The History of Dutchess County*. Poughkeepsie, N.Y.: S. A. Matthieu, 1909.

Heckewelder, John. *History, Manners, and Customs of the Indian Nations Who Once Inhabited Pennsylvania and the Neighboring States*. Philadelphia, 1819. Reprint. New York: Arno Press, 1971.

An Historical Sketch of the Congregational Church, Stockbridge. Stockbridge, Berkshire County, Mass., 1888.

History of Berkshire County, Massachusetts, with Biographical Sketches of Its Prominent Men. 2 vols. New York: J. B. Beers & Co., 1885.

Hopkins, Rev. Samuel. *Historical Memoirs, Relating to the Housatunnuk Indians: or, An Account of the Methods used, and Pains taken, for the Propagation of the Gospel among that heathenish-tribe*. Boston: S. Kneeland, 1753.

_____. *Historical Memoirs Relating to the Housatonic Indians*. New York: William Abbatt, 1911. Reprint. New York: Johnson Press, 1972. [Note: This is a considerably edited version of the 1753 edition cited above.]

Hubbard, Rev. William. *The History of the Indian Wars in New England*. Vol. I. Ed. Samuel G. Drake. New York: Kraus Reprint Co., 1969.

Huey, Paul and Ralph Phillips. *The Early History of Nassau Village 1609-1830*. Nassau, NY: Nassau Free Library, 1976.

Huntting, Isaac. *History of Little Nine Partners of North East Precinct and Pine Plains, New York*. Vol. I. 1897. Reprint. Rhinebeck, NY: A Palatine Reprint, 1974.

Innes, Stephen. *Labor in a New Land*. Princeton, New Jersey: Princeton University Press, 1983.

Jackson, Joseph. *American Colonial Architecture*. Philadelphia: David McKay Co., 1924.

Jameson, J. Franklin, ed. *Narratives of New Netherland 1609-1664*. Charles Scribner's Sons, 1909. Reprint. New York: Barnes and Noble, Inc., 1967.

Johnson, Eric S. *Discovering the Ancient Past at Kampoosa Bog, Stockbridge, Massachusetts*. Amherst, Mass.: University of Massachusetts Archeological Services, 1996.

Johnson, Sir William. *The Papers of Sir William Johnson*. Albany: The University of the State of New York, 1957.

Jones, Electa Fidelia. *Stockbridge, Past and Present*. Springfield, Mass., 1854.

Joseph, Stanley. "The Yorker, Van Valkenburgh." *de Halve Maen Magazine*. Vol. lxiii, No. 2. The Holland Society, New York, (1990): 4-8.

Karner Brook Watershed: A Proposal for Nomination as an Area of Critical Environmental Concern. Northampton, Mass.: Massachusetts Office of Environmental Affairs, 1991.

Kaufmann, Kenn. *Lives of North American Birds*. Boston: Houghton Mifflin Co., 1996.

Keith, Herbert F. *History of Taconic and Mount Washington from 1692 to 1892*. Berkshire Courier, Great Barrington, MA, 1912.

Lafitau, J.F. *Customs of the American Indians Compared with the Customs of Primitive Times*. (1724) Vol. 2. Ed. by W. N. Fenton and E. L. Moore. Toronto: Publications of the Champlain Society 49.

Leder, Lawrence H., ed. *The Livingston Indian Records 1666-1723*. Quarterly Journal of the Pennsylvania Historical Association. Vol. XXIII, No. 1. (January, 1956).

"Letters from John Stoddard," *New England Historical & Genealogical Register*. Vol. XX. Boston: New England Historic-Genealogical Society, 1886.

Loskiel, Rev. George Henry. *History of the Mission of the United Brethren Among the North American Indians*. Germany, 1788. Trans. into English by Rev. Christian Latrobe, London, 1793.

Map Collectors' Circle. Vol. III. London: Durant House, 1966.

McDermott, William, ed. *Eighteenth Century Documents of the Nine Partners Patent, Dutchess County, New York*. Vol. X. Collections of the Dutchess County Historical Society. Baltimore, Maryland: Gateway Press, 1979.

Miles, Lion. "The Red Man Dispossessed," in *The New England Quarterly*, Vol. 67, no. 1 (March 1974): 46-76.

_____. "The Stockbridge Indian Massacre Continued." *Journal of the Native American Institute*. Vol. 2, No. 1 (Winter 1999): 1-7.

Moeller, Roger, ed. "Some Thoughts on Late Woodland Ecology," *Journal of Middle Atlantic Archeology*. Vol. 12 (1996): 61-66.

Morrill, William F. "The Spur at the Heel of the Manor." *The Livingston Legacy*. Ed. Richard T. Wiles. Bard College, 1987: 38-66.

Munsell, J., ed. *The Annals of Albany*. 10 vols. Albany: Joel Munsell, 1850-1859.

New York State. *New York at the Jamestown Exhibition*. (Exhibit catalog prepared by Cuyler Reynolds, Norfolk, Virginia, 1907). Albany: J. B. Lyon Company, 1909.

O'Callaghan, E. B. ed. *Calendar of Indorsed Land Papers (New York Colonial Manuscripts)*. 1864. Reprint. Harrison, New York: Harbor Hills Books, 1987.

O'Callaghan, E. B., ed. *Documentary History of the State of New York*. 4 vols. Albany: Weed, Parsons & Co., 1849-1851.

O'Callaghan, E. B. and others, eds. *Documents Relative/Relating to the Colonial History of the State of New York*. 15 vols. Albany: Weed, Parsons & Co., 1853-1857.

Oerter, Maurice Frederick. *A Book of Remembrance, The Tragedy of Gnadenhutten*. Gnaden-hutten Sesqui-Centennial Committee of the Ohio State Archeological and Historical Society: 1932.

Old Fort Hunter and Queen Anne Chapel. Comp. Edward J. Sheehan. St. Johnsville, NY: Improved Order of Red Men and Degree of Pocahontas, 1937.

Old Miscellaneous Records of Dutchess County. (The Third Book of the Supervisors and Assessors). Poughkeepsie, NY: Vassar Brothers' Institute, 1911.

Orcutt, Samuel. *The Indians of the Housatonic and Naugatuck Valleys*. Hartford, Connecticut: 1882.

Pettee, Julia. *The Rev. Jonathan Lee and His Eighteenth Century Salisbury Parish: The Early History of the Town of Salisbury, Connecticut*. Salisbury, Conn.: The Salisbury Association, Inc., 1957.

Piwonka, Ruth. *A Portrait of Livingston Manor 1686-1850*. Friends of Clermont, 1986.

_____. *Historic Resources in the Town of Kinderhook; A Reconnaissance Survey*. Town of Kinderhook, New York, 1989.

Pope, Franklin Leonard. *The Western Boundary of Massachusetts*. Pittsfield, Mass., 1886. Pittsfield, Mass.: Berkshire Family History Association Reprint, 1994.

Preiss, Lillian E. *Sheffield, Frontier Town*. North Adams, Mass.: Sheffield Bicentennial Committee, 1976.

Quinney, John. "Celebration of the Fourth of July, 1854." *Wisconsin Historical Society, Collections*. Vol. 4/5 (1858): 313-320.

Rawls, Walton H., ed. *The Century Book of the Long Island Historical Society*. New York: The Long Island Historical Society, 1964.

Reed, Newton. *Early History of Amenia*. Amenia, NY: De Lacey and Wiley, Printers, 1875.

Reichel, William C. *Memorials of the Moravian Church*. Volume I. Philadelphia: J. B. Lippincott & Co., 1870.

Richter, Daniel K. "Rediscovered Links in the Covenant Chain: Previously Unpublished Transcripts of New York Indian Treaty Minutes, 1677-1691." *Proceedings of the American Antiquarian Society*. Volume 92, Part I. Boston: April 21, 1982, pp. 45-85.

Ruttenber, E.M. *History of the Indian Tribes of Hudson's River*. Albany, NY: J. Munsell, 1872.

Sedgwick, Charles F. *A History of the Town of Sharon, Litchfield County, Conn., From Its First Settlement*. Hartford, Conn., 1842.

_____. *General History of the Town of Sharon, Litchfield County, Conn., From Its First Settlement*. Second Edition. Amenia, NY: Charles Walsh, Publisher, 1877.

_____. *General History of the Town of Sharon, Litchfield County, Conn., From Its First Settlement*. Third Edition. Amenia, NY: Charles Walsh, Publisher, 1898.

Skinner, Alanson. "Notes on Mahikan Ethnology." *Bulletin of the Public Museum of the City of Milwaukee*. Vol. 2, no. 3 (January 20, 1925).

Smith, de Cost. *Martyrs of the Oblong and Little Nine*. Caldwell, Idaho: Caxton Printers, Ltd., 1948.

Smith, James H. *History of Dutchess County, New York, with Illustrations and Biographical Sketches*. (1882) Reprint. Interlaken, NY: Heart of the Lakes Publishing, 1980.

Smith, J. Michael. *Wappinger Land Transfers, 1680-1737: Social Political Interaction Between Hudson Valley Indian Proprietors*. Hudson, NY: Research Journal of the Native American Institute, 1999.

Smith, Peter. "Indian Personal Name Entries in Peter Smith's Indian Blotter," *New York History*. Vol. 28. Cooperstown, NY: State Historical Association, 1947, pp. 466-469.

Snow, Dean. "The Architecture of Iroquois Longhouses," *Northeast Anthropology*. No 53 (Spring, 1997), pp. 61-84.

Speck, Frank. "The Mohegan Indians," *Anthropological Papers of the American Museum of Natural History*. Vol. III. New York: Hudson-Fulton Publication, 1909.

Stocker, Harry Emilius. *A History of the Moravian Church in New York City*. New York City, 1922.

Stokes, I. N. Phelps. *The Iconography of Manhattan Island*. Vol. 2. New York: Robert H. Dodd, 1916.

Strickland, William. *Journal of a Tour in the United States of America 1794-1795*. New York: New-York Historical Society, 1971.

Taylor, Charles. *History of Great Barrington, Berkshire County, Massachusetts*. Great Barrington, Mass.: Clark W. Bryan & Co., 1882.

Van der Donck, Adriaen. *A Description of the New Netherlands*. Ed. Thomas F. O'Donnell. Syracuse University Press, 1968.

Van Laer, A. J. F. trans. and ed. *Van Rensselaer-Bowier Manuscripts*. Albany: University of the State of New York, 1908.

Van Laer, A. J. F., ed. and Jonathan Pearson, trans. *Early Records of the City and County of Albany*. 4 vols. Albany: University of the State of New York, 1869-1919.

Wadsworth, Benjamin. "Wadsworth's Journal." *Collections of the Massachusetts Historical Society*. (Vol. 31 or Vol. 1 of the Fourth Series), pp. 102-110.

Walling, Richard. *Death in the Bronx*. Hudson, NY: Native American Institute, 1999.

Westmeier, Karl-Wilhelm, *The Evacuation of Shekomeko and the Early Moravian Missions to Native North Americans*. Lewiston, NY: Edwin Mellen Press, 1994.

Wheeler, Rachel Margaret. *Living Upon Hope: Mahicans and Missionaries, 1730-1760*. UMI Dissertation Services, 1998.

(Williams, Roger). *What Cheer, Netop! Selections from a Key Into the Language of America*. Ed. R. W. Haffensreffer. Bristol, Rhode Island: Brown University, Museum of Anthropology, 1986.

Wolley, Charles. *A Two Years' Journal in New York [1678-1680]*. 1902. Reprint, Harrison, NY: Harbor Hill Books, 1973.

Wood, William. *New England's Prospect*. Amherst, Mass.: University of Massachusetts Press, 1977.

Wraxall, Peter. *An Abridgement of the Indian Affairs*. Cambridge: Harvard University Press, 1915.

Wright, Harry Andrew, ed. *Indian Deeds of Hampden County*. Springfield, Massachusetts: 1905.

Wyss, Hilary E. "Historical Memoirs: Stockbridge, New Stockbridge and the Nostalgia of Conversion." Chapter Three. Stockbridge Library Historical Collection.

Zeisberger, David. *History of the North American Indians*. Eds., Archer Butler Hulbert and William Nathaniel Schwarze. Marietta, Ohio: Ohio State Archeological and Historical Society, 1910.

Appendix A:
Recorded Land Transactions

Note: Since *The Mohicans and Their Land 1609-1730* was published in 1994, additional Indian deeds given in Mohican territory prior to 1730 have come to light. These early deeds are included here, as well as many deeds dating from 1730 to 1818. For the previous list of Mohican land transactions, see Appendix A of *The Mohicans and Their Land 1609-1730*.

No. 1, June 27, 1666, Columbia County, NY
LOCATION: "two hundred acres of meadow called Nehuseke or Nenewoskeek along the Seepus (stream), Kinderhook." Maps show a large tract including the whole of Stuyvesant Landing with a river front about one mile, going the same width inland a little southeast about three miles to the Van Alstyne neighborhood. (Collier, *A History of Old Kinderhook*, p.46; New York Archives, Land Papers, Vol. 1: 11, not listed in the *Calendar*) PURCHASER: Thomas Powell and others.
PAYMENT: unknown.
INDIANS INVOLVED: Taukamakeheke.

No. 2, May 9/19, 1667, Columbia County, NY
LOCATION: land called by the Indians "Machack koeske" lying on both sides of the Kinderhook Creek south of Valatie, bounded on the south by a creek at the present Luykas Van Alen House Historic Site. (Piwonka, *Historic Resources in the Town of Kinderhook*, 78, 86; NYSL, Manuscripts and Special Collections, Mss. Kinderhook Deeds) PURCHASER: Evert Luycasse, Jan Hendrickse de Bruyn, Dirk Wessels Ten Broeck, Pieter Van Alen.
PAYMENT: 5 kettles, 3 guns, 5 cloth garments, 50 fathom seawant, 6 axes, 6 adzes, 6 bars of lead, and 4 cupped handfuls of gunpowder.
INDIANS INVOLVED: Awequen, and his brother, Machackmatock Wissiau, and their blood relations. Indian witnesses were Mahasock, alias David, and Cawennenock.

No. 3, December 26, 1672, Greene County and Albany County, NY
LOCATION: land along the Hudson River, extending twelve miles inland, for the Coeymans Patent. (NYHS, Mss., Van Rensselaer, Killian) PURCHASER: Barent Pieterse Coeymans.
PAYMENT: unknown.
INDIANS INVOLVED: Maghsapeet (Mahakniminaw) in the name of Brownis, Caekonapit, NahontNarmoes, Janaman, and Tielhuysem. For names of relations, see August 22, 1709.

No. 4, July 28, 1688 (Patent Date), Dutchess County, NY
LOCATION: A tract of land lying at Red Hook on the east side of Hudson's River, opposite Magdalen Island, beginning at a creek called Matambesom. (*Calendar of Land Papers*, pp. 35, 71, 747) PURCHASER: Peter Schuyler.
PAYMENT: not known.
INDIANS INVOLVED: not known.

No. 5, July 7, 1697, Columbia County, NY
LOCATION: a piece of land "on Roeloff Jansens Kill a Litle above the farm Belonging to said Robt Livingston where Johannes Dyckman now Lives with all the Right and title that wee the said My Lady and Manhagh have or hereafter might Claime to as farr as the said Robt Livingston's Patent for the Said Roeloff Jansens Kill extends." Another source describes this land as extending south of the Roeloff Jansen Kill. Robert Livingston wrote that "I have an Indian deed of the Squas MyLady and Manhagh dated the 7th day of July, 1697." (NYSL, Livingston Papers, Microfilm, Vol. 18: 27; Brooklyn Historical Society, Livingston Family Papers; Rawls,

Century Book, p. 53; the signatures are pictured in Grumet, *The Lenapes*, p. 46) PURCHASER: Robert Livingston.
PAYMENT: two fathoms of duffels, some powder, shot, and rum for Tsioas and his brother.
INDIANS INVOLVED: Mylady (woman), Manhagh (woman), Goose, Tsioas, son of Manhagh, and his brother, Winnigh Po. The two women drew rectangular human figues for their signatures. Witness was "Pennonack a Westenhook Indian." On August 14, 1697, in an addendum to this deed Goose declared that he was present at the sale of the above land to Robert Livingston who purchased all the land to the high hills, and that he was employed by the two women as agent to dispose of the land to Livingston. See also April 19, 1725, below.

No. 6, October 1, 1703, Berkshire County, MA
LOCATION: land lying on the Westenhook Creek, from an Indian burying place called Kaphack, on both sides of the creek north to a fall or rift called by the Indians Sassgtonack, into the woods westerly to the bounds of Kinderhook and Patkook, and eastward into the woods four English miles. (Albany County Hall of Records, Deeds, Book 4:272-273) PURCHASER: Col. Peter Schuyler, Maj. Dirck Wessels, Capt. John Johnson Bleeker and Mr. John Abeel.
PAYMENT: 110 beavers and 12 otters.
INDIANS INVOLVED: Tapaset and Pittonack (Pinonock), heirs of the deceased Indian named Mataset, on behalf of others. Witnesses were Mackhataw and Onasakwa.

No. 7, October 2, 1703, Berkshire County, MA
LOCATION: land on the Westenhook Creek, north of the previous purchase, from the falls called Tapgtonak (Sapgtnack, Sassgtonack) and running north on both sides of the creek to another rift called by the Indians Packwack, and into the woods to the bounds of the Colony of Rensselaerswyck and Claverack. This was an unusual contract; the Indians conveyed the land with the understanding the buyers would get a patent for it but reserve it for the Indians. The buyers resigned the lands for the Indians' settlement, until such time as the Indians might be willing to receive the full payment for the lands. (NYHS, Misc. Mss., Peter Schuyler) PURCHASER: Peter Schuyler, Dirk Wessels, John Johnson Bleeker, John Abeel.
PAYMENT: 12 1/2 beavers, six duffel coats and other goods.
INDIANS INVOLVED: Tapamet (Tapaset) and Pinonock (Pittonock), heirs of the Indian called Mataset, deceased, in behalf of Indians called Akamaagkamin (Attamagkamin) and his brother Sokam (Sokaen) and all other Indians with any claim to the land at Westenhook.

No. 8, November 5, 1703, Dutchess County, NY
LOCATION: a tract of 7500 acres near Amenia and Wassaic which ran to a high mountain called Weeputting Mountain, then southwesterly along the ridge of a mountain. (Isaac Huntting, *History of Little Nine Partners*, p. 17) PURCHASER: Richard Sackett.
PAYMENT: not known
INDIANS INVOLVED: Wusumpe, Tamquash, Yong-sing-pom-kin-feet, Occumbus, Wyawaw, and Younghans' squaw on behalf of her sons. "Crays wigwam," a loaf-shaped structure, was shown on the survey map for the patent. The deed was signed in Woodbury, Connecticut.

No. 9, September 3, 1704, Berkshire County, MA
LOCATION: land on a creek called Westenhook, beginning from a falls called Sapgtanok and running northerly on both sides of the creek to another falls called Pachwack, and from there up the creek to a place called by the Indians Squegkanekaneck and Kapakagh, into the woods eastward the whole length four English miles deep, and west to the bounds of Kinderhook and the Colony of Rensselaerswyck. (Albany County Hall of Records, Deeds 4: 311) PURCHASER: Peter Schuyler, Dirk Wessels, John Johnson Bleeker and John Abeel.
PAYMENT: value of sixty beaver skins.
INDIANS INVOVED: Sankhank, Cagkarricseet (Catharickseet), and Wallegnaweek on behalf of all their relations.

No. 10, October 20, 1704, Dutchess County, NY
LOCATION: land in the northeast corner of Dutchess County for the tract known as the Little Nine Partners. The land encircled on the west, north and east the tract purchased by Richard

Sackett of the Indians in 1703. (Huntting, *History of Little Nine Partners*, pp. 8, 19; for date and Indian names see MOA, Box 113, F. 5, Item 1) PURCHASER: Samson Sheldon Broughton, Rip Van Dam, Thomas Wenham, Roger Mompesson, Peter Fauconier, Augustine Graham, Richard Sackett, Robert Lurting and including George Clark.
PAYMENT: not known.
INDIANS INVOLVED: Nopamukqno, Wunnupee, Tisqueake, Tonowoactum. Witnesses were Crays, Promish, Rob'n, Foeshes and Quantamimo.

No. 11, August 22, 1709, Greene County, NY; Albany County, NY
LOCATION: On this date, Indians of Catskill testified in a boundary dispute between Kiliaen Van Rensselaer and Barent Pietersen Coeymans that their chief sold to Barent Pietersen Coeymans on December 26, 1672 land from Jan Bronk's Kill north of Coxsackie north to a marked tree at the middle of Jan Reyers Island (called by the Indians Sietpaghack) and westward the same width as far as his right extended, which was about twelve miles from the river. (Dunn, *The Mohicans and Their Land*, p. 291; NYHS, Mss. Van Rensselaer, Kiliaen) PURCHASER: Barent Pietersen Coeymans.
PAYMENT: the Indians were reported to be fully paid and contented.
INDIANS INVOLVED: Maghah (Magakemmena), alias Maghsapeet, also known as Mahaknimi-naw, sachem of Catskill, deceased, was the original seller, in his own name and in the name of Brownis, Caeukonapit, NahontNarmoes, Janaman and Tielhysem, deceased; he (Maghsapeet) was uncle of some of the testifying Indians and related to the others. Those who testified to this effect in 1709, were: Ambamet (Ampamit, from Schodack), Bononap (Penonamp, Ampamit's brother), Wawanaghea, Nawanaqugheet, Annabesem (a woman), Anekehoes, Nanaquogqut (a woman), Koewama, and Tonwehees (Ampamit's brother). Relationships were detailed in the text as follows: Ambamet was the son of Brownis; Nanaghakea was the widow of Brownis; for Nawanequocheek (Nawanaqugheet), no relationship was stated; Annabesem was the sister of Magakemmena alias Maghshapeet; Anakekoes (Onekehoes) was brother of the said Maghshapeet; Nanaquogkat (Nanaquogqut) was grandchild of Magshapeet; Koewamo, cousin of Maghshapeet; Tonwehees, brother of Ampamet.

No. 12, May 11, 1713, Columbia County, NY
LOCATION: within Livingston Manor, an area called "Gochkomekkok" at Tachkanick, which the Indians had reserved to themselves, was sold. (Referenced in: NYSL, Livingston-Redmond Mss, Roll 10; Livingston Papers, v. 18, Indian Conveyance of Gochkomekkok; Rawls, *Century Book*, p. 63) PURCHASER: Robert Livingston.
PAYMENT: not known.
INDIANS INVOLVED: not known.

No. 13, May 13, 1718, Columbia County, NY
LOCATION: the Mohicans desisted their claim to woodland and meadows on the north side of the Manor of Livingston, close to where Nicholas Jansen lived. (BHS, Livingston Family Papers F.19: 13) PURCHASER: Robert Livingston.
PAYMENT: payment was the cancelation of debts owed to Robert Livingston by a Mohican family group, in exchange for giving up all their claims to land on the north line of Livingston Manor.
INDIANS INVOLVED: Catharickseet, his wife named Nanakem, Nanakem's daughter Mawemeen and her sister Shano, and also her brother, a young Indian named Koehak. The women were accompanied to the signing by several Indians.

No. 14, August 22, 1719, Litchfield County, CT
LOCATION: A tract on the west side of the Housatonic River in the Colony of Connecticut known by the name of Weatauk, now part of Salisbury. "Begining at the falls [probably Great Falls, near present Falls Village] of said river and runing thence up the River to a little run of water which comes into said River thence runing up the Run of Water to a Lake called Kokonhamok [Lake Washinee?] thence runing with a strait line to the end of a hill called Weeatauwash [Wetauwanchu?] thence along the said hill to the first station of said Bounds at the afore

said falls of the said River." (Salisbury, Connecticut, Deeds 3: 504) PURCHASER: William White and Abraham Van Deusen.
PAYMENT: thirty pounds lawful money of New York.
INDIANS INVOLVED: Katrokseet (Catharickseet), Takomp, Conekamow (woman), Jhenem (woman); with Indian witnesses Jhawinon, Sankoonakehek, and Mamanitiseckhan (Shabash or Abraham, of Shekomeko). Guttatomow, a sister of Takomp, signed a quitclaim August 16, 1720.

No. 15, January 27, 1721, Litchfield County, CT
LOCATION: The Mohicans of Weatauk sold the tract south of the Great Falls to Laurence Knickerbacker and another Dutchess County farmer, Johannes Dyckman. Knickerbacker had bought the land from Thomas Welles. The land lay "on the west side of Oussatunuck or Stratford River beginning at the Upper Falls of said River to the southwards of Weatauk thence running along the side of a hill called Wetawanchu by the bounds of the land which William White and Abraham Van Dusen have formerly purchased of the Indians two miles . . .Runing with a straight line to a mile above the falls of a brook called by the Indians Washokastanook thence running south three miles thence running easterly to the aforesaid River thence running up the said river to the first station. . . ." (Connecticut Archives, Towns and and Lands, First Series, Vol. 7, Doc. 245a) PURCHASER: Laurence Knickerbaker and Johnnes Dyckman.
PAYMENT: twenty pounds.
INDIANS INVOLVED: seventeen Mohicans were listed as the sellers: Kenanaquin alias Corlar (Metoxon), Wikacheam, Sakowenakeek, Makmekqueam (woman), Anckaheanawa, Aushewakoheek, Nawes, Janpanetan, Peet, the son of Shuhekan, Mahokhaunt, Naqatoo, Mamauntisekan (Abraham of Shekomeko), Watnakaw, Konohunnawak, Maquaquas, Shuhanemow, Tickanenah, all Indians of the "Nation of the Mohokanders." Signers of the deed were: Kennanaquen alias Corlar, Wikacheam, Sakewenakok (Sakowenakeek), Mamaqueam (Makmequeam, woman), Kanahanwa (Anckaheanawa, woman), Memaquas (woman). Witnesses were four more Mohicans: Pemiote, Shuhekan, Kawetunk, and Bachus.

No. 16, (no date), 1721, Columbia County, NY
LOCATION: Indian release of Waintas. (Referenced in NYSL, Microfilm, Livingston Papers, Roll 10) PURCHASER: Robert Livingston.
PAYMENT: not known.
INDIANS INVOLVED: not known.

No. 17, February 19, 1722, Columbia County, NY
LOCATION: land at Wichquapakhat, near the entrance to the Connecticut spur of Livingston Manor; also a release by Indians of all claims on Robert Livingston. (Referenced in NYSL, Microfilm, Livingston Mss., Vol. 18: 37; in Rawls, Century Book, p. 63) PURCHASER: Robert Livingston.
PAYMENT: not known.
INDIANS INVOLVED: not known.

No. 18, (no date) 1724, Dutchess County, NY
LOCATION: north line of Livingston Patent; the Indians gave a quit claim on the Livingston north line. (Referenced in NYSL, Microfilm, Livingston Mss., Roll 10) PURCHASER: Robert Livingston.
PAYMENT: not known.
INDIANS INVOLVED: not known.

No. 19, April 25, 1724, Berkshire County, MA
LOCATION: land at Sheffield, Great Barrington, and part of Stockbridge and Lee was sold to the committee appointed by the General Court to purchase land on the Westenhook River from the Indians for two future towns. The Indians reserved for themselves a tract running from the river to the New York boundary, south of present South Egremont. (Wright, Indian Deeds of Hampden County, pp. 116-118; Dunn, The Mohicans and Their Land, p. 307) PURCHASER: members of the Settling Committee.

PAYMENT: 460 pounds in money, 3 barrels of cider, 30 quarts of rum.
INDIANS INVOLVED: Conkepot (Konkapot), Poneyote (Poniote), Pota wakeont, Naunausquan, Wanenocow, Naunauquin, Conconaughpeet, Paunopescennot, Covconoseet, Naunhamiss, Sunkhonk, Popaqua, Taunkhonkpus, Tatakim, Saunkokeke, Cancanwap,
Saunkewenaugheag, Manchewanseet, John Vangilder, Ponaskanet.

No. 20, April 19, 1725, Columbia County, NY
LOCATION: land on the Livingston Patent south line: Tsioas, Indian son of Manhagh (Manhaet),
complained that he and his brother received nothing of the goods intended for them in the
sale of land by his mother, Manhagh, and an Indian woman known as "My Lady" in July,
1697. He promised that if Livingston would bestow on him a gift, they would never make any
claim to the land in the Manor. After examining a map, the Indians approved of Livingston's
settling Jan Tys Smith and Frederick Proper at Pachowasit, the land lying above Jurian
Decker's on both sides of Roelof Jansens Kill. Both farmers were present. (BHS, Livingston
Family Papers, 1974.18.F.15) PURCHASER: Robert Livingston.
PAYMENT: Livingston gave Tsioas two fathoms duffles, some powder, shot and rum for himself
and his brother, Winnigh Po.
INDIANS INVOLVED: Tsioas (also known as Shabash and as Abraham of Shekomeko) and his
brother, Winnigh Po. Also present was Gauwanan, the son of My Lady.

No. 21, (no date) 1726, Litchfield County, CT
LOCATION: Richard Sackett, located near Amenia, bought thousands of additional acres from
the Mohicans, much of which was in Connecticut in the area of Sharon, extending within two
miles of the Housatonic River. (Sedgwick, *The Town of Sharon* (1877), pp. 13-14; 1726 date
given in Newton Reed, *Amenia*, p. 15) PURCHASER: Richard Sackett.
PAYMENT: not known.
INDIANS INVOLVED: Metoxon and others.

No. 22, September 7, 1727, Rensselaer County, NY
LOCATION: an island in the Hudson River near Schodack, today's Schodack Landing. This deed
was displayed in an exhibition of 1909. (New York State, *New York at the Jamestown Exposi-
tion*, p. 265) PURCHASER: Jeremiah Van Rensselaer, Lord and Patroon of Rensselaerswyck.
PAYMENT: not known.
INDIANS INVOLVED: not known; one signed with the mark of a horse.

No. 23, June 19, 1729, Litchfield County, CT
LOCATION: A tract lying in the north west corner of Salisbury, at or near the place known by
the name of Weatauk, beginning at the Massachusetts line opposite a pond called Panaheconnok and running southward to said pond and from the pond southward on the high land till
opposite the Great Falls in the Housatonic River, then turning eastward to said falls and from
the falls running southwest with a straight line to a pond called Tautauquanockpaucok and
from the pond west to where the division line between the governments of New York and
Connecticut would be set and running up the said line till it met with the Massachusetts line;
thus, bounded north on the Massachusetts line and east on the lands purchased by the people
of Weataugue (Weatauk) and the Great River and south on the lands purchased by Dyckman
in part and part on Hinman and Knowles or lands purchased by Richard Sackett and west on
the line to be set between the governments of New York and Connecticut. (Connecticut Archives, Colonial Land Records, Vols. 4-5, document 440) PURCHASER: Andrew Hinman
and Thomas Knowles, both of Woodbury.
PAYMENT: 30 pounds.
INDIANS INVOLVED: Matauckson (Metoxon), Sausenauckhege, Muckaneege, Pauqennapeet,
Nanaconett, Neshanees, Indians of Weatauk in the Colony of Connecticut.

No. 24, August 4, 1729, Columbia County, NY
LOCATION: land on a stream that emptied into the Claverack Creek; the tract, beginning at the
beaver dam, ran up on both sides or banks of the said stream as far as Gysbert Shap's pasture
fence. It extended in breadth on both sides to the foot of the hill. The 1729 deed was translated

from the Dutch original in 1762, when a patent was requested. In the 1762 patent, the land was described as beginning on the east side of the Kinderhook Creek by the high falls commonly called Major Abraham's fall, on the bounds of Kinderhook, being bounded "by the Wishto. . ., the Claverocks Creek, the Kenderhooks Creek and on the other side by the Kings woods." The acreage requested in 1762 was 3590 acres, of which only part was represented by the Indian purchase given. (New York Archives, Indorsed Land Papers, 16: 109) PURCHASER: Coenraat Borghart.
PAYMENT: thirty pounds.
INDIANS INVOLVED: Sankiedahock, SankernSchoeck, Wennenaeske (a woman), unidentified Indian witnesses.

No. 25, (no date), 1731, Berkshire County, MA
LOCATION: four hundred acres (possibly 600 acres) lying "between Egremont Plain and North Egremont," within the Indian Reserved Land. (Taylor, *History of Great Barrington*, pp. 79-80; Keith, *History of Taconic and Mount Washington*, p. 23) PURCHASER: Capt. John Spoor.
PAYMENT: 30 pounds and a suit of clothes.
INDIANS INVOLVED: Konkapot and others.

No. 26, (no date), 1731, Berkshire County, MA
LOCATION: a farm of 600 acres on Under Mountain Road "which included Berkshire Hills School" in Sheffield. (Keith, *History of Taconic and Mount Washington*, p. 23) PURCHASER: Dirck Spoor.
PAYMENT: not known.
INDIANS INVOLVED: not known.

No. 27, August 7, 1734, Greene County/Schoharie County, NY
LOCATION: a tract of 2000 acres on the west side of the "Bleuw hills of Catts kill, Bounded along Each Side of the Chawtickignack krick to the Schowherres [Schoharie] crick and along on Each Side of the afore Said Schowherres krick to the nearest falls to Schowherre. . . ." (New York Archives, Indorsed Land Papers 11: 104) PURCHASER: Daniel Denton of Orange County.
PAYMENT: forty-four pounds eight shillings
INDIANS INVOLVED: Sinhow, Kagwap, Namakeme, Pawau, Kehogqua, Aghkeame; Indian witness was Mamtowat.

No. 28, August 7, 1734, Schoharie County, NY
LOCATION: a tract of 2000 acres on the west side of the "Bleuw Hills of Kats Kill, Bounded along Each Side of Chawtickignack Krick to the Schowherres [Schoharie] Krick and then along on Each Side of the Afore Said Schowherres Krick to the nearest fall to Schowherre." (New York Archives, Indorsed Land Papers 11: 105) PURCHASER: Michael Dunning of Orange County.
PAYMENT: forty-four pounds, eight shillings.
INDIANS INVOLVED: Sinhow, Kagwap, Pawau, Namakeme, Kekogqua, and Aghkeame were the native proprietors and sellers. Indian witnesses was Mamtowat. This sale and two others in the area were protested by the Mohawks, who claimed the River Indians had stolen and sold to Daniel Denton, Michael Dunning and Vincent Matthews about 6000 acres of their land. A survey for the land was returned October 5, 1734.

No. 29, November 8, 1734, Greene County, NY
LOCATION: land at Coxsackie, bounded northerly by the west line of the Manor of Rensselaerswyck, southerly by the lands granted to John Bronck and Marten Gerritse Van Bergen, easterly by the Hudson River, and westerly by the high woods called by the Indians Stichtekock. (New York Archives, Indorsed Land Papers 11: 142) PURCHASER: Edward Collins and Thomas Williams of Albany.
PAYMENT: sixty pounds in merchandise.
INDIANS INVOLVED: Mataksin Alias Corler, Amawanck Alias Jan d'backer, Towetemack (woman), Nanamema (woman), Quaemkees (woman).

No. 30, December 24, 1735, Berkshire County, MA
LOCATION: A tract of land situated near Westenhook, bounded by the south side of the road
leading from Jan Van Alstyne's to Westenhook known as Kackpacack beginning at a marked
tree, southerly one English mile, then easterly four English miles, then northerly one English
mile, and then westerly to the place of beginning. (Mss., Dec. 24, 1735 Indian Deed to Jacob
Lansing, Westen Hook, N.Y. (sic), NYHS) PURCHASER: Jacob Lansing.
PAYMENT: fifty pounds in money and goods.
INDIANS INVOLVED: Chienome; Nancusquah (also spelled Nanusquah) (a woman); and Mahitkees.

No. 31, October 22, 1736, Berkshire County, MA
LOCATION: Part of Sheffield: a tract of Indian land at Sheffield was exchanged for land north of
Monument Mountain formerly occupied by a farmer, Aaron Gardenier, from Kinderhook, Albany County, NY. "Whereas the General Court of the Province of Massachusetts Bay, Did
on the 25th and 26th of March 1736 Authorize and Impower. . .[John Stoddard and others] to
dispose of the lands that are reserved to the Housatunnock Indians in the Town of Sheffield
and mentioned in the Committees Report in order to make satisfaction so far as the Same will
go to the owners and proprietors of the land granted by the said Assembly to the said
Housatunnock Indians above the Monument Hill or mountain . . . .for and in consideration
of a right of four hundred acres of land above the said Monument Mountain this day quitted
and released to the government of Massachusetts Bay for the use of the said Housatunnock Indians by Aaron Gardenier of Kinderhook [the Committee] Have Disposed of one fourth part
of sd Reserved lands viz, one fourth part of the meadow or Intervale land reserved to sd Indians and lying by the River Housatunnock which fourth part is sixteen acres of meadow and begins at the Mouth of a Small Brook that emtieth it Self into Housatunnock River Eastwardly,
and is bounded on the South by a west line Drawn from the Mouth of sd Brook which line is
the Northern boundary of Capt. Van-all[styne]s meadow land and from thence it Extends
Northerly between sd Housatunnock River and a Swamp till it makes the quantity of Sixteen
acres And also the Swamp lying between sd Sixteen acres of meadow and the Road that leads
from John Vangilders to Capt. Van-alls[tyne's] meadow Together with one fourth part of the
upland lying between the aforesd Road on the East and a west line Drawn from the Mouth of
the aforesd Brook on the South and a west line drawn from a beach tree which Stands by a
Small run of water at a little Distance South from Green River and at the right hand of the
path at the North East Corner of the hill whereon the Indians lately Dwelt, Extending westward as far as the Town of Sheffield Extends. . . ." Note the reference to the Indian village.
The Committee gave one fourth part of the meadow reserved to the Indians together with the
swamp and one fourth part of the upland to Aaron Gardenier, reserving land for a highway
across the land. (Wright, Indian Deeds of Hampden County, pp. 134-135) PURCHASER: John
Stoddard, Ebenezer Pomroy and Thomas Ingersole, a committee acting for the General Court.
PAYMENT: an exhange of land.
INDIANS INVOLVED: Housatunnock Indians. No individuals signed in agreement for this ex-
change.

No. 32, June 2, 1737, Berkshire County, MA
LOCATION: Tyringham, Monterey, New Marlboro, Sandisfield and part of Otis: a tract of wilderness land in the then county of Middlesex, bounded by the colony line on the south, east
by the Farmington River, north by wilderness or Province land in part and partly on Upper
Housatunock and on the west by Sheffield and Upper Housatunock. (Hampden County Registry of Deeds, Bk. L, pp. 351-352; Wright, Indian Deeds of Hampden County, pp. 138-140) PUR-
CHASER: Nahum Ward and Ephraim Williams. This land was for four townships authorized
by the General Court. The deed was witnessed by John Sergeant and Timothy Woodbridge
and acknowledged on June 12, 1737 by John Stoddard.
PAYMENT: three hundred pounds in money.
INDIANS INVOLVED: John Pophnehounauwok alias Kunkapot, Poniote, Pelawuhkout (Patawuhkont) alias Skannaup, Wenaumpe, Wequagun, Umpeathhow, Naunowsquah, of
Housatunock, Indian planters, and in behalf of Nicholas Mhutkees alias Uhwaunmut (Uk-

waernnuit), Neshawuh, Sauseehhoot, and Aunow waumpummuhgseet. All signed the deed. (These names appeared three times in the deed. Some of them were spelled differently each time. The variations have been placed in parenthesis where they radically alter the pronunciation.)

No. 33, July 11, 1737, Greene County, NY
LOCATION: land near the Katts Kill Hills. The 3,470 acre tract, in the present-day Kiskatom area east of Palenville, began on the north side of a brook called by the Indians Kiskatameneegtack, on the west side "of a high rounde hill called Waweiantepachook." Indian locations in the deed included a pond of water called Hyiastuk and a brook called Napeesteegtock, as well as the brook called Kisktameneegtack. (New York Archives, Indorsed Land Papers 12: 88; 13: 72, 78) PURCHASER: John Poole, Timothy Green and Martin Van Bergen on behalf of themselves and two others.
PAYMENT: fifteen pounds.
INDIANS INVOLVED: the seller was Noch Kaweme. Indian witnesses were: Kagawap, Saheak, and Nesho, all men.

No. 34, July 22, 1737, Greene County, NY
LOCATION: a tract on the east side of the Katts Kill Mountains. Boundaries included trees marked with three notches and other trees marked with capital letters. Also mentioned were the Fly (Vly) Kill, and the Dwoss Kill. The survey of the parcel was done on three days in July in the presence of Nagh Jan. (New York Archives, Indorsed Land Papers 12: 89) PURCHASER: Valentine Herman and Fredrick Rouw.
PAYMENT: twenty-six shillings. A note on the deed says the seller was paid July 22, 1737.
INDIANS INVOLVED: Nagh Jan, native proprietor. The deed notes that one Vallendein (Valentine) Fihrer was sworn to "surely and faithfully in the best of his skill to interpret the within mentioned deed of purchase to the within mentioned Nagh Jan."

No. 35, October 24, 1737, Berkshire County, MA
LOCATION: Part of Egremont: land lying in the Indian reservation. The reservation extended, according to this deed, from a beech tree by Samuel Harmon's land, on the west side of the Housatonic River, running south about three quarters of a mile to a brook and from there west to the foot of Taconic Mountain, and from there about three quarters of a mile north, from which point the line ran east to the place of beginning; one part of this reserved land lay within the bounds of Sheffield and one part extended west beyond the bounds of Sheffield to the foot of Taconic Mountain. The signers gave to their friend, John Vangilder, one half of all the land from the west bounds of Sheffield to the foot of Taconic Mountain, specifically the south half of that section, below a line running west nine degrees north through the middle of the land. (Hampden County Registry of Deeds, Bk. N, p. 574; Wright, *Indian Deeds of Hampden County*, pp. 141-142) PURCHASER: The land was a gift to John Vangilder, a Mohican Indian who had a farm there.
PAYMENT: the land was given "out of love and esteem."
INDIANS INVOLVED: John Pophnehaunauwah (Konkapot), Skannop, and Poniote, all of Housetunnok.

No. 36, October 25, 1737, Berkshire County, MA
LOCATION: Pittsfield: A tract of land six miles square, on the main branch of the Housatonic River, "about sixteen miles northward of the place where Cuncupot [Konkapot] now dwells, and at the place where Unkamet's Road, so called, that leads from Albany to Northampton, crosseth said branch; beginning at said crossing, extending two miles eastward and four miles westward, three miles northward and three miles southward, extending every way from said point until it embraces six miles square of land. . . ." The lease was to extend for nine hundred and ninety-nine years. (Wright, *Indian Deeds of Hampden County*, p. 136) PURCHASER: John Stoddard of Northampton.
PAYMENT: annual rent of six pounds in public bills or its equivalent in silver, payment to be made on the twentieth of October annually, and the lessors to have the right to re-enter and take possession, if payment was delayed twenty-one days.

INDIANS INVOLVED: the deed was signed by Jacobus Coocheecomeek (also spelled Cohqua-
hegameek), Mahtookamin (also spelled Matakeamin) and Wampenum, all "formerly of
Menanoke or the Island in the Hudson below Albany [Moesimus Island, opposite Schodack
Landing], now planters in the Indian Town on Housatonic River. . . ." In a document of Octo-
ber 10, 1738 (see below) the Indian names were spelled as follows: Jacobus Coohquahegameek,
Muhtacomin and Wampanon.

No. 37, January 9, 1738, Columbia County, NY
LOCATION: 1500 acres at a place called by the Indians Petan Nook, [also Petann Hook] east of
the lands patented to Dirck Wessels and Gerrit Teunise, to the north of the patented lands of
the Township of Kinderhook, and south of the patented lands of Jeremiah Van Rensselaer.
The deed mentions the dwelling house of John Van Alstyne and a small brook which spreads
into three branches. (New York Archives, Indorsed Land Papers 12: 124; 15: 188) PUR-
CHASER: Johannis Van Deusen and Johannes Van Derpoel.
PAYMENT: one hundred pounds and a mare.
INDIANS INVOLVED: Sankewenageek (Umpachanee) and Anna, his wife, were sellers. The
boundaries were marked out in his presence. Indian witnesses were Nectionhak and Quaent,
both men.

No. 38, May 20, 1738, Columbia County, NY
LOCATION: a tract on both sides of Kinderhook Creek beginning at a white oak tree marked
with a cross on the north bounds of the Patent of Burger Huyck, John Van Alstyne and oth-
ers near a small brook running out of a pond, and continuing, after several points, to a "White
Oak tree Marked With the Picktor [picture] of an Indian," returning along the boundaries of
Huyck, Van Alstyne and others to the place of beginning. (New York Archives, Indorsed
Land Papers 12: 134) PURCHASER: Johannis Van Deusen and Johannis Van Derpool.
PAYMENT: twenty-five pounds.
INDIANS INVOLVED: Kagkahoot and Wanekenaes.

No. 39, September 11, 1738, Berkshire County, MA
LOCATION: Pittsfield, Lanesboro and part of Cheshire: land to the north of the upper town
(Stockbridge) at Housatunnok, ten miles above the hoplands, extending on both sides of the
Westenhook or Sheffield River six miles and in length along the river twelve miles. (Wright,
Indian Deeds of Hampden County, pp. 143-144; copies also at The Stockbridge Library Histori-
cal Collection) PURCHASER: Jacob Wendell: On May 28, 1735, the General Court at Boston granted to the town of Boston the right to lay out and sell three tracts of land, each six
miles square, in the unappropriated lands of the province. Jacob Wendell, a merchant of Boston, purchased one of these undefined tracts at auction June 13/30, 1737. He then obtained
this tract of Indian land for his proposed town.
PAYMENT: 120 pounds current money of the Province.
INDIANS INVOLVED: "Masinamake *Alias* Solomon, one of ye Mahekander Indians." His name
at the end was spelled Masalamack. Witnesses were Kankepot (Konkapot) and Sankewenageek.
Also witnessing the transaction were Timothy Woodbridge and Aaron V. Dyke.

No. 40, October 10, 1738, Hampshire County, MA
LOCATION: the claim of an Indian who was not present at the original signing of an earlier deed
of October 25, 1737 (see above) for the tract of land six miles square at present Pittsfield was ac-
knowledged, and he signed off, "Having already taken Sufficient security for my part or Pro-
portion of the Annual rents of sd Lands & being entirely satisfied and content therewith. . . ."
The deed "lying on Unkameets also Ketunkameets road leading from Albany to Northamp-
ton. . . " measured from the place where the road crossed the main branch of the Housatonic
River. (Berkshire Athenaeum, Pittsfield, Massachusetts, Indian Deed presented by James D.
Colt, 1889) PURCHASER: John Stoddard.
PAYMENT: his share of the annual rents.
INDIANS INVOLVED: The signer was Maukenenmeet (alternately spelled Moskenamawg else-
where in the deed) "now of the Shawanos Country in the Province or Government of Pensil-

vania. . . formerly of the Place now Called the Indian Town on Housatonnuck river." The Indian witness was Yocon (Yokun).

No. 41, October, 1738, Litchfield County, CT
LOCATION: This purchase was intended to clear the Indian title to lands confiscated from New York owners after the 1731 colony boundary dispute between New York and Connecticut was settled, so that the Township of Sharon could be established. It also included Weatauk (Salisbury) land. According to Indian complaints, the purchase was deceitful and took land they never intended to sell. See text for a discussion of Indian relations in Sharon. (Sedgwick, *History of the Town of Sharon* (1877), p. 15)
PURCHASER: Thomas Lamb, acting for the Colony of Connecticut and the Proprietors of the Township of Sharon. The Township was formed, and lots sold, in October 1738. (Sedgwick, *History of the Town of Sharon* (1877) pp. 17, 31; *Historical Addresses Delivered by Hon. Samuel Church and Ex-Gov. A. H. Holley*, p. 7) PURCHASER: Thomas Lamb, on behalf of the Governor and Company of the Connecticut Colony.
PAYMENT: eighty pounds and assorted victuals and clothes.
INDIANS INVOLVED: "signed by the marks of many Indians, who described themselves as of the Indian nation, belonging to Muttapacuck [Muhheekunnuk]. The name of one of the signers of this deed. . .was Toccunuc." Toccunuc was Metoxen.

No. 42, (no date), 1740, Berkshire County, MA
LOCATION: one half of the Indian Reserved Land remaining in Egremont, near Gilder Hollow, on which Andrew Karner already lived. "The land extended west to the mountain, 860 rods from the west line of Sheffield." The lease was for ninety-nine years. (Massachusetts Archives, Vol. 118, page 567, given in Taylor, *History of Great Barrington*, p. 71) PURCHASER: Andrew Karner.
PAYMENT: the land was a gift.
INDIANS INVOLVED: Konkapot and others.

No. 43, (no date), (1740), Berkshire County, MA
LOCATION: one mile square and fifty acres at Stockbridge over which there was no dispute, sold "about nine years past," was mentioned in the report of a General Court Committee submitted in December, 1749. The one mile square included much swampy broken land, to compensate for which the buyer requested an additional 150 acres. The Indians complained at a General Court Committee hearing in 1749 that some of them had not approved this sale, and that only fifty acres extra, not 150 acres, should be included. Although the sale of the land was without Court permission as required, and there was some question about whether the Indians understood the deed would include the extra 150 acres, yet, as the money was for houses "in the Infant state of the town," and as the buyer, Timothy Woodbridge, had spent "the prime of his life and most of his estate in the service of the Indians," the Committee recommended confirming the land to Woodbridge. (The Stockbridge Library Historical Collection, 73–1.27) PURCHASER: Timothy Woodbridge.
PAYMENT: not known.
INDIANS INVOLVED: nine Stockbridge Indians who had purchased and paid for the land from other Indians.

No. 44, October 18, 1740, Berkshire County, MA
LOCATION: land in Stockbridge about one and a half miles from Houstonic River, being a tract of land surveyed and granted as an equivilant for Jehoikim's meadow, purchased by Ephraim Williams, John Sergeant and others, bounded southerly and westerly on Stockbridge township lines and on all other sides joined to unappropriated lands, "it being four Thousand acres as an Equivalent Laid out and granted by the General Court for the use above." (The Stockbridge Library Historical Collection, m73–1.24) PURCHASER: Timothy Woodbridge, schoolmaster.
PAYMENT: forty-five pounds.

INDIANS INVOLVED: Paul Ompeathow of Stockbridge, and Nicholas alias Tantuhpusseet, Mehmeech (a woman), and Shekaunenuty (a woman), "of Shouanoos [Shawnees] but now Residents at Stockbridge." Witness was Aaron Sonkewenaukheek (Umpachanee).

No. 45, December 12, 1741, Columbia County, NY
LOCATION: a tract called Mawighanunk, to the northeast of Kinderhook, about 15 miles from the Hudson River, beginning by a waterfall on the Kinderhook River, "which said fall is called by the Indians Kasesjewack [for Keesiewey, a Mohican of the seventeeth century] takin[g] in all the lands and woodlands on both sides of the said river two miles on each side thereof to a certain place called by the natives Mogongh kamigh, Then up the southeast branch of the said river to a place called by the natives Mohanack and from thence with a straight line to the foot of a hill called by the natives Wapeem watsjoe and in duch [Dutch] de Karstenge Bergh, always keeping a brath [breadth] of two English miles in each side of the kill till you come by the foot of the said hill called Karstenge Bergh the whole brath of the tract is four English miles. . . ." (New York Archives, Indorsed Land Papers 13: 111, 156) PURCHASER: Stephen Bayard and Cornelis Van Schaack, on behalf of themselves and John Babtiste Van Renselaer, Johannis Van Deusen, Barent Vosburgh and Jacobus Van Renselaer.
PAYMENT: thirty-four pounds current money.
INDIANS INVOLVED: Jeremiah Kagahoot, Waneekenes and Adam Watanikmeth, "three of the Tribe of the Indjans Commonly Called Moheekans. . .proprietors." All were men.

No. 46, April 26, 1743, Litchfield County, CT
LOCATION: At the northeast corner of the town of Salisbury was land which the Indians felt they had not sold (see 1738 deed by Lamb, above). In addition, they claimed additional land around their improvements, as well as 200 acres of woodland, and a narrow strip along the south end of the township obtained (fraudulently) by Lamb in 1738. "After the charter to the Town [Salisbury] was granted, and as late as 1742, the Indians made claim to lands here: and in October of that year, Daniel Edwards, of New Haven, was appointed to purchase of the Indians, two miles square, at the northeast corner of the town, and to deliver to one Tocconuc [Metoxon], two blankets to resign his claim." (Binzen, *Mohican Lands and Colonial Corners*, pp. 119-121; Connecticut Archives, Indian Papers, Series I, Vol. I, Document 246) PURCHASER: Daniel Edwards, of New Haven, for the Town of Salisbury.
PAYMENT: sixty pounds.
INDIANS INVOLVED: The elderly and principal persons at Stockbridge directed Edwards to a family represented by Tautaupusseet, an Indian man who was not present, and an Indian woman called Shekannennoti, his sister, together with a fourteen-year old, Kowannun, child of another brother. The deed for five thousand acres was translated to these two, with the understanding that Tautaupusseet would sign on his return, and witnessed by the Stockbridge Indian elders. The deed was left with Rev. Sergeant, minister at Stockbridge, until Tautaupusseet's return. The two blankets were not given to Metoxon because he was not present.

No. 47, January 6, 1743, Greene County, NY
LOCATION: land called Stighcook (Stighkoke) west of Coxsackie containing 2560 acres, and another tract of 100 acres lying between the river and Stighcook, on the north side of a brook called the Stoney Kill and on the west side of the old Catts Kill footpath. (New York Archives, Land Papers 13: 134, 142; *History of Greene County* p. 240) PURCHASER: Casparis Bronck and Hendrick Remsen. In addition, Gerrit Van Bergen and Martin Van Bergen were applicants on the license to purchase of 9 April 1742.
PAYMENT: goods to the value of thirteen pounds ten shillings.
INDIANS INVOLVED: Hermain Backer, Tawightamow (woman), Kowghan (woman), Aquahannit, Tantaghoes.

No. 48, August 7, 1744, Berkshire County, MA.
LOCATION: Richmond and part of Lenox: the tract began at the northeast corner of Stockbridge township and from there ran east to the Housatonic River, north along the river to the south bounds of Poontoosuck (Pittsfield) township. It was bounded on the north by the township

line as far as it ran, and the same line was to be continued west until it came to the dividing line between the province of Massachusetts Bay and New York, then south as far as the northwest corner of Stockbridge, then east along the north line of Stockbridge until it came to the beginning. Excepted out of the tract were parcels purchased by Ephraim Williams and Timothy Woodbridge. (Hampden County Registry of Deeds, Bk Q, pp. 88-89; Wright, *Indian Deeds of Hampden County*, pp. 145-147) PURCHASER: Jocom (Jehoiakim) Yocon and Mohtockaumum, both of Stockbridge.

PAYMENT: twelve pounds New York money.

INDIANS INVOLVED: John Neekkuchewohkaumun and Tushauneak were the sellers. Witnesses were Aaron Sonkewenenaukheek (Umpachanee) and Solomon Waunaupaugus, Timothy Woodbridge, schoolmaster, and John Wauwaumpequunnaunt.

No. 49, September 1, 1745, Greene County, NY
LOCATION: land lying on "the southside of the Land of Jeremiah Van Rensselaer, Esq., of Boath sids of Cats Cils [Creek] Called in the comon. Its Begening Easterly one quarter of an english mile of an Injon [Indian] wigguam where one Injon named Corler, or Commonly By the natifs, Metoxson, now livfs'in. So westerly one inglish mile on or about north tow [two] Inglish miles thence about Easterly one inglish mile then about Suther [southerly] by two Inglish miles." (New York Archives, Indorsed Land Papers, 14: 9) PURCHASER: Hendrick Remsen.

PAYMENT: goods and chattels to the sum of six pounds.

INDIANS INVOLVED: Teweghtemap (woman), Sinhuw, Quisquantan, Kaghawap, Chapekewak, and Panquammage were listed at the beginning of the document. The names were spelled as follows at the end of the deed next to the Indians' marks: Sinhow, Quisquatom, Kagkewap, Pamquammage, Golwamagh, Chapekewogh.

No. 50, November 4, 1745, Berkshire County, MA
LOCATION: Part of Lee or Lenox: a tract of land at a place called Housatunnok bounded west by lands of Ephraim Williams and the Rev. Stephen Williams, and east partly on the Housatonic River, "it being a grant made by the general court of this Province to the sd Laribee of five Hundred acres the same has been Surveyed and a plan Returned unto the General Court and accepted. . . ."(Wright, *Indian Deeds of Hampden County*, pp. 147-148) PURCHASER: John Laribee of Boston. This 500 acres was apparently granted without a specific site; Laribee had negotiated with the Mohicans for some of their unsold territory.

PAYMENT: fifteen pounds.

INDIANS INVOLVED: John Konkopot alias Pophnehonauwoh of Stockbridge. He described himself as the sole owner; he signed, as usual, with the track of a single turkey foot.

No. 51, May 16, 1747, Litchfield County, CT
LOCATION: The Indians at Wequadnach (Sharon, Connecticut) petitioned for recognition of their village tract, which they claimed they had never sold, and protested incursions by proprietors and squatters. (Connecticut Archives: Indian Papers, Series 2, Vol. 2, document 103) PURCHASER: none involved

PAYMENT: this was not a sale; no payment was involved.

INDIANS INVOLVED: signers of the petition were Sauchewawaha alias Benjamin, Timothy alias Cowpoise, Umpawahanit alias Jonathan, Ackawahanit alias Bartholomew, and Tsacoke alias David. Their English lawyer was William Spencer.

No. 52, December 5, 1748, Greene and Albany counties, NY
LOCATION: two tracts, southward of lands of Jeremiah Van Rensselaer, near lands of Johannis Holenbeck: one of 590 acres began "on the north side of Catts kill [creek] where a small Run of water falls off a steep bank of rocks on the south end of a piece of Low Land & opposite to a Point of Land made by a short Turn of the sd Cats kill. . ." with a piece across the Catskill; the second tract of 1500 acres began on the south side of the Catskill creek where the Shingle Kill entered it and extended beyond a point where a stream called by the Indians Naghtenak entered the Catskill. (New York Archives, Land Papers 14: 18, 20, 26, 32) PURCHASER: Henry Remsen.

PAYMENT: goods to the full value of forty-five pounds.

INDIANS INVOLVED: Tewightemow (woman), Squans, Naghkawiment, Kaghawap, Abraham, Arrent (possibly Metoxon?) and Otiwigh (woman). Marten Van Bergen certified that Jan Hallenbeck interpreted the deed to the best of his skill to the Indians and that the goods were given to them in his presence. Antony Kag, Pet Tap, and Lenard Larke were Indian witnesses.

No. 53, December 9, 1748, Greene County, NY

LOCATION: November 27, 1747, a license was given to purchase a tract of "vacant land as yet unpurchased of the Native Indian proprietors thereof," north of lands near the Catskill patented to Francis Salisbury, Marte Van Bergen and others. The land was "Adjoining on the South Line of the Mannor of Renselaerswyck and bounded on the West by the Blue [Catskill] Mountains, having on the East Coghsaghy (Coxsackie) Containing about Six Thousand Acres Which your Petitioners being desirous to purchase in his Majesty's Name In Order to enable them to obtain his Majesty's Letters Patent for Four Thousand Acres thereof." (New York Archives, Land Papers: 14: 17) Subsequently, a tract to the northward of Catskill belonging to Salisury and Van Bergen was surveyed and purchased. "This said Tract Begins in the north bounds of said lands or Patent of Salisbury and Van Berghen one Chain to the Eastward of where sd north bounds Crosses a Creek or brook Called Poeteek's Creek & Runs from thence North Ten Degrees west Twenty five Chains to the most southerly Corner of a tract of Land Granted to the said Casparis Bronk & then along the sd Tract North fifty degrees West one Hundred & Sixty chains. . . ." The tract, which continued where a small run of water fell into the creek and ran down the Catskill to the lands of Salisbury and Van Bergen, grew to 8,000 acres. The surveyor of the above tract, Cadwallader Colden, Jr., wrote "That as the weather was cold the Indian owners would not go themselves to see it Surveyed but Sent five of their young Indians who see it marked out conformable to the Bounds set forth in the deed." (New York Archives, Indorsed Land Papers 14: 27, 34, 39) PURCHASER: Abraham and William Salisbury, and Casparis Bronk.

PAYMENT: forty pounds current money.

INDIANS INVOLVED: Squans, Naghka, Penenenit, Tewightamow (woman), Abraham, Nanemogh (woman). Witnesses were Arrent (possibly Metoxon), Peet Rap, and Lark Lenard. Marten Van Bergen certified that Teunis Van Vaghten was sworn to "Interpret trully and faithfully According to the best of his skill between the Indians & Purchasers." Both Van Bergen and Colden, the surveyor, certified that the Indians received twenty pounds of the money and acknowledged they had formerly received the like sum.

No. 54, June 9, 1750, Berkshire County, MA

LOCATION: Peru and parts of Cummington, Dalton, Hinsdale, Middlefield, Washington and Worthington: a tract beginning at the southeast corner of Poontoosuck (Pittsfield) and from there running east nineteen degrees and twenty minutes south until it comes to Westfield River, then running north six and a half miles up the river, then running west nineteen degrees and twenty minutes north until the line meets the northeast corner of Poontoosuck, and from there bounded on the east side of Poontoosuck to the place of beginning. (Hampden County Registry of Deeds, Bk. 1; Wright, *Indian Deeds of Hampden County*, pp. 149-150) PURCHASER: Johannis Mtoksin, Gentleman, a Mohican of Stockbridge.

PAYMENT: five hundred pounds New York money.

INDIANS INVOLVED: The sellers were Benjamin Kewnonaunaunt "ye Indian King" (chief sachem of the Mohicans at the time), Jehoiakim Yokim, Peter Pophqumnaupeet and Robert Nungkauweaunt, all of Stockbridge, Gentlemen. Witnesses were Isaac Wnaupey and David Nauneknick.

No. 55, November 25, 1750, Greene County, NY

LOCATION: a tract containing 4530 acres adjoining the patent of the Great Flatts or Lonenburgh [Athens]. The land ran from a point north of Joachim Janse's house near the Old Catskill Footpath inland to Poteck Creek and upward along the creek to land of Abraham and William Salisbury and Casparus Bronck, then to the corner of land of Casparus Bronck, then to land of Mattys Hoogteling, and back to the Lonenburg Patent. (New York Archives, Indorsed Land Papers 14: 64, 91, 95, 103, 105) PURCHASER: Jacob Roseboom, John Jacobus Roseboom, and John G. Roseboom.

PAYMENT: not known.
INDIANS INVOLVED: not known; the Indian deed was presented to the Council but is not included in the Land Papers file.

No. 56, October 17, 1750, Greene County, NY
LOCATION: a tract of 3408 acres south of Rensselaerswyck, "beginning by lands pattented to Henry Lane and Hendrick Remsen on the west side of Kats Crik [Catskill Creek] thirteen Chain downstream of Kats Crik from where a crik called Matenit falls into Kats crik, whereon now stands a sawmill of Henry Lane and Hendrick Remsen, thence East across Kats Crik to Lands of Abraham Salsbury and Company thence along patented lands to Kats Crik where it joyns Ranselor [Rensselaer] thence west along the Manner of Ranselor Eighty Chains that breath down Kats Crik to lands of Henry Lane and Hendrick Remsen and to the place where it first begun." (New York Archives, Indorsed Land Papers 14: 86, 100, 111) PURCHASER: Thomas Lane and Joris H. Remsen of the City of New York
PAYMENT: six pounds.
INDIANS INVOLVED: Nagewamet and Teweghtemap (woman). The deed contains a certification by a justice of the peace that the boundaries were inserted in the deed in his presence and that the Indians were actually paid and the deed signed by them in his presence. Capt. William Van Bergen of Cats Kill interpreted between the Indians and purchasers.

No. 57, October 4, 1751, Berkshire County, MA
LOCATION: three acres in Stockbridge with the frame of a house partly covered standing on it. Bounded south by the highway (the street to the Meetinghouse), west by the highway that comes off the hill by the side of Mr. Jones' lot, north by Clerk Pixley's land, and east by the home lot on which stands the house where Jacob Naunompetonk lives. (Berkshire County Middle District Registry of Deeds, Bk. 2, p. 241) PURCHASER: Rev. Mr. Jonathan Edwards.
PAYMENT: thirty dollars or nine pounds.
INDIANS INVOLVED: Ephraim Nunqueen. His name was given as "Ephraim Naunaunquan alias Bockus" in an October 14, 1763 consent to this sale by Joseph Pynchon and John Ashley. Pynchon and Ashley were appointed to investigate Indian land sales, about which there had been complaints, by the General Court of October 5, 1757.

No. 58, December 5, 1751, Berkshire County, MA
LOCATION: eight acres in Stockbridge lying on the street that leads through the plain to the Meetinghouse, together with one dwelling house and barn, bounded eastwardly on land of Mohkhowwawseet. (Berkshire County Middle Registry of Deeds, Bk. 2, pp. 239-240) PURCHASER: Rev. Mr. Jonathan Edwards, minister.
PAYMENT: 100 pounds.
INDIANS INVOLVED: Jonas Etowwauhkaum and James Chenequen, of Stockbridge, hunters.

No. 59, February 15, 1752, Berkshire County, MA
LOCATION: a tract in Stockbridge on both sides of the highway going up the hill from Samuel Brown's towards Col. Williams', bounded north by Samuel Brown, east by land for a road and partly by land lately in possession of Capt. Ephraim Williams, south by land laid out to Solomon Waunnepougos and west by the highway from Brown's to the Meetinghouse. Approved by Ashley and Pynchon. (Berkshire County Middle Registry of Deeds, Bk.2, pp. 237-238) PURCHASER: Rev. Jonathan Edwards of Stockbridge.
PAYMENT: thirty pounds.
INDIANS INVOLVED: Adam Wautonkaumeet, Jacob Cheeksunkun, Bartholomew Aughhunnit, Hannah Quullautowatuk, and Elizabeth Mauchenouwaushguh, Indians of Stockbridge.

No. 60, May 1, 1752, Berkshire County, MA
LOCATION: twelve acres in Stockbridge on the opposite side of the highway from Joseph Woodbridge's farm or settling lot and opposite his dwelling house, bounded north on the highway that leads to the mills, south on the river, east on a small run of water that runs from the street to the river through the westerly part of the land laid out to Deacon Pophquunaupeet's house lot, west at a white oak marked by the road and to run from there to a white oak tree on the

side of the mountain, then to the river to a great stump standing on the bank. Approved by Ashley and Pynchon. (Berkshire County Middle Registry of Deeds, Bk. 2, pp. 237-238) PURCHASER: Jonathan Edwards.
INDIANS INVOLVED: Robert Nungkauwaut of Stockbridge, hunter alias husbandman.

No. 61, July 24, 1752, Litchfield County, CT
LOCATION: The Wequadnach Mohicans gave up their claims and sold their village site. The site was described as a parcel of land in the Town of Sharon containing an estimated fifty acres, "abutting South upon the land said Thomas Barnes bought of Joseph Skinner; North upon Salisbury line; West upon the Pond called the Indian Pond, and extending East so far as to take in all Our improvements in said Township of Sharon, it being the whole of what Land We claim in said Township." (Charles F. Sedgwick, *General History of the Town of Sharon*, (1877), pp. 188-189) PURCHASER: Thomas Barnes.
PAYMENT: fifty pounds.
INDIANS INVOLVED: Nequitimaug alias Moses, and Bartholomew. Other Indians protested this sale.

No. 62, July 28, 1752, Greene County, NY
LOCATION: a tract of 6000 acres southward of the Manor of Rensselaerswyck and on the north side of the Catskill Creek. (New York Archives, Indorsed Land Papers 14: 174; 15: 7) PURCHASER: Teleman Cuyler, Joris Johnson, and Henry Remsen, Jr.
PAYMENT: not known.
INDIANS INVOLVED: not known. The Indian deed, although mentioned, is not included in the document file.

No. 63, May 15, 1753, Berkshire County, MA
LOCATION: land in Stockbridge bounded west by the river, east by land improved by Elias Vanschaack, north by land of Ephraim Williams and partly on land in possesion of said Vanschaack, and south by land belonging to David Naunauneekaunuck, being part of the home lot originally laid out to Richard More, by estimation containing fourteen acres more or less. (Stockbridge Library Historical Collection, m73-1.29 (5)) PURCHASER: The Indian Proprietors of Stockbridge, planters.
PAYMENT: fifty pounds to Ephraim Williams, the seller.
INDIANS INVOLVED: The Indian Proprietors (no Indian names given).

No. 64, June 29, 1754, Albany, Rensselaer and Columbia counties
LOCATION: several Mohicans petitioned the Governor of New york and the Council asking redress for lands they owned which they stated had been surveyed and patented without their having been paid. The lands listed were: a tract of land at a place called Wohnockkaumechkuk, lying east of Mr. Hoffman's and running south some miles (Little Nine Partners patent); a tract at the upper part of Claverack or the south part of Kinderhook; a tract on the east side of the Hudson opposite Albany beginning about two miles from the river and running south until it comes near to the Hudson; a part of an Island called Rensselaer's Island, lying a little below Albany, the "south part of which has never been purchased of any of us"; a large tract of land on the east of Kinderhook and reaching several miles to the east, "which we understand by information is taken up by Mr. Ransler" (given up by Van Rensselaer, this area was later called King's District); and a large tract of land called Tovichchook. The signers implied there were other lands unpurchased: "We have given but general hints reflecting our lands, but Relying on your Honours goodness to see that Justice be done. . . ." An added note at the end of the document affirmed the ownership right of the signers: "We underwritten being old men and acquainted with the rights and claims of the Muhheekkaunuck tribe of Indians witness that the persons prefering this petition are the owners of the lands (by decent [descent] and native right) that are set forth in this petition." (New York Archives, Land Papers 15: 110) PURCHASER: none.
PAYMENT: none; this document is not a sale.
INDIANS INVOLVED: The signers were Thomas Sherman, Peter Pophqumnaupeet, Johoiakim Yokum, Jacob Checksonkun, Mohkhowwauweet, and Sausseekhoot. Signers of the added

note at the end were: John Pophnehonnoksook, Adam Wantonkuhmett, Khusquauntaum, Solomon Wannumpaugus, and David Nannauneckkaunuck.

No. 65, February 19, 1755, Berkshire County, MA
LOCATION: a triangular parcel of five acres in Stockbridge on the north side of Housatunnock River between Jonathan Edwards' dwelling house and the river. Bounded south and southwest by the river, eastwardly by land belonging to Mahwaweet or his wife Wawneneeme, north-wardly and northwesterly by the brow of the meadow hill which is between Housatunnok River and the highway that leads to the meetinghouse, coming to a point westwardly by the meeting of the river and hill. (Berkshire County Registry, Middle District, Deeds, Bk. 2, pp. 234-235) PURCHASER: Jonathan Edwards.
PAYMENT: 10 pounds 2 shillings and six pence.
INDIANS INVOLVED: Jehoiakim Shawwanunn (Sawanun) of Stockbridge.

No. 66, September 25, 1755, Berkshire County, MA.
LOCATION: a small tract in Stockbridge, being the north part of a lot laid out to John Skushawmh, a Stockbridge Indian. The lot lay in the southerly part of the township on the east side of the Road leading from Stockbridge to Sheffield, bounded north on land of Stephen Nash, east on Konkopot's Brook, west on the road, and extending southerly as far as to make up fifty acres, the south bounds adjoining the residue of the said lot. (Hampden County Regis-try, Bk. Y, p. 262; Wright, *Indian Deeds of Hampden County*, pp. 151-152) PURCHASER: Joab, a Negro man, a freeman of Stockbridge, and farmer.
PAYMENT: thirteen pounds, six shillings and eight pence.
INDIANS INVOLVED: The land had been allotted to John Skushawmh; he petitioned the Bos-ton General Court for permission to sell part of his land for the support and maintenance of himself and his family. The Court appointed John Worthington to investigate and make the sale on behalf of John Skushawmh, if Worthington approved. Worthington judged it "abso-lutely Necessary" that the land and produce on it should be sold.

No. 67, May 25, 1756, Columbia County, NY
LOCATION: Hillsdale: a large tract intended for a township lying west of Sheffield, beginning at a heap of stones on Taukonnuck (Taconic) Mountain about one mile and a half south of the road from Sheffield to Claverack, then running west five and a half miles, then running north seven miles, then running east five and a half miles, then running south to the heap of stones which marked the place of beginning. The first line from the heap of stones was to vary as might be most suitable for the Township, and the other lines were to be conformed to the first line. (Hampden County Registry of Deeds, Bk. Y, p. 575; Wright, *Indian Deeds of Hampden County*, pp. 153-154) PURCHASER: Robert Noble, Thomas Whitney, Japhet Hunt and John McArthur, living on land west of Sheffield.
PAYMENT: two hundred pounds in money.
INDIANS INVOLVED: Peter Pohquunnaupeet, John Wauwaumpequannaunt, Wepookqshuht, Benjamin Kaukewenoh, Josiah Waumuhhewey. Witnesses were David Naunaunehennuk and Muttuhkummun.

No. 68, June 1, 1756, Berkshire County, MA
LOCATION: Part of Sheffield and Egremont: land situated in and near the township of Sheffield, being the whole of the land that the Indians reserved to themselves in the town, bounded southerly on the line between the Indian land and the third division and easterly on the Housa-tonic River, running from there northerly to the upper side of the land reserved by the Indi-ans and then running west that width to the line between New York Colony and Massachusetts, together with whatever belongs to the freehold. (Hampden County Registry, Bk. Y, p. 379; Wright, *Indian Deeds of Hampden County*, pp. 155-156) PURCHASER: John Vanguilder, a Mohican Indian, described as a husbandman living west of Sheffield.
PAYMENT: the land was given "for the love and affection I have and Do bear unto John Vanguil-der. . .and for many other good Causes and Considerations me hereto moving, as well as Sun-dry Sums of money and other presents."

INDIANS INVOLVED: Noch Namos, "Indian woman now of the Fishkills in Dutches County in the Province of New York formerly of Housatunnock."

No. 69, September 27, 1756, Columbia County, NY
LOCATION: Austerlitz (Spencertown): land lying north of and adjoining a township granted to Capt. Robert Noble and others lying west of Sheffield and Stockbridge (see May 25, 1756). The land conveyed was described as follows: bounded south on the township granted to Capt. Robert Noble and others, beginning at the north east corner of said town and running west seven degrees north to the northwest corner of Noble's town to a stake and stones there, thence north fifteen degrees east five miles one and a quarter and nine rods, thence east seven degrees south six miles and forty four rods thence south to the first mentioned bounds, containing twenty thousand seven hundred and twenty-two acres and a half. (Wright, *Indian Deeds of Hampden County*, pp. 158-160) PURCHASER: One sixth of the tract went to a large number of settlers listed in the deed, and a one hundred and thirty-second part went to the following people, among whom were some of the Vangilder family: Samuel Sedgewick, John Wadsworth, Ebenezer Warner, Eliather Rue, Menis Griswold, Joseph Bailey, Elisha Hatch, William Hambleton, Benjamin Chase, Philip Callender, John Callender, William Whitney, William Spencer, Samuel Lee, David Allen, Joseph Gillet, Milborough Vanvalkemburgh, Jacob Vanvalkemburgh, Henry Vangilder, Joseph Vangilder and Mathew Vangilder. Eleven members of the Spencer family were included and town was called Spencer Town.
PAYMENT: Two hundred and thirty pounds New York currency.
INDIANS INVOLVED: the sellers were Peter Pophquunnaupeet and John Pophnehonuuwoh (Konkopot). Indian witnesses were Jehoiakim Yokun and Isaac Waunaumpeh.

No. 70, October 29, 1756, Berkshire County, MA
LOCATION: Part of Egremont and Alford, described as land west of Sheffield, bounded east on Sheffield, "South on the land called the Indian Land on which John Vanguilder and Andrew Carner lives," (see deeds of October 24, 1737 and June 1, 1756) west by the Township lately laid out to Robert Noble and others, called Nobles Town, north as far as Nobles Town extended, and from the northeast corner of that town to run east to the Stockbridge west line. Large amounts of land previously sold were exempted from the grant: to Timothy Woodbridge, Stephen Kelcey, Ebenezer Hamblin, Ebenezer Warner, John Hamlin, Eliatha Kew, Elnathan Brunson, Robert Watson, Anthony Hopkins, Micah Hopkins, Daniel Kelcey, Stephen Kelcey, Jr., Jonah Fortin, and Simon Cook–that part of the described tract which lay at the north end was to include that part of the tract which these last mentioned persons had purchased of Shouanun and Quinnuhquant, "of which the sd persons have an Instrument under the hands of sd Shouanun and Quinnauquant Describing the Said Purchase." Further, to Peter Sharp the Indian sellers had granted two hundred acres of the tract lying where Peter lived, bounded and surveyed to him, for which Peter Sharp had a conveyance from Shouanun and Quinnauquant. Further, they gave to Isaac Spoor, Cornelius Spoor, Jacob Spoor and Jonathan Nash each five hundred acres to be taken up within the purchase made by their father, John Spoor (see undated c. 1731 deed to Capt. John Spoor, above). Further, they granted to Nehemiah Messenger one eighty-fourth part of the tract. In addition, they sold to a list of eighteen people the one hundred and twelfth part of the tract. (Hampden County Registry of Deeds, Bk. Y, p. 669; Wright, *Indian Deeds of Hampden County*, pp. 161-164) PURCHASER: The multiple buyers were organizing a town. Each was to receive his proportion or share. The long list (not given here) included Samuel Winchel, Jr., John Vangilder, Jacob Vangilder, and Catherine the daughter of John Van Guilder (the wife of Hezekiah Winchel), each to have one sixtieth part of the premises.
PAYMENT: twenty pounds from the first group and an additional 230 pounds.
INDIANS INVOLVED: John Pophnehonnuhwoh (Konopot), Peter Pophnepeet (Pophquunnaupeet), Jehoiakim Yokun, Isaac Wenaumpeh (Waunehowoh, Wauunaumpeh), Quans, Joseph Quinnauquant, Jehoiakin Shonanun (Kouaunun, Shouanun, Kanaunun), and Quanponwos (a woman). Peter Pophnepeet did not sign but was a witness, along with CouauNun (Kouaunun). All were of Stockbridge.

No. 71, March 15, 1757, Columbia County, NY

LOCATION: Copake: a large tract "bounding South on the South Boundaries of the sd Province [of Massachusetts] North on a Line Drawn Parralell to sd Line [and] Seven Miles Distante from sd Province line which is on the Township Sold To Robert Noble & others in part East on the Great Mountain Called Tauconock Mountain (That is the Steep Mountain West on a Line to be Drawn Parralell To Hudson River at Twelve Miles Distance from the River) which sd Tract of Land is Supposed to be from East to West in Length about Eight Miles Exclusive of any Legall Conveyance that have been given by any of Our Indian Ancestors. . . ." This tract and the tract sold to Robert Noble were supposed to be within the boundary of Massachusetts. (Wright, *Indian Deeds of Hampden County*, pp. 165-167; Livingston Records, Indian deed "on which the insurgents first founded their claim,"copy made Sept. 17, 1792, BHS; Hampden County Registry of Deeds, Bk Y, 595; Berkshire County Middle Registry, Bk. 1, pp. 144-147, approved January 19, 1793) PURCHASERS: John Hollenbeck, William Hollenbek, "son to sd John Michael Hollanbeek," Andres Rease, John Rease, William Reas, Jr., Nicholas Reas, Henry Brasee, Andres Brasee, John Brasee, Christoper Brasee, Andres Brasee, the said Robert Hollenbeek, John Hollenbeck, Jr., Richard Hollenbeck, Michael Hollenbeck, Jr., Abraham Hollenbeck, and many other men, including members of the Vanguilder family: John Vanguilder, Nicholas Vanguilder, Joseph Vanguilder, John Vanguilder, jr., Mathew Van Guilder, Henry Vanguilder, Jacob Vanguilder, Andreas Vanguilder, Hezekiah Winchel, Pelatiah Winchel, and Wau Hock Indian; the list included other participants.

PAYMENT: five hundred and sixty one pounds New York money in hand paid and well secured to be paid by John Hollenbeek.

INDIANS INVOLVED: Benjamin Kaukeweneckenaunt, Sachem, and Maukcuwewet, hunter, both of Stockbridge. The deed was signed by these two men and witnessed by: Peter Pophquannaput, Capt. Jacob Cheeksaunkum, Jehoyaim Jackin (Yokun), Lt. Jacobus Naunaughtoneh, Timothy Cowpas, David Wawunmeagkuuh (spelled Naunauneaugknick in Berkshire County Middle Registry of Deeds, Bk. 1, pp. 144-47), Isaac Weanaumpe, Johannes Nahhson (Mtohksin), and Moses Mukhehuenwenget (Nukhihwawweye).

No. 72, March 29, 1757, Berkshire County, MA

LOCATION: Part of Mount Washington: a large tract bounded south by the south bounds of the province, north by a line to be drawn parallel to the south line at seven miles distant from it (which was in part on the township lately sold to Robert Noble and others and in part west on the township that was lately sold at Tahcanock to John Halenbeck and others), east on the top of the first great ledge of the mountain called Tahconock mountain west of Sheffield and of the house of John Vanguilder. (Wright, *Indian Deeds of Hampden County*, pp. 168-169) PURCHASER: John Dibble and others; the tract was to be divided into forty-eight "rights." Some investors had more than one right. Once again, the Vangilders and Winchells, (John Vangilder and his children and their spouses) with Indian connections, were among those listed as participants and granted rights. (Hampden County Registry of Deeds, Bk. 1, pp. 11-12; Wright, *Indian Deeds of Hampden County*, pp. 168-169)

PAYMENT: seventy-five pounds.

INDIANS INVOLVED: Benjamin Kokhkewenaunaut, Jehoiakim Yokun, Jacob CheekSuankun, Joseph Quannukkaunt, and Mokhwauwouweet. Witnesses were Jacob NaunauphCaunk, John Wauwaupequnnaunt, Johannis Mtohksin.

No. 73, April 26, 1757, Berkshire County, MA

LOCATION: contested land (the Gore) west of present West Stockbridge, lying between West Stockbridge and the east line of Spencertown, now Austerlitz. It was bounded south partly by land called the Shauwaunan purchase and partly on land of David Ingersoll and was to extend north as far as the Township of Stockbridge extended. This tract was paid for by people already settled on the land without an Indian deed and by others anxious to settle there. The deed was not recorded until 1774. (Garnett, *West Stockbridge, Massachusetts*, pp. 3-5; Berkshire County Registry, Middle District, Deeds, Bk. 12, p. 28.) PURCHASER: those of whom the Indians demanded payment were: Jeremiah Omstead, Joseph Fleming, Jabez Omstead, William Virgin, James Saxton, Jonah Westover, Abraham Andrus, Japhet Hunt, Peter Ingersoll, and John Mills and John Burgat.

PAYMENT: sixty pounds, New York currency.

INDIANS INVOLVED: John Pophnehonnuwoh (Konkapot) and Jehoiakim Yokun; an Indian witness was Johannis Mtohksin. The Indians promised a deed as soon as the grant was approved by the General Court.

No. 74, April 27, 1757, Berkshire County, MA.

LOCATION: Part of Lee: a tract on the Housatonnic River lying partly on the east and partly on the west side of the river, bounded west by the Stockbridge town line, north partly on the grant of Col. Ephraim Williams and partly on the grant taken up by Capt. Laribee, south on the north line of Upper Sheffield Township, east on the Province's unappropriated lands, containing 1,560 acres. The land had been surveyed and a plan laid out. (Hampden County Registry, Bk. 1, p. 25; Wright, *Indian Deeds of Hampden County*, pp. 170-172) PURCHASER: Issac Winslow, James Bowdoin, Esq., Thomas Flucker, John Smith, Norton Quincy, Jonathan Williams and heirs of John Franklin.

PAYMENT: twenty-eight pounds, ten shillings and six pence.

INDIANS INVOLVED: John Pophnehonnuhwok and Robert Nungkauwot.

No. 75, May 25, 1757, Berkshire County, MA

LOCATION: a tract of country land lying west of Sheffield where Mathew Van Guilder was developing a farm, beginning southwest of Nicholas Van Guilder's by the road that goes from John Van Guilder's to Sheffield at a crotched pine tree, then westward on the fence between Hendrick Van Guilder and Matheus Van Guilder, to the foot of Black Rock Mountain, from there to the northwest corner of David Winchell's land and from there eastward forty rods on the dividing line, then north on the road to the beginning, being 118 acres within Mathew Van Guilder's line. (Berkshire County Registry, Middle District, Deeds, Bk. 12, pp. 134-135) PURCHASER: the land was a gift to Matheus (Matthew) Van Guilder.

PAYMENT: in consideration of the sufferance of Matheus Van Guilder in Albany Goal [jail] paid by twenty stone, "the receipt we acknowledge."

INDIANS INVOLVED: Daniel Nimham, Rhoda Ponoant. Witnesses were David Naunaunecknek and Joseph Shauquethqueat. By the time the deed was recorded, May 30, 1774, Rhoda Poneoat (Ponoant) was deceased.

No. 76, July 4, 1757, Berkshire County, MA.

LOCATION: Part of Alford: land lying westerly of Stockbridge and partly west of Sheffield and joining on the west lines of the two towns, that is, on the southwest corners of Stockbridge and the northwest corner of Sheffield and contained about 1,005 acres. (Wright, *Indian Deeds of Hampden County*, pp. 173-175) PURCHASER: David Ingersoll.

PAYMENT: fifty pounds.

INDIANS INVOLVED: Mokhowwowweet and Joseph Quinnauquaunt, Jehoiakim Yokun, and Benjamin Kockhewenaunt (Kokhwauwweet), all of Stockbridge, are named at the beginning of the deed. Joseph Quinnauquant did not sign at the end of the deed, nor did he appear before the Justice of the Peace to acknowledge the deed. Indian witnesses were Benjamin Kokhhkewenaunt, and Jonas Bkwweiukeuo (a misspelling).

No. 77, May 4, 1758, Berkshire County, MA.

LOCATION: parts of Adams, Cheshire, New Ashford and Williamstown: land on the north side of a new township called New Framingham; the full contents of six miles in width and seven miles in length, to be laid out adjoining on the north side of said township in regular form. The deed specifically freed the purchaser from any encumbrances, suggesting that the money was going directly to debtors. (Hampden County Registry of Deeds, Bk. 1, p. 84; Wright, *Indian Deeds of Hampden County*, pp. 176-177) PURCHASER: Johannis Mtoksin, of Stockbridge, "Indian interpreter and Gentleman."

PAYMENT: two hundred thirty pounds.

INDIANS INVOLVED: Jehoiakim Yokim of Stockbridge was the seller and Johannis Mtoksin, the buyer. Indian witness was Isaac Wenaumpee.

No. 78, November 22, 1758 Columbia County, New York
LOCATION: Canaan: settlement had begun in 1754. Following Indian protests that the land had not been paid for, this deed was obtained from the Stockbridge Indians and recorded in Sheffield. The bounds were described as beginning at a heap of stones about a mile west of Stockbridge's northwest corner and extending north along Pontoosuck's west line to Van Dusen's purchase. The tract of six miles square included a pond on Aspetuch Mountain and the high pinnacle of rocks called Peckquhpan. (Dunton, Anna Mary, *Reflections Canaan, New York Bicentennial 1976*, p. 2) PURCHASER: led by Asa Douglas, the 1758 signers were: Jeremiah Andruss, Gideon Ball, Asahel Beebe, John Beebe, Solomon Beebe, Charles Belding, Augustian Bryan, Jr., Jacob Bunce, Jonathan Chipman, Ozias Curtiss, John Dean, Nathan Dean, Solomon Deming, Asa Douglas, John Ensign, Daniel Farrand, Tim Hallaberd, Joseph Hanchett, Abraham Hollenbeck, William Holmes, Daniel Horsford, Elisha Hurlburt, Samuel Keep, Joseph Kellogg, John Knickerbocker, Jonas Marsh, James Mickels, Samuel Robbins, Zebulon Robbins, David Russell, Elijah Russell, Jonathan Russell, Samuel Russell, Stephen Russell, Andrew Stevens, William Warner, Gamaliel Whiting, Benjamin Willard, David Wright, David Wright, Jr., Elizas Wright, Samuel Wright, and Solomon Wright. Note: These were not necessarily all original settlers, as some land had changed hands even before the Indian deed.
PAYMENT: 250 pounds money of New York.
INDIANS INVOLVED: Isaac Whnaumpeti, Cornelius Nawwaukele, Jacob Naunauhblaunk, Benjamin Kokhkewnauhnaut (also spelled Kokh kow nau nautt elsewhere in this deed), Jehoikim Yokum, Peter Pophquanauput, Johannes Mattocson, and Ephraim Mauttaukumum. Timothy Woodbridge, their adviser, also signed. The deed guaranteed the buyers against further claims and future sales by any Indians.

No. 79, May 24, 1758, Berkshire County, MA
LOCATION: Parts of Cummington, Plainfield, Savoy and Windsor: "one certain township of land. . .bounding Southerly on ye North Side of ye Said Johannis Mtohksin own land[,] the Southwest Corner of said Township to begin Six miles East of a new Township commonly called . . . New Framingham. . .& from thence to run East Nineteen Degrees & twenty minits South Six miles on sd Johannis Mtohksin own land then Turning & runing Northerly Six miles then Turning & running westerly Six miles Then turning and runing Southerly Six miles to the Southwest corner where the bounds first began. . . ." (Wright, *Indian Deeds of Hampden County*, pp. 178-179) PURCHASER: Johannis Mtohksin of Stockbridge, Indian Interpreter and Gentleman.
PAYMENT: two hundred eighty pounds New York money.
INDIANS INVOLVED: Benjamin Kaukewenauhnaunt King of an Indian Tribe belonging to Stockbridge, and Jehoiakim Yokin Indian Planter of Stockbridge. They sold the land to another Indian of Stockbridge, Johannis Mtohksin. Indian witness was Isaac Wnaupey.

No. 80, July 10, 1758, Berkshire County, MA
LOCATION: part of Adams, Cheshire, Clarksburg, Florida, Monroe, North Adams and Savoy: land for two townships, each to be the full size of six miles in width and seven miles in length and each to be laid out in a regular form. The southwesterly corner of the land began at the northeasterly corner of the new township called New Framingham, and from there was to run northerly and easterly to include both the townships. (Wright, *Indian Deeds of Hampden County*, pp. 180-181) PURCHASER: Johannis Mtohksin of Stockbridge, Indian Interpreter and Gentleman.
PAYMENT: six hundred pounds New England money.
INDIANS INVOLVED: Jehoiakim Yokun of Stockbridge, Indian Claimer and Gentleman. Indian witness was Benjamin Kokhkeweenaunaut. The buyer was a Mohican Indian.

No. 81, June 1, 1759, Berkshire County, MA
Location: land in Stockbridge on the east side of the county road leading from Stockbridge to Pontoosuck, being part of the land given to Poniote and others as an equivilent for land lying in Sheffield called the Indian lands. The land was bounded north on the Old Housatonnock Line, east by the east line of Stockbridge, south by land laid out to Shaunaup but lately sold to Timothy Edwards and west by the road, containing thirty-four acres, two roods and thirty-

five perch. (Berkshire County Registry, Middle District, Deeds, Bk. 2, pp. 243-244) PUR-
CHASER, Timothy Edwards, student.
PAYMENT: twelve pounds and nineteen shillings, New York money.
INDIANS INVOLVED: Rhoda Quanponwos and Sarah Dummekonwoh, of Stockbridge, basket-
makers.

No. 82, June 1, 1759, Berkshire County, MA
LOCATION: in Stockbridge near the northeasterly part of the "present Improvements" on the
    east side of the road leading to Pontoosuck, part of a tract given to Shaunaup and others as an
    equivilent for their land in Sheffield called the Indian land, containing about sixty-seven acres,
    three roods and thirty-six perch. The land was bounded by the above road and land sold by Jo-
    hanis Mtohksin to Josiah Jones, Jr., southwardly by the aforesaid lands and land of John
    Konkapot, east by the east line of Stockbridge, and north by land lately belonging to heirs of
    Poniote in the possession of Edwards. (Berkshire County Registry, Middle District, Deeds,
    Bk. 2, p. 245) PURCHASER: Timothy Edwards.
PAYMENT: 49 pounds and three pence, New York money.
INDIANS INVOLVED: Johannis Mtohksin, Interpreter, of Stockbridge, and Isaac Waunaumpoh.

No. 83, July 25, 1759, Berkshire County, MA
LOCATION: a lot in Stockbridge, bounded north by a lot laid out to Solomon Wunnaubaugin,
    westerly and southerly by a lot laid out to John Wauwaumpeguunnaunt, deceased, now in the
    possession of the deceased's widow, and easterly by land belonging to Deacon James Willson.
    (Wright, *Indian Deeds of Hampden County*, pp. 182-183) PURCHASER: Cornelious Van-
    schaack of Kinderhook.
PAYMENT: thirteen pounds, New York money.
INDIANS INVOLVED: Josiah Muhhuttauwee, husbandman and hunter, of Stockbridge.

No. 84, May 16, 1760, Rensselaer County, NY
LOCATION: land in Nassau and Schodack; the Indians conveyed to Joseph Primmer a tract of
    land north of Hoag's Pond, present Nassau Lake. The future lake area was known as the bea-
    ver dam or the *vly* (marsh), as Hoag's Pond was not impounded until about 1790. The Prim-
    mer Indian deed was in possession of the family as late as the 1880s, but its present
    whereabouts is unknown. (French, *Gazetteer of the State of New York*, 1861, p. 557; Nathaniel
    Bartlett Sylvester, *History of Rensselaer Co., New York*, p. 420) PURCHASER: Joseph Prim-
    mer.
PAYMENT: not known.
INDIANS INVOLVED: a group of Stockbridge Indians; their local chief was Kesh-o-mawck, also
    spelled Ka-she-ke-ko-muck.

No. 85, May 16, 1760, Rensselaer County, NY
LOCATION: land in Nassau village. (J. H. French, *Gazetteer of the State of New York, no publisher,
    1861, p. 557.* Also, Nathaniel Bartlett Sylvester, *History of Rensselaer Co.*, Everts & Peck, 1880,
    p. 420.) PURCHASER: Hugh Wilson.
PAYMENT: not known. The deed has not been located.
INDIANS INVOLVED: "At the time a few families of the Stockbridge Indians were living where
    Mr. Hoag's orchard now stands [west side of present Elm Street, Nassau Village]. They called
    their village On-ti-ke-ho-mawck; and their chief was named Kesh-o-mawck."

No. 85, May 20, 1761, Berkshire County, MA
LOCATION: 270 acres, lying 276 rods north of Stockbridge, 100 rods west of land laid out to
    Timothy Yocun. (Berkshire County Registry, Middle District, Deeds, Bk. 1, p. 194) PUR-
    CHASER: Cornelius Van Schaack.
PAYMENT: 40 pounds.
INDIANS INVOLVED: John Mtohksun and Hannah, his wife: "land given to us the said John
    and Hannah by our late honored father Jehoiakim Yokun in his last will and testament."

No. 86, May 20, 1761, Washington County, NY
LOCATION: at White Creek, land on both sides of a brook or rivulet "Called by the Indians
Tightillijagtihook, by the white People the South Branch of Batten Kill, Bounded on the
south by the Pattent of Wallomsack; on the west by Sawyers and Lansings Purchase, on the
North by Batten Kill and on the East the high mountains." (New York Archives, Indorsed
Land Papers 16:49) PURCHASER: Arent Corlaer and Nicholas Lake, both of New Jersey.
PAYMENT: fifty Spanish Dollars.
INDIANS INVOLVED: Jacob, alias Schenk. He was, according to a statement in the deed, the
only remaining Indian of the tribe of Schaghticoke Indians who all had deserted to Canada.
(The group left in 1754.)

No. 87, August 12, 1761, Berkshire County, MA
LOCATION: fifty acres in Stockbridge, lying on the south of the Orphan House farm in Stock-
bridge, touches Johannis Muttaukson's lot. (Berkshire County Registry, Middle District,
Deeds, Bk. 1, pp. 40-42) PURCHASER: a gift to Rev. Stephen West.
PAYMENT: pursuant to a grant of the Great and General Court: voted by the Indian Proprietors
to the Rev. Mr. Stephen West "to encourage him to settle in the Work of the Ministry in said
Stockbridge."
INDIANS INVOLVED: John Pohnehonnukwok, Benjamin Kokhkewenaunaunt, and Johannis
Mtohksin.

No. 88, December 23, 1761, Greene County, NY
LOCATION: parts of Durham, Cairo, Windham and Greenville, four tracts of land: the first
(1298 acres) began at a waterfall on the south side of the brook called Catskill and was measured from land formerly granted to Henry Lane and Henry Remsen; the second (500 acres)
lay on the west side of the Catskill mountains and was in the Batavia Patent; the third tract (48
acres) lay about eight miles to the west, on the west of a brook called Schoharie Creek, opposite land formerly granted to Vincent Meatheus (Matthews) and others, along the Schoharie
Creek and on the north end of a small piece of low ground called Elks plain, where a small
run of water emptied into Schoharie Creek; and the fourth parcel (295 acres) began at the most
southerly bounds of the tract granted to Vincent Meatheus and others. (New York Archives,
Indorsed Land Papers 16: 106) PURCHASER: William Van Bergen, Marten Gerretse Van Bergen and James Umphrey, Jr.
PAYMENT: fourteen pounds.
INDIANS INVOLVED: Tamphampamet, Panenamet, Nishogkampenine, Canekeskoha, Shepokass (all men). Appended to the deed was the certification by Marten Van Bergen, Justice of
the Peace, that he had faithfully interpreted the deed to the Indians to the best of his ability.

No. 89, July 19, 1762, Berkshire County, MA
LOCATION: one whole right of land in the District of Egremont, beginning at the southeast cor-
ner at a marked white oak tree, then northerly on the highway to Prisclas Smith's land, then
westerly to the foot of the mountain, and from there south to the Indians' land or line. (Berk-
shire County Registry, Middle District, Deeds, Bk. 1, p. 285) PURCHASER: Meray [Mary]
Vangilder.
PAYMENT: fifty-five pounds.
INDIANS INVOLVED: Hezekiah Winchel of Egremont, husbandman, Catrite Winchel, spelled
Catharen Winchel in the acknowledgment. She was the daughter of John Vangilder.

No. 90, August 20, 1762, Berkshire County, MA
LOCATION: thirty-seven acres, north on Joab's land which was land formerly belonging to
Mary, south on land laid out to Ebenezer Poopoonnuck, east on a brook called Konkapot's
Brook, west on the highway from Stockbridge to Great Barrington. (Berkshire County Regis-
try, Middle District, Deeds, Book 1, p. 306) PURCHASER: Elias Willard, Benjamin Willard,
Joseph Willard of Stockbridge.
PAYMENT: 15 pounds.
INDIANS INVOLVED: Mary Wepuckshuh, an aged Indian woman belonging to Stockbridge.
She had petitioned the General Court and received permission to sell the land. The transaction

was supervised and approved by Timothy Woodbridge, the Indians' Justice of the Peace. At this time, Indians could not sell their land without the approval of the General Court.

No. 91, January 12, 1763, Berkshire County, MA.
LOCATION: with exceptions, all the land in the Province, bounded north on the divisional line between Massachusetts and New Hampshire, south by the line between Massachusetts and Connecticut, being fifty miles more or less, bounded on the west at twelve miles east of Hudson's River or otherwise where the dividing line would be established between Massachusetts and New York on the limits west of Massachusetts, and bounded east on the Westfield River, being thirty-six miles in breadth more or less. "Excepting and reserving for our Selves and our Heirs the Town of Stockbridge as granted and patented by [a] former Great and General Court and also a Tract of Land adjoyning to the North part of said Stockbridge bounding East on said Housatunnock River South on the North line of said Stockbridge North on the South line of Pittsfield to run west to the Province of New York Saving to the said Great and General Court Such Tracts of lands as have been heretofore Granted within the last described Tract or parcel of Reserved land." (Hampden County Registry of Deeds, Bk. 4, pp. 833-835; Wright, *Indian Deeds of Hampden County*, pp. 184-187; Berkshire County Registry, Middle District, Bk. 2, p. 172) PURCHASER: the Great and General Court of the Province of the Massachusetts Bay, their grantees and assigns.
PAYMENT: 1700 pounds money of the Province of Massachusetts (reduced from 1800 pounds, see note appended to deed. Because of negotiations, the deed was not recorded until June 20, 1763.)
INDIANS INVOLVED: Benjamin Kokhkewenaunaut Chief Sachem of the Mohhekunnuck River Indian or Housatunnock Tribe, John Pophnehonnuhwoh alias Konkaupot, Jacob Cheeksonkun, David Naunauneekaunuck, Solomon Uhhuhwawnuhmut, Robert Nungkauwot, John Naunauphtaunk, Gentlemen; Johannis Mhtocksin, Interpreter, Mokkhowwowweet, Ephraim Waunaunqueen, Isaac Wepuckshuh, Daniel Poochose, Daniel Quans, Ephraim Paumpkhaunhaum, Timothy Yokun, Joseph Quinnauquaunt, Hendrick Pooponkseet, Nimham, Jonas Etuakom, Daniel Minek, Waunaunmpeh, all of the said Mohheekkunnuck River Indian or Housatunnock tribe, inhabitants and residents of Stockbridge in the County of Berkshire and Province of the Massachusetts Bay in New England, "Hunters and Claimers of the land lying in the Western part of said Province of the Massachusetts Bay from the Great River called Hudsons River on the west part and a River called Westfield River on the East part."

No. 92, April 22, 1763, Berkshire County, MA
LOCATION: 140 acres in Stockbridge, beginning at a hemlock tree 18 perch east of the brook on which Elias Van Schaack and some Indians once began to erect a sawmill. (Berkshire County Registry, Middle District, Deeds, Bk. 2, pp. 143-144) PURCHASER: Elijah Williams of Stockbridge.
PAYMENT: this was a rental lease, although patently intended to contravene the law that Indian land at Stockbridge could not be sold without the approval of the General Court. The seller was "to receive rents and for divers other valuable considerations [*i.e.* his debts] for 500 years," with yearly rent of a peppercorn.
INDIANS INVOLVED: Robert Naungkauwaunt, yeoman, of Stockbridge.

No. 93, January 21, 1765, Berkshire County, MA
LOCATION: a tract in Stockbridge, adjoining the road that goes from Stockbridge to Kinderhook and lies on the west side of the brook on which stands the sawmill built by Deacon Brown and others. (The Stockbridge Library Historical Collection) PURCHASER: Larrance Linch of Stockbridge.
PAYMENT: three pounds.
INDIANS INVOLVED: Margaret, of Stockbridge, widow of Paul Ompeatkhow, deceased. Witness was Solomon Uhhaunnuhwaunnuhmut.

No. 94, February 5, 1765, Berkshire County, MA
LOCATION: this was in form a mortgage for three acres of meadowland lying in Stockbridge, but it was actually a sale, a way of buying Indian land when it was forbidden to do so. The land was bounded west on land belonging to Abraham Naunaumpatonk, north on Great Honnigs

Land, east on land belonging to Jacob Wenaumpey and south on the river, "all of said Lot both Plowing Land and Grass Land. . .for security of said sum of three pounds." The text included a promise "Whenever the way may or can be made lawful to Execute a good Deed of Sale." (The Stockbridge Library Historical Collection) PURCHASER: Elias Willard, Benjamin Willard, Joseph Willard, of Stockbridge.

PAYMENT: debt of three pounds.

INDIANS INVOLVED: the seller was John Naunauhphtaunk (also spelled Naunaumpatonk). Johannes Mtohksin was a witness.

No. 95, September 20, 1765, Berkshire County, MA

LOCATION: a grant of land to be laid out in Stockbridge containing sixty acres formerly granted to Jacob Scautcaw at a meeting of the proprietors, and in part of the right that belonged to Capt. Konkapot, deceased, for surity of the sum of twenty pounds, until the said sum of twenty pounds might be paid with the lawful interest, within two years. (The Stockbridge Library Historical Collection) PURCHASER: Benjamin Willard.

PAYMENT: mortgage of land for twenty pounds worth of good merchantable goods paid by Benjamin Willard of Stockbridge.

INDIANS INVOLVED: Robert Naungkawant (Nungkauisaut) and Jacob Scawtcauw (who signed with turtle), hunters, both of Stockbridge. It is likely Jacob Scawtcaw was Konkapot's son, Jacob, and that Robert was Jacob's brother or son. Note that Konkapot had died. Witnessing the deed was Jacob Cheeksaunkun.

No. 96, (no date), Berkshire County, MA

LOCATION: a tract in Stockbridge. A survey reads: "Surveyed and Laid out to Wautaunkghmeet Alias Unkaumug fifty acres of Land beginning at Waunumpaugus' Northeast Corner & Running from Thence North 16 degrees East fifty Perch & then West 16 degrees North one hundred & Sixty Perch and then South 16 degrees West fifty Perch and from Thence directly to the Place where this Survey first began." (The Stockbridge Library Historical Collection) PURCHASER: the owner was to be Wautaunkghmeet.

PAYMENT: As this was a plot allocated by the Proprietors from the Indian land at Stockbridge, there was no payment. However, Timothy Dwight, the surveyor, was paid for his work. Surveys for the many parcels of Indian land distributed by the Mohican Proprietors were a drain on their finances.

INDIANS INVOLVED: Wautaunkghmeet alias Unkaumug.

No. 97, March 25, 1766, Albany and Greene counties, NY

LOCATION: "Beginning on Hudsons River opposite to the South end of the Island commonly called John Ryerse's Island [Smack's or Shad Island, opposite Bethlehem] lying in the said River and running West from the said River twelve Miles, thence North to the Line of the Colony of Rensselaerwyck thence along the said Line as it runs Westerly to the Schoharie Kill thence across the said Kill to the North bounds of the Patent formerly Granted to Johannes Hardenbergh and others commonly called the Great Patent thence along the bounds of the said last mentioned Patent as the same runs Southwestwardly to the head of the Katers Creek or Kill thence along the said Katers Creek or Kill upon the several courses of the same down to the mouth thereof where it empties itself into Hudsons River and thence up the Stream of Hudsons River to the place of Beginning. And also all the Islands lying in Hudsons River abreast of the last described Tract of Land and in general all other the Lands and Tracts pieces and parcels of lands belonging to our said Tribe in the County of Albany aforesaid or to either of us." This deed ceded to the King all unpatented lands belonging to the Catskill Indians so the Governor, Sir Henry Moore, could grant them to the purchasers. (Van Bergen Family Papers, mss. 14665, Manuscripts and Special Collections, NYSL) PURCHASER: Henry Andrew Franken, John French, John Morin Scott, Joseph Blanchard, Marte Gerritsen Van Bergen, Thomas Synot, William Caine, Hugh Dennison and Daniel Dennison, on behalf of themselves and others.

PAYMENT: fifty pounds from the purchasers and also five shillings representing the King's interest. The sale was made at a public meeting, as required by an order of the King, after complaints of frauds and abuses. The meeting was held at Fort George in the City of New York.

INDIANS INVOLVED: At the beginning of the deed are listed: Agcontioneck, otherwise called
William; Nochquaweemuth, otherwise called Hendrick; Tomhampemet, otherwise called Cornelius; Anaweem, otherwise called John De Backer; Tomhomquameesga, otherwise called
Philip; "being and effectually representing the whole Tribe of the Katts Kill Indians." Signers
at the end of the deed were the above and Weenhop. Signing yet again to certify that they had
received their payment were: Aghcontioneck, Weenhop, Nochquawemuth, Tomhampamep,
Anaween, and Tomhamquamesqua. All were men. The text states that Tomhampamet (Cornelius) was acting on behalf of his father, Paneenanet, otherwise called John, who was unable
to attend. These participants were described as the remainder of the Catskill Indians.

No. 98, May 25, 1766, Berkshire County, MA
LOCATION: a parcel of fifty acres in Stockbridge, part of the land laid out to Jonas Etuakom
(Etowaukaum) and James Cheenequin, as parts of his rights in Stockbridge, the lot to be taken
out of said lot which contains 150 acres, one quarter and nineteen rods. (The Stockbridge Li-
brary Historical Collection). PURCHASER: Larrance Linch of Stockbridge, yeoman.
PAYMENT: thirty pounds New York currency.
INDIANS INVOLVED: Solomon Uhhaunnauwauhmut.

No. 99, May 29, 1766, Berkshire County, MA
LOCATION: This unusual deed was titled "Articles of Agreement" and was a contract for a tract
of land twelve miles square English measure, to be taken in any place the buyer thought
proper out of such lands as the Mohicans at present claimed in North America as their lawful
inheritance. (The Stockbridge Library Historical Collection, m.73–1.33 (3)) PURCHASER:
William Gregg, Jr.
PAYMENT: Provided the Indian claims were confirmed, Gregg was to get his twelve miles square
on a lease for 999 years, paying to the Indians Jacob, Solomon and John, representing their
constituents, the Indians of the Mohheekaunuck Tribe and original natives of Hudson's River,
ten shillings annually. In addition, he was to support the three Indians for three years in England, where they were going in order to lay their claims before the King; he was to lay the Indian claims before the King; Gregg also was to transport them there and back. He was to
supply them with "sufficient Meat, Drink, apparel, Lodging and washing fitting Gentlemen,
and shall and will further pay to them the sum of Thirty pounds New York Currency each by
the year, amounting, on the whole, to the three, to the sum of ninety pounds York money by
the year." In exchange, the Indians agreed to be at Gregg's disposal in London, to do his reasonable commands, and not to absent themselves during the term agreed.
INDIANS INVOLVED: Jacob Cheeksaunkun, Solomon Uhhaunuhwaunukmut, and John Naunauphtaunk, of Stockbridge, Gentlemen, impowered by the Indians of the Mohheekaunuck
Tribe. Indian witness was Daniel Nimham (a Wappinger sachem who lived at Stockbridge,
who also had land claims).

No. 100, July 5, 1766, Berkshire County, MA
LOCATION: seventy acres in the northwest part of Stockbridge, bounded north on the town
line, east on land laid out to Josiah Wawnchauy and partly on undivided land, south and west
on undivided land. (Berkshire County Registry, Middle District, Deeds, Bk. 5, p. 121) PUR-
CHASER: Elijah Williams of Stockbridge.
PAYMENT: twenty-eight pounds, two shillings, and six pence.
INDIANS INVOLVED: Ephraim Paunphpaunhaum of Stockbridge.

No. 101, July 5, 1766, Berkshire County, MA
LOCATION: called the Rattlesnake Mountain, land that was in common and undivided north of
what was called the old Housatonnock line, extending to the north line of Stockbridge. From
the east line of the town between the old Housatonnock line and the north line to the east side
of the Great Pond and west at the north end of the pond as far as a brook that runs from the
northward into the pond. Also one hundred acres lying west of the brook as far as the proprietors' grant made as an equivalent for the land Solomon Uhhaunnuhwaunnuchmut took up
and sold to George Dudley, being about sixty acres on the east side of the brook. All the lands
remaining undivided and not taken up by the English or Indian Proprietors. This land was in-

cluded in a divisional deed made between the English and Indians. (Berkshire County Registry, Middle District, Deeds, Bk. 22, pp. 181-182) PURCHASER: Josiah Jones, Joseph Woodbridge, Elijah Williams, Josiah Jones, Jr. and Erastus Sergeant.

PAYMENT: 150 pounds to the Indian proprietors of the undivided lands of the town of Stockbridge.

INDIANS INVOLVED: Benjamin Kokhewenaunaut and Johannis Mtocksin in the name of the Indian Proprietors. This land was approved for sale for the payment of the Indians' debts.

No. 102, May 30, 1767, Berkshire County, MA

LOCATION: three parcels in Stockbridge, "one Tract or Lot Lying west of the pond Brook (so Called) & Bounding Easterly by Said Brook north by Land belonging to the heirs of Paul ImpechHow De'd. [deceased] west by Common Land according to the Survey on Record of the Indian proprietors Book of Record & to Run so far South from Sd north [line] as to make fifty acres. also one other Lot of Land Lying west of Enoch Slossons Land Beginning at the Southwest corner of Sd Slossons land Thence Running west. . .then Turning & Running north. . .to a Stake & Stones by the Road Leading to Richmont then Turning & Running East. . .to a Black Burch Tree marked thence north. . .to a Stake & Stones thence East. . .to the west Bounds of Said Slossons Land thence Running South. . .to the North East Corner of Land Granted to Stephen Nash. Sd Tract of Land Contains Thirty Two acres with allowances for Swag of Chain & the Road that Runs Thro Sd land. also one other Lot of Land Lying Northwesterly of the last Described lot on the Road afore Sd bounded as followeth begins at a witch Hazel Tree Standing a Little East of the Road a going Down the mountain that Leads to Richmonts thence Running west. . .to a Beach Tree marked thence South 9 degrees East & 1 Rod to a Stake & Stones thence East . . .north. . . to a Ledge of Rock thence 20 Rods to the Bounds first begun at this Last Tract Contains 28 Acres of Land with allowance for swag of Chain and 4 Rods for the Road that Runs thro Sd Land." (The Stockbridge Library Historical Collection). PURCHASER: Samuel Brown of Stockbridge.

PAYMENT: fifty-two pounds York money.

INDIANS INVOLVED: Jonas Etowaukaum of Stockbridge (spelled Itoaukaum at the beginning of the deed).

No. 103, June 13, 1767, Berkshire County, MA

LOCATION: this was a mortgage for the 120 acres of land granted to Jehoiakim Mohkhowwauweet by the Indian Proprietors in Stockbridge on the westerly part of the township. (Berkshire County Registry, Middle District, Deeds, Bk. 22, pp. 181-182) PURCHASER: Elijah Williams of Stockbridge.

PAYMENT: sixteen pounds: if Jehoiakim repaid to Elijah the sum of sixteen pounds within one year with interest then the above mortgage was void, but if he failed, Elijah would pay Jehoiakim thirty-four pounds exclusive of the sum already paid and take the land. The deed was not recorded until July 27, 1785.

INDIANS INVOLVED: Jehoiakim Mohkhowwauweet.

No. 104, September 2, 1767, Berkshire County, MA

LOCATION: fifty acres in Stockbridge bounded north on Laurance Finches' land, east on Deacon Brown's mill brook, south on undivided lands or Thomas Sherman, west on his own land. (Berkshire County Registry, Middle District, Deeds, Bk. 5, p. 276) PURCHASER: Cornelius Van Schaack, Kinderhook trader.

PAYMENT: thirty pounds New York money.

INDIANS INVOLVED: Solomon Uhhaunauwaunaumut of Stockbridge.

No. 105, September 3, 1767, Greene County, NY

LOCATION: this deposition defined the boundary between the Mohicans of Catskill and the Esopus Indians, a step necessary following the deed of March 25, 1766, given above. Indian ancestors had said the bounds between the Esopus Indians and the Catskill Indians ran from the Creek called Tendeyagkameka, on which the mill of Jacobus Persen stood in 1767, nearly west to a hill a little to the north called Pessawenkouck, where Isaac Post then lived. The Esopus said they never had sold any land to the Esopus settlers further north than to the creek Ten-

deyagkameka; the name meant a point from which water falls. The great fall at the mouth of this creek had been noted as the north boundary of Esopus lands a century earlier, in March, 1677. The stream was known in Dutch as the Sagers Kill (Sawyer's Creek); in 1676 the Esopus Indians gave title to the creek and adjacent land as far as the borders of the Catskill Indians to "the Old Sawyer." (Mss. 6812 and 6819, Manuscripts and Special Collections, NYSL) PUR-CHASER: none; Marten Van Bergen was among the purchasers of 1766; he presented testimony he had obtained from the Esopus and Catskill Indians resolving the south boundary claimed by the Catskill Indians.
PAYMENT: no payment for the information is mentioned.
INDIANS INVOLVED: Allameetahat, an Esopus sachem who in Dutch was called *Piet Tap*, said that he had always heard the above information about the line from his father, who was called Newachquany, and from his uncle, who was called Schawenack. Another Indian, Annawee-meet, a Catskill Indian called in Dutch *Jan De Backer*, of the age of thirty years or upwards, gave the same information about the line. Van Bergen testified the two Indians were sober.

No. 106, April 6, 1768, Berkshire County, MA
LOCATION: land in Stockbridge in the meadow on the north side of the river, being one half of the lot bought from Abraham Naunauphpataunk, the west half of the said lot estimated to contain four acres: bounded north by land belonging to Johannis Mtauwampey, west by John Naunauphpataunk, south by Elizabeth Wnaumpey, and east by land belonging to Abraham Brinsmaid. (The Stockbridge Library Historical Collection) PURCHASER: Phinehas Morgan.
PAYMENT: twelve pounds.
INDIANS INVOLVED: David Pixley was the seller; this deed is included because of the Indian references.

No. 107, June 15, 1768, Berkshire County, MA.
LOCATION: a tract in the Town of Stockbridge laid out for Capt. Jacob Naunauphtaunk, sixty acres of land to the westwardly side of a large brook called Laupauquk, beginning at a corner of some land laid out to Col. Williams. This sale was made to "discharge the debt of the heirs of the said Jacob Naunaughtaunk." Approved by Timothy Woodbridge and John Ashley. (The Stockbridge Library Historical Collection) PURCHASER: Theophilus Westover.
PAYMENT: thirty-two pounds.
INDIANS INVOLVED: John Naunauhphtaunk, Gentleman; Abraham Naunauhphtaunk, yeoman; Jacob Naunauhphtaunk, yeoman; Jehoiakim Naunauhphtaunk, hunter.

No. 108, July 2, 1768, Berkshire County, MA
LOCATION: land in Stockbridge on the southerly side of the highway that crossed the plain by the meeting house. It lay opposite Matthew Cadwell's home lot on the other side of the road, and was bounded northwardly on the road crossing the plain, westwardly on the road that went through the meadow, eastwardly on land of Johonnis Wautuawaumpehs, and south-wardly upon the land that Joseph Woodbridge had in possession. This was all the land that lay on the east side of the road on the plain that was originally laid out to Muhskenaumauk. (The Stockbridge Library Historical Collection, m73–1.29 (3)) PURCHASER: Phinehas Morgan of Stockbridge.
PAYMENT: five pounds.
INDIANS INVOLVED: Rhoda Quonpunwas of Stockbridge. Witness was John Nounauhphtauk.

No. 109, May 25, 1769, Berkshire County, MA
LOCATION: a house lot in Stockbridge about 80 rods south from Samuel Brown's house, bounded easterly by the road leading from Brown's house to the Meeting House, south by land belonging to Jehoiakim Yokun's heirs, and partly on land of Asa Bement, north by land of Jacob Cheeksonkun and westerly near to the pond brook, so called, being fifteen acres of land with a dwelling house on it. (The Stockbridge Library Historical Collection, m73–1.24 (4)). PURCHASER: Samuel Brown.
PAYMENT: fifty-two pounds ten shillings York money.

INDIANS INVOLVED: Hendrick Pauponkseet, a Stockbridge Indian, hunter, and his wife Elizabeth Pauponks[eet]. She signed off on her right of dower and future widow's power of a third in the property. Witness was Johannis Mtohksin.

No. 110, July 9, 1769, Berkshire County, MA
LOCATION: fifty acres of land in the common and undivided land of Stockbridge. The land began at the northeast corner of the 140 acre lot formerly laid out to Robert Nungkawwot, went northeast to the south line of a fifty acre lot formerly laid out to Jehoiakim Shouwunnohghuek, alias Weame, then westward along his south line to the southwest corner of Weame's lot, then southwest to a point in the north line of Nungkawwot's 140 acres, and returned east to the starting point. The plot was surveyed by John Southgate October 7, 1772. The survey was recorded October 28, 1779, by Timothy Woodbridge. (The Stockbridge Library Historical Collection, m73–1.27 (1)) PURCHASER: David Naunauneekaunuck.
PAYMENT: none mentioned.
INDIANS INVOLVED: The land was granted by the Indian Proprietors, not named.

No. 111, July 27, 1769, Berkshire County, MA
LOCATION: a tract of fifty acres in Stockbridge granted by the Indian Proprietors "to be taken up in any Part of the undivided land in the town of Stockbridge." (Berkshire County Registry, Middle District, Deeds, Bk. 25, pp. 170-171.) PURCHASER: Elijah Williams.
PAYMENT: fifteen pounds
INDIANS INVOLVED: Jehoiakim Mauhaunaunut of Stockbridge, yeoman.

No. 112, August 17, 1769, Berkshire County, MA
LOCATION: the lot lying in Stockbridge containing thirteen acres was bounded east by the road leading from Brown's house to the Meetinghouse, south by land belonging to Brown, north by land also belonging to Brown in part and partly belonging to Azariah Williams and land belonging to the Widow Weeaumee, an Indian woman. (The Stockbridge Library Historical Collection, m73–1.25) PURCHASER: Samuel Brown.
PAYMENT: seventy pounds.
INDIANS INVOLVED: Jacob Cheeksonkun (Cheeksaunkun) and his wife, Mary Cheeksaunkun. She signed away her right of dower.

No. 113, August 17, 1769, Berkshire County, MA
LOCATION: "one certain Tract. . .Scituate in the Town of Stockbridge aforesaid and in the Meadow on the North side of the River containing by estimation Eight Acres be it more or less Butted and Bounded as follows (viz) South and West on the River, North partly on Land belonging to the Heirs of John Wauwaumpeequnnaunt and partly on Land belonging to Duoohauquees and Eastwardly partly on Land belonging [to] Benjamin Kohkewenaunaunt and partly on Land belonging to Johannis Mtohksin. . . ." (The Stockbridge Library Historical Collection) PURCHASER: David Pixley, Jr. of Stockbridge.
PAYMENT: twenty-four pounds lawful money.
INDIANS INVOLVED: Timothy Youkun.

No. 114, August 17, 1769, Berkshire County, MA
LOCATION: a tract in the Town of Stockbridge in the meadow on the north side of the river containing about eight acres, bounded south and west on the river, north partly on land belonging to the heirs of John Wauwaumpeequnnaunt and partly on land belonging to Duoohauquees and eastwardly on land belonging to Johannis Mtohksin. (The Stockbridge Library Historical Collection) PURCHASER: David Pixley, Jr. of Stockbridge.
PAYMENT: twenty-four pounds.
INDIANS INVOLVED: Timothy Youkun.

No. 115, September 24, 1770, Berkshire County, MA
LOCATION: not a deed but a survey by Bill Williams, surveyor: it is included because it confirms that Benjamin was chief sachem. Fifty acres of land in Stockbridge in the Indian common land on the west side of the mill brook adjoining a pitch laid out to Lt. David Pixley, part on the

north end and part on the south end of said pitch. The land shown in the attached map was west of the mountain. (The Stockbridge Library Historical Collection) PURCHASER: David Pixley, Jr.
PAYMENT: not noted.
INDIANS INVOLVED: Indian common land, no names noted except at top "on the right of Ben, Sachem."

No. 116, December 11, 1771, Berkshire County, MA
LOCATION: land in Stockbridge beginning at the southeast corner of a forty-acre lot which Samuel Churchill bought of the Indians lying on the east side of the mountain that lies on the west side of the great pond, from there west on the south line of the lot lately owned by Benjamin Norton to the top of that mountain, then southerly on the top of the mountain to the north side of land owned by Samuel Brown, then east to the first bounds. (The Stockbridge Library Historical Collection) PURCHASER: Samuel Brown, Jr.
PAYMENT: forty shillings.
INDIANS INVOLVED: David Naunaunakauneek and Johannes Mtohksin, acting as a committee empowered by the Indian proprietors to sell some Indian land for the benefit of the proprietors.

No. 117, December 17, 1771, Berkshire County, MA
LOCATION: land in Stockbridge, part of a tract originally laid out for Paul Ompeatkhow, on the west side of the brook called Brown's Mill Brook, bounded east on the road that crossed said lot by Cadwell's over to Eleazar Slosson's and south on Slosson's land, west on land belonging to Daniel Phelps, north partly on the road that goes to Kinderhook, partly on land belonging to Tarra Zinch and partly on land of John Hambleton and partly on land of Enoch Slosson. (The Stockbridge Library Historical Collection, m73 1.22 (3)) PURCHASER: Daniel Phelps.
PAYMENT: sixty pounds.
INDIANS INVOLVED: David Naunauneekqunuck and Elisabath Nauwohtohkhonnuhwoh, wife of David, both of Stockbridge, planters.

No. 118, April 14, 1773, Rensselaer County, NY
LOCATION: land bounded easterly on Neapmooke Patent, northeast by Hoosick Patent, then west and south on the Patent belonging to John Matthews, then south and southeast on Pittstown line, containing by estimation 1000 acres. (Albany County Hall of Records, Deeds, Book 10, p. 210) PURCHASER: William Shephard of Pittstown.
PAYMENT: thirty pounds.
INDIANS INVOLVED: Solomon Ukkaunauwaunnmut, Timothy Youkon, and Johannis Mtokksin, of Stockbridge in Berkshire County, Massachusetts Bay of New England.

No. 119, April 14, 1773, Rensselaer County, NY
LOCATION: About 4000 acres of land bounded south on the Manor of Rensselaerswyck, southeast on the Hoosick Patent, northeast on St. Coick (Sankhaick) Patent and north on the same, northwest on the Neapmooke Patent, west and southwest on Pittstown. (Albany County Hall of Records, Deeds, Bk. 10, p. 211) PURCHASER: William Shephard of Pittstown.
PAYMENT: one hundred pounds of the Colony of New York.
INDIANS INVOLVED: Solomon Ukkaunauwaunnmut, Timothy Youkon, Johannis Mtokksin, of Stockbridge, Berkshire County, Massachusetts Bay of New England, Indians.

No. 120, April 30, 1772, Berkshire County, MA
LOCATION: fifty acres of land in the northwest part of Stockbridge, bounded east on a lot laid out to Jehoiakim Mauhauwauweet now owned by William Tuller. For other bounds, the deed refers the reader to the survey in the Indian Proprietors' book. (Berkshire County Registry, Middle District, Deeds, Bk. 22, p. 183. PURCHASER: Elijah Williams.
PAYMENT: sixteen pounds, ten shillings.
INDIANS INVOLVED: Johannis Mtohksin. This deed was not recorded until July 29, 1785.

No. 121, September 27, 1776, Berkshire County, MA

LOCATION: ninety acres in Stockbridge, being two grants made made by the Indian Proprietors for debts, "beginning at the southwest corner of Jehoicim's lot, north to a stake and stones in said Jehoicim's north line,. . . to a white birch on the mountain. . . to the beginning." (Berkshire County Registry, Middle District, Deeds, Bk. 14, pp. 13-14) PURCHASER: Benjamin and Joseph Willard.
PAYMENT: Forty-five pounds (the line following is missing from the deed)
INDIANS INVOLVED: Solomon Uhhaunnauwaunmut, Johannis Mtohksin and Joseph Shawquethqueat of Stockbridge were a committee empowered to sell the land for the payment of some Indian debts.

No. 122, April 11, 1780, Berkshire County, MA
LOCATION: one acre taken from a four acre lot lying westerly of Mr. John Sergeant's land, bounded west and north by Benjamin, Joseph and David, brothers of said Rhoda. (Berkshire County Registry, Middle District, Deeds, Bk. 13, p. 365) PURCHASER: Daniel James.
PAYMENT: four pounds.
INDIANS INVOLVED: Abraham Konkpot and Rhoda, his wife, both of Stockbridge, Indians.

No. 123, November 9, 1780, Berkshire County, MA
LOCATION: one acre in Stockbridge. The purchaser previously had bought one acre, see April 11, 1780. (Berkshire County Registry, Middle District, Deeds, Bk. 13, p. 362) PURCHASER: Daniel James.
PAYMENT: four pounds.
INDIANS INVOLVED: Abraham Konkpot (Konkapot) and Rhoda, his wife, both of Stockbridge.

No. 124, March 10, 1781, Berkshire County, MA
LOCATION: a tract of twenty acres in Stockbridge bounded east on Benjamin Mautaukmun's land, north by the river, westerly partly on David Naunaunkanuk's land, partly on John Kurthuse's land and partly on Jacob Kunkapot's land, south on Samuel Hatch's land. (Berkshire County Registry, Middle District, Deeds, Bk. 22, pp. 183-184) PURCHASER: Elijah Williams of Stockbridge.
PAYMENT: 61 pounds, 15 shillings, 7 pence.
INDIANS INVOLVED: Joseph Shawquethquat, Chief of the Stockbridge Indians and Benjamin Waununauwut of Stockbridge, hunter. This deed was not recorded until January 24, 1786.

No. 125, November 26, 1781, Berkshire County, MA
LOCATION: a tract in Stockbridge containing two acres and sixteen rods of ground, lying on the west side of the road about ninety rods south from the great bridge called the Orphan House Bridge and beginning at a stake and stones at the north end of the crossway on Mrs. Willard's line, running south 39 degrees west eighteen rods to a stake and stones, running then north 68 degrees west thirty-nine rods to a stake and stones then east two degrees south forty-eight rods to the beginning. (Berkshire County Registry, Middle District, Deeds, Bk. 23, pp. 20-22) PURCHASER: Lott Rew of Stockbridge.
PAYMENT: six pounds.
INDIANS INVOLVED: Jehoiakim Mtohksin, gentleman.

No. 126, March 7, 1785, Berkshire County, MA
LOCATION: Ninety acres, sixty acres of which was laid out on the right of Jonas Wauwohnumuwaus in Stockbridge, running from Seth Norton's southwest corner, northeast to land belonging to Johannis Mtoksin's heirs, west to a point in the east line of a fifty acre lot laid out to Benjamin Waunihnauwut, then southwest, then to the corner of Johannis Mtoksin's ninety acre lot now owned by Mrs. Judith (Heyer?) and then to the beginning. (The text contains an illegible line.) (The Stockbridge Library Historical Collection, M73-1.29) PURCHASER: John Sergeant (Junior) of Stockbridge.
PAYMENT: fifty pounds.
INDIANS INVOLVED: Jehoiakim Waunaupnutonhg (Naunseptonk, Naunonpetonk) and Jacob Mauwanssumun (Waumausnum, Waumausum).

No. 127, April 13, 1785, Berkshire County, MA
LOCATION: two acres of the farm in Stockbridge on which Johannis Mtohksin late of Stock-
bridge, deceased, lived and in that part of the town which Johannis gave to Jane by his last will
and testament. (Berkshire County Registry, Middle District, Deeds, Pittsfield, Bk. 28, p.439)
PURCHASER: conveyed by will to Jane Konkapot.
PAYMENT: no payment involved.
INDIANS INVOLVED: Johannis Mtohksin, deceased; John Konkpot and Jane (his wife).

No. 128, May 4, 1785, Berkshire County, MA
LOCATION: land in the southeast corner of Stockbridge, being all the land not taken by grants
heretofore made by the same, "said grant being made to me, the said John, on the 25th day of
April last. This conveyance having preference thereto." (Berkshire County Registry, Middle
District, Deeds, Bk. 20, p. 267) PURCHASER: Ira Seymour, Stockbridge.
PAYMENT: fifteen pounds
INDIANS INVOLVED: John Konkpot (Konkapot), Stockbridge Indian.

No. 129, February 7, 1786, Berkshire County, MA
LOCATION: a tract in Stockbridge beginning two rods southwest of the northeast corner of a six-
acre lot which Jehoiakim Mtohksin held by deed from Jehoiakim Naunnumpeetenkq. It was
bounded east on the highway and west on Mrs. Judith Thayer's line and south on the remaining part of the six-acre lot, and was in the northeast corner of a forty acre lot formerly laid out
to Jacob Nawnaumppeetenkq, deceased. (Berkshire County Registry, Middle District, Deeds,
Bk. 23, pp. 22-23) PURCHASER: Amos Hager.
PAYMENT: eight pounds.
INDIANS INVOLVED: Jehoiakim Mtohksin of Stockbridge, Gentleman. The sale was approved
by John Sergeant (Jr.) and Joseph Woodbridge, in their role as examiners of the sales and leases
made by the Moheakunnuk Tribe of Indians.

No. 130, March 14, 1794, Berkshire County, MA
LOCATION: all the land in the southeast corner of Stockbridge granted to John Kunkapot by the
Indian proprietors April 25, 1785. (Berkshire County Registry, Middle District, Deeds, Bk. 52,
p. 400) PURCHASER: Ira Seymour of Stockbridge.
PAYMENT: twenty pounds.
INDIANS INVOLVED: "John Kunkapot of Tuscarory, otherwise of New Stockbridge in the
State of New York, Indian. . . County of Herkimer."

No. 131, November 6, 1810, Berkshire County, MA.
LOCATION: land in Stockbridge bounded southerly by a highway, westerly by Elijah Deming's
land, northerly and easterly by land owned by Thaddeus Pomeroy, being the land on which
Lucretia Ninham last lived, containing an estimated one half acre. (Berkshire County Registry,
Middle District, Deeds, Bk. 49, p. 135) PURCHASER: Oliver Partridge of Stockbridge.
PAYMENT: fifteen dollars.
INDIANS INVOLVED: Jacob Konkepot, of New Stockbridge in the County of Oneida, of the
State of New York, yeoman.

No. 131, September 7, 1818, Berkshire County, MA
LOCATION: a tract of land containing about four acres, being the part within Stockbridge of a
road formerly reserved by the Indian proprietors to lead from Stockbridge to Sheffield, of an
undescribed width but afterwards surveyed by order of the county court and laid four rods in
width. (Stockbridge Library Historical Collection, m73-1.29 (4)) PURCHASER: David Goo-
drich.
PAYMENT: ten dollars.
INDIANS INVOLVED: Hendrick Aupaumut, sachem, David Neshoonhuk, Solomon I. Hendrick, Abner W. Hendrick, and Solomon U. Hendrick, "counselors of the Muhheeconuck
tribe of Indians, formerly proprietors of the town of Stockbridge, who now reside in New
Stockbridge." The three men besides Aupaumut and David Neshoonhuk were Hendrick Aupaumut's brother named Solomon I. and his sons Abner W. and Solomon U.

Appendix B
Index to Mohican Personal Names, Locations, and Relationships

Women are marked with an asterisk (*). For additional information, check the appropriate deed in Appendix A, under the year given. For some individuals, material from the text has been added.

AARON, see Umpachanee.

ABRAHAM

1748: with others, he sold two tracts on Catskill Creek.

1748: he sold, with others, land west of Coxsackie.

ACKAWAHANIT, see Bartholomew.

ADAM, see Wautonkaumeet.

AGHCONTIONECK (William).

1766: with others, he signed a deed releasing all land belonging to the Catskill Indians in (then) Albany County.

AGHEAME

1734: with others, he sold land along the Scoharie Creek.

1734: he sold land with others along the Schoharie Creek.

AKAMAAGKAMIN, Attamagkamin; his brother was Sokam.

1703: land was sold in his behalf on the Westenhook Creek.

AMAWANCK, see Anaweem.

AMPAMIT, Abamet, Ampamet, also called Ampamet Sinho (Sinhow); chief sachem of the Mohicans in the 1730s; his village was on Moesimus Island at Schodack; his son was Paumaumpausoo of Stockbridge.

1703: Ampamit, his older brother, Aquatso (empowered by his mother, Wanenagkela), and Menonampa, another brother, signed a deed.

1707: Ampamit was a joint owner of Schodack land.

1709: he testified about the 1672 land for the Coeymans Patent; his mother, father, brothers and relatives were named.

1722: he complained to Governor Burnet at an Indian conference about sales of rum and Indians being cheated in land sales.

1722: Ampamit was chief of an island in the Hudson.

1730: Ampamit sold part of Moesimus Island. His village of four houses was shown on a survey map of the island.

1733: he was first of seven signers for land east of Kinderhook.

1739: Ampamit's son was baptized at Stockbridge.

1744: his Indian village on the island was noted by a traveler.

ANAWEEM, Ananween, Amawanck, alias John de Backer, Jan d'backer.

1734: with others, he sold land at Coxsackie.

1766: with others, he signed a release of all unpatented land belonging to the Catskill Indians.

ANEKEHOES

1709: he testified about the land for the Coeymans patent. The deed said he was the brother of Magshapeet (Mahakniminaw).

*ANCKAHEANAWA, Knahanwa.

1721: with others, she sold land on the Housatonic in Salisbury.

*ANNA (Hannah), her husband was Sankewenageek (Umpachanee).

1738: they sold land at Petan Hook in Columbia County.

*ANNALESEM, Annabesem.
1709: she testified about the land for the Coeymans patent. The deed said she was the sister of
      Maghshapeet (Mahakniminaw).
ANNAWEME, see Weame.
ANNIMAPAW, see Winnigh Po.
ANTONY KAG
1748: he was witness to a sale of two tracts on the Catskill.
AQUAHANNIT
1743: with others, he sold land west of Coxsackie.
ARRENT (Dutch name, possibly referring to Corlaer/Metoxon).
1748: with others, he sold two tracts on Catskill Creek.
1748: he was a witness to the sale of land west of Coxsackie.
AUGHUNNIT (Bartholomew), Ackawahanit.
1747: with others, he petitioned for recognition of the Indian village at Wequadnach (Sharon, Con-
      necticut).
1752: with Moses Nequitimaug, he sold the Wequadnach village site.
1752: with others, sold Stockbridge land on the road up the hill.
AUNAUWAUNEEKHHEEK (Jeremy), Wanneeck. (See Chapter 8.)
1734: described as from Keenameek (Kaunaumeek), he sold land on the Kinderhook Creek.
1737: as the chief at Kaunaumeek, he invited John Sergeant to speak there.
1739: he returned from a visit to the Shawnees with messages.
AUNOW WAUMPUMMUHGSEET
1737: a deed for townships east of Stockbridge was signed on his behalf.
AUPAUMUT (Hendrick). (See Chapter 10.)
1818: as sachem, with counselors, sold four acres at Stockbridge.
AUSHEWAKOKEEK
1721: with others, he sold land on the Housatonic at Salisbury.
AWEQUEN
1667: with his blood relations, he sold land south of Valatie.
1667: his brother was Machackmatock Wissiau.
BACHUS (nickname, meaning god of wine, reveler); see Ephraim Bochus.
BACKER, see Hermain Backer.
BARTHOLOMEW, Bertholomew, alias Ackawahanit; see Aughhunnit.
BENJAMIN, see Sauchewawha.
BENJAMIN KOKHKEWENAUNAUT (King Ben); see Kokhkewenaunaut.
BKWWEIUKEUO, (Jonas) (likely a misspelling for Etowaukaum).
1757: he witnessed the sale of land for part of Alford.
BOCHUS, Ephraim, see Naunaunquan, Wohnaunqueen.
BONONAMP, Penonamp, Menonampa, Manounip Sinho, (Ampamit's brother).
1703: with family members, he sold a Columbia County woodland.
1707: with brothers Aquoatch (Aquatso) and Ampamit (Aanpamit) he gave a confirmation deed for
      Van Rensselaer Indian purchases.
1709: testified about the 1672 land sale for the Coeymans Patent.
1730: he was one of four Mohicans who sold land on Moesimus Island.
1733: with Ampamit and others, he sold land in Columbia County.
BROWNIS, Brown, Prownish; father of Ampamit, husband of Nanagakea, also spelled
      Wanenagkela. He was dead before 1709.
1672: land for the Coeymans Patent was sold in his name.
1704: witness to land sale for the Little Nine Partners Patent.
CAEKONAPIT
1672: land for the Coeymans Patent was sold in his name.
1709: he was deceased before 1709.
CAGKARRICSEET, see Catharickseet.
CANCANWAP, see Kagawap.
CANEKESKOHA
1761: he sold land with others in the Batavia patent.
1761: with others, he sold Greene County land near Batavia.

CATHARICKSEET (Cornelius), Katrukseet, Cagarricseet, other spellings; his father was Goose.
1704: with two others, he sold land on Westenhook Creek.
1712: he helped locate the pile of stones called Wawananwasick on the Van Rensselaer-Livingston line.
1714: he helped a surveyor lay out the Livingston Patent line.
1718: he, wife Nanakem, her daughter, sister and brother, with others, gave up their claim on the north Livingston line in exchange for cancellation of debts.
1719: with others, he sold land in Salisbury, Connecticut.
1743: mentioned in a letter by Philip Livingston as an old Indian.
1743: went with surveyor Charles Clinton to the southeast corner of the Livingston Patent.
1744: he was a Moravian convert.
CAWENNENOCK:
1667: he was a witness to a deed south of Valatie.
CHAPEKEWAK, Chapekewogh.
1745: with others, sold land near Metoxen's wigwam at Freehold.
CHEEKSUNKUN (Capt. Jacob), Cheeksonkun, CheekSaunkun; his wife was Mary. He was a leader in the Seven Years War.
1752: with others, sold Stockbridge land on the road up the hill.
1754: with other Stockbridge leaders, petitioned the Governor of New York for redress of lands patented without pay to the Indians.
1757: witnessed a deed for land at Copake.
1757: signed a deed for part of Mount Washington.
1763: with others, sold the last tribal land except Stockbridge and a tract north of it.
1765: he witnessed a mortgage given by Robert Nungkauweaunt and Jacob Scautcaw.
1766: empowered by the tribe, he signed a contract for a tract twelve miles square out of Mohican lands on a lease of 999 years, in exchange for a trip to England to lay Indian claims before the King.
1769: with his wife, he sold thirteen acres in Stockbridge.
1769: his land was north of the Pauponskeet's house lot.
*CHEEKSUNKUN (Mary); wife of Jacob Cheeksunkun.
1769: with her husband, she sold thirteen acres in Stockbridge. She signed away her right of dower.
CHENEQUEN (James), Chineagin; his brother was Jonas Etowaukaum.
1751: with his brother, he sold eight acres on the street through the plain.
CHIENOME
1735: with others, sold land at Westenhook.
COHQUAHEGAMEEK (Jacobus), Coocheecomeek.
1737: with others, he sold land for Pittsfield; he was formerly of the Island in the Hudson below Albany.
CONCONAUGHSEET, Cauconaughseet.
1724: with others, sold land for two townships on the Housatonic.
*CONEKAMOW
1719: with others, she sold land near Salisbury, Connecticut.
CORLAR, Corlaer, see Metoxon.
CORNELIUS, see Catharickseet.
CORNELIUS, see Nawwaukele.
CORNELIUS, see Tomhampemet.
COVCONOSEET
1724: signed a deed for two townships on the Housatonic River.
COWPOISE (Timothy), Cowpas.
1747: with others, he petitioned for recognition of his Wequadnach village tract.
1757: he witnessed a deed for Copake.
CRAYS (a nickname).
1704: his wigwam near Amenia was shown on a survey for Richard Sackett.
1704: he witnessed the land sale for the Little Nine Partners.
DANIEL MINEK, see Minek.
DANIEL NIMHAM, see Nimham.
DANIEL POOCHOSE, see Poochoose.

DANIEL QUANS, see Quans.

DAVID NANNAUNECKKAUNUCK, Naunemneekkaunuck, Nauneknick, Wawunmeagkuuh, see Nannauneckkaunuck.

DAVID, see Neshoonuk.

DAVID, see Tsacoke.

DONOWOACTUM

1704: among others, sold land for the Little Nine Partners Patent.

*DUMMEKONWOH (Sarah)

1759: she sold part of the Stockbridge land laid out to Ponniote and others.

1759: the deed says she was a basketmaker.

EBENEZER, see Poopoonah.

*ELIZABETH, see Mauchenouwaushguh.

*ELIZABETH, see Pauponkseet.

EPHRAIM, see Paumpkhaunhaum.

EPHRAIM, see Waunaunqueen.

ETOWAUKAUM (Nicholas, also Claes).

1710: he went to England with three Iroquois. See Chapter 6.

1734: of Kaunaumeek, he sold land on the Kinderhook Creek.

ETOWAUKAUM (Jonas), Etuakom, Etowwauhkaum, Itoaukaum; son of Umpachanee and Anna; grandson of Etowaukaum.

1734-1735: as an eight-year-old boy, he spent the winter at New Haven with John Sergeant and attended school. His brother was James Chenegun.

1751: with his brother, he sold eight Stockbridge acres on the street through the plain.

1757: he was a witness to a sale of land for part of Alford.

1763: with others, he sold all remaining unsold tribal land except Stockbridge and a tract north of it.

1767: he sold three parcels in Stockbridge.

FOESHES

1704: witness to land sale for the Little Nine Partners patent.

GAUWANAN

1697: he was named as the son of My Lady in a deed.

1725: he was witness to a claim by Shabash of Shekomeko.

GOLWAMAGH

1745: with others, sold land near Metoxen's wigwam at Freehold.

GOOSE, Gose, see Tataemshatt.

*GUTTATAMOW, a sister of Takomp.

1685: she was a proprietor of the land called Tachkanick (Taconic), sold to Robert Livingston.

1720: she was paid for land near Salisbury, Connecticut.

HANNAH, see Quullautowatuk.

HENDRICK, see Aupaumut.

HENDRICK, Wautonkauwot, Woompookseet, Pooponkseet, see Wautonkauwot.

HENDRICK (Abner W.); he was a son of Hendrick Aupaumut.

1818: with other counselors, he sold four acres at Stockbridge.

HENDRICK (Solomon U.); he was a son of Hendrick Aupaumut.

1818: with other counselors, he sold four acres at Stockbridge.

HENDRICK (Solomon I.); he was a brother of Hendrick Aupaumut.

1818: with other counselors, he sold four acres at Stockbridge.

HERMAIN BACKER

1743: with others, sold land west of Coxsackie.

IMPECHHOW (Paul).

1767: land of heirs of Paul Impechhow, deceased was mentioned.

ISAAC WEPUCKSHUH, see Wepookqshuht.

ISAAC WNAUMPEE, see Wenaumpe.

JACOB, see Cheeksunkun.

JACOB, see Naunompetonk.

JACOB, see Schenk.

JACOB, see Vasnanghtouk.
JACOBUS COOCHEECOMEEK, see Cohquahegameek.
JAMES, see Chenequen.
JAMES, see Wohcoheekcomuck.
JANAMAN
1672: land for the Coeymans Patent was sold in his name.
1709: he was deceased before 1709.
JANPANETAN
1721: with others, sold land on the Housatonic at Salisbury.
JEHOIAKIM, see Mauhaunaunut.
JEHOIAKIM, see Shawwanunn.
JEHOIAKIM, see Yocun.
JENKINS (Jehayasin, Jehoiakim).
1757: he witnessed a deed for land at Copake.
JEREMIAH, see Kagahoot.
JEREMY, see Aunauwauneekhheek.
JHAWINON
1719: witnessed the sale of land near Salisbury, Connecticut.
*JHENEM
1719: with others, she sold land near Salisbury, Connecticut.
JOAB, a Negro man, a Stockbridge farmer and freeman.
1756: he bought the north half of an Indian lot in Stockbridge.
JOHANNES NAHHSON, see Metoxon.
JOHANNIS MTOHKSIN, see Metoxon.
JOHN DE BACKER, see Anaweem.
JOHN NAUNAUPHTAUNK, see Naunauphtaunk.
JOHN NEEKKUCHEWOHKAUMUN, see Neekkuchewohkaumun.
JOHN POPHNEHOUNAUWOK, see Konkapot.
JOHN SKUSHAWMH, see Skushawmh.
JOHN VANGILDER, see Vangilder.
JOHN WAUTAUNKUMEET, see Wautaunkumeet.
JOHN WAUWAUMPEGUUNNAUNT, see Wauwaumpegquunnaunt.
JONAS, see Etowaukaum.
JONATHAN, see Umpawahanit.
JOSEPH QUINNAUQUANT, Joseph Quinney, see Quinnauquant.
JOSIAH, see Muhhuttauwee.
KAGAHOOT
1738: he sold land on both sides of the Kinderhook Creek.
1741: with other Mohicans, sold a tract northeast of Kinderhook.
KAGAWAP, Cancanwap, Kakewap, Kagwap, Kaghawap, Kagkewap.
1724: with others, sold land for two townships on the Housatonic.
1733: he signed a deed for land east of Kinderhook.
1734: he sold land on the Schoharie Creek, outside of Mohican territory, but possibly given to him
    because he lived among the Mohawks. He was listed by the Mohawks as one of those who had
    stolen their land.
1734: with others, he sold land on the Schoharie Creek.
1737: he witnessed a land sale at Kiskatom, east of Palenville.
1745: with others, he sold land on the Catskill (Creek).
1745: with others, sold land near Metoxen's wigwam at Freehold.
1748: he sold two tracts on Catskill Creek, with others.
*KANAHANWA, see *Anckaheanawa.
KASHEKEKOMUCK, Keshomawck
1760: he had a village called Ontikehomawuck at later Nassau Village.
1760: he sold land north of Hoag's Pond, Nassau.
KATROKSEET, Katrukset, see Catharickseet.
KAWETUNK
1721: witnessed a land sale on the Housatonic in Salisbury.

KEKOGQUA
1734: with others, he sold land along the Schoharie Creek.
1734: he sold land with others along the Schoharie Creek.
KENNANAQUEN, see Metoxon.
KESHOMAWCK, see Kashekekomuck.
KHUSQUANTAUM
1750: he signed a note to a petition for redress.
KOEHAK
1718: he was the brother of Mawemeen. The family claimed land on the north line of Livingston
    Patent.
KOEWAMA
1709: he testified about the 1672 land for the Coeymans patent. The deed said he was the cousin of
    Maghshapeet.
KOKHKEWENAUNAUT (Benjamin, King Ben), Kewnonauaunt, Kankewenagheeh,
    Kaukewenoh, Kokhwauwweet, Kaukeweneckenaunt; chief sachem of the Mohicans by 1750.
1750: as "Indian King." he sold land with others east of Pittsfield.
1752: he was a witness to a sale of land for Pittsfield.
1756: with others, he sold land for a township west of Sheffield.
1757: with Maukcuwewet, sold land at Copake, "on which the insurgents based their claim."
1757: with others, sold land for part of Mount Washington.
1757: signed, with others, and was a witness for sale of land encompassing part of Alford.
1758: with others, he sold land to Asa Douglas for Canaan.
1758: in a deed he was again identified as "King of an Indian Tribe belonging to Stockbridge"; with
    Jehoiakim Yokin he sold land to Johannis Mtohksin.
1758: he witnessed a sale by Jehoiakim Yokun to Johannis Mtohksin.
1761: with others, he sold fifty acres in Stockbridge.
1763: identified as "Chief Sachem of the Mohhekunnuck River Indian or Housatunnock tribe,"
    with many others he sold the remaining unsold tribal lands, excepting Stockbridge and a tract
    north of it.
1766: in the name of the Indian proprietors, he and Johannis Mhtocksin sold part of Rattlesnake
    Mountain to pay Indian debts.
1770: the "right of Ben Sachem" is mentioned in a survey.
KONKAPOT (Abraham); a son of Konkapot, his wife was Rhoda.
1780: with Rhoda, he sold one acre off a four-acre lot.
1780: with Rhoda, he sold one acre in Stockbridge.
KONKAPOT (Jacob); he was a son or grandson of Konkapot.
1810: he sold one half acre land in Stockbridge; he was of New Stockbridge at that time.
*KONKAPOT (Jane)
1785: a deed for two acres mentions the farm of Johannes Metoxen (Mtohksin) was willed to her.
KONKAPOT, (Capt. John) Kunkapot, Kankopot, Cunkpot, John Pophnehounauwok (various
    spellings): born about 1690, dead by 1765. A sachem; his village was called Wnahktukuk. His
    sons probably were Abraham, Robert, John and Jacob.
1724: with others, he sold land for townships at Westenhook, known as Housatunnuk.
1737: with others, he sold land for four towns: Tyringham, Monterey, New Marlboro, Sandisfield,
    and part of Otis.
1737: with others, he confirmed land to John Vangilder in the Indian Reservation west of Sheffield.
1738: he witnessed a sale of land by Solomon Masinamake.
1745: he sold a tract of land, part of Lee or Lenox.
1749: sale of 50 acres to Timothy Woodbridge approved in 1749.
1750: he signed a note at the end of a petition for redress.
1756: with Peter Pophquunnaupeet, he sold land for the town of Austerlitz.
1756: with others, he sold land for part of Egremont and Alford.
1757: with Nungkauwot, he sold land on the Housatonic for Lee.
1761: with others, he sold fifty acres in Stockbridge.
1763: with many others, he sold the remaining tribal lands, except Stockbridge and a tract north of
    it.
KONKAPOT (John, Jr.), Kunkapot; a son or grandson of Konkapot.

1785: he signed for two acres willed to Jane Konkapot by Johannis Mtohksin.

1785: he sold all land remaining in the southeast corner of Stockbridge granted to him April 25, 1785.

1794: of Tuscarory, he sold land in Stockbridge granted by the Proprietors April 25, 1785.

*KONKAPOT (Rhoda); her husband was Abraham Konkapot.

1780: with Abraham, she sold one acre off a four-acre lot.

1780: with Abraham, she sold one acre in Stockbridge.

KONOHUNNAWAK

1721: with others, he sold land on the Housatonic in Salisbury.

KOWANNUN (Jehoiakim), Shonanun, Kouaunun, Kanaunun; child of a brother of Tautau-pusseet and Shekannennoti, of the Shawnees.

1743: he was fourteen years old when the Weatauk deed was signed.

1756: he was listed in a deed for part of Egremont and Alford.

*KOWGHAN

1743: with others, she sold land west of Coxsackie.

LENARD LARKE, Larke Lenard.

1748: witness to the sale of two tracts on the Catskill Creek.

1748: he witnessed a land sale west of Coxsackie.

MACHACKMATOCK WISSIAU

1667: with his blood relations, he sold land south of Valatie.

1667: his brother was Awequen.

MAGHSAPEET, MAGHAH, MAGAKEMMENA: see Mahakniminaw.

MAHAKNIMINAW (Joris), also Machack Niemanauw, Matit Niminaw, Maghsapeet, Magakem-mena, Magah, Maetsepack. See deed of August 22, 1709 for a list of his relatives.

1657-1663: chief of Catskill, served as a mediator in Esopus Wars.

1661: he was one of four sellers of an island below Albany.

1672: sold land on behalf of himself and others for Barent Pietersen Coeymans' Patent on the present Albany County south line.

1678: with others, sold flats and woods at Leeds, New York.

1679: his land on the Kinderhook is mentioned in a deed.

1682: as sachem, with eight Esopus Indians, he sold land on a bay below Catskill.

1682: as Joris, he signed a treaty with Maryland and Virginia.

1709: he was deceased before 1709.

MAHASOCK (David).

1667: he was a witness to a deed south of Valatie.

MAHITKEES

1735: with others, he sold land near Westenhook.

MAHOKHAUNT

1721: he sold land on the Housatonic in Salisbury, Connecticut.

MAHTOOKAMIN, see Muhtacomin.

*MAKMEKQUEAM, Mamaqueam, Nanakem.

1718: she was the wife of Catharickseet and a "daughter's daughter of William Emigh."

1721: she signed a deed for land on the Housatonic near Salisbury.

MAMANITISECKHAN, see Maumauntissekun.

*MAMAQUAN, Memaquas

1721: not the same person as Mamaqueam. The two women both signed the same deed for land on the Housatonic in Salisbury.

*MAMAQUEAM, see Makmequeam.

MAMTOWAT

1734: he was a witness to a sale of land on the Schoharie Creek.

1734: witnessed a sale of land on the Schoharie Creek.

MANCHEWANSEET, Mauchewauseet.

1724: with others, sold land for two towns on the Housatonic River.

*MANHAGH, Manhaet; married Argoch (Agotach); mother of Abraham (Maumaunitissekun); she died in war; see Chapter 9.

1697: with My Lady, sold land called Pachowasit, on Roelof Jansen Kill.

MAQUAQUAS

1721: with others, sold land on the Housatonic in Salisbury.

*MARGARET, see Ompeatkow.

*MARY, Meray, see Wepuckshuh.

MATAKEAMIN, Omaghtaghkemen, see Muhtacomin.

MATASET

1703: deceased, his heirs were mentioned in a Westenhook deed.

*MAUCHENOUWAUSHGUH, Elizabeth.

1752: with others, sold Stockbridge land on the road up the hill.

MAUHAUNAUNUT (Jehoiakim).

1769: he was given a tract of fifty acres by the Indian Proprietors to be taken up in any part of the undivided land at Stockbridge.

MAUKENENMEET, Moskenamawg, Maukcuwewet.

1738: he received payment for land at Pittsfield; he lived in the Shawnee country in Pennsylvania but was formerly of Stockbridge.

1757: he sold land at Copake, on which the anti-rent insurgents based their claim to land in the mountains.

MAUMAUNITISSEKUN (Abraham), Mamanitiseckhan, Shabash, Shaveous, Tsioas; his mother was Manhagh (Manhaet), his brother, Winnigh Po. See Chapter 9.

1696: Tsioas, a son of Manhagh, was mentioned in a deed.

1697: sold land, with others, on the Roeloff Jansen Kill.

1719: he witnessed the sale of land at Weatauk (Salisbury).

1721: with others, sold land on the Housatonic River in Salisbury.

1725: received goods from Livingston for land on Roelof Jansen Kill.

MAUWANSSUMUN (Jacob), Wasmausnum, Waumausum.

1785: he sold land laid out on the right of Jonas Wauwohnumuwaus.

"MAWEMEEN

1718: she was the daughter of Nanakem, Catharickseet's wife.

MCHHEHUENWENGET (Moses), probably the same as Moses Nequitimaug of Wequadnach.

1757: he witnessed a deed for Copake.

*MEHMEECH

1740: with others, she sold Stockbridge land to Timothy Woodbridge. She was of the Shawnees but a resident of Stockbridge.

METOXON, Matuackson, Mtoksin, Mutohksin; alias Corlaer or Corlar; called Kennanaquen and Toccunuc; an important chief living in the Salisbury, Connecticut area. He relocated to Greene County, New York.

1704: he sold land near Sharon, Connecticut to Richard Sackett.

1721: he signed the deed for land on the Housatonic near Salisbury.

1726: he sold, with others, land in Sharon to Richard Sackett.

1729: he sold land in Salisbury, Connecticut, on the river.

1729: he sold land on the Housatonic at Weatauk, Connecticut.

1734: he sold land, with others, at Coxsackie, Greene County.

1738: he sold land at later Sharon.

1738: he was one of the signers for land obtained by Thomas Lamb at Sharon, Connecticut.

1743: he was to have two blankets to resign his claim at Salisbury, but was not at the signing.

1743: he was not present when the deed for Weatauk was signed.

METOXON (Jehoiakim), Mtohksin.

1786: he sold a six-acre lot in Stockbridge with the approval of John Sergeant, Jr. and Joseph Woodbridge, examiners of Mohican sales and leases.

METOXON (Johannis), Metoxen, Mtohksin, Mattocson, Nahhson; he is described as an interpreter and a gentleman. His wife was Hannah.

1750: he purchased from fellow Mohicans a tract west of Pittsfield.

1757: he witnessed a deed for Copake.

1757: he witnessed a deed for part of Mount Washington.

1758: he purchased Indian land for a new town near New Framingham.

1758: with others, he sold land to Asa Douglas for Canaan.

1758: he purchased township land adjoining his own land.

1758: he purchased land for two townships from other Indians.

1759: he sold part of a tract given to Shaunaup (Skannaup) and others as equivilent land. This suggests he was an heir of Skannaup.

1761: he and wife Hannah sold land given to them by "our late honored father Jehoiakim Yokun" in his will.

1761: with others, he sold fifty acres in Stockbridge.

1763: with others, he sold all remaining unsold tribal land except Stockbridge and a tract north of it.

1765: he witnessed a mortgage of three acres in Stockbridge.

1766: in the name of the Indian proprietors, he and Benjamin Kohkhewenaunaut sold land on Rattlesnake Mountain to pay Indian debts.

1769: he witnessed a sale by the Pauponskeets of a house lot.

1771: he, with David Naunaunakauneek, acted as a committee to sell Indian land for the proprietors. They sold a piece of land on the mountain.

1772: he sold fifty acres in the northwest part of Stockbridge.

1776: he sold ninety acres; he, Solomon Uhhaunnauwaunmut, and Joseph Shawquethqueat were a committee empowered to sell land to pay Indian debts.

1781: he sold a two-acre tract near the Orphan House Bridge.

1785: he was deceased; a deed says he had willed a farm in Stockbridge on which he lived to Jane Konkapot. Two acres were conveyed. John Konkapot also signed.

MHUTKEES (Nicholas) alias Uhwaunmut or Ukaernnuit. Possibly Nicholas Claes.

1737: land for four townships was sold in his behalf.

MINEK (Daniel).

1763: with others, he sold all remaining unsold tribal land except Stockbridge and a tract north of it.

MOHKHOWWAUWEET (Jehoiakim), Mokhwauwouweet.

1754: with other Stockbridge leaders, petitioned New York's Governor for redress of patents issued without pay.

1757: signed a deed for part of Mount Washington.

1757: with others, sold land for part of Alford.

1763: with others, sold all remaining unsold tribal land except Stockbridge and a tract to the north of it.

1767: he gave a mortgage for his Stockbridge land to Elijah Williams.

MOSES, see Mchhehuenwenget.

MOSES, see Nequitimaug.

MOHTOCKAUMUM, see Mahtookamin.

MTAUWAMPEY (Johannis).

1768: his land was north of Abraham Naunauphpataunk's.

MTOHKSIN, see Metoxon.

MUCKANEEGE

1729: with others, he sold land at Weatauk, Connecticut.

MUHHUTTAUWEE (Josiah), Waumuhhewey.

1759: as "husbandman and hunter," he sold a lot in Stockbridge.

MUHTACOMIN (Ephraim), OmaghTaghKemen, Mahtookamin, Matakeamin, Mohtockaumum, Muttuhkummun, Mauttaukumum; he was formerly from Ampamit's village on Moesimus (Menanoke) Island below Albany.

1730: he witnessed the sale of part of Moesimus Island.

1737: with others, he sold land for Pittsfield; the deed states he was formerly of Menanoke, the Island in Hudson's River below Albany.

1744: with Jehoiakim Yocun, bought land in Richmond and Lenox.

1744: with Jehoiakim Yocon, he purchased land at Stockbridge.

1756: he witnessed the sale of a township west of Sheffield.

1758: with others, he sold land to Asa Douglas for Canaan.

*MY LADY (nickname); her son was Gauwanan.

1697: sold land, with Manhagh, on Roelof Jansen Kill.

NAGHKA, possibly the same person as Naghkawiment.

1748: with others, sold land west of Coxsackie.

NAGHKAWIMENT, Nagewamet.
1748: with others, he sold two tracts on the Catskill Creek.
1750: with Teweghtewap, a woman, he sold land in Greene County.
NAGH JAN
1737: he sold a tract on the east side of the Catskill mountains.
NAHHSON, Johannes, see Metoxon.
NAHONT NARMOES
1672: land for the Coeymans Patent was sold in his name.
1709: he was deceased before 1709.
NAMAKEME
1734: with others, sold land along the Schoharie Creek.
1734: sold land along the Schoharie, with others.
NANACONETT
1729: with others, sold land at Weatauk, Connecticut.
*NANAGHAKEA, see Wawanaghea.
*NANAKEM, see Mamaqueam.
*NANAMEMA
1734: with others, she sold land at Coxsackie.
*NANAQUOGQUT
1709: she testified about land for the 1672 Coemans Patent. The deed said she was a grandchild of
    Magshapeet.
*NANCUSQUAH, Nanusquah.
1735: with others, she sold land at Westenhook.
*NANEMOGH
1748: with others, she sold land west of Coxsackie.
NAUNAUQUIN (Ephraim), Naunaunquan, Nunqueen, Bockus, Bachus.
1721: witnessed the sale of land on the Housatonic in Salisbury.
1724: with others, sold land for two townships on the Housatonic.
no date: fifty acres were surveyed for him.
1751: he sold land in Stockbridge to Jonathan Edwards.
NAUNAUPHTAUNK (Abraham), Naunaumphpataunk, Naunauphtaunk.
1765: his land was west of land belonging to John Naunauphtaunk.
1768: David Pixley sold one half of the lot he bought from Abraham Naunaphpataunk.
1768: he was an heir of Capt. Jacob Naunauphtaunk.
NAUNAUPHTAUNK (Lt. Jacob, Capt. Jacob, Jacobus), Naunaughtoneh, Naunauneauughtnick.
1757: he witnessed a deed for Copake.
1757: he witnessed a deed for part of Mount Washington.
1758: with others, he sold land to Asa Douglas for Canaan.
1768: sixty acres were sold to pay the debts of the heirs of Capt. Jacob Naunauphtaunk. His heirs
    who signed the deed were: John N., Gentleman; Abraham N., yeoman; Jacob N., yeoman;
    and Jehoiakim N., hunter.
NAUNAUPHTAUNK (Jacob).
1768: he was an heir of Capt. Jacob Naunauphtaunk.
NAUNAUPHTAUNK (Jehoiakim).
1768: he was an heir of Capt. Jacob Naunauphtaunk.
NAUNAUHPHTAUNK (John)
1763: with others, he sold all remaining unsold tribal lands except Stockbridge and a tract north of
    it.
1765: he mortgaged three acres of Stockbridge meadowland, promising a deed for the land when
    lawful.
1765: he mortgaged a tract of meadowland in Stockbridge, bounded west by land of Abraham Nau-
    naumpatonk and east by Jacob Wenaumpey.
1766: impowered by the tribe, he signed a contract for a tract twelve miles square out of Mohican
    lands on a lease of 999 years, in exchange for a trip to England to lay Indian claims before the
    King.
1768: his land was mentioned in a neighbor's deed.
1768: he was an heir of Capt. Jacob Naunauphtaunk.

NAUNAUNECKKAUNUCK (Ensign David), Naunuuneekaunuck, Naunaunehennuk, Naunauneekqunuck, Nauneknick, Wawunmeagkuuh; his wife was Elisabath Nauwohtohkhonnuhwoh.

1750: he witnessed a sale of land east of Pittsfield.

c.1750 (no date) sixty acres was surveyed for his first proprietor's lot. He received fifteen acres for
carrying the chain for all surveys then made.

1754: he signed a note at the end of a petition for redress.

1756: he witnessed the sale of a township west of Sheffield.

1757: he witnessed a deed for Copake.

1757: he witnessed a deed for Mathew Vangilder's land.

1763: with many others, he signed a deed for all remaining tribal land except Stockbridge and a
tract north of it.

1771: he, with Johannis Mtohksin, acted as a committee to sell Indian land for the proprietors.
They sold land on the mountain.

1771: with his wife, he sold land in Stockbridge.

1778: fifty acres granted by the proprietors was surveyed for him.

1768: he witnessed a deed given by Rhoda Quonpunwas of Stockbridge.

NAUNEKNICK, David, see Naunauneckaunuck.

NAUNHAMIS

1724, with others, sold two townships on the Housatonic River.

NAUNOMPETONK, Jacob, Naunauphcaunk, Naunauhblaunk

1751: his house was mentioned in a neighbor's deed.

NAUNOWSQUAH, Naunausquan

1724: with others, he sold two townships on the Housatonic.

1737: with others, he sold four townships near Stockbridge.

1769: he received fifty acres granted by the Indian Proprietors.

*NAUWOHTOHKHONNUHWOH (Elisabath); she was the wife of David Naunauneckaunuck
(Naunauneekqunuck).

1771: with her husband, she sold land in Stockbridge.

NAWANAQUGHEET

1709: he testified about land for the 1672 Coeymans patent.

NAWANEQUOCHEEK, Nawanaqugheet.

1709: he testified about the 1672 Coeymans land sale.

NAWES

1721: with others, he sold land on the Housatonic in Salisbury.

NAWWAUKELE (Cornelius).

1758: with others, he sold land to Asa Douglas for Canaan.

NAYATOO

1721: sold land, with others, in Salisbury, Connecticut.

NECTIONHAK

1738: he witnessed a land sale at Petan Hook, Columbia County.

NEEKKUCHEWOHKAUMUN (John).

1744: with Tushauneak, he sold land at Stockbridge.

NEQUITIMAUG, Quotomack, alias Moses.

1747: he signed a petition to the Connecticut Assembly.

1752: with Bartholomew Ackawahanit, he sold the Wequadnach Indian site.

NESHANEES

1729: with others, he sold land at Weatauk, Connecticut.

NESHAWUH, Nesho.

1737: a deed for four townships was signed on his behalf.

1737: he witnessed a sale of land at Kiskatom, near Palenville, New York.

NESHOONUK (David).

1818: with others, he sold four acres of land at Stockbridge.

NICHOLAS, see Etowaukaum.

NICHOLAS, see Mhutkees.

NICHOLAS, alias Tautuhpusseet.

1740: Nicholas, a Shawnee, sold Stockbridge land to Timothy Woodbridge.

NIMHAM, Daniel; he was a Wappinger sachem who lived at Stockbridge. He died fighting for American independence in the Revolution.

1763: with others, he sold all remaining Mohican unsold tribal land except Stockbridge and a tract north of it.

1766: he was witness to a contract for land in exchange for a trip of Mohican and Wappinger representatives to lay land claims before the King.

NISHOGKAMPENINE

1761: with others, he sold land in the Batavia Patent.

1761: he sold, with others, land in Greene County near Batavia.

NOCH KAWEME

1737: he sold land near the Catskills, known as Kiskatom.

*NOCH NAMOS, "Indian woman now of the Fishkills in Dutches County. . . formerly of Housatunnock." Possibly mother of John Vangilder.

1756: gave the whole of her interest in the Indian reserve at Sheffield to John Vangilder, with love and affection.

NOCHQUAWEEMUTH (Hendrick); possibly the same as Noch Kaweme, above.

1766: he signed a deed for Greene County land, also releasing all land belonging to the Catskill Indians.

NOPAMUKQNO

1704: he signed a deed for the Little Nine Partners patent.

NUNGKAUWEAUNT (Robert), Nungkauwot; alias Konkapot; he was the son or grandson of Konkapot and was termed a hunter and husbandman.

1750: with others, sold land east of Pittsfield.

1752: he sold twelve acres in Stockbridge.

1757: with Konkapot, sold land on the Housatonic for Lee.

1763: with others, sold all remaining unsold tribal lands except Stockbridge and a tract north of it.

1763: as a way of selling 140 acres, he gave a lease for 500 years to Elijah Williams.

1765: with Jacob Scautcaw, a son of Konkapot, Robert mortgaged land formerly belonging to Capt. Konkapot.

1769: his 140 acre lot was mentioned in a deed.

OAUL (Paul).

1740: a Shawnee, he sold Stockbridge land to Timothy Woodbridge.

OCCUMBUS

1703: with others, sold Dutchess County land to Richard Sackett.

OIHAEKOAM

1721: with others, sold land on the Housatonic near Salisbury.

OMAGHTAGHKEMEN, see Muhtacomin.

*OMPEATKOW (Margaret); in 1765, she was the widow of Paul Ompeatkow.

1765: she sold land in Stockbridge.

OMPEATKOW (Paul), Umpeathow, Umpeatkow, Impechhow; his wife was Mararget.

1737: with others, he sold four townships near Stockbridge.

1740: with others, sold land at Stockbridge to Timothy Woodbridge.

1765: his wife was a widow.

1767: land of heirs of Paul Impechhow, deceased, was mentioned.

*OTIWIGH

1748: with others, she sold two tracts inland on Catskill Creek.

PANENAMET, Penenemit, Paneenanet.

1748: with others, he sold land west of Coxsackie.

1761: sold land with others near Schoharie, in the Batavia Patent.

1761: with others, sold land inland in Greene County near Batavia.

1766: the father of Tomhampamet, Panenamet could not attend a sale.

PANQUAMMAGE, Pamquammage.

1745: sold land near Metoxen's wigwam near Freehold.

PAUL UMPEATHKOW, see Ompeatkow.

PAUMPKHAUNHAUM (Ephraim).

1763: with others, he sold all unsold land in Massachusetts, excepting Stockbridge and a tract of land north of it.

*PAUPONSKEET (Elizabeth), Pauponks.
1769: with her husband, she sold a house lot. She signed off on her right of dower and widow's third.
PAUNOPESCENNOT
1724: with others, sold two townships in Massachusetts.
PAUPONSKEET (Hendrick); his wife was Elizabeth.
1769: with his wife, he sold a house lot in Stockbridge.
PAUQENNAPEET
1729: with others, he sold land at Weatauk.
PAWAU
1734: with others, sold land along the Schoharie Creek.
1734: sold land with others along the Schoharie Creek.
PEET, he was the son of Shuhekan
1721: with others, sold Salisbury land on the Housatonic River.
PEET RAP, see Pet Tap.
PELAWUHKOUT, Patawuhkont, alias Skannaup; see Skannaup.
PEMOTO, Pemiote, see Poniote.
PENENEMIT, see Panenamet.
PENNONACK, Pittonack, Pinonack, a Westenhook Indian.
1668: a deed mentions a creek called Pittanock in Columbia County.
1679: among sellers of flats on Kinderhook Creek.
1697: he was witness to a sale on the Roelof Jansen Kill.
1703: he and Tapaset were heirs to Mataset. They signed deeds for land on the Westenhook Creek (Housatonic River).
1703: with Tapaset, as heir to Mataset, he sold land on behalf of other Indians.
PENONAMP, see Bononap.
PETER, see Pophqumnaupeet.
PET TAP, Peet Rap
1748: he was witness to sale of two tracts on the Catskill.
1748: he was witness to sale of land west of Coxsackie.
PONASKANET
1724: with others, sold land for two towns on the Housatonic River.
PONIOTE, Poneyote, Panneyote, also Pemoto/Pemiote.
1721: witnessed a sale of land on the Housatonic in Salisbury.
1724: he was among Mohicans who sold townships on the Housatonic.
1737: with others, sold four townships near Stockbridge, Mass.
1737: with Konkapot and Skannaup, he gave land to John Vangilder.
1738: Joseph Van Gilder later remembered that about 1738 Panneyote was very old.
1759: land given to him as an equivalent for Indian land lying at Sheffield was mentioned in a deed.
*PONOANT (Rhoda), Poneoat, Quanponwos, Quonpunwas; she and Sarah Dummekonwoh were heirs of Poniote.
1756: with others, she sold land for part of Egremont and Alford. The deed said Rhoda was a Stockbridge basketmaker.
1757: with Daniel Ninham, she gave land to Mathew Vangilder, who was in Albany jail.
1759: with Sarah Dummekonwoh, she sold land given to Poniote and others (as an equivalent for Indian land at Sheffield) to T. Edwards. The deed said Sarah was a basketmaker.
1759: a deed said the land of T. Edwards belonged to heirs of Poniote.
1768: she sold land in Stockbridge for five pounds.
1774: before the 1757 deed was recorded in 1774, she had died.
POOCHOOSE (Daniel).
1763: with others, he sold all remaining unsold tribal lands except Stockbridge and a tract north of it.
POOPONKSEET (Hendrick).
1763: with others, he sold all remaining unsold tribal land except Stockbridge and a tract north of it.
POOPOONAH (Ebenezer). (See Chapter VII.)
1734: the first Mohican baptized at Stockbridge, he spoke English.

POPAQUA

1724: with others, sold two townships on the Housatonic.

POPHNEHOUNAUWOK, Pophnehaunauwah (various spellings), see Konkapot.

POPHQUMNAUPEET (Deacon, Peter), Pauquennapeet, Bukquunnawpeet, Pohquunnaupeet, Pophnepeet, Pophquannaput.

1729: with others, sold land at Weatauk, Connecticut.

1750: with others, sold land east of Pittsfield.

1752: his house lot is mentioned in a neighbor's deed.

1754: with other Stockbridge leaders, petitioned the Governor of New York for redress for lands patented without pay.

1756: sold a township tract, with others, west of Sheffield.

1756: witness to sale of land for Egremont and Alford.

1757: witnessed a sale of land at Copake.

1758: sold, with others, land to Asa Douglas for Canaan.

POTAWAKEONT

1724: with others, sold townships on the Housatonic.

1756: he and Konkapot sold a tract which became Austerlitz.

1756: he witnessed a sale for part of Egremont and Alford.

PROMISH, see Brownis.

*QUAEMKEES

1734: with others, she sold land at Coxsackie.

QUAENT

1738: he witnessed a land sale at Petan Hook, Columbia County.

*QUANPONWOS (Rhoda), see Ponoant.

QUANS (Daniel).

1756: with others, sold land for part of Egremont and Alford.

1763: with others, he sold all remaining unsold tribal lands except Stockbridge and a tract north of it.

QUANTAMINO

1704: witness to land sale for the Little Nine Partners patent.

QUINNAUQUANT (Joseph), Joseph Quinney, Quannukkaunt.

1756: with others, he sold land for part of Egremont and Alford, which included land he and Shawwanum sold earlier.

1757: sold land for part of Mount Washington.

1757: with others, sold land for part of Alford.

1763: with others, he sold all remaining unsold tribal lands except Stockbridge and a tract north of it.

QUISQUANTAN, Quisquatom.

1745: with others, he sold land near Metoxen's wigwam in Freehold.

*QUULLAUTOWATUK, Hannah.

1752: with others, sold Stockbridge land on the road up the hill.

RHODA, see Ponoant.

ROBERT NUNGKAUWEANT, see NUNKAUWEANT.

ROB'N (Robin).

1704: witness to land sale for the Little Nine Partners patent.

SAHEAK

1737: he witnessed a sale of land at Kiskatom, near Palenville.

SAKOWENAKOK, SANKOONAKEHEK, Saunkokehe, Sankewenageek, see Umpachanee.

SANKERN SCHOECK

1729: with others, sold land on the east side of the Kinderhook Creek.

SANKHANK

1704: with others, he sold land on the Westenhook Creek.

SANKIEDAHOCK

1729: with others, sold land on the east side of the Kinderhook Creek.

SARAH, see Dummekonwoh.

SAUCHEWEWAHA, alias Benjamin.

1747: he was among Wequadnach Indians who petitioned for recognition of their village tract.

SAUNKEWENAUGHEAG
1724: with others, sold land for two towns on the Housatonic River.
SAUSEEHHOOT, Sausseekhoot
1737: a deed for townships east of Stockbridge was signed on his behalf.
1754: with other Stockbridge leaders, he petitioned the New York Governor for redress of patents isssued without pay.
SAUSENAUCKHEGE
1729: with others, he sold land at Weatauk, Connecticut.
SCHENK, (Jacob)
1761: he sold land at White Creek. He was the last of the Schaghticoke Indians. All the others had gone to Canada.
SHABASH, see Maumauntisseckhan.
*SHANO
1718: she was the daughter of Nanakem, Catharickseet's wife.
SHAWQUETHQUEAT (Joseph), Shawquethquat.
1757: he witnessed a deed for land near Mathew Vangilder's.
1776: he, Solomon Uhhaunnauwaumut and Johannis Mtohksin, were a committee empowered to sell land to pay Indian debts; they sold ninety acres.
1781: as "Chief of the Stockbridge Indians," with Benjamin Waununauwut, he sold twenty acres in Stockbridge.
SHAWWANUNN (Jehoiakim), Shonanun, Kouaunun.
1755: he sold a five-acre triangular parcel in Stockbridge.
1756: he witnessed the sale of land for Egremont and Alford, which included land he and Quinnauquant sold earlier.
*SHEKAUNENUTY, Shekannennoti, the sister of Tautaupusseet.
1740: with others, she sold Stockbridge land to Timothy Woodbridge. She was of the Shawnees, now a resident of Stockbridge.
1743: she signed a deed selling 5000 acres at Weatauk.
SHEPOKASS
1761: with others, he signed a deed for land in the Batavia Patent.
1761: he sold, with others, Greene County land near Batavia.
SHERMAN, (THOMAS)
1754: with other Stockbridge leaders, he petitioned the Governor of New York for redress for lands patented without pay
SHONANUN, see Shawwanunn.
SHOUWUNNOHGHUEK (Jehoiakim), alias Weame.
1772: his lot was mentioned in a survey.
SHUHANEMOW
1721: with others, sold land on the Housatonic River in Salisbury.
SHUHEKAN, his son was named Peet.
1721: signed a deed for land on the Housatonic in Salisbury.
SINHOW, Sinhuw
1734: with others, he sold land on the Schoharie Creek.
1734: sold land with others along the Schoharie Creek.
1745: sold a tract west of Catskill, near Metoxen's wigwam.
SKANNAUP, Skannop, Skannout, Shaunaup, Pelawuhkout, Patawuhkont
1737: with others, he sold townships east of Stockbridge.
1737: with Konkapot and Poniote, he gave land to John Van Gilder.
1738: Joseph van Gilder later remembered that about 1738 Skannaup was grey with age, and older than Ampamit, who was in his 60s.
1759: the land laid out for Skannaup was mentioned in a deed.
SKUSHAWMH, John
1755: the north part of a lot laid out to him was sold, to support him and his family.
SOKAM, Sokaen, brother of Akamaagkamin.
1703: land at Westenhook was sold in his behalf.
SOLOMON, see Masinamake.
SOLOMON, see Uhhuhwawnuhmut.

SOLOMON, see Waunaupaugus.
SONKEWENAUKHEEK, see Umpachanee.
SPANKEWENOGEEK, see Umpachanee.
SQUANS
1748: with others, sold two tracts inland on the Catskill Creek.
1748: with others, sold land west of Coxsackie.
SUNKHONK
1724: with others, sold land for two townships on the Housatonic.
TAKOMP, his sister was Guttatamow.
1719: with others, sold land near Salisbury, Connecticut.
TAMPHAMPAMET (Cornelius), Tomhampemet; he was the son of Paneenanet, alias John.
1761: he sold land, with others, on "the Elks plain" in the Batavia Patent.
1761: with others, sold four tracts in Greene County near Batavia.
1766: signed, with others, a release of all unpatented land belonging to the Catskill Indians. He was
    acting on behalf of his father, Paneenanet, otherwise called John, who could not attend.
TAMQUASH:
1703: sold Dutchess County and Connecticut land to Richard Sackett.
TANTAGHOES
1743: with others, he sold land west of Coxsackie.
TAPASET, Tapamet
1703: sold land on the Westenhook Creek, with Pennonack.
TATAEMSHATT (Gose, Goose, nickname), Tattamshatt; the father of Catharickseet; Tataem-
    shatt's brother was Waquassamo (Michiel).
1682: as a Catskill sachem, he signed an agreement with Lord Baltimore.
1683: he was among Mohicans who sold land on the Roelof Jansen Kill to Robert Livingston.
1685: the land of Tataemshatt, near Tachkanick, was west of Westenhook.
1685: with Michiel, he sold land at Tachkanick to Livingston.
1697: named a guardian of Manhagh's children, he was employed by My Lady and Manhagh to sell
    land to Robert Livingston on the Roelof Jansen Kill, extending to the high hills.
1703: an heir of Mataset, sold Westenhook land on behalf of others.
TATAKIM, Tatarkim
1724: with others, sold land for two townships on the Housatonic River.
TAUKAMAKEHEKE
1666: he sold land at Kinderhook.
TAUNKHONKPUS
1724: with others, sold land on the Housatonic for two towns.
TAUTUHPUSSEET, Tautaupusseet, alias Nicholas
1740: with others, sold land at Stockbridge to Timothy Woodbridge.
1743: he was not present when the Weatauk deed was signed.
*TEWIGHTAMOW, Teweghtemap, Tawightemow, Towetemack.
1734: with others, she sold land at Coxsackie
1743: with others, she sold land west of Coxsackie.
1745: sold land, with others, west of Catskill, near Metoxen's wigwam.
1748: sold, with others, two tracts inland on Catskill Creek.
1748: with others, she sold land west of Coxsackie.
1750: with Nagewamet, she sold land south of Rensselaerwyck.
THOMAS, see Sherman.
TICKANENAH
1721: with others, sold land on the Housatonic River in Salisbury.
TIELHUYSEM (Dutch nickname having to do with houses).
1672: land for the Coeymans Patent was sold in his name.
1709: he died before 1709.
TIMOTHY, see Cowpoise.
TIMOTHY, see Yokun.
TISQUEAKE
1704: with others, signed for land for the Little Nine Partners.
TOCCONUC, Tossonee, see Metoxon.

TOMHOMQUAMEESGA (Philip).

1766: with others, he signed a release for all remaining land belonging to the Catskill Indians.

TONOWOACTUM

1704: with others, signed for land for the Little Nine Partners.

TONWEHEES, Tawahees, brother or half-brother of Aquatso, Ampamit, and Penonamp.

1685: he conveyed the tract called Tachkanik.

1707: with others, he confirmed previous Van Rensselaer deeds.

1709: he testified about land for the Coeymans Patent. The deed said he was the brother of Ampamet.

TSACOKE (David).

1747: with others, he petitioned for recognition of their Wequadnach village tract.

TSIOAS, see Maumauntissekun.

TUSHAUNEAK

1744: with John Neekkuchewohkaumun, he sold land at Stockbridge.

UHHUHWAWNUHMUT (Solomon), Uhhaunnauwaunmut.

1738: he sold land for Pittsfield, Lanesboro and part of Cheshire.

1763: with others, he signed a deed for all remaining unsold tribal lands except Stockbridge and a tract north of it.

1765: he was witness to a sale of Stockbridge land.

1766: he sold fifty acres in Stockbridge, part of the land laid out to Jonas Etowaukaum and James Chenequin, as part of his rights.

1776: he, with Johannis Mtohksin and Joseph Shawquethqueat, were a committee empowered to sell land for the payment of Indian debts. This sale was for ninety acres.

1766: empowered by the tribe, he signed a contract for a tract of twelve miles square to be taken out of Mohican lands on a lease of 999 years, in exchange for a trip to England to lay Indian claims before the King.

1767: he sold fifty acres in Stockbridge.

UHWAUNMUT, Ukwaernnuit, see Mhutkees (Nicholas).

UMPACHANEE (Aaron), Sakewenakok, Sonkewenaukheek, Spankewenogeek, Sankewnageek, Sankekeke, known as Lieutenant after 1734. His wife was Anna (Hannah).

1719: witnessed the sale of land near Salisbury, Connecticut.

1721: he signed a deed for land on the Housatonic in Salisbury.

1724: with others, sold land for two townships on the Housatonic.

1738: with his wife, Anna, he sold 1500 acres at Petan Hook, in later Columbia County.

1738: Joseph van Gilder (born about 1720), remembered in 1768 Umpachanee was the former sachem of the Mohicans. Van Gilder noted that about 1738 Umpachanee was over sixty years of age. Umpachanee died in 1751.

1738: he was a witness at the sale of land to Jacob Wendell.

1740: with others, sold Stockbridge land to Timothy Woodbridge.

1744: he was a witness to a land sale at Stockbridge.

UMPAWAHANIT (Jonathan).

1747: with others, he petitioned for recognition of the village tract at Wequadnach.

UMPEATHHOW, see Ompeatkow.

VANGILDER (John), Vangelder, Van Guilder. His son was Joseph.

1724: with others, sold land for two towns on the Housatonic River.

1726: according to son, Joseph, the family moved from (later) Great Barrington to Sheffield about this year.

1737: he received a confirmation deed for his land in the Indian Reservation, west of Sheffield, from fellow Mohicans.

1756: he received from Noch Namos her interest in the land that the Indians reserved in Sheffield, for the love and affection she had for him.

VANGILDER (Mary, Meray).

1762: she bought a right of land in Egremont from Hezekiah Winchel and Catharen Winchel.

VANGILDER (Mathew, Matheus).

1757: 118 acres of the land he was improving west of Sheffield was a gift to Mathew Van Gilder, who was in Albany jail.

VASNANGHTOUK (Jacob).

1757: he witnessed a deed for Copake.

WALLEGNAWEEK

1703: with others, sold land on the Westenhook Creek.

WAMPANON, Wampenum.

1737: with others, he sold land for Pittsfield; he was formerly of Menanoke, the Island in Hudson's River below Albany.

WANEKENAES, Waneekenes.

1738: he sold land on both sides of the Kinderhook Creek.

1741: with others, he sold a tract northeast of Kinderhook.

WANENOCOW

1724: among others, sold two townships on the Housatonic.

WAQUASSAMO (Michiel, Machiel); his brother was Tataemshatt.

1685: with others, he sold land called Tachkanick on the Roelof Jansen Kill.

1697: he was named a caretaker of Manhagt's children.

WASSAMPAH (John), Tschoop.

1740: he lived at Shekomeko when the mission was forming. See Chapter 9 for information about his life.

WATNAKAW

1721, with others, sold land on the Housatonic River in Salisbury.

WAUMUHHEWEY (Josiah).

1756: with others, sold land for a township west of Sheffield.

WAUNAUAUNQUEEN (Ephraim).

1763: with others, he sold all remaining unsold tribal land except Stockbridge and a tract north of it.

WAUNAUMPEH, Isaac, see Wenaumpe.

WAUNAUPAUGUS (Solomon), Waunumpaugus.

1744: he witnessed a deed for Stockbridge land.

1750: he signed a note at the end of a petition for redress.

no date: he received fifty acres according to a survey.

WAUNAUPNUTONHG (Jehoiakim), Naunseptonk, Naunonpetonk.

1785: he sold land adjacent to the lot of Benjamin Waunihnauwut.

WAUNUNAUWUT (Benjamin), Waunihnauwut.

1781: a hunter, he sold twenty acres in Stockbridge.

1785: his land is mentioned in an adjacent land sale.

WAUTONKAUMEET (John, also Adam), Watonkuhmett, Watanikmeth

1737: he was second in importance at Kaunaumeek; he had been baptized a Catholic. He moved to Stockbridge with his children.

1741: with others, he sold a tract northeast of Kinderhook.

1750: he signed a note at the end of a petition for redress.

1752: with others, sold Stockbridge land on the road up the hill.

WAUTONKAUWOT (Hendrick), Wautaunkghmut, alias Unkaumug.

1771: his land in Stockbridge was surveyed.

WAUWAUMPEGQUUNNAUNT (John).

1744: he witnessed a Stockbridge deed.

1756: he sold a township, with others, west of Sheffield.

1757: he witnessed a deed for part of Mount Washington.

1759: he was deceased; his land was in possession of his widow.

*WAWANAGHEA, Wanenagkela, Nanaghakea; wife of Brownis (Promish), mother of Aquatso, Ampamit, Penonamp and Tonwahees.

1703: with sons, she sold woodland in northwest Columbia County.

1709: she testified about the land for the Coeymans Patent. The document said she was the widow of Brownis.

WAWUNMEAGKUUH, see Nannauneckkaunuck, David.

WEAME, see Shouwunnohghuek.

WEENHOP

1766: he signed a deed releasing all remaining land belonging to the Catskill Indians.

WENAUMPE (Elizabeth), Wnaumpey.

1768: her land was south of Abraham Naunauphpataunk's.

WENAUMPE (Isaac), Wenaumpee, Wnaupey, Waunaumpoh, Weananumpee, Whnaumpeti; possibly Isaac Wunnupee, of Dutchess County.

1737: with others, sold four townships near Stockbridge.

1750: witnessed sale of land east of Pittsfield.

1756: he witnessed a sale of land which became Austerlitz.

1756: with others, sold land for Egremont and Alford.

1757: he witnessed a deed for Copake.

1758: he was a witness at a sale for a new township.

1758: with others, he sold land to Asa Douglas for Canaan.

1758: he witnessed a deed to Johannis Mtohksin.

1759: with Johannis Mtohksin, he sold land formerly laid out for Skannaup and others.

1763: with others, he sold all remaining unsold tribal land except Stockbridge and a tract north of it.

WENEPACK

1732: he was among sellers of 12,000 acres northeast of the Hoosick Patent. His mark was a turtle.

*WENNENAESKE

1729: with others, she sold land on the east side of the Kinderhook Creek.

WEPOOKQSHUHT (Isaac), Wepuckshuh.

1756: with others, he sold a township west of Sheffield.

1763: with others, he sold all remaining unsold tribal lands except Stockbridge and a tract north of it.

WEPUCKSHUH (Mary).

1762: with permission of the court, she sold thirty-seven acres of her own land. She was an aged woman of Stockbridge.

WEQUAGUN

1737: with others, sold four townships near Stockbridge.

WIKACHEAM

1721: he signed a deed for land on the Housatonic in Salisbury.

WINNIGH PO, Annimapaw, brother of Maumauntissekun.

1697: a deed for land on the Roelof Jansen Kill mentions he is the son of Manhagh.

1725: he received goods from Livingston for an earlier sale of land on Roelof Jansen Kill.

WOHCOHEEKCOMEEK (James).

no date: fifty acres were surveyed for him.

WOHNAUNQUEEN, alias Ephraim Bochus, see Naunaunquin

WOOMPOOKSEET (Hendrick).

no date: his fifty acres of land was surveyed.

WUNNUPEE, Wusumpe.

1703: among sellers of Dutchess County land to Richard Sackett.

1704: signed a deed for the Little Nine Partners Patent.

WYAWAW

1703: among sellers of Dutchess County land to Richard Sackett.

YOCUN (Jehoiakim), Yokun, Yocon, Yocum, Yokim.

1738: he witnessed a delayed payment to Maukenenmeet.

1744: with Mohtockaumum, he purchased land at Stockbridge.

1748: sold land east of Pittsfield, with others.

1750: sold land east of Poontoosuck (Pittsfield).

1754: with other Stockbridge leaders, petitioned the Governor of New York for redress for lands patented without pay.

1756: he was a witness to a sale of land which became Austerlitz.

1756: he sold, with others, land for part of Egremont and Alford.

1757: he witnessed the deed for Copake.

1757: with others, signed a deed for part of Mount Washington.

1757: signed with others for land encompassing part of Alford.

1758: he sold land to Johannis Mtohksin for a new township.

1758: he sold land, with others, to Asa Douglas for Canaan.

1758: with Benjamin Kaukewenauhnaunt, he sold land to Johannis Mtohksin.
1758: he sold land to Johannis Mtohksin for two townships. Yokun was identified as an Indian owner and gentleman.
1761: by May, 1761, his will was mentioned in a deed. He left land to Hannah Mtohksin, wife of Johannis Mtohksin.
1769: land owned by his heirs was south of Pauponskeet's lot.
YOKUN (Timothy), Youkun; his father probably was Jehoiakim Yocun.
1763: with others, he sold all remaining unsold tribal land except Stockbridge and a tract north of it.
1769: he sold a tract of eight acres in Stockbridge.
1761: his land at Stockbridge was east of Hannah Mtohksin's land, according to a deed.
1763: with others, he sold all the unsold land in Massachusetts except Stockbridge and a tract north of it.
YONGSINGPOMKINSEET
1703: among sellers of Dutchess County land to Richard Sackett.
*YOUNGHANS' SQUAW, the Indian wife of a German named Younghance or of an Indian using that name.
1703: among sellers of Dutchess County and Connecticut land to Richard Sackett, on behalf of her sons.

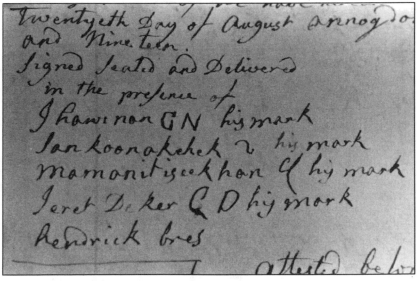

Mamanitiseckhan (Maumaunitissekun), also known as Shabash or Abraham of Shekomeko, was a witness to a deed for land near Weatauk in 1719.
Hampden County Registry of Deeds, Springfield, Massachusettes

Index

369

About the cover

Artist L. F. Tantillo's magical painting, "The Mohican Grandfather," shows a village group absorbed in a tale told by an elder on a bluff above the Hudson River. Tantillo, renowned for his luminous paintings of marine scenes and historical moments, recreates the look and feel of an event only after extensive research. He holds a graduate degree in architecture from the Rhode Island School of Design. His works have appeared in books, periodicals, and television documentaries. Signed, limited-edition, giclée prints of "The Mohican Grandfather" (image size: 21" x 14") are available from L. F. Tantillo Fine Art: 518-766-4542; www.lftantillo.com.

About the author

The holder of Masters' degrees in English and History, Shirley Wiltse Dunn has worked as a teacher, museum interpreter, and historic preservation consultant and was a founder of the Dutch Barn Preservation Society. She is the author of *The Mohicans and Their Land, 1609-1730*, published by Purple Mountain Press in 1994 and now in its third printing. In recognition of her research on Dutch farm locations, she was honored as a *Fellow* by the Holland Society of New York. She became interested in the Mohicans two decades ago while studying Indian deeds for early properties in the Albany, New York, area. A devoted grandmother, she lives with her husband in Rensselaer County.